TM

References for the Rest of Us! ™

The Healthy Heart For Dummies®

Cheat Sheet

Eight Guidelines for Heart-Healthy Nutrition

- Limit saturated fat intake to less than 10 percent of total calories and total fat intake to less than 30 percent of total calories.

- Limit cholesterol intake to less than 100 mg per 1,000 calories and no more than 300 mg a day.

- Increase the amount of carbohydrate in the diet to 50-55 percent of the total calories or more, emphasizing complex carbohydrates.

- Limit sodium intake to no more than 1 gram per 1,000 calories and not more than a total of 3 grams a day (preferably no more than 2400 mg).

- Protein should comprise approximately 15 percent of total calories.

- If you consume alcoholic beverages, do not exceed 1 to 1.5 ounces of alcohol per day (approximately one shot of distilled spirits or two glasses of wine or two beers).

- Do not consume more calories than are required to maintain your best body weight.

- Consume a variety of food.

Keys to Modifying Your Risk Factors for Heart Disease

- Control high blood pressure. Optimal blood pressure is 120/80 mm Hg or below.

- Control your cholesterol levels. Desirable levels are below 200 mg/dl. The lower the better.

- Accumulate at least 30 minutes of moderate physical activity on most, if not all, days.

- Maintain your body weight at healthy levels — a body mass index between 19 and 25.

- If you smoke, quit.

Five Keys to Staying with Your Physical Activity Program

- **Set a time and place.** Plan at least one activity like a short walk at lunch and other opportunities will fall in place.

- **Be prepared.** Adopt a mindset that emphasizes more physical activity.

- **Include family and friends**.

- **Have fun.** You'll stay with something you like.

- **Prioritize.** Make getting physical activity as important a priority as other objectives in your life.

The Healthy Heart For Dummies®

Cheat Sheet

Tips for Lowering Stress

- **Modify factors that can compound stress.** Get enough rest. Don't overconsume caffeine. And so on.
- **Live in the present.** Quit fearing the future or regretting the past. Make the most of today.
- **Get out of your own way.** Don't dwell on the negative or indulge in negative self talk.
- **Take time out.** Step away from it all for ten minutes a day. Take a stroll. Meditate. Nap. Tune into the calm.

Warning Signs of Heart Attack

Even if you've never had a single sign of trouble, call 911 and go straight to the hospital for prompt evaluation if you have any of these warning signs of heart attack.

- Uncomfortable pressure, fullness, squeezing, or pain in the center of the chest lasting more than a few minutes
- Pain spreading to the shoulders, neck, or arms
- Chest discomfort with lightheadedness, fainting, sweating, nausea, or shortness of breath

Questions to Ask the Doctor

When you are being evaluated for heart disease or any other condition, asking these questions can help you get the information you need.

- What is my diagnosis?
- What tests will I need to undergo?
- Do these tests have any side effects or dangers?
- What is the recommended treatment?
- What are the potential side effects of the treatment?
- What treatment choices are available?
- Should I be asking any other questions?
- Is there any source of information that I can read about my diagnosis?

Major Risk Factors for Coronary Artery Disease

- High blood pressure
- Elevated cholesterol
- Cigarette smoking
- Inactive lifestyle
- Obesity

For Dummies™: Bestselling Book Series for Beginners

The Healthy Heart FOR DUMMIES®

by James M. Rippe, M.D.

IDG BOOKS WORLDWIDE

IDG Books Worldwide, Inc.
An International Data Group Company

Foster City, CA ◆ Chicago, IL ◆ Indianapolis, IN ◆ New York, NY

The Healthy Heart For Dummies®

Published by
IDG Books Worldwide, Inc.
An International Data Group Company
919 E. Hillsdale Blvd.
Suite 400
Foster City, CA 94404
`www.idgbooks.com` (IDG Books Worldwide Web site)
`www.dummies.com` (Dummies Press Web site)

Library of Congress Catalog Card No.: 99-66494

ISBN: 0-7645-5199-X

Printed in the United States of America

10 9 8 7 6 5 4 3 2 1

1B/QS/RS/ZZ/IN

Distributed in the United States by IDG Books Worldwide, Inc.

Distributed by CDG Books Canada Inc. for Canada; by Transworld Publishers Limited in the United Kingdom; by IDG Norge Books for Norway; by IDG Sweden Books for Sweden; by IDG Books Australia Publishing Corporation Pty. Ltd. for Australia and New Zealand; by TransQuest Publishers Pte Ltd. for Singapore, Malaysia, Thailand, Indonesia, and Hong Kong; by Gotop Information Inc. for Taiwan; by ICG Muse, Inc. for Japan; by Intersoft for South Africa; by Eyrolles for France; by International Thomson Publishing for Germany, Austria and Switzerland; by Distribuidora Cuspide for Argentina; by LR International for Brazil; by Galileo Libros for Chile; by Ediciones ZETA S.C.R. Ltda. for Peru; by WS Computer Publishing Corporation, Inc., for the Philippines; by Contemporanea de Ediciones for Venezuela; by Express Computer Distributors for the Caribbean and West Indies; by Micronesia Media Distributor, Inc. for Micronesia; by Chips Computadoras S.A. de C.V. for Mexico; by Editorial Norma de Panama S.A. for Panama; by American Bookshops for Finland.

For general information on IDG Books Worldwide's books in the U.S., please call our Consumer Customer Service department at 800-762-2974. For reseller information, including discounts and premium sales, please call our Reseller Customer Service department at 800-434-3422.

For information on where to purchase IDG Books Worldwide's books outside the U.S., please contact our International Sales department at 317-596-5530 or fax 317-596-5692.

For consumer information on foreign language translations, please contact our Customer Service department at 1-800-434-3422, fax 317-596-5692, or e-mail rights@idgbooks.com.

For information on licensing foreign or domestic rights, please phone +1-650-655-3109.

For sales inquiries and special prices for bulk quantities, please contact our Sales department at 650-655-3200 or write to the address above.

For information on using IDG Books Worldwide's books in the classroom or for ordering examination copies, please contact our Educational Sales department at 800-434-2086 or fax 317-596-5499.

For press review copies, author interviews, or other publicity information, please contact our Public Relations department at 650-655-3000 or fax 650-655-3299.

For authorization to photocopy items for corporate, personal, or educational use, please contact Copyright Clearance Center, 222 Rosewood Drive, Danvers, MA 01923, or fax 978-750-4470.

About the Author

Dr. Rippe is a graduate of Harvard College and Harvard Medical School with post graduate training at Massachusetts General Hospital. He is the founder and director of the Center for Clinical and Lifestyle Research and Associate Professor of Medicine (Cardiology) at Tufts University School of Medicine.

Dr. Rippe is founder and director of the *Rippe Health Assessment at Celebration Health*. This is a series of comprehensive health evaluations for high performance individuals conducted at the state-of-the-art medical and fitness facility of Celebration Health in Orlando, Florida.

Dr. Rippe is regarded as one of the leading authorities on preventive cardiology, health and fitness and healthy weight loss in the United States. Under his leadership the Center for Clinical and Lifestyle Research has conducted numerous research projects on cardiovascular risk-factor reduction, fitness walking, weight loss, running, basketball, bodybuilding, cycling, rowing, cholesterol reduction, and low-fat diets. Laboratory members have presented over 120 papers at national, medical, and scientific meetings in the last ten years. Dr. Rippe has written over 200 publications on issues in medicine, health and fitness, and weight management. He has also written or edited 25 books, including 15 medical texts and 10 books on health and fitness for the general public, including *Fitness Walking* (Perigee, 1985), *The Sports Performance Factors* (Perigee, 1986), and *Fitness Walking for Women* (Perigee, 1987). Both walking books were recipients of National American Health Book Awards. His book on executive fitness, *Fit for Success*, was published by Prentice Hall Press in June 1989. His book on walking and weight loss, *The Rockport Walking Program*, was published in fall 1989. Another one of his books, *The Complete Book of Fitness Walking* was published by Prentice Hall Press in June 1990. His book, *The Exercise Exchange Program*, combining exercise and proper nutrition, was published in February 1992. *Fit Over Forty*, published in 1996, explores lifestyle issues related to cardiovascular health, particularly for individuals over the age of 40, and focuses on motivating people to take the simple steps to take charge of their health and lives.

Dr. Rippe also edits a major text book that teaches physicians about diverse aspects of cardiovascular medicine and the impact of lifestyle decisions on good health. This text book, *Lifestyle Medicine*, (Blackwell Science, 1999) is the first text book to guide physicians in the diverse aspects of how to incorporate lifestyle recommendations into the practice of modern medicine. His intensive care text book, *Irwin and Rippe's Intensive Care Medicine* (4th edition, 1998; co-edited with Dr. Richard Irwin) is the world's leading text book on intensive and coronary care.

Dr. Rippe serves as Medical Director for TBG Development and developed corporate fitness programs for a variety of companies including Allstate Life Insurance and The Shimizu Corporation. He serves as Chairman of the Advisory Board for the "Healthy Growing Up" program — a curriculum linking health and fitness for children that was made available free of charge to every school system in the United States in 1992.

Dr. Rippe's work has been featured on The Today Show, Good Morning America, PBS "BodyWatch," CBS Morning and Evening News, CNN, and in a variety of print media including the *New York Times, New York Times Magazine, L.A. Times, Wall Street Journal* and many monthly publications. He comments regularly on health and fitness for *USA Today, American Health,* and *Prevention.* He served for three years as Medical Editor for the Television Food Network (TVFN).

In 1989, Dr. Rippe was named Fitness Educator of the Year by the International Dance Exercise Association (IDEA). In 1990 he was named one of the 10 national "Healthy American Fitness Leaders" by the United States Jaycees and the President's Council on Physical Fitness and Sports. In 1992, he received a Lifetime Achievement Award from IDEA.

A lifelong and avid athlete, Dr. Rippe maintains his personal fitness with a regular walk, jog, and weight training program. He holds a black belt in karate and is an avid windsurfer, skier, and tennis player. He lives outside of Boston with his wife, television news anchor Stephanie Hart, and their three children, Hart, Jaelin, and Devon.

Dedication

To Stephanie, Hart, Jaelin, and Devon, who make my heart sing and provide the cornerstone for my personal program to maintain a healthy heart.

ABOUT IDG BOOKS WORLDWIDE

Welcome to the world of IDG Books Worldwide.

IDG Books Worldwide, Inc., is a subsidiary of International Data Group, the world's largest publisher of computer-related information and the leading global provider of information services on information technology. IDG was founded more than 30 years ago by Patrick J. McGovern and now employs more than 9,000 people worldwide. IDG publishes more than 290 computer publications in over 75 countries. More than 90 million people read one or more IDG publications each month.

Launched in 1990, IDG Books Worldwide is today the #1 publisher of best-selling computer books in the United States. We are proud to have received eight awards from the Computer Press Association in recognition of editorial excellence and three from Computer Currents' First Annual Readers' Choice Awards. Our best-selling ...For Dummies® series has more than 50 million copies in print with translations in 31 languages. IDG Books Worldwide, through a joint venture with IDG's Hi-Tech Beijing, became the first U.S. publisher to publish a computer book in the People's Republic of China. In record time, IDG Books Worldwide has become the first choice for millions of readers around the world who want to learn how to better manage their businesses.

Our mission is simple: Every one of our books is designed to bring extra value and skill-building instructions to the reader. Our books are written by experts who understand and care about our readers. The knowledge base of our editorial staff comes from years of experience in publishing, education, and journalism — experience we use to produce books to carry us into the new millennium. In short, we care about books, so we attract the best people. We devote special attention to details such as audience, interior design, use of icons, and illustrations. And because we use an efficient process of authoring, editing, and desktop publishing our books electronically, we can spend more time ensuring superior content and less time on the technicalities of making books.

You can count on our commitment to deliver high-quality books at competitive prices on topics you want to read about. At IDG Books Worldwide, we continue in the IDG tradition of delivering quality for more than 30 years. You'll find no better book on a subject than one from IDG Books Worldwide.

John Kilcullen
Chairman and CEO
IDG Books Worldwide, Inc.

Steven Berkowitz
President and Publisher
IDG Books Worldwide, Inc.

Eighth Annual
Computer Press
Awards ≥1992

Ninth Annual
Computer Press
Awards ≥1993

Tenth Annual
Computer Press
Awards ≥1994

Eleventh Annual
Computer Press
Awards ≥1995

Author's Acknowledgments

It would be impossible to cite all of the individuals who have provided advice and support during the time it took to complete this book. However, several deserve special recognition for their significant contributions.

First, I would like to acknowledge and applaud the superb writing and editorial skills of my main collaborator, Mary Abbott Waite. This is the second book project (following *Fit Over Forty*), on which Mary Abbott and I have collaborated. Mary Abbott is a dream writing partner. She has taken complex medical topics and edited my thoughts in a way that makes the message clear, concise, and user-friendly (and, we hope, at times even a little humorous!). Mary Abbott not only writes well but also is a superb researcher. She verified a number of topics which I introduced in various chapters by performing considerable outside research from a variety of other expert sources. She has often added interesting and helpful tips and anecdotes that come either from her own experience or from her friends and relatives.

Second, my Editorial Director and good friend, Beth Porcaro applied her formidable organization skills to keep this whole process moving forward and on time. Beth manages to accomplish an unbelievable amount of work while maintaining great judgment and a wonderful sense of humor.

The recipes in this book were organized and edited (and in a few cases developed!) by two superb research nutritionists working in my laboratory, the Center for Clinical and Lifestyle Research. Amy Myrdal, MS, RD and Angela Harley Kirkpatrick, RD, are consummate professionals — not only do they have a superb grasp of nutrition, but they also have a wonderful touch for editing and a great love of food. I also would like to commend and thank top chefs from around America who wrote the recipes that are included in this book. These include:

Hans Bergmann, Garrett Cho, Alfonso Constriciani, Felicien Cueff, Danielle Custer, John Harris, Constantin Kerageorgiou, Bruce Molzan, Mario Norcera, Donna Nordin, Walter Pisano, Sylvain Portay, Nora Pouillon, Mary Ann Saporito Boothroyd, Michael Schwartz, Mark Tarbell, Norman Van Aken, and Carl Walker.

Titles, restaurant names, and restaurant locations for the contributing chefs can be found with their recipes.

The initial concept for this book was developed by my friend and Senior Acquisitions Editor at IDG Books, Tami Booth in conjunction with my Literary Agent, Reid Boates. Tami and Reid are not only terrifically bright and hard working professionals, but they are also good friends. Their support, collaboration, and advice throughout this whole process has been invaluable. Colleen Totz, Project Editor at IDG Books, did a superb job from start to finish.

I am also indebted to the talented research staff at my laboratory, the Center for Clinical and Lifestyle Research in Shrewsbury, Massachusetts. Under the superb direction of Research Director, Diane O'Brien, RN, BSN and Clinical Research

Development Director, Deirdre Morrissey, MA, our staff of 20 healthcare and research professionals manage to keep a busy laboratory humming along while freeing up time for me to tackle major writing projects such as this.

Many of the clinical insights from this book are employed on a daily basis at my clinical facility, the *Rippe Health Assessment at Celebration Health*. My superb staff there including Chris Young, RN, Clinic Manager; Rick Wassel, Director of Sales and Marketing; Sara McCoy, my Executive Assistant; and Kim Hamilton, Carol Benson, Andrea Elrod, and Tara Geise, MS, RD have all provided useful insights and ongoing clinical validation of many of the concepts discussed in this book.

My professional colleagues have been a source of continuing intellectual stimulation throughout my career as a cardiologist. I would like to particularly acknowledge Dr. Joseph Alpert, Chief of Medicine at the University of Arizona who was an early mentor at Harvard Medical School and has continued to support and fuel my interest in preventive cardiology. Dr. Ira Ockene, Professor of Medicine and Director of the Preventive Cardiology program at UMass Medical School was an early mentor in invasive cardiology and coronary care and has continued to help clarify my thinking in all aspects of preventive cardiology. My friend and colleague Dr. Richard Irwin has taught me a great deal about both the practice of medicine and the writing and editing of books.

My responsibilities and commitments as a cardiologist and researcher, teacher, consultant, and writer require meticulous attention to details and schedules. My Executive Assistant, Carol Moreau, does an almost miraculous job in keeping all of these strands of my life intertwined with considerable grace and competence and never loses her cool.

Last, but certainly not least, my darling wife, Stephanie Hart Rippe, has provided the safe harbor without which none of these voyages, literary or otherwise, would be conceivable. While supporting my intense work schedule and often outlandish travel arrangements, she has grounded me with her love and inspired me with her courage, beauty, and intelligence. In addition, she has given me three beautiful daughters: Hart Elizabeth Rippe, Jaelin Davis Rippe, and Devon Marshall Rippe. Our capable assistant and "oldest daughter" Natasha Koeberg and her compatriot Julie Wells have provided invaluable assistance in managing our ever growing brood. These six individuals who together comprise the "Rippe Women" continue to make it all worthwhile and have convinced me that I am not only the luckiest but also the most loved man in the universe.

To all of these individuals and many others who have helped along the way, my heartfelt gratitude. I hope the final product reflects the strength, commitment, and caring of all those who made it possible. In a small way, I hope that this book helps people who are either engaged in an ongoing battle against the number one killer — heart disease — in our country or who are seeking to prevent it, by providing useful facts, information, and above all motivation to live a heart-healthy lifestyle.

Publisher's Acknowledgments

We're proud of this book; please register your comments through our IDG Books Worldwide Online Registration Form located at http://my2cents.dummies.com.

Some of the people who helped bring this book to market include the following:

Acquisitions, Editorial, and Media Development

Project Editor: Colleen Totz

Executive Editor: Tammerly Booth

Technical Editor: Julia H. Indik, M.D., Ph.D

Editorial Coordinator: Maureen Kelly

Acquisitions Coordinator: Karen Young

Associate Permissions Editor:
Carmen Krikorian

Editorial Manager: Kristin A. Cocks

Media Development Manager:
Heather Heath Dismore

Editorial Administrator: Michelle Hacker

Production

Project Coordinator: Regina Synder

Layout and Graphics: Amy M. Adrian, Kate Jenkins, Tracy Oliver, Jill Piscitelli, Doug Rollison, Brent Savage, Jacque Schneider, Janet Seib, Maggie Ubertini, Dan Whetstine

Special Art: Kathryn Born

Proofreaders: Laura Albert, Vickie Broyles, John Greenough, Rebecca Senninger, Susan Sims, Charles Spencer

Indexer: Ty Koontz

Special Help:

Corey Dalton, Jennifer Ehrlich, Donna Frederick, Sherri Fugit, Anita Snyder

---

General and Administrative

IDG Books Worldwide, Inc.: John Kilcullen, CEO; Steven Berkowitz, President and Publisher

IDG Books Technology Publishing Group: Richard Swadley, Senior Vice President and Publisher; Walter Bruce III, Vice President and Associate Publisher; Joseph Wikert, Associate Publisher; Mary Bednarek, Branded Product Development Director; Mary Corder, Editorial Director; Barry Pruett, Publishing Manager; Michelle Baxter, Publishing Manager

IDG Books Consumer Publishing Group: Roland Elgey, Senior Vice President and Publisher; Kathleen A. Welton, Vice President and Publisher; Kevin Thornton, Acquisitions Manager; Kristin A. Cocks, Editorial Director

IDG Books Internet Publishing Group: Brenda McLaughlin, Senior Vice President and Publisher; Diane Graves Steele, Vice President and Associate Publisher; Sofia Marchant, Online Marketing Manager

IDG Books Production for Dummies Press: Debbie Stailey, Associate Director of Production; Cindy L. Phipps, Manager of Project Coordination, Production Proofreading, and Indexing; Tony Augsburger, Manager of Prepress, Reprints, and Systems; Laura Carpenter, Production Control Manager; Shelley Lea, Supervisor of Graphics and Design; Debbie J. Gates, Production Systems Specialist; Robert Springer, Supervisor of Proofreading; Kathie Schutte, Production Supervisor

Dummies Packaging and Book Design: Patty Page, Manager, Promotions Marketing

◆

The publisher would like to give special thanks to Patrick J. McGovern, without whom this book would not have been possible.

◆

Contents at a Glance

Cartoons at a Glance

By Rich Tennant

"Well, everything turned out perfect! Scarecrow has a brain, the lion found his courage, and the Tin Man got a harp."

page 5

"Of course you're better off eating grains and vegetables, but for 6¢. Valentine's Day, we've never been very successful with, 'Say it with Legumes'."

page 39

"Be just a minute, folks. We got a hole between the atria and both ventricles, and a tricuspid valve that looks deformed. Once we get it patched up, you'll be on your way."

page 109

"Be just a minute, folks. We got a hole between the atria and both ventricles, and a tricuspid valve that looks deformed. Once we get it patched up, you'll be on your way."

page 167

"You know, anyone who wishes he had a remote control for his exercise equipment is missing the idea of exercise equipment."

page 289

Fax: 978-546-7747
E-mail: richtennant@the5thwave.com
World Wide Web: www.the5thwave.com

Table of Contents

Part IV: Understanding and Controlling Heart Disease 167

Chapter 13: Tests and Procedures: When Each Is Used and What They Tell Us 169

Introduction

. . . .

Consider the following facts:

- One American dies of heart disease every 33 seconds — almost one million deaths each year.

- Almost one in four Americans has one or more types of heart disease.

- Considering all risk factors for heart disease — high blood pressure, high cholesterol, smoking, being overweight, physical inactivity — there is no family in America that is untouched by heart disease.

- Whatever your age, sex, and ethnicity, whatever your current heart health, you can acquire the knowledge and take action to work toward a healthier heart and the benefits that go with it.

As you hold this book in your hand to read these facts, your heart is beating away in your chest sustaining your life. Although it's about the size of a clenched adult fist and weighs less than a pound, your heart beats 40 million times a year and generates enough force to lift you 100 miles into the atmosphere. What an amazing — and absolutely essential — machine!

Why This Book?

The Healthy Heart For Dummies is a commonsense guide for everyone. In this book, I give you some advice, simple diagrams, and yes, even an occasional stern lecture about simple things that you can do every day to maximize your cardiac function. You'll also find some basic strategies and lifestyle plans to reduce your risk of the major forms of heart disease.

You may ask, what if you (or loved ones) already have heart disease? You have come to the right place. I run the largest exercise, nutrition and cardiac lifestyle research laboratory in the world, I am also a board-certified cardiologist and editor of the major intensive care textbook in our country. I have personally performed thousands of heart catheterizations and taken care of many people with all forms of heart disease. I will rely on that background and the many important conversations that I have had with patients to give you some simple advice about the common conditions related to heart disease. I explore some facts related to coronary artery disease, angina, heart attacks, hypertension, heart failure, and many other conditions. Along the way, I hope to answer those questions that I suspect many of my patients had but may have been afraid to ask.

When you were born, you were given one heart and one life. It is up to you to make the best of both. This book's goal is to provide simple, straightforward information and answers to help you do just that.

How This Heart Owner's Manual Is Organized

"Begin at the beginning," instructs the King of Hearts in *Alice in Wonderland*. Since that's sound advice, let's go.

Part I: The Heart and Heart Health

Part I provides the basic information you need to begin to take control of your heart health: Chapter 1 covers why you need to care more about your heart; Chapter 2 explains how the heart works; and Chapter 3 describes the conditions and activities that put the heart at risk for disease.

Part II: The Healthy Heart Lifestyle Plan

Modern science has shown that simple strategies based on proper nutrition, physical activity, weight management, and mind/body connections can both prevent and help control heart disease — to say nothing of making you wealthy and wise!

These chapters detail all the facts and resources you need to design your own personal lifestyle plan for keeping your heart healthy for a lifetime or for working in partnership with your physician to prevent and/or control heart disease. Chapters 4 and 5 offer compact guidelines for heart-healthy nutrition and all the resources you need to custom design a healthy menu that fits your taste and lifestyle. As a special bonus at the end of the book, you'll find a special section containing 35 great heart-healthy recipes by America's leading chefs.

To heartwise (and great) eating, you'll want to add physical activity. Chapter 6 covers the whys, wherefores, and benefits of physical activity. Chapter 7 helps you spring into action with a customized, personal exercise plan. Chapter 8 offers tips about drawing on the power of mind/body connections to reduce stress and achieve success.

Part III: Preventing Heart Disease: The Big Four

You can do a great deal to prevent heart disease if you control four conditions that are major contributing causes of heart disease: elevated cholesterol, high blood pressure, smoking, and being overweight. These chapters cut right to the heart of what you need to know about each of these conditions and what you can do about them, on your own and with the help of your physician and other experts as necessary or advisable. Chapter 9 corrals high blood pressure (hypertension), Chapter 10 tackles cholesterol and other fats, Chapter 11 stamps out smoking, and Chapter 12 weighs in on healthy weight loss and management.

Part IV: Understanding and Controlling Heart Disease

Speaking of the dangers of the Great Depression, President Franklin Roosevelt observed that "the only thing we have to fear is fear itself." Fear of heart disease — that you either have it or may get it — can be immobilizing. Modern science and medicine offer many strategies to prevent, diagnose, control, and manage this public health enemy number one. As a heart owner, you will find that knowledge is power. Each chapter in this section takes the mystery and fear out of the common conditions that can plague the heart and gives you the "ammunition" you need to fight back as you work in partnership with your physician and other medical allies.

Chapter 13 is a quick, dummy-friendly guide to all the tests and procedures used in evaluating heart health and problems. Then I look at the most common heart conditions experienced by Americans. Chapter 14 covers coronary artery disease, which is the leading cause of death from heart disease and is associated with a wide variety of serious syndromes including angina (chronic chest pain) and heart attack. Chapter 15 looks at heart attacks and Chapter 16 gives you strategies for cardiac rehabilitation after heart attack. Then I turn to other common conditions — rhythm disturbances in Chapter 17, heart failure (as in congestive heart failure) in Chapter 18, and in Chapter 19, other cardiac conditions such as valvular heart disease, pericardial disease, and congenital abnormalities (conditions that some people are born with). Chapter 19 also looks at the heart in pregnancy and discusses what to do about other medical issues if you have underlying heart disease.

Is heart disease ever reversible? I look at all the evidence in Chapter 20. I explore alternative therapies in Chapter 21. And Chapter 22 gives you everything you need to know about working with your doctor in a few easy pages.

Part V: The Part of Tens

If you skip the rest of the book and do nothing but memorize the ten tips in each of these four chapters, your heart will thank you.

Oh, and go to the Appendix to check out 35 of the tastiest and healthiest dishes ever set before mortal man and woman. If you thought healthy eating had to be boring, you underestimated some of America's leading chefs.

Icons Used in This Book

This icon signals physiological and scientific information about the heart. But don't worry — all technical stuff is presented in plain English.

You find facts, practices, and insights that promote or enhance heart health at the sign of this icon.

The fields of health, fitness, and medicine abound with ideas — some very popular — that have no basis in fact or that are outdated. When it ain't so, we say so.

This icon indicates practical suggestions you can put to work to help you reach your heart health goals.

Think of this icon as a caution flag.

Part I
The Heart and Heart Health

"Well, everything turned out perfect! Scarecrow has a brain, the lion found his courage, and the Tin Man *got* a harp."

In this part . . .

In this part, you find the basic information you need to begin to take control of your heart health. First, I share with you why you ought to care about your heart if you want to make the most of life. Then it's time to explore how that miracle machine that is your heart works — cardiac anatomy covered painlessly in one easy chapter. Then you get an overview of what behaviors and conditions increase your risk of developing heart disease and what you can do about them.

Chapter 1

Heart Health and You

· ·

In This Chapter

▶ Why care about heart health?

▶ The bad news about heart disease in the United States

▶ The good news about prevention and control of heart disease

▶ Concerns for women, African Americans, parents, and older adults

▶ Lifetime benefits of a healthy heart

▶ Why knowledge is power

· ·

*W*hy is the heart so magical for all of us? Why do we tell our loved ones that they live inside our hearts? Why do we say that someone with enormous courage has "tremendous heart"? Why are lovers said to die of a broken heart? And why do we all know exactly what that song means when it says, "I know a tear would glisten if once more I could listen to that gang that sang *Heart of My Heart*"?

All of us have an emotional attachment to this miraculous pump that is inconceivable for any other organ. Would a tear glisten if somebody sang about their lungs or their pancreas?

One Heart, One Life

The heart captivates our imaginations for good reason — human health, daily performance, and life itself depend on the heart. The heart and the cardiovascular system have amazing sophistication, strength, and durability. At the same time, the health of the heart rests on a fragile balance. When even small parts of its complex machinery are a little bit out of whack, the heart can cause great discomfort, pain, and even death.

Given the emotional energy we attach to our hearts and its crucial importance to life itself, most of us are pretty ignorant about the heart and how it works. We know we can't live without one. We know that heart disease is pretty common in our society and more than a little scary. So we'd like to avoid heart disease, if we could, but most of us are a little fuzzy on how to go about doing that. Meanwhile, our lives are so busy that we just keep hustling on, depending on our hearts to keep us going at full speed.

Think about that scenario for a minute. Not too smart, right? None of us would buy an expensive automobile and fail to learn even the basics about how to keep it performing up to its capabilities. Yet, we often give scant attention to preventive maintenance for our hearts, which are at once much simpler than a fancy car and infinitely more complex. Maybe the very sturdiness of our heart causes us to take it for granted until something goes wrong.

A pump that makes beautiful music

Because the heart is a pump, we often speak of it in mechanical terms. But I find it helpful also to think of the heart as functioning somewhat like a fine symphony orchestra.

In a symphony orchestra, over 100 musicians bring their talents together in a closely coordinated, precisely–timed performance to make music for the audience. So it is with the heart. Seventy times a minute, electrical impulses start in a small group of heart cells (the conductor) near the top of the heart and alert every cell in the heart muscle (the musicians) that it is time to contract. Each cell instantly responds — the heart springs into action, contracting to eject three quarters of the blood within it out into the lungs or the rest of the body. Simultaneously, the four heart valves either open or shut to guide the flow of blood. (The performance has begun.)

If you start to exercise (pick up the tempo), the healthy heart can smoothly accelerate from 70 to 180 beats per minute or even faster, and the amount of blood being sent on its way to exercising tissues can rise from a gallon a minute to the dizzying amount of eight gallons a minute. (Bravo!) So, the healthy heart is like a finely tuned orchestra, a beautiful thing to behold, making beautiful music in a seemingly effortless fashion.

When the music dies

But what if something goes wrong? What if one of the valves fails or the arteries supplying the heart get clogged or maybe even if part of the heart muscle dies? Rather than making music, the heart's impaired performance begins to produce "noise." Or to return to the heart's reality as a mechanism, it malfunctions and is no longer able to do its job of keeping the body fully functional. At worst, it stops entirely, and life stops with it.

It's your life

At birth, each of us is given one heart and one life. Most of us want to live that life to its fullest. Our desire to live as long, productively, and happily as possible provides the best reasons for caring about our hearts:

- Poorly functioning heart = poor quality of life
- No heart = no life

Beyond this stark reality, there are many more specific reasons that ought to be important to us — and spur us into action.

Why Care About Heart Health?

Heart disease is public health enemy number one in America. In one or another of its manifestations, heart disease touches virtually every family in the United States. Consider these startling facts:

- Almost 60 million Americans — almost one in every four — have one or more types of heart disease.
- Heart disease and stroke cause more than one of every two deaths — more deaths than all other diseases combined.
- An individual is over 10 times more likely to die of heart disease than in an accident and more than 30 times as likely to die of heart disease than AIDS.
- Heart disease is an equal opportunity killer. It is the leading cause of death in both men and women and in all ethnic and racial groups in the United States.
- If money is the most important thing in your life, you might like to know that the yearly estimated cost of cardiovascular disease in the United States is $286.5 *billion*.

As a cardiologist, I've seen these statistics made all too real in the lives of too many patients. Like many cardiologists, I initially trained in the most highly technical of fields, heart catheterization. I spent literally thousands of hours in the heart cath lab, wearing a lead apron as I manipulated catheters around people's hearts. One day, as I was performing yet another catheterization on yet another individual who had suffered a serious heart attack, I started thinking, *there must be a better way*. I felt like a farmer trying to grab the tail after the horse had already gotten out of the barn. I vowed then that I was going to find a way to shut that door before the horse ever left its stall by keeping that heart healthy rather than just trying to repair damage that had already occurred. Sharing this heart owner's manual with you is part of that commitment, which for twenty years has been the focus of my practice and research in cardiology.

The good news

The "bad news" facts about heart disease are real, but they aren't the only news. Extensive research has proved that there are many things that we can do in our daily lives that will preserve and maximize the health of our hearts — even if you already have heart disease. Consider these "good news" facts:

- Individuals who get regular physical activity cut their risk of heart disease in half.
- Individuals who stop smoking cigarettes can return their risk of heart disease and stroke to almost normal levels within five years after stopping.
- Overweight individuals who lose as little as 5 to 10 percent of their body weight can substantially lower their risk of heart disease.
- Simple changes in what you eat can lower blood cholesterol.
- The deaths from heart disease declined 20 percent in the last decade largely based on lifestyle measures.

So, who should care?

Who should care? Everybody. Because everyone can do lots to reduce the risk factors for heart disease, as you see in Chapter 3. Young or old. Man or woman. Totally healthy or coping with heart disease or other health problems. All ethnic and racial backgrounds. Within these groups, however, there are some associated facts and conditions that should raise your consciousness about why paying attention to heart health should be important to you.

Why care, if you are a woman?

Although heart disease is an equal opportunity killer, many people, both men and women, continue to think that heart disease is primarily a *man's* problem. Wrong!

- More women die of heart disease than men in the United States.

- While men do suffer heart attacks an average of 10 years earlier than women, after menopause women catch up. Within the year after a heart attack, 42 percent of women will die as compared to 24 percent of men.

- Women are less likely to know the warning signs for heart attack.

- Women smokers have a six times greater risk of heart attack than nonsmoking women.

- Amazingly, some recent surveys have shown that women are more afraid of breast cancer than cardiovascular disease. While there is no question that breast cancer is a serious disease, only one woman in 27 dies from breast cancer, while one in two dies from heart disease.

In the final analysis, heart disease is at least as dangerous for women as it is for men.

So, if you are a woman who has bought this book for a man in your life, think again. Keep this copy for yourself and buy another for him! There is just as much in this book for you as there is for men.

Why care, if you're African American?

Heart disease is the leading cause of death for African Americans, just as it is for all Americans. Although every individual is different, as a group, African Americans have a higher incidence of certain conditions that contribute to the risk of heart disease.

- African Americans develop high blood pressure at earlier ages than white Americans and at any decade of life, more have high blood pressure, which is a risk factor for both heart disease and stroke.

- African Americans are 2.5 times more likely to die from stroke than European Americans.

- Although heart disease is a leading cause of death for all women, black women, ages 35 to 74, have a death rate from heart disease nearly 72 percent higher than white women.

- African Americans are twice as likely as non-Hispanic whites to have diabetes, a contributing factor to developing heart disease.

While much current research seeks to determine the causes of the higher incidence of high blood pressure among African Americans, African Americans can prevent and control hypertension and other risk factors by adopting appropriate lifestyle practices.

Why care, if you already have heart disease?

Even if you have coronary heart disease or have had a heart attack, clinical research shows that working with your physician in a supervised program to reduce your risk factors for heart disease is highly beneficial and even life saving.

- If you have coronary artery disease, modifying risk factors such as high blood pressure, high blood cholesterol, physical inactivity, and being overweight can reduce your risk of a future heart attack or the need for coronary artery bypass surgery, and add years to your life.

- In clinical studies, persons who had experienced a heart attack or unstable angina and who lowered their total cholesterol by 18 percent and LDL cholesterol by 25 percent experienced a 24 percent decrease in death from cardiovascular disease compared to a control group. The need for bypass surgery was reduced by 20 percent.

- Appropriate physical activity or exercise improves the ability of persons with angina or persons who have had a heart attack or coronary surgery to perform their daily activities comfortably.

- Weight loss can help lower cholesterol levels and help control blood pressure and diabetes — conditions that contribute to continued progress of heart disease.

- If you smoke and have had a heart attack, quitting smoking significantly reduces your risk of a second heart attack or sudden death.

Why care, if you're a parent?

The incidence of heart disease is, of course, very rare among children and youth. But the roots of heart disease are firmly planted in childhood. As we have become a nation that spends more time in front of the TV or computer screen, commuting in our cars and eating out, our children are learning lifestyle behaviors and developing health conditions that may make them *more,* rather than *less,* likely to develop heart disease and other health problems. The good (and bad) habits of a lifetime usually begin in childhood. As parents we want to set examples for our children and encourage them to adopt practices that optimize their future health.

- An estimated 4.1 million teenagers, ages 12 to 17, smoke. Over 43 percent of high school students use tobacco products, and the percentage continues to grow. Smoking is a major contributor to heart disease, cancer, and other health problems.

✔ Approximately 50 percent of American teenagers get no regular physical activity.

✔ More than one in five children and youth, aged 6 to 17, is overweight, another risk factor for heart disease.

Why care, if you are older?

Unfortunately, many Americans expect that "heart trouble" will be part of their older years. That need not be so. And if you are older and even if you already have heart disease, you can do a lot to avoid being part of these statistics:

✔ Approximately 84 percent of deaths from heart disease occur in people over 65.

✔ Persons over 65 account for about 85 percent of deaths from heart attack.

✔ After age 55, the incidence of stroke doubles with each decade of life.

✔ The most frequent cause of hospitalization for people over 65 is congestive heart failure.

✔ In America, the older we get, the fatter we get. We're twice as likely to be overweight at 65 than we were at 35 — a risk for heart disease we absolutely can control.

So what's the bottom line?

There is no question that heart disease is a serious enemy — the biggest enemy. But, it is equally true that you can tame this enemy by using a few simple daily lifestyle practices as your defense. All you need is a little planning, consistency, and knowledge.

Ipsa scientia potestas est. Knowledge is power. (That Latin should get you ready for some of the medical terms I have to use occasionally. Besides, I'm a doctor, so what did you expect?) The rest of *The Healthy Heart For Dummies* is full of the information to empower you to take charge of your heart health.

Benefits of Heart Health

If the morbid statistics outlined previously in this chapter haven't scared you into the conviction that it's time to get righteous about taking care of your heart, consider the wonderful upside.

- **Improved overall health**. Many of the steps that benefit your heart health will also improve your total health and fitness, to say nothing of your good looks.

- **Increased functionality**. Use it or lose it, goes the old saying. A healthy heart increases the probability that you will be able to stay active, mobile, and engaged in pursuits that interest you for a long, long time.

- **Economic benefits**. The healthier you are, the lower your health care costs, the more money in your pocket for more fun things.

- **Longevity**. Keeping your heart healthy is not an iron-clad guarantee that you'll live longer, but considering the heart disease mortality rates reviewed, even we card-carrying "Dummies" can figure out that keeping our hearts healthy can keep the grim reaper away longer.

- **More fun. Less excitement for your family**. Nothing slows you down or scares the family like a heart attack. Angina pain, angioplasty, coronary artery bypass surgery, and other common outcomes of heart disease aren't picnics in the park either.

Chapter 2

Anatomy and Destiny: The Heart and Cardiovascular System

*H*ere it is, shown in Figure 2-1: Your heart. My heart. Every human heart. Not much to look at, is it? The average adult heart is about the size of a clenched fist and weighs under a pound. But our lives depend on our hearts. The heart is the "engine" that keeps our bodies functioning. Now, your brain may be telling you that the heart is "just a pump," but without it even the mighty, controlling, thinking brain is nothing but dead meat.

In this chapter, I discuss how your heart and cardiovascular system are structured — their anatomy — and how they accomplish their amazing work. I also show how a sound knowledge of the anatomy of your heart can make a big difference in the destiny of your life.

Can you skip this chapter? Sure, but I wouldn't. Even if you begin to hyperventilate (or snooze) at the mere idea of technical stuff, don't forget that knowledge is power. You'll be glad you got a grip on these basics. Understanding the amazing beauty and structure of the heart helps you better understand strategies for keeping your heart healthy. If you already have heart disease, understanding more about your heart helps you be a better partner in your health care.

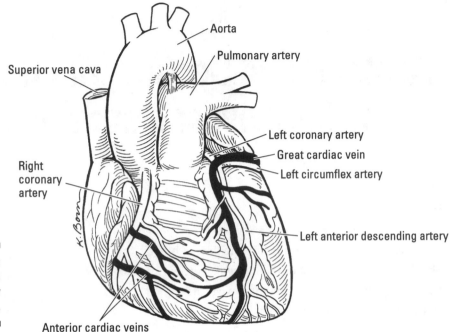

Aorta

Pulmonary artery

Superior vena cava

Left coronary artery

Great cardiac vein

Left circumflex artery

Right coronary artery

Left anterior descending artery

Figure 2-1:
A typical healthy heart.

Anterior cardiac veins

The Heart

The heart is located in the center of the chest cavity. About one-third rests beneath the breastbone, or *sternum,* and two-thirds rests to the left of the midline of the body. The breastbone, rib cage, muscles, and other structures of the chest wall protect the heart. In the average adult, the heart pumps 5 quarts of blood a minute at rest and 25 to 30 quarts per minute at maximum effort. In highly trained athletes working at maximum effort, the amount of blood pumped per minute can run as high as 40 quarts.

The heart muscle

The walls of the heart are made up of a unique muscle called the *myocardium* (*myo* = muscle and *cardium* = heart; pronounced *my'-o-car'-dee-um*). This muscle is the only one of its kind in the body because it must have oxygenated blood at all times to survive. In contrast, other muscles, such as those of the arms and legs, while still highly dependent on oxygenated blood can also perform briefly in the absence of oxygen (as when you dash from your car to the store during a rain shower). This luxury is denied to the heart. For the heart to keep beating, the arteries that feed the heart, the *coronary arteries*, must deliver a continuous supply of oxygenated blood. That's why the narrowing of these arteries, also known as *coronary artery disease (CAD)*, is so dangerous to the heart. When the coronary arteries become narrowed, a series of adverse events ensues, starting with *angina (an'-gin-uh)*, or chest pain, and ranging all the way to heart attack and, potentially, sudden death.

The heart as a pump

The heart is a magnificent four-chambered pump that has two jobs:

- ✔ To pump blood to the lungs to get oxygen
- ✔ To pump the oxygenated blood to the rest of the body

To fulfill these tasks, the heart has two sides, as shown in Figure 2-2. The two main pumping chambers of the heart, called *ventricles,* are located at the bottom of the heart. Sitting above the ventricles are two small booster pumps called *atria* (or *atrium,* if you are talking about just one). The right ventricle pumps the deoxygenated blood which has returned from the body through the veins and right atrium out into the lungs where it gets a new supply of oxygen. The blood then returns to the heart, first entering the left atrium and then the left ventricle. The left ventricle pumps the oxygenated blood through the arterial system out to the rest of the body where it feeds every vital organ — in fact, every single living cell you have. A thick muscular wall called the *septum* separates the left and right ventricles. Valves regulate the flow of blood in and out of the heart and from chamber to chamber.

The heart valves

The heart has four valves, which act a bit like cardiac traffic cops because they determine what direction the blood flows, how much of it flows and when to stop it from flowing. Take a look at the position of the four valves and how they direct blood flow through the heart, as illustrated in Figure 2-3.

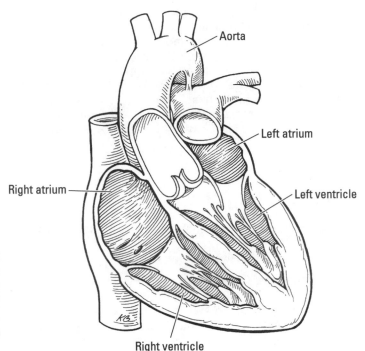

Aorta

Left atrium

Right atrium

Left ventricle

Figure 2-2:
The four
chambers of
the heart.

Right ventricle

✔ The *tricuspid* valve, so-called because it has three *cusps,* or flaps, opens
to allow blood to flow into the right ventricle when the heart is relaxed
and closes to prevent blood from going back into the body when the
heart contracts.

✔ The *mitral* valve *(my'-trul),* which resembles a bishop's mitered hat,
controls the blood flow between the left atrium and the left ventricle.
(The next time you see the Pope in full regalia, think of the hat that he
wears as resembling the structure of a mitral valve in the heart.)

✔ The *pulmonic* valve controls the flow of blood from the right ventrical
to the pulmonary artery supplying the lungs. (This is called *pulmonic*
because the Latin word for lungs is the root word for *pulmonary.*)

✔ The *aortic* valve, which separates the left ventricle from the aorta, opens
to allow blood flow to the body when the heart contracts and closes
when the heart relaxes to prevent blood from flowing back into
the heart.

To the cardiologist, the heart valves literally make "music to the ear." (See
why in Chapter 19.)

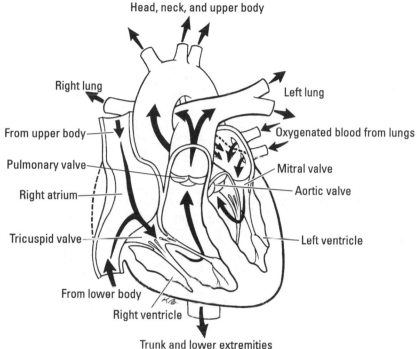

Head, neck, and upper body

Right lung

From upper body

Pulmonary valve

Right atrium

Tricuspid valve

From lower body

Right ventricle

Left lung

Oxygenated blood from lungs

Mitral valve

Aortic valve

Left ventricle

Trunk and lower extremities

Figure 2-3:
The valves
of the heart
and how
they work.

The coronary arteries

Three large coronary arteries and their many branches supply blood to the
heart. As you can see in Figure 2-4, two coronary arteries branch off one main
trunk which is called the *left main coronary artery*. One of these branches
runs down the front of the heart, so in medspeak it is naturally called the *left
anterior descending artery*. (*Anterior* is just a fancy word for *front*.) The second
branch of the left main coronary artery circles around and supplies the side
wall of the heart so it is called the *left circumflex artery*. The third main coronary artery, which typically comes off of a separate trunk vessel, is called the
right coronary artery. It supplies the back and bottom walls of the heart.
Significant narrowing of any of these coronary arteries causes the symptom
of angina, which is typically characterized as chest pain. (I discuss angina in
detail in Chapter 14.) An acute blockage of one these arteries causes a heart
attack, and the heart muscle that had formerly been supplied by the blocked
artery dies.

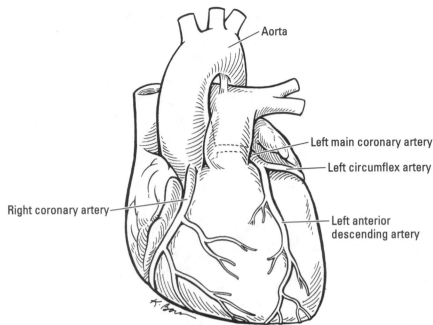

Aorta

Left main coronary artery

Left circumflex artery

Right coronary artery

Left anterior descending artery

Figure 2-4:
The coronary arteries.

Mechanics may tell you that the most important thing you can do to keep your car healthy is change the oil frequently. Well, keeping these coronary arteries clear, free-flowing, and doing their job for the heart is the most important thing you can do to keep your heart healthy for a lifetime. So, this book shares a number of strategies to help you do just that.

The electrical system

Surprised to hear that the beating of the heart is controlled by an electrical system? Many folks are shocked to hear this. But it's true — and even more exciting, because your cardiac electric company is the mechanism that enables pacemakers and defibrillators (those dramatic standbys of TV doctor dramas) to work. This system is controlled by a group of specialized cells that spontaneously discharge, sending electrical currents down specialized nerves and tissues, alerting all the other heart cells that it is time to discharge and causing the heart to contract — for most folks about 70 to 80 times a minute when at rest. When any of these electrical structures become diseased or disordered, *arrhythmias (ay-rith'-mee-uhs),* or heart rhythm disturbances, occur. (More about these in Chapter 17.)

The pericardium

The entire heart rests in a thin sac called the *pericardium* (*peri* = around and *cardium* = heart). The thin-walled pericardium normally rests right up against the walls of the heart and is lubricated by a thin layer of body fluids to allow the heart to slide easily within it. However, this sac around the heart can become inflamed, resulting in chest discomfort or even compromised heart function. (You can check out these conditions, called *pericarditis,* in Chapter 19).

The Rest of the Cardiovascular System

A pump is useless without the rest of the plumbing, which in our bodies is called *the cardiovascular system.* Take a quick look at how it all fits and functions together.

The lungs

The lungs rest on either side of the heart and take up most of the space in the chest cavity, as shown in Figure 2-5. The lungs are a complex series of air sacs surrounded by a complex, highly branching network of blood vessels. Their sole purpose in life is to receive the deoxygenated blood from the heart, chock the red corpuscles full of fresh oxygen, and send them back to the heart for delivery to the body. To facilitate the rapid flow and reoxygenation of enormous amounts of blood, this heart-to-lung-to-heart circuit is a low pressure system; that means that the heart does not have to exert very great force with each contraction to move blood through this system.

The arteries

As oxygenated blood returns to the left side of the heart, it is pumped out to the body through the *aorta,* the major artery in the body, and into the rest of the arterial system to feed the whole body. Because the body is fairly large, compared to the heart, the heart exerts force to push oxygenated blood throughout the body, and the arteries also have muscular walls to help push the blood along. This force exerted against resistance of the artery walls creates a high pressure system. At the same time, this high-pressure system is very *elastic* to allow the arteries to expand or contract to meet the needs of various organs and muscles whether they are working or at rest.

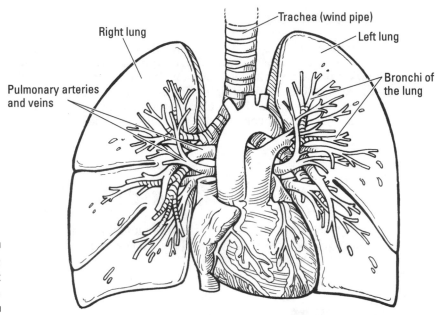

Right lung

Trachea (wind pipe)

Left lung

Pulmonary arteries and veins

Bronchi of the lung

Figure 2-5:
The heart and lungs.

Each time the left ventricle contracts, it pumps blood into the arterial system, which in turn expands to accept the surge of blood. However, this expansion of the arterial system does not occur as rapidly as the heart contracts. Therefore, when the heart relaxes, there is still pressure in the arterial system and blood continues to move forward to the body. The contraction of the left ventricle is called *systole (sis'-tuh-lee)*. When the heart relaxes, the pressure falls somewhat as the blood continues to flow in the arterial system. This relaxation of the heart is called *diastole (dye-ass'-tuh-lee)*. Your *blood pressure* is determined by measuring the amount of pressure in the arteries during both the systole and diastole. (Read more about blood pressure in Chapter 9.)

The capillaries

To get nourishing blood to each individual cell, the arterial system divides and redivides into a system of ever smaller branches, ultimately ending up in a network of microscopic vessels called *capillaries*, which deliver the oxygenated blood to the working cells of every organ and muscle in the body. This amazing network of branching microscopic vessels would put even the most complex digital network to shame! A section of body tissue no bigger than the head of a pin has between 2,000 and 3,000 capillaries.

The veins

After oxygen leaves the capillary system, the deoxygenated blood and waste products from the cells are carried back through the body in the *veins*. The veins from the legs ultimately come together in a very large vein in the middle of the body called the *inferior vena cava (vee'nuh cay'vuh)*, and all the veins in the upper part of the body come together in a large vein called the *superior vena cava*. These veins discharge blood into the right atrium of the heart to be pumped into the right ventricle and out to the lungs again to start the whole process over again. You can see this circular flow of blood through the heart in Figure 2-3.

What Determines Your Heart Rate?

In addition to its internal electrical system, the heart has profound linkages to the nervous system, which allows additional control of the heart rate. Two main branches of the involuntary nervous system interact with the heart — the *sympathetic nervous system* and the *parasympathetic nervous system*. In simple terms, the sympathetic nervous system helps the heart speed up and the parasympathetic nervous system helps the heart slow down. I discuss rhythm problems in Chapter 17.

Sympathetic nervous system

The sympathetic nervous system typically directs the heart to speed up during periods of exercise or strong emotion. For example, we can feel our heart beat faster when we are angry, upset, or frightened. These responses probably go back to the survival needs of earliest human history. Chapter 8 looks more fully at the reasons why. For now let's concentrate on the how. The sympathetic nervous system acts both through direct nerve links to the heart and through chemical substances which reach the heart through the blood stream. In everyday speech, we say we can feel our adrenaline pumping. When the heart speeds up, it is known in medicine as *tacchycardia (tack'-ih-car'-dee-uh)*. Of course, this is highly beneficial when you are exercising, but it is not so good when the accelerated rate results from disordered electrical impulses found in many people with heart disease. (See Chapter 17 for further discussion of heart rhythm problems).

Parasympathetic nervous system

The parasympathetic branch of the nervous system acts as a trusty, unobtrusive housekeeper that keeps such functions as breathing and digestion perking along without any need for conscious thought on our part. (Imagine how complex life would be if you had to stop and think each time you wanted to breathe.) The parasympathetic nervous system can also direct the heart to slow down, both through direct nerve links to the heart and through release of a chemical called *acetylcholine* into the bloodstream.

The slowing of the heart is called *bradycardia (bray'-dee-car'dee-uh)*. When individuals are in great shape physically, they may have a very healthy bradycardia. However, in certain disease states, the heart rate can be too slow, resulting in inadequate blood flow to the tissues.

In certain circumstances, the parasympathetic nervous system can even be "tricked" into causing an inappropriately slow heart rate. The resulting brief period of inadequate blood flow to the brain usually causes a fainting episode. Fainting is the brain's safety valve because when it decides the heart is not sending it enough blood, the brain sends the body crashing "to ground" where in horizontal position the brain will automatically get its share of the blood flow, whether or not the heart is going fast or slow.

The Heart at Rest and at Work

Now that you know what all the parts are, it's time to see how they work together. Let's start with most Americans' favorite position — relaxing on the couch.

The view from the couch

While you are sitting still, your heart is beating at 70 to 80 contractions a minute (unless you are very fit, but more about that later). With each contraction, the right ventricle discharges three-quarters of the blood it contains into the vessels of the lungs where it gets oxygenated. At the same time, the left ventricle is discharging three-quarters of the blood that it contains into the aorta and arterial system to feed all the organs and muscles. All four heart valves are working together controlling both blood flow into and out of the heart and making sure that no blood goes in the opposite direction. (Wouldn't it be nice if our traffic cops were so efficient!)

The arterial system is dilating each time the left ventricle empties into it and speeding blood on its way to the various working tissues. How much blood goes to each tissue is determined by what that muscle or organ needs to do.

If you have just eaten a big meal, for example, the heart, brain, parasympathetic nervous system, and arteries all have decided that more blood should go to the organs in the gastrointestinal tract to help them with the work of digesting that low fat, cardiac-healthy meal that you just ate.

The view from the track

But say that after reading this book, you have decided that you are going to exercise regularly. (Good idea!) Exercise poses a different challenge to the heart as compared to rest. Extra blood flow must go to the exercising muscles and also to the coronary arteries to feed the heart muscle itself so that it can pump out the extra blood required for exertion.

Fortunately, this is no problem for the healthy heart. Once again, all systems work in concert. Extra blood is pumped from the heart, extra blood flow courses down the coronary arteries which dilate to accept this extra flow. The heart valves continue to direct the blood in the proper direction and the electrical system, with a little boost from the nervous system, starts to generate more beats per minute. At the same time, the cardiac muscle relaxes a little bit, allowing more blood to be pumped out during each beat.

In addition, the nervous system, working with the arterial system, has caused some parts of the arterial circulation to expand or dilate to send more blood to the working muscles and other parts to constrict or narrow to divert blood away from areas where it is not as needed during exertion. The good news is that if you exert yourself on a regular basis, the heart and the rest of the cardiovascular system begin to become more efficient and prepare for the regular exercise sessions.

Anatomy Is Destiny

Well. . . at any rate, the condition of your heart's anatomy is your health's destiny. When all parts of the heart and cardiovascular system are healthy and functioning well together, it is a beautiful system. But the heart is a muscle. Like any muscle, it works best if you keep it in shape and if you avoid injury.

The conditioned heart

Like any muscle, a conditioned heart is stronger and better able to meet the demands the body places on it. Human bodies were designed to be in motion. And the motion of physical activity keeps the heart tuned up.

- Literally hundreds of studies have shown that individuals who adopt the simple habit of daily physical activity substantially reduce their risk of developing various heart problems, most notably, coronary artery disease.

- The conditioned heart enables individuals to accomplish the activities of daily living with comfort as well as plenty of breath and energy.

- The more conditioned the heart, the lower the resting heart rate, the less work the heart has to do in a lifetime.

The deconditioned heart

In contrast to the active individual, the individual who leads a sedentary lifestyle can actually experience a deconditioned heart. The deconditioned heart is less efficient at doing its work and has to work harder to get adequate blood flow throughout the body.

- Do you avoid the stairs because climbing two or three flights leaves you extremely short of breath?

- Do you circle a parking lot numerous times looking for a space right in front of the store to make sure that you don't have to walk much?

- Do you watch sports on television rather than participate in them with friends and family?

If you answered yes to any of these questions, you're a prime candidate for a deconditioned heart. And a deconditioned heart is the first step in a slow slide down a long slope toward a sick heart. But it's not too late to get that heart in shape. This book shows you how.

The diseased heart

A sedentary lifestyle coupled with unhealthy practices such as poor nutrition, weight gain, and cigarette smoking or certain health conditions such as high blood pressure, high cholesterol, or diabetes can severely alter the basic cardiac structures and lead to a disordered anatomy that can create a very unhappy destiny. A short list of the things that can go wrong includes blocked arteries, high cholesterol, high blood pressure, angina, heart attack, heart failure, and sudden death. The bottom line is that many of the cardiac problems that people experience are brought on by years of neglect and failure to abide by even the most basic of cardiac healthy lifestyle principles. (Nature makes a few mistakes, too, but even in those cases, personal choices often complicate the problem.) The good news is that even years of neglect can be largely turned around if you pay attention to the basic principles of a cardiac healthy lifestyle. In this book, I will show you how — starting in the next chapter with all the things that put at risk the miraculous organ we call our heart.

Chapter 3

Life's Risky Business: Minimizing Your Risk of Coronary Heart Disease

In This Chapter

▶ What's a risk factor anyway?

▶ Why two risk factors are double trouble and three are even worse

▶ The big six risk factors that we can all control

▶ Three risk factors you cannot control (but need to watch for)

▶ New risk factors that you may have never heard of

▶ New information on clustering of risk factors

▶ How risk factors differ in women and in men

▶ A self test you can take to estimate your risk of heart attack

*1*n the history of medicine, risk factors are a relatively new concept. In fact, before World War II, when men (and it usually was men) and women died suddenly, it was thought to be an act of God. Even if people knew that someone died of a heart attack, the cause of the heart attack was not linked to any personal habits or actions. How else could you explain that our soldiers were sent off to battle with cigarettes as a reward for a job well done, that Camel cigarettes were advertised as "the doctor's choice," or that no one thought twice about consuming enormous steaks without trimming the fat? To borrow a phrase (one unfortunately co-opted by a cigarette manufacturer), "We've come a long way, baby!"

What Is a Risk Factor Anyway?

Just as the name suggests, a *risk factor* is something that increases your risk of developing a chronic condition. In the case of cardiac health, a risk factor is either a personal habit or practice or a characteristic that increases your risk of developing coronary heart disease.

We have learned, and continue to learn, about these factors primarily through a number of long-term studies of very large groups of people such as the Framingham Heart Study, which has followed the lifestyle and health record of 10,000 men and women in great detail over fifty years.

In medicine, some risk factors for heart disease are classified as major, meaning that they at least double your risk of heart disease. That is not to say that other risk factors are unimportant, just that the current research data for these risk factors does not demonstrate the level of danger demonstrated by the major risk factors. But these other risk factors can still contribute in significant ways to your risk of heart disease.

Table 3-1	Risk Factors for Developing Coronary Artery Disease	
Major Risk Factors	*Other Risk Factors*
Hypertension	Diabetes
Elevated Cholesterol	Family history of premature heart disease
Cigarette Smoking	Male gender
Inactive lifestyle	Age
Obesity	Stress

Emerging risk factors

Every day scientists are learning and publishing more about other risk factors which certainly contribute to coronary artery disease. For example, these newer studies have added to our knowledge of other suspected risk factors, such as a high consumption of alcohol, elevated levels of homocysteine (an amino acid), low levels of antioxidants and abnormal blood clotting. In the future, as research provides more data, these risk factors will undoubtedly be classified as either major or other risk factors.

Double trouble and more—multiplying risks

One aspect of risk factors that makes them particularly dangerous is their tendency, when you have two or more, to multiply the effects of each other rather than to add to each other. As you can see in Figure 3-1, which is based on data from the Framingham Heart Study, individuals who have a single risk factor double their risk of developing heart disease. With two risk factors present, the risk quadruples. But when three risk factors are present, the risk of heart disease increases between eight and twenty times! Having two or three risk factors, unfortunately, is not unusual. In fact, risk factors have a distinct tendency to cluster, as I discuss later in this chapter.

Figure 3-1: Eight-year risk of CHD (per 1,000) according to number of coronary risk factors (Framingham Heart Study).

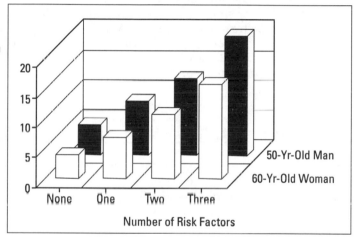

Heading trouble off—controlling risk factors

For all the major risk factors and a couple of the others, what you helped create, you can change.

- ✔ By controlling risk factors, you can substantially lower your risk of ever developing coronary heart disease. In medicine, we call the prevention of a disease entity in the first place *primary prevention.*

- ✔ If you already have coronary heart disease, controlling risk factors usually decreases your risk of having further complications and manifestations from this condition. This attempt to prevent further problems is called *secondary prevention.*

Interpreting risk factors—one size does not fit all

Before I discuss risk factors and their reduction in more detail, it is important to understand that controlling or treating a given risk factor may mean different things for different individuals. Just like in clothing, one size does not fit all. For example, a mildly elevated cholesterol in a young woman with no other risk factors — say 215 mg/dl — requires a certain level of treatment. On the other hand, the same level of elevated cholesterol in a 60-year-old man who has already suffered a heart attack might signal *red alert* to his cardiologist.

Because the young woman with elevated cholesterol has a relatively greater risk of developing coronary heart disease sometime in her life than a young woman who does not have elevated cholesterol, her elevated cholesterol should be treated. But her situation is not as immediately threatening and she does not need to be treated as aggressively as the 60-year-old man with heart disease and elevated cholesterol. Because his elevated cholesterol comes in the context of his already having heart disease, therapy for this man would be much more intensive.

Six Risk Factors That You Can Control

Although risk factors are often classified as *major* factors or *other* factors, it's probably even more educational to divide risk factors into those that you *can* modify and those that you *cannot* modify. So that's the way I discuss them, starting the risk factors that you can tackle successfully.

Hypertension

Since landmark studies conducted in the 1960s, there has been no serious doubt that elevated blood pressure represents a very substantial risk factor for both coronary heart disease and stroke. Hypertension appears to be particularly dangerous in terms of the likelihood of developing a stroke. (For an in-depth discussion of hypertension, see Chapter 9.)

Hypertension is extremely common in the United States, probably because of our nutritional habits, propensity to gain weight, and sedentary lifestyle. Over one-fourth of the entire adult population in the United States suffers from hypertension. By the time that an individual reaches the age of 60, he or she has a greater than 60 percent chance of having an elevated blood pressure.

Once again, the good news is that daily habits and practices, such as appropriate weight control, sound nutrition, and regular physical activity can profoundly diminish the likelihood of ever developing hypertension in the first place and can significantly contribute to the effective treatment of elevated blood pressure.

Elevated cholesterol

By now, almost everyone knows that it is bad to have a high cholesterol level in your blood. When it comes to risk of heart disease, however, elevated blood cholesterol is one of a number of lipid problems (problems with fats in the blood) that can significantly elevate your risk of heart disease. The abnormalities which are particularly dangerous include an elevated total cholesterol, elevated LDL cholesterol, low HDL cholesterol, elevated triglycerides or any combination of the four.

The good news is that by following appropriate lifestyle measures and, in some instances, utilizing medicines which are now available, this risk factor for coronary heart disease can be very effectively managed. You can get all the definitions, evidence, and strategies for better controlling cholesterol levels in Chapter 10.

Tobacco use

With all the information available about health, heart disease, and cigarette smoking, any smoker who fails to understand that smoking poses a very serious threat to his or her health must have been hiding incommunicado in a wilderness cave for the last 20 years. Reams of data present a very stark, negative picture: Cigarette smoking (and the use of other tobacco products) is the leading cause of premature death in the United States each year, claiming over 400,000 lives.

While cigarette smoking has declined, unfortunately about 25 percent of the adult population still smokes cigarettes. Shockingly, while many adults successfully struggle to quit cigarette smoking, an estimated 3,000 children start smoking every day.

The health consequences of cigarette smoking are very severe.

> ✔ An individual who smokes cigarettes triples his or her risk of heart disease and increases his or her risk of lung cancer by a whopping 3,000 percent.

> ✔ In addition, individuals who smoke risk harming the health of others. Individuals with coronary heart disease can have angina attacks provoked by being in a smoke filled room.
>
> ✔ Cigarette smoking tends to lower HDL cholesterol (the good guys).

In an otherwise bleak picture, there is outstanding good news:

> ✔ Stopping smoking lowers the risk of coronary heart disease.
>
> ✔ Individuals who quit smoking can anticipate adding two to three years to their life expectancy.
>
> ✔ Smoking cessation also improves blood lipids. In one study, LDL cholesterol decreased over 5 percent and HDL cholesterol increased over 3 percent in individuals who stopped cigarette smoking.

Quitting is so important (and so tough) that Chapter 11 is devoted to the facts and strategies you need to find the ways and means — and support — to stamp out smoking in your life.

Physical inactivity

In 1994, faced with overwhelming evidence, the American Heart Association added the first new "major" risk factor in twenty-five years — a physically inactive lifestyle. Physical inactivity also contributes significantly to a number of the other major risk factors, such as high blood pressure, perhaps elevated blood cholesterol, and often obesity. But if you get off your duff and get active, you can turn this sad picture around. (See Chapters 6 and 7 for help.) A physically active lifestyle not only reduces that specific risk factor for heart disease, but also has a positive impact on these other major risk factors for heart disease.

Obesity

In 1998, obesity joined the list of major independent risk factors for heart disease. Obesity also contributes to many other risk factors, such as hypertension and elevated cholesterol and other abnormal lipids.

Unfortunately, in the last 10 years, the prevalence of obesity has grown a shocking 34 percent. Over one out of every three adults is now obese. By obese, I mean at least 20 percent over desirable body weight. That's not as fat as most people think, either. For example, if your optimal weight is 150 pounds and you weigh 180 — just 30 pounds overweight — you are technically obese even if you think you still look pretty good.

Obesity increases the risk of coronary artery disease in a number of different ways.

✔ Obesity interacts with many other risk factors for coronary heart disease, including high blood pressure, Type 2 diabetes, and cholesterol problems.

✔ Obese people are particularly likely to suffer from clustering of risk factors. In fact, an obese individual has a 70 percent chance of having at least one other risk factor for heart disease, a 50 percent chance of having at least two other risk factors for heart disease, and a 20 to 25 percent chance of having three other risk factors for heart disease!

✔ Obesity leads to dangerous lipid abnormalities that increase the risk of heart disease. These include elevated blood triglycerides, an elevated LDL cholesterol, and a depressed HDL.

✔ Carrying extra weight around the abdomen (sometimes called *abdominal obesity* or *apple-shaped obesity*) is particularly dangerous in terms of its risk of coronary heart disease.

Weight loss reduces risk. See Part II of this book for a lifestyle plan to help you achieve this goal. Remember, obese people do not die because they are too fat; they die of heart disease.

Diabetes mellitus

Approximately 14 million people in the United States, or 6 percent of the adult population, suffer from diabetes mellitus. Over 95 percent of these individuals have Type 2 or "adult onset" diabetes. Diabetes represents a significant risk factor for coronary heart disease. In fact, coronary heart disease is by far the leading cause of death in individuals with diabetes.

Individuals with diabetes often have multiple blood lipid abnormalities including elevated blood triglycerides and elevated LDL cholesterol and a depressed HDL. Having this particular constellation of lipid abnormalities spells triple trouble! For reasons that are not totally clear, women with diabetes have an even greater risk of heart disease than men with diabetes.

By working with your physician if you have diabetes, however, you can lower many of the complications of diabetes and also control your blood lipids. Daily steps that you can take to help control diabetes include weight loss if you are overweight, regular physical activity, and proper nutritional habits.

Risk Factors for Heart Disease That You Cannot Modify

Now I come to three risk factors that you can't modify: your age, gender, and family history. Having one or more of these non-modifiable risk factors makes it particularly important that you pay close attention to those risk factors which you can modify.

- ✔ **Age:** Age is considered a significant risk factor for coronary heart disease for men if you are above the age of 45 and for women if you are above the age of 55 or have undergone premature menopause without estrogen replacement therapy.

- ✔ **Gender:** Men are more likely to develop coronary heart disease than women. Furthermore, the onset of symptoms for coronary heart disease typically occurs 10 years later in women than in men. It is important, however, to point out that coronary heart disease remains the number one killer in *both* men and women in the United States. Coronary heart disease becomes particularly prevalent in women after menopause. Over the age of 65, both men and women have approximately the same risk for coronary heart disease.

- ✔ **Family history:** Coronary heart disease tends to occur more frequently in some families than in others. If you come from a family where premature heart disease has occurred in a brother, sister, father, or mother, this clearly increases your risk of coronary heart disease. By premature coronary heart disease, we mean that any first degree male relative (father or brother) has had a definite diagnosed heart attack or sudden death before age 55 or that any first degree female relative (mother or sister) has had one of these events before age 65.

Emerging Risk Factors for Coronary Heart Disease

Recent research has continued to identify other risk factors that may increase or decrease your risk for coronary heart disease. Although conclusive evidence for some of the following areas is not yet available, it is still worthwhile to discuss them with your physician.

- ✔ **Alcohol:** The relationship between alcohol and coronary heart disease is complex. Several studies have shown that moderate alcohol consumption may actually be associated with decreased risk of coronary heart disease. Moderate consumption means no more than one to two glasses of wine per day, one to two beers per day, or one and a half ounces of distilled spirits a day. Individuals who do not currently consume alcohol, however, should not use this as a justification to start. Furthermore, higher levels of alcohol consumption, (three alcoholic drinks per day or more) are associated with an increased risk of high blood pressure and heart disease (and motor vehicle accidents).

✔ **Homocysteine:** *Homocysteine* is an amino acid that is a building block of proteins in the body. However, some studies show that elevated concentrations of homocysteine in the blood can be associated with increased risk of coronary heart disease. Fortunately, relatively simple measures, particularly taking additional folic acid (also called folate) can decrease blood homocysteine levels in individuals who have elevations of this amino acid.

In order to obtain the appropriate level of folate, most scientists have encouraged individuals to consume 400 micrograms of folate per day. Since this information is very new, you should consult with your physician about whether or not a blood homocystine level should be obtained on you. But whatever the impact of folate on heart disease risk, consuming 400 mcg of folic acid daily is a reasonable health decision and absolutely mandatory for women of childbearing age.

✔ **Low levels of antioxidants:** In recent years, antioxidants have been hyped by the popular media as the cure *du jour* for several conditions including risk of heart disease. It is true that several studies have supported the concept that low levels of antioxidants in blood may increase the risk of coronary heart disease. These findings have led some physicians to recommend that individuals who are either at increased risk for coronary heart disease or who have established heart disease take supplementary antioxidants such as Vitamin E, Vitamin C, and/or beta-carotene. This recommendation, which remains controversial, is not included as part of the current generally accepted standard risk factor reduction recommendations. But further studies are underway to clarify whether or not this is a reasonable recommendation. Most recent studies in this area have suggested that antioxidants do not lower the risk of heart disease.

✔ **"Type A" personality and stress:** Without a doubt, linkages exist between the mind and the heart, physical as well as emotional. Individuals who exhibit "type A" behavior — those who are persistently rushed and unhappy and particularly those who face the world with high levels of hostility — are at increased risk for heart disease. If you experience high levels of stress in your life, it is worthwhile to explore ways of lowering this stress. (See Chapter 8 for strategies.)

✔ **Abnormal blood clotting:** In the last ten years, substantial evidence has emerged indicating that how one's blood clots is part of the process of acute coronary artery disease. Certain rare clotting abnormalities clearly increase the risk of coronary heart disease for some individuals. But at this time, using blood clotting parameters to determine an individual's risk of coronary heart disease is highly experimental. If you have questions concerning whether or not this rare problem relates to you, discuss it with your physician.

Clustering of Risk Factors

Most physicians tend to be splitters rather than lumpers. As a result, when we are educating folks about heart disease, we physicians have probably often underestimated the strong tendency for risk factors to cluster in individuals. Such clustering is particularly true for overweight individuals, who, in addition to excess weight, often have one or more other risk factors for heart disease. This condition makes them particularly susceptible to dying from heart disease. The reason for this probably relates to abnormalities caused by fat cells in general and abdominal fat cells in particular.

If you are overweight, you should make it a point to discuss with your physician whether or not you have other risk factors for heart disease in addition to your obesity. The odds are that you do. At the risk of sounding like a stuck record, let me note again that many of the lifestyle measures I discuss throughout this book will be particularly valuable in simultaneously reducing multiple risk factors for heart disease. And weight loss in and of itself is a highly effective way of reducing multiple risk factors for heart disease.

Assessing Your Risk Factors — a Quiz

Many tests are available to help individuals assess their risk of developing coronary heart disease in general and first heart attacks in particular. This test, based on data from the Framingham Heart Study, will help you assess your risk of having a first heart attack. It will also give you a good idea of where you can work to modify your risk factors.

First Heart Attack Risk Test

This test will help you figure your risk of a first heart attack. Fill in your points for each risk factor. Then total them to find out your risk.

_____ **Age (in years): Men**
    0 pts. less than 35; 1 pt. 35-39; 2 pts. 40-48; 3 pts. 49-53; 4 pts. 54+

_____ **Age (in years): Women**
    0 pts. less than 42; 1 pt. 42-44; 2 pts. 45-54; 3 pts. 55-73; 4 pts. 74+

_____ **Family History**
    2 pts. A family history of heart disease or heart attacks before age 60.

_____ **Inactive lifestyle**
    1 pt. I rarely exercise or do anything physically demanding.

_____ **Weight**
    1 pt. I'm more than 20 lbs. over my ideal weight.

_____ **Smoking**
   1 pt. I'm a smoker

_____ **Diabetic**
   1 pt. Male diabetic; 2 pts. Female Diabetic

_____ **Total Cholesterol Level**
   0 pts. Less than 240 mg/dl; 1 pt. 240-315 mg/dl; 2 pts. More than 315 mg/dl

   HDL Level (Good cholesterol)

   0 pts. 35-59mg/dl 1; pt. 30-38 mg/dl; 2 pts. Under 30 mg/dl; 1pt. Over 60 mg/dl

_____ **Blood Pressure**
   I don't take blood pressure medication; my blood pressure is:
   (*use your top or higher blood pressure number*)
   0 pts. Less than 140 mmHg; 1 pt. 140-170 mmHg; 2 pts. Greater than 170 mmHg
        (or)
   1 pt. I am currently taking blood pressure medication.

_____ **Total Points**

If you scored 4 points or more, you could be at above the average risk of a first heart attack compared to the general adult population. The more points you score, the higher your risk. (Based on data from The Framingham Study, as adapted by Bristol Meyer Squib.)

Leading a Cardiac-Healthy Lifestyle

While life can be a risky business, you can lower your risk of coronary heart disease by adopting healthy habits and actions in your daily life. You'll find a lot of information and tips throughout the rest of this book to help you learn more about how and why. Many of the measures such as proper nutrition, increased physical activity, and weight management can simultaneously lower many risk factors for heart disease. Following these guidelines of a cardiac healthy lifestyle is particularly important for individuals who are predisposed to a higher risk of CHD by virtue of their age, sex, or previous family history. Adopting a heart-healthy lifestyle is your best defense against the leading killer of both men and women in the United States.

Part II
The Healthy Heart Lifestyle Plan

The 5th Wave   By Rich Tennant

"Of course you're better off eating grains and vegetables, but for St. Valentine's Day, we've never been very successful with, 'Say it with Legumes'."

In this part . . .

In this part, I show you how simple strategies based on proper nutrition, physical activity, weight management, and mind/body connections can both prevent and help control heart disease — to say nothing of making you wealthy and wise! These chapters provide all the facts and resources you need to design your own personal lifestyle plan for keeping your heart healthy for a lifetime or for working in partnership with your physician to prevent and/or control heart disease. There are nutrition facts and resources for custom designing a heart-healthy eating plan that fits your taste and lifestyle. In addition to overall strategies for effective physical activity, I provide a 12-week walking program that you can use or adapt to other aerobic workouts. Finally, you find tips to help you draw on the power of mind/body connections to reduce stress and achieve success.

Chapter 4

Nutrition for a Healthy Heart

· ·

· ·

*A*s far as your heart goes, you are what you eat. Sound nutrition is critically important to heart health. Many people get hung up on one aspect of heart healthy nutrition, such as lowering cholesterol. Although this is certainly important (as discussed in Chapter 10), there are many other vital aspects of heart-healthy nutrition that people often forget.

Nutrition Is Not a Four-Letter Word

The word *nutrition* grows out of an ancient Latin word meaning "to nourish" or "to suckle." How splendidly the root meaning of this word illustrates what eating well and eating right is all about, because mother's milk is a perfect blend of just the right amount of the nutrients that babies need for a good start. Likewise, good nutrition for all of our lives should mean good eating from the balanced variety of foods needed to support life and health.

In spite of all the food and diet hype you hear, the guidelines for healthy eating shared in this chapter are simple and tested by experience and science. Adopting them as the foundation of your enjoyment of food will work toward a healthy heart and optimal health. So don't let the word *nutrition* scare you; just think good eating for good health.

You are what you eat — the bad news

Make no mistake about it, what you eat affects your health. The Surgeon General's Report on Nutrition and Health reminds us that eight out of the ten leading causes of death in the United States have a nutrition or alcohol component. And heading the list as the number one killer is cardiovascular disease. In fact, the over-consumption of *dietary* fat in the United States and the inevitable result of added *body* fat are two major contributing factors to the continuing epidemic of heart disease in the United States.

You are what you eat — the good news

Whatever trouble people eat themselves into, however, they can eat themselves out of! Even though poor food choices such as eating too much dietary fat contribute to significant health problems, including heart disease, adopting some simple, commonsense approaches to modifying your food choices for the better can lower your risk of heart disease, as well as help control weight problems and improve health, happiness, and quality of life. It will not, however, bring back a good five-cent cup of coffee or improve the return on your IRA. You can't have everything.

Choose Healthy Pleasures

Food pervades our lives. Food is not only necessary for life itself, it is also part of virtually every social or family occasion and celebration that people participate in. It is possible to eat a heart-healthy diet without sacrificing the multiple pleasures of great food beautifully prepared. In short, it is possible to improve your cardiac health without being a food cop.

Many people, however, suffer from the misconception that healthy cooking takes all of the pleasure out of eating by making food taste bland and unappetizing. No way! In fact, many of the top chefs in America now are working with recipes that are not only healthy low-fat variations, but also are a pleasure to consume. Many home chefs are pretty expert, too — so why not you! To support you in this effort, in the Appendix we share with you some of these heart-healthy recipes developed by some of America's top chefs. The next chapter also gives you lots of tips on how you can modify your own ways of cooking and eating for better health and great taste.

Guidelines for Eating Right While Eating Well

In the late 1980s, the American Heart Association (AHA) and the American Dietetic Association (ADA), as well as a number of other major health and nutrition organizations in the United States, developed some basic principles for healthy nutrition. The guidelines that they generated, while designed to promote overall good health, constitute the core of heart-healthy living. Although literally thousands of scientific studies over a number of years inform these guidelines, they are simple and common-sensical.

Lower the amount of fat in your diet

It is not by chance that the first recommendation involves fat intake. Although during the last two decades dietary fat consumption has declined from 40 percent to 34 percent of total calories consumed, North Americans still eat too much fat. The over-consumption of fat in the diet is so dangerous that the Surgeon General's report on nutrition cited eating too much fat as the number one nutritional problem facing Americans today.

Eating too much fat contributes to two significant health problems: elevated cholesterol and obesity, both of which have clear links to increased risk of cardiac disease. A high-fat diet has also been linked to both diabetes and colon cancer. Finally, eating lots of fat, which has 9 calories per gram as compared to 4 calories per gram for carbohydrates and protein, contributes to the over-consumption of calories by most Americans.

For these reasons, you need to lower the total amount of fat in your diet to less than 30 percent of total calories and, in particular, to lower the amount of saturated fat in your diet to less than 10 percent of total calories. Saturated fat needs to be restricted, because it contributes directly to elevating blood cholesterol and developing atherosclerosis, often called *hardening of the arteries* (see Chapter 10).

There are basically three types of fat:

- ✔ **Saturated fat** typically comes from animal sources, although some fats from plants such as cocoa butter, palm oil, and coconut oil are also saturated. Typically, saturated fats are solid at room temperature.

✔ **Monounsaturated fat** comes from vegetable sources, such as olive, canola, and peanut oil, and is typically liquid at room temperature. Recent evidence has suggested that monounsaturated fats, particularly as consumed in a Mediterranean diet that features olive oil, can significantly lower the risk of heart disease by raising HDL without raising total cholesterol. More on Mediterranean diets in a moment.

✔ **Polyunsaturated fat** also comes primarily from vegetable sources and is typically liquid at room temperature. Corn oil and most other salad oils are examples of polyunsaturated oils. Unsaturated fats, however, can be turned into solid form and thus into saturated fat through the process of hydrogenation. That's why vegetable shortenings and stick margarine are high in saturated fat even though the manufacturing process may have started with a polyunsaturated and/or monounsaturated oil.

Table 4-1 outlines the common food sources for each type of fat.

Table 4-1	Common Sources of Fats by Type	
Saturated Fats	*Monounsaturated Fats*	*Polyunsaturated Fats*
Animal Sources	*Animal Sources*	*Animal Sources (of omega-3 fatty acids)*
Cheese	Chicken	Fish
Butter	Fish	
Milk		*Plant Sources*
Meat	*Plant Sources*	Walnuts
Beef, pork, chicken, lamb, and so on	Vegetable oil	Filberts
Eggs	Pecans	Soft margarine
Lard	Olive Oil	Almonds
	Canola Oil	Mayonnaise
Plant Sources	Stick margarine	Soybean oil
Coconut oil	Peanut oil	Corn oil
Palm kernel oil	Peanut butter	Sunflower oil
Palm oil	Cottonseed oil	Safflower oil
Cocoa butter (chocolates)	Avocados	Sesame oil

Saturated fat alert

Saturated fat, often hidden, lies in wait for us. When you know where to look for it, you can trim the amount you consume without sacrificing good eating.

✔ **Visible fat on all meat; chicken and turkey skin.** Trim what fat you can see.

✔ **Processed meats — hot dogs, salami, lunch meat, sausage.** These meats can get 75 percent or more of their calories from saturated fat. Select fat-free products or put one slice of salami with sliced lean turkey for all the flavor and ¼ the fat.

✔ **Butterfat, present in cream and whole milk and products made with them. Luxury ice cream is loaded.** Select skim or 1 percent milk; low-fat or nonfat sour cream, cream cheese, and cottage cheese. Look for ice cream treats that are nonfat or lower fat.

✔ **Vegetable fats such as palm oil and hydrogenated vegetable fats, present in prepared mixes and foods (cookies, bakery goods, cake mixes).** Check out the list of ingredients on the label.

✔ **Fried and processed foods — those chips, that frozen dinner or pizza.** Again check out the fat on the label. If you've got to have those puff-a-pops, pick the one with the least fat/saturated fat.

Lower cholesterol consumption

Elevated blood cholesterol is a clearly established risk factor for coronary artery disease (see Chapter 10). For this reason, the AHA has recommended that we strive to keep our cholesterol below 200 mg/dl. When blood cholesterol rises above 200 mg/dl, the risks of heart disease start to rise dramatically. From a dietary point of view, the first line of therapy for elevated cholesterol is to lower both saturated fat and cholesterol consumption. Unfortunately, the average adult in our society consumes over 400 mg of cholesterol a day, over 33 percent higher than the recommended maximum of 300 mg. To put this in perspective, there are 215 mg of cholesterol in the egg yolk of an average egg. That's why the AHA recommends that adults consume no more than 4 egg yolks per week. (Egg whites are cholesterol-free.)

Increase the amount of carbohydrates in the diet to 50-55 percent of total calories

Carbohydrates, particularly the complex carbohydrates found in fruits, vegetables, and grains, are the mainstay of a heart-healthy way of eating. Other great sources of these complex carbohydrates are whole-grain products such as cereals, rice, pasta, and breads.

Look Mom, low cholesterol!

Cholesterol, which is found exclusively in animal tissue, is particularly present in eggs and organ meats. Here some tips for avoiding it.

Eggs. Most people know that eggs are high in cholesterol. One egg yolk has 300 mg. But you can have your eggs and avoid cholesterol too.

✔ Substitute two egg whites (0 mg cholesterol) for one whole egg in most any recipe where the egg doesn't star.

✔ Use egg substitute or cholesterol-free egg products.

✔ For scrambled eggs/omelets, use one whole egg and one white instead of two whole.

✔ Use an egg substitute.

Organ meats. Liver, for instance, is just loaded with cholesterol. One 3-oz slice of beef liver has 410 mg; one chicken liver has 125 mg. So if you like organ meats, save brains, sweetbreads, gizzards, hearts, and kidneys for a treat. If you hate liver, here's an excuse never to eat it again.

There has been a tremendous amount of misinformation about carbohydrate in the diet in the last few years. Many so called "experts" have blamed carbohydrate consumption for the increased incidence of obesity in the United States. Nothing could be further from the truth. It is the *over consumption of calories* coupled with *inadequate physical activity* that has led to the explosion of obesity in our country.

In addition to providing complex carbohydrates, fruits, vegetables, and whole-grain products often contain other substances of great benefit for cardiovascular health. For example, fruits, vegetables and whole-grain products are very high in fiber. The under-consumption of fiber has clearly been associated with increased risk of heart disease. Everyone should be consuming approximately 25 grams of fiber from natural dietary sources every day, and yet the sad truth is that most folks eat only about 50 percent of this.

In addition, fruits and vegetables contain many other substances that lower the risk of both heart disease and cancer. These may include naturally occurring *antioxidants* and other *phytochemicals*. For these reasons, every major, responsible nutritional organization has recommended that people consume a minimum of five servings of fruits and vegetables on a daily basis. Yet, shockingly, only 10 percent of the American public consumes this level of fruits and vegetables.

Limit sodium intake

Although these guidelines recommend a daily maximum limit of three grams of sodium, the average adult in the United States consumes over twice that much — six to eight grams of sodium per day. Most of this is in the form of common table salt, although a lot of sodium is also present in many processed foods. The major reason to limit sodium intake has to do with its association with high blood pressure. In societies where less sodium is consumed, the incidence of high blood pressure is dramatically lower than it is in the United States. In fact, the AHA now recommends that for heart-healthy eating, everyone should try to consume no more than 2,400 mg of sodium daily (rather than 3,000 mg/3 grams). If individuals with hypertension would pay attention to strict limitations on salt consumption and control their weight, many would be able to manage blood pressure without medications.

Limit protein intake to 15 percent of your total calories

The average American eats much more protein than necessary — or optimal — for good health. And this bad habit has been reinforced by so-called fitness and nutrition experts who have recently advocated increasing protein above what is already consumed in the American diet. Some of these "experts" recommend a protein consumption of 30 percent of calories, more than twice that recommended by extensive scientific research and the consensus guidelines based on that research. Recommending such large amounts of protein is bad advice. While eating a high protein diet may help with short-term weight loss, there may be a significant price to pay. Usually, high-protein diets are also high in fat and may increase cholesterol.

Catch those carbos

Fruits, vegetables, and grains seem to come in almost endless variety. Eating more complex carbohydrates is easy and full of flavor.

✔ Get whole grains at breakfast by picking cereals, breads, and muffins made with whole grains (and not too much sugar).

✔ Choose fruit for snacks and for dessert.

✔ Think fruit juice rather than soft drink for that afternoon thirst quencher/pick-me-up.

✔ Feature vegetables, pastas, and grains at dinner, not meat. Avoid fatty or cream sauces and gravies.

✔ Avoid empty sugar carbohydrates in candy and snacks.

✔ Once a week, try one new vegetable or fruit or a new way of fixing them.

✔ Choose the bread, reject the spread. It's usually not the bread that has too many calories; it's the butter, oil, or jam you put on it.

There is also a popular misconception that increased protein consumption is important to athletic performance and to muscle building, yet there is not a shred of scientific evidence to support these beliefs.

If you consume alcohol, do so in moderation

From a cardiovascular stand point, alcohol consumption is a complex issue. Moderate alcohol consumption has actually been shown to lower the risk of heart attack. Yet, alcohol is also loaded with calories and may, therefore, contribute to weight gain. Furthermore, excessive alcohol consumption actually carries a cardiovascular risk by increasing blood pressure and acting in adverse ways on the cardiac muscle itself.

The reason that moderate alcohol consumption may lower the risk of heart attack seems to come from two actions of alcohol. First, alcohol raises the HDL level in the blood (the good cholesterol), and this increased HDL is associated with decreased risk of heart disease. Second, some forms of alcoholic beverages impede blood clotting. Blood clotting is a dangerous process that contributes to heart attacks. Red wine (as well as red grape juice), in particular, seems to impede blood clotting. While the actual substances in red wine that contribute to this effect are not fully understood, it is thought that a particular class of compounds called *flavonoids*, found in the skins of grapes, which are left on longer in making red wine than white wine, make a major contribution to decreased blood clotting.

Moderate alcohol consumption is generally defined as one shot of distilled spirits or two glasses of wine or two beers on a daily basis. Levels of alcohol consumption beyond that carry unacceptable health risks.

Slack off the salt

Four easy steps can significantly lower the amount of salt in your diet:

✔ Never salt food without tasting it.

✔ Increase your intake of fruits and vegetables and natural products that have minimal or no salt in them.

✔ Take the salt shaker off the table.

✔ Cut down on processed foods and "fast" foods, which are usually loaded with salt.

If you are a snack addict, the market now has a number of low-fat and reduced-salt products such as reduced-salt baked corn chips, pretzels, or potato chips.

Do not consume more calories than required to maintain your best body weight

Obesity is a major risk for a variety of health consequences, but particularly for heart disease. About 75 percent of all mortality associated with obesity comes from the increased risk of heart disease. (For a full discussion of the cardiovascular risk of obesity, see Chapter 12.) While decreased consumption of fat calories will decrease the risk of obesity, all calories from any source do count. The reason so many Americans are overweight is that they consume too many calories, period.

Consume a variety of foods

In the United States, we are blessed with a food production and processing system that makes an almost infinite variety of edibles available. Faced with all these choices, you need to make wise ones. To guide in this process, the U.S. Department of Agriculture and the Department of Health and Human Services have generated a plan — the Food Guide Pyramid — that incorporates variety as well as good health practices. The AHA has adapted this pyramid guide slightly to represent an optimal heart-healthy diet as illustrated in Figure 4-1.

Protein aplenty

It doesn't take much effort to consume adequate protein:

- Eating two 2 to 3 oz servings of fish, lean meat, or poultry provides an adequate daily protein intake

- One egg or two egg whites has protein equal to one ounce of meat or fish.

- Enjoy smaller portions of meat in combination main dishes such as pasta, stir-fries, or casseroles — just remember to avoid high fat.

- Consider tofu (soy bean curd) in stir-fries and casseroles for good protein with relatively low fat.

- Choose bean dishes, particularly combos such as beans and rice or beans and pasta, for a good source of protein and fiber.

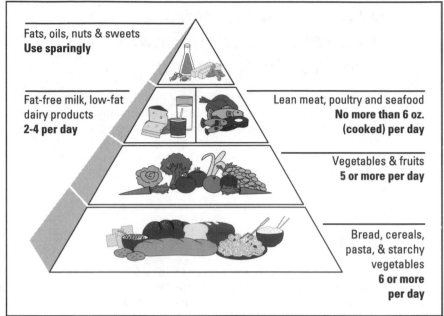

Figure 4-1:
The AHA
food
pyramid.

Just a glance shows you what to emphasize in your daily food choices. If you look a little more closely, you can see that the number of servings are also indicated. The number of servings can seem large — a sure recipe for weight gain — unless you realize that the legal definition of a serving used by the food professionals is much smaller than we citizens in the land of the bigger burger, overstuffed potato, and all-you-can-eat buffets realize. After all, you'd never consider a measly one-half cup of spaghetti a serving, would you? So for an image adjustment, consult the sidebar "What's a serving?"

Three Key Rules for Healthy Eating

Sometimes the most important principles for healthy eating are the simplest ones and yet they are often ignored. If your head is whirling with the guidelines just discussed, here are just three simple heart-healthy practices that you can adopt immediately to make an enormous difference.

Rule #1: Eat a healthy low-fat breakfast

The well-respected nutrition writer Jane Brody was once asked the most important nutritional practice that she had learned in her twenty-five years of writing about nutrition. She said, "We should breakfast like a king, lunch like a prince, and supper like a pauper." Unfortunately, many of us do exactly the reverse. There are many health and nutrition reasons to consume a good, low-fat breakfast. Here are just a few.

✔ **Breakfast skippers tend to gain weight.**

Why? People who skip breakfast don't get the calories they need when they need them — early in the morning. As a result, they tend at mid-morning to gorge themselves on a doughnut or load up on a cup of coffee with sugar and cream. This is a recipe for weight management disaster!

✔ **It is important to match calorie consumption with calorie expenditure.**

Consuming more of your calories in the morning gets you ready to face the demands of an active day. If you eat most of your calories at night and then go to bed, the body thinks that it is time to store those calories, contributing to weight gain.

✔ **Breakfast is a great time to consume fiber.**

Many people get up to 25 percent of their daily fiber at breakfast. With so many high-fiber breakfast cereals now available, it's easy to increase fiber consumption, which lowers the risk of heart disease.

✔ **Breakfast is a great time to consume fruits and vegetables.**

Pour yourself a tall glass of orange juice and put a sliced banana on your cereal, and you are 40 percent of the way to the recommended daily minimum of five servings of fruits and vegetables a day.

✔ **What is the perfect breakfast?**

It is hard to top a bowl of whole grain cereal (whole grain oat cereal is probably the best, because the soluble fiber further lowers cholesterol) with some sliced fruit, a glass of orange juice, and a piece of whole-grain toast and a cup of coffee or tea, all with skim milk. You say you prefer grapefruit, prune or tomato juice, and low-fat oat-bran muffins for variety? That's great. You've got the general idea.

Rule #2: Eat at least five servings of fruits and vegetables every day

Fruits and vegetables are important both for what they do contain and what they don't. Fruits and vegetables are loaded with fiber, antioxidants, and other chemicals, all of which can lower your risk of heart disease. In addition, fruits and vegetables are extremely low in sodium and have no fat, so they do not increase blood cholesterol. Eating fruits and vegetables also benefits people who have high blood pressure. A recent study showed that individuals with high blood pressure who consume a diet containing high levels of fruits and vegetables and low-fat dairy products were able to significantly reduce their blood pressure.

What's a serving?

When scientists, registered dietitians, and food pyramid guides talk about servings, here are some of the typical amounts they have in mind for one serving.

Grain products
1 slice of bread

½ cup dry cereal

½ cup cooked rice, pasta, or cereal (like oatmeal)

Vegetables
1 cup raw leafy vegetables (lettuce, cabbage)

½ cup cooked vegetable

6 oz vegetable juice

Fruits
1 medium fruit (apple, pear, orange)

¼ cup dried fruit

½ cup fresh, frozen or canned-in-juice (not syrup) fruit

(a serving of some fruits such as strawberries or watermelon can be a cup or more)

6 oz fruit juice

Dairy products
1 cup skim or 1% milk

1 cup nonfat or low-fat yogurt, nonfat cottage cheese

1 oz cheese (about 1 inch cube of cheddar, jack, or swiss)

Meat, poultry, fish 2-3 oz cooked

Nuts, seeds
1½ oz/ ⅓ cup nuts (peanuts, pecans, walnuts, cashews)

2 tbsp. seeds (sunflower, pumpkin)

Rule #3: Drink pure water

Folks tend to neglect the natural and healthful practice of drinking pure water. Instead, they substitute beverages that contain sugar, caffeine, or fat (milkshakes!). Caffeine and fat may either increase blood pressure or increase the risk of heart disease. Empty sugar calories can lead to over-consumption of calories and weight gain.

Special Issues in Nutrition for Heart Health

While low-fat, low-cholesterol eating is the cornerstone for heart-healthy nutrition, some additional "tidbits" on sound practices and some controversies can help you build on this solid, nutritional core:

✔ **Whole grain oats.** Careful studies have shown that eating adequate amounts of whole grain oats can further reduce cholesterol up to 5 to 6 percent over and above cholesterol reduction achieved from low fat nutrition. To put this in perspective, for every 1 percent reduction in cholesterol, there is a 2 percent decrease in the likelihood of coronary artery disease. The amount of oats needed to achieve these benefits can be obtained in one good size bowl of Cheerios or similar oat cereal every day.

✔ **Fish.** Recent studies have shown that individuals who consume fish at least once a week lower their incidence of sudden death from cardiac disease. This is just one more reason to eat fish — one of the most complete and healthy foods you can eat. It is a great source of protein and is low in saturated fats.

Shellfish (shrimp, lobster, oysters, clams, and so on) does contain a lot of cholesterol, but because it has virtually no saturated fat, it also can certainly be contained in a heart-healthy diet.

✔ **Butter versus margarine.** For years, cardiologists advised people to limit their intake of butter and choose margarine, particularly soft margarine, instead. Then, in 1994, a number of articles, including one from the Harvard School of Public Health, suggested that the *trans-fatty acids* found in margarine were worse both for cholesterol and LDL than butter. Of course, people screamed that once again the experts had misled them. My advice on this is to limit your intake of *both* butter and margarine. As I have already said, drizzling a little olive oil, with its beneficial monounsaturated fats, on your bread is a much better choice than either margarine or butter.

✔ **Nutrition for athletes and physically active people.** Sometimes athletes and physically active people feel that they need to eat special diets to meet the demands of their physical activity. (Certain advertisements do their best to push this idea while hyping their product.) But the nutritional needs of highly active or athletic people change in only one way — these individuals can consume a few more calories without weight gain because they are burning more calories. Sound nutrition for physically active people is based on the same principles that we have already described for heart-healthy nutrition for nonactive people.

✔ **Fad diets.** Unfortunately, people who are trying to lose weight often get sucked into fad diets. Recent popular diets include those that advocate increasing the amount of protein in the diet, as well as ones that advocates increasing the amount of fat in the diet. Although these diets have achieved a certain popularity for weight loss, they are not good from a cardiovascular standpoint. Both approaches can significantly raise your cholesterol.

Other fad diets may promote supposedly scientific practices (often food combinations) that make your body burn fat more rapidly in heretofore unknown or secret ways. Unfortunately, whatever their claims, most of these diets have no basis in scientific fact. An even more important argument against them, however, is that even if one should lose weight in the short-term by using them, that weight loss usually cannot be sustained nor can health benefits be realized, because the diets do not foster balanced, healthy approaches to eating for the long term.

Other Components of a Healthy Lifestyle

Nutrition is of great importance to a heart-healthy lifestyle, but please remember that it is not a magic bullet. If you pay attention to sound nutritional practices and combine them with managing your weight and incorporating regular physical activity in your life, you have achieved three of the most important pillars of daily lifestyle habits and actions that can contribute to an overall heart-healthy lifestyle.

The Mediterranean Diet: A recipe for cardiovascular health

For a long time, we've known that the countries around the Mediterranean Sea seem to have a lower incidence of heart disease than most other countries. It has been argued that the so-called *Mediterranean Diet,* which is high in monounsaturated fats (largely from olive oil) and grains and vegetables, makes a major contribution to the low incidence of heart disease in this region. Monounsaturated fats seem to both raise the HDL (the good cholesterol) while not raising total cholesterol. Both the American Heart Association and the American Dietetic Association have increasingly used Mediterranean style diets as recommendations for lowering your risk of chronic disease. One downside of any oil, however, is that it is loaded with calories. Just remember to use it in moderation.

Chapter 5

Personal Nutrition: Designing Your Own Menu

• •

In This Chapter

▶ Evaluating your eating habits now

▶ Setting goals for improvement

▶ Planning a custom menu to fit your lifestyle

▶ Model plans/options for heart-healthy eating

▶ Eating out without falling off your plan

• •

*A*ll the guidelines and tips for heart-healthy nutrition shared in the last chapter do no good unless you put them to work in your daily life. That's what this chapter is about — giving you a road map for success and resources for the adventure. To succeed in reaching your personal nutritional objectives, you must

✔ Understand your challenges

✔ Evaluate how you eat now

✔ Set some goals for improvement

✔ Plan a custom menu to fit your tastes and lifestyle (and your family's)

What Are Your Challenges to Success?

The trouble with teaching our stomachs new ideas, as an ancient Roman almost said, is that they have no ears to hear. Food (along with clothing and shelter) is one of the big three necessities of life. You might say that eating is the first thing on our minds when we're born and, for many of us, hardly diminishes in importance for the rest of our days. Sharing food, as we observed before, is also central to many family, social, and business occasions. No wonder we develop fixed preferences and patterns related to such a core component of our lives.

Examining and understanding how you feel about food and how you settle into comfortable eating patterns is the first step to unlocking the prison of habit. It's also the first step in a great adventure — one that will be full of fun, good eating, and (to be totally truthful) the occasional culinary disaster. But what's adventure without a little risk?

Your success, like mine, in adopting heart-healthy ways of eating means:

- Looking at the challenge of planning your personal menu as an opportunity for discovery, not deprivation

- Relying on sound, scientifically supported information, not the headlines from the latest small study or most recent food fad

- Making choices for change that fit your tastes, schedule, and lifestyle, not those of some ideal mortal

- Using your common sense and judgment while still being willing to experiment

Evaluating How You Eat Now

For most people, how you *think* you eat and how you *actually* eat often differ. So the only accurate way to evaluate if and where you need to make modifications in what you eat is to keep a record for several days of everything you put in your mouth — pencils and other inedibles excepted. Yes, that's as tedious as it sounds, but the results may surprise you. They will certainly be useful.

Set up a daily log

Begin by making a log sheet that contains the categories shown in the following sample. You can create a log sheet on your computer, use pages in your daily scheduler or a notebook, or draw a master copy by hand and photocopy it. Your log need not be fancy, just clear to you.

Daily Food Log			
Meal (When & Where)	*Food Item*	*Serving (Number/size)*	*Food Group(s)*

What to record on the log

✔ Include the meal or occasion for eating (breakfast, snack, drinks with friend, and so on) and when and where you ate.

✔ Under "food item" list the exact items eaten.

✔ Indicate how many servings of the item you ate, using the serving sizes presented in Chapter 4. That's not as dumb as it sounds. For example, we often eat two pieces of toast for breakfast; that would count as two bread/starch servings. In a pasta main dish, you may eat 1½ cups of spaghetti or linguine; that counts as 3 servings in the same food group. You don't have to be a mathematician or carry around measuring cups; just estimate as accurately as you can.

✔ Determine which food group or food groups the food item belongs to: Bread/cereal/pasta/starch, Vegetables, Fruits, Dairy foods, Meat/fish/eggs, Fats/oils, Sugars, Water.

✔ Combination and prepared foods may need to be broken into servings in separate food groups to make up the total portion consumed. For example, a typical side portion of macaroni and cheese might equal 1 serving of pasta and 1 of dairy food; a small order of french fries might equal 1 bread/starch and 1 fat serving. Again, your best estimate is okay.

✔ Record every thing you eat and drink, not just major meals and snacks. That peppermint or handful of snack mix from the office community stash counts.

Keep your log for at least three consecutive days. Make one of the days a Saturday or Sunday because most folks eat differently on the weekend. For greater accuracy, keeping the log for four or five days is better; seven days, practically perfect.

Analyze your current eating pattern

After three or more days of dedicated jotting and estimating, your log is a goldmine of raw data. Your objective is to see how what you eat now stacks up against the nutritional guidelines that I outline in Chapter 4. First, do a brief, informal analysis to get an overview of what nutritional areas need work. Then you can be as detailed as you like — I give you tips to help.

1. Look for patterns and habits

Start by reviewing your logs for general patterns and trends. Ask questions such as the following:

✔ Does anything leap out at you — a pattern, habit, or type of food?

✔ What types of food do you tend to emphasize? Do your meals, for instance, emphasize vegetables and grain products? Or do they emphasize meat? If you're vegetarian, how's your balance of vegetables, grains and oils, for example?

✔ Do you favor fried foods over other, lower-fat methods of preparation? Eat a lot of sauces or butter on your veggies?

✔ How much do you snack? When? On what?

✔ Do you consume a wide variety of foods or stick to a few favorites?

✔ What's your general impression of how many sugar-rich or fat-rich foods you consume?

✔ What about salty things?

✔ How often do you eat out? Do your food choices differ when you eat out from when you eat at home or take lunch? How?

2. Compare your average intakes to the recommendations of the Food Guide Pyramid

This step helps you quantify your observations from the preceding section.

✔ On your log, figure the total number of servings in each food group over all days and divide that by the number of days you recorded to get your average daily servings of food types.

✔ Compare your pattern of eating by food group and number of servings to these recommended levels: Bread/cereal/pasta/starch, 6-8; Vegetables, 3-5; Fruits, 3-5; Dairy foods, 2-4; Meat/fish/eggs, 2; Fats/oil, 0-8; Sugars, 2; Water, 8 (8 oz serving). Recommendations for vegetarians are the same except for Meat substitutes, legumes, nuts 2-3; Dairy foods, 0-3, and Bread/grains, up to 11.

✔ In what areas are you eating less than recommended?

✔ In what areas are you eating more?

✔ Are you eating a lot less or a lot more in any areas?

✔ In what areas do these comparisons suggest you need to make changes? Describe and quantify those changes for yourself as a foundation for setting goals.

3. Compare your average intakes to the Nutritional Guidelines for Eating Right While Eating Well

If you want to be more precise, if you are overweight, or if you already have heart disease or a medical condition for which your physician has recommended a change in your eating habits, you may want to make a more detailed analysis than the first two steps provide by comparing your intake to the nutritional guidelines I present in Chapter 4. You can do this in a general way by using the information in the chapter, but the most accurate and useful analysis requires the resources of a food composition guide. For greatest accuracy, you may want to determine various facts about the makeup of your food choices such as calories, grams of fat (by type: saturated, monounsaturated, and polyunsaturated), protein, and carbohydrates, sugars, fiber, sodium, cholesterol, and various vitamins and minerals:

✔ If you have access to the Internet, you can use a splendid, free program that helps you accurately analyze your complete intake. Developed by the University of Illinois, the *Nutritional Analysis Tool* (www.ag.uiuc.edu/~food-lab/nat/nat.cgi) enables you to input each food, servings eaten, your age and gender, and then it performs a complete analysis of the nutritive value of those foods — including all the categories in the guidelines.

✔ The U.S. Department of Agriculture researches and makes available food composition data. Its Food Nutrition Information Center offers the food composition databases of the U.S. Nutrient Data Bank and other such resources as "Fast Food Facts" online (www.nal.usda.gov/fnic/).

✔ Various food composition guides from commercial publishers are available in bookstores. Just make sure that the one you purchase has all the categories you need and is based on a reputable source, such as USDA research.

✔ Don't overlook the resources of your physician's office. If you like, ask them to recommend a registered dietitian or other professional nutrition expert who can not only help you analyze how you eat now but also help you plan your personal menu for improvement.

Finding a dietitian

Did you know that anybody, no matter their training or expertise, can call themselves a "nutritionist"? For professional help in planning new ways of eating, I recommend that you consult a registered dietitian. That "RD" after the professional's name means that he or she has earned a professional degree (or degrees) in nutrition and has successfully completed the national credentialing exam and other qualifications set by the Commission on Dietetic Registration of the American Dietetics Association (ADA). You can reach the Nationwide Nutrition Network, the ADA's referral service, at 1-800-366-1655.

Set Goals for Improvement

Your next step is to set the goals you want to work toward with your personal menu or eating plan.

1. **Keeping before you the results of your self-evaluation (including the list of nutritional changes that you develop in step 2 and your doctor's recommendations, if any), make a list of goals you want to accomplish and the nutritional modifications that can help you meet those goals.**

2. **Consider personal factors and preferences that influence your food choices and menu planning, such as**

   - Convenience or speed of preparation

   - Taste preference

   - Habit

   - Family needs

   - Availability

   - Health conditions, such as food allergies

3. **Prioritize your goals. Decide which ones are most important, which steps you want to undertake first.**

Plan Your Personal Menu

Your approach to planning your menu can be as individual as your personality. There is no one right way to do it. First and last, you must translate your goals into action-oriented steps that work for you.

When it comes time to pack lunch or fix dinner, lots of us share the problem of the highrise steel-worker who always ate lunch aloft with his buddies. Each day he'd grab a sandwich from his lunch box, peek underneath the bread, and say, "Peanut butter! I hate peanut butter!" as he tossed it off the highrise. Finally a co-worker asked, "Why don't you ask your wife not to give you peanut butter?" To which the indignant worker replied, "You leave my wife out of it — I make my own sandwiches!"

Faced with the immediate task of planning and making meals, many of us also suffer brain cramp and opt for the same old thing. So you're going to need to think ahead. Find a couple of quiet hours when you can dream and drool over what you'd enjoy as well as be hardheaded about the most efficient way to accomplish those great meals.

The following tips and resources should make it easier.

Schedule your prioritized goals and modifications for action

A concrete plan with a timeframe for action may help you not only get going but also carry through.

- ✔ **Make a worksheet or timeline**. You can make a list with target dates in a notebook, on your computer, or on a calendar. The idea is to list concrete action steps. For example, add one vegetable dish at dinner, eat one meatless main meal and one meatless lunch a week, and eat fruit for an afternoon snack at least three times a week.

- ✔ **Start with the easiest modifications and changes**. Set yourself up for success by beginning with those modifications that you think you can accomplish most easily.

- ✔ **Take one step at a time**. Don't try to make every change at once. Gradually introduce your modifications. Experiment with new ways of preparation and new dishes by picking only one or two a week to try. Giving yourself a chance to adapt to new ways of eating increases your long-term success.

Plan actual menus for several days

Using your goals and the nutritional guidelines in Chapter 4, plan menus you and your family would like for three or four days. A simple list of dishes is fine — and you can do that even if you don't cook!

Here are some tips for planning a menu:

✔ Select favorite recipes or dishes that fit the guidelines.

✔ Think of favorite recipes that you can easily modify. (For example, using a leaner cut of meat, low-fat/non-fat dairy product, baked rather than fried, and so on.)

✔ Keep an eye out for new heart-healthy ideas and recipes. Newspapers and magazines often present low-fat or otherwise heart-healthy dishes. Online sources are growing every day.

✔ Plan meals and snacks to fit your personal preference. If, for instance, you like a lighter lunch and a morning and afternoon snack, distribute the appropriate servings in that manner.

Five tips to add zip

Cutting fat, cholesterol, and sodium shouldn't mean cutting flavor. Keeping these five items on hand gives me lots of ways to zip up a meal while eating low fat and low salt.

✔ **Vegetable and Fruit Salsas.** From party dips to dressing for salads or vegetables or sauces for fish, salsas are versatile. Find a good prepared salsa to keep on hand (watch out for sodium) and experiment with your own freshly made combinations.

✔ **Chilis.** Some like it hot! Supermarkets these days offer a good range of peppers hot and hotter. And for the pantry shelf, there are hundreds of hot sauces. You use so little that sodium's not usually a problem. From the Caribbean to Asia and the whole globe in between, every style of cooking has creative uses for the pepper. It's a kick that won't hurt you.

✔ **Mustards.** Did you know there are *hundreds* of different mustards? They can substitute for traditional fats in dressing everything from sandwiches to entrees. Some can be pretty high in sodium, but a little goes a long way.

✔ **Balsamic (and other) vinegars.** A good balsamic vinegar is so nutty and sweet that lots of folks enjoy it alone as a salad dressing. Try the many specialty and flavored vinegars available to add a piquant touch to much more than salads.

✔ **Fresh herbs**. Or dried. Dill, basil, cilantro, thyme, rosemary, oregano, chives. . . just the names make my mouth water. Supermarkets are now carrying a wider range of fresh herbs and many are easy to grow, even as pot plants. After you've seen what fresh basil can do for a tomato or for pasta or what a rosemary sprig and lemon juice can do for a grilled fish filet or chicken breast, you'll be looking for more herbal opportunities.

Use a model eating plan for guidance

If planning your own menus sounds like too much work or you need to prime your imagination, you might want to follow any of several model plans that have been based on sound research and for which there are lots of resources.

✔ The term **Mediterranean Diet** is more appropriately used to describe an approach to eating, rather than a specific diet, that is typical of Italy, Greece, and other countries surrounding the Mediterranean Sea. These cuisines are typically low in saturated fat and red meat and high in the consumption of plant products — grains, fruits, vegetables, and olive oil (a heart-healthy monounsaturated fat). The Mediterranean diet is featured in a number of good books. There are also numerous online sources for additional information and recipes. Entering "Mediterranean diet" on your web browser will lead you to lots of options — just don't forget your heart-healthy guidelines when selecting recipes. And don't ignore those oil calories.

✔ Although **The DASH Diet** was designed as part of a research study that tested the effect of dietary patterns on preventing and lowering high blood pressure, it offers an excellent approach for general heart health. (DASH stands for Dietary Approaches to Stop Hypertension.) The eating plan reduces total and saturated fat intake and emphasizes fruits, vegetables, and low-fat dairy foods. It is also low in sweets. Read all about the DASH Diet on its official Web site (http://dash.bwh.harvard.edu). The National Heart, Lung, and Blood Institute, the study sponsor, publishes a 16-page booklet with menus that may be downloaded from its Web site (www.nhlbi.nih.gov), or write to the NHLBI Information Center, P.O. Box 30105, Bethesda, MD 20824-0105.

✔ Explore a **food guide pyramid.** The Food Guide Pyramid developed by the U.S. Department of Agriculture to illustrate its "Dietary Guidelines for Americans" has inspired a number of adaptations. When based on sound science, these can be very helpful.

   • A 30-page booklet on "The Food Guide Pyramid," developed by the USDA and its Center for Nutrition Policy and Promotion, can be a very helpful resource for developing your own menu. Download it from their Web site (www.usda.gov/fcs) or, for a small fee, order Home and Garden Bulletin Number 252 from the Consumer Information Center, Pueblo, CO 81009. (Order their free catalog with other resources by calling 1-888-878-3256.)

   • Read more about vegetarian possibilities on the Web site of the American Dietetic Association (www.eatright.org). Be sure to check out the useful information in their position paper on vegetarian diets. The ADA also has a number of useful publications available in bookstores and through their online marketplace.

- For pyramid guides that offer healthy approaches to eating based on traditional ethnic cuisines such as Latin American, Mediterranean and Asian plus Vegetarian cuisines, check out the material developed by Oldways Preservation & Exchange Trust in cooperation with the Harvard School of Public Health (www.oldwayspt.org).

Check that label!

Convenience foods are a growing share of the American food dollar. Zipping into the market for a prepared entree and sides from the freezer or ready-to-go counter may aid your schedule but what about your healthy eating plan? Use the label to aid your selection.

As the sample label illustrates, the label describes the serving size and for each serving gives the total calories, calories from fat, and the amount of important nutrients in grams and percentage of recommended daily intake.

Yep, that sausage pizza with extra cheese that gets two-thirds of its calories from fat (70 percent of total daily recommended intake) and contains 60 percent of the day's sodium — and that's just one slice — is probably not your best choice for a quick-grab supper. At least on a regular basis. But those store-prepared chicken fajitas look more promising. You've got the idea.

Nutrition Facts

Serving Size ½ cup (114g)
Servings Per Container 4

Amount Per Serving

Calories 90   Calories from Fat 30

	% Daily Value*
Total Fat 3g	5%
Saturated Fat 0g	0%
Cholesterol 0mg	0%
Sodium 300mg	13%
Total Carbohydrate 13g	4%
Dietary Fiber 3g	12%
Sugars 3g	
Protein 3g	

Vitamin A	80%	•	Vitamin C	60%
Calcium	4%	•	Iron	4%

* Percent Daily Values are based on a 2,000 calorie diet. Your daily values may be higher or lower depending on your calorie needs:

		Calories	2,000	2,500
Total Fat	Less than		65g	80g
Sat Fat	Less than		20g	25g
Cholesterol	Less than		300mg	300mg
Sodium	Less than		2,400mg	2,400mg
Total Carbohydrate			300g	375g
Fiber			25g	30g

Calories per gram:
Fat 9   •   Carbohydrate 4   •   Protein 4

More nutrients may be listed on some labels.

Every two or three months, prepare a Menu Rut Buster

With all the activities we pack into hectic lives, we mere mortals often fall into ruts. After you've found modifications and recipes that work (and that the whole family will eat), it's human nature to slip into serving the same things, going to the same restaurants, taking the same lunch until boredom sabotages your plan. Send the Menu Rut Buster to the rescue.

When you bog down in a rut, take a quiet hour some evening or Sunday afternoon and get out the magazines, the torn newspaper scraps with a promising low-fat recipe, and a couple of cookbooks you've been meaning to explore more (don't forget my Heart Healthy Recipes). Then take a piece of paper and divide it into 15 or 20 squares. In each square, place one new dish (maybe two if they're simple), then add other dishes that are already part of your repertoire to make a meal. A square could be lunch, dinner, weekend brunch, party snacks — in no particular order, just whatever the new ideas suggest. On the square also note where the recipe is found and make a separate list of any ingredients to purchase on the next shopping trip. (Small sticky notes work well for the ingredient list.) Put the Rut Buster up on the fridge door, ready for instant consultation the next time boredom or fatigue threatens. A hint: Anyone in the family can contribute a square.

Is Ketchup a Vegetable? Tips for Heart-Healthy Dining Out

Eat at some fast food joints on a regular basis, and you certainly would have to count ketchup as a vegetable to have any hope of eating your daily quota. And don't even think about avoiding excess fat! But dining out need not be so fraught with peril for your healthy eating goals. If you keep these simple tips in mind, you can eat out, eat well, and eat right.

> ✔ **Select a restaurant that can help you stay on plan.** Whether you're headed out for fine dining or fast food (or anything in between), you can choose a restaurant that can help you meet your goals. For example, a sandwich shop where you can select a lean stuffing and fixings may be a better choice than a place that offers only burgers and fries. The same sort of distinctions can apply to better restaurants as well.

✔ **Order wisely to make the menu work for you**. Almost any restaurant offers items and/or methods of preparation that you can enjoy with a cheerful heart. Make the menu work for you with wise selections:

- Broiled, baked, or roasted rather than fried
- Vegetable or clear sauces rather than butter or cream sauces
- Steamed veggies rather than creamed or fried
- Dressing on the side for salad

✔ **Practice portion control.** "Bigger is better" seems to be the watchword for restaurant portions these days. When presented with a plate heaped with enough for two or three, resist temptation — eat what you need, and take the rest home to Fido or leave it. If the restaurant deserves a repeat visit, maybe you can share that great dish with a friend. Also, order an appetizer as an entree.

✔ **Enjoy the occasional blowout.** Remember that Greek tyrant Procrustes who chopped off visitors to fit his guest bed? That's not what heart-healthy eating is about. If a big, juicy steak with all the trimmings or a classic French dinner with rich sauces and great wines is your idea of the proper way to celebrate, *bon appetit!* One meal won't do you in. Healthy eating is about moderation and balance overall.

More resources for developing your personal menu

These three resources can provide a basic library to support your efforts and to help you judge how to evaluate the many resources available online and in print.

✔ *American Dietetic Association's Complete Food and Nutrition Guide* by Roberta Laison Duyff. 1996. You can order it online from ADA (www.eatright.org) or by phone (1-800-877-1600, Ext. 5000).

✔ *Month of Meals* published by the American Diabetes Association gives you a lot of ideas for different types of meals even if you aren't diabetic. I like it because each breakfast menu has the same nutritional value as any other breakfast menu, so you can mix and match. Ditto for lunch and dinner. Plus the book is arranged so that you can easily select individual meals from separate days while knowing it'll all add up right! Order by phone from the American Diabetes Association (1-800-232-3472) or online (www.diabetes.org).

✔ *Dieting For Dummies,* prepared by experts from the American Dietetic Association, can give you additional help in planning for weight loss and healthy weight management. Available in your local bookstores.

Chapter 6

Exercise and the Heart: Keep It Pumping

. . . .

In This Chapter

▶ Why exercise reduces the risk of heart disease

▶ What happens to the heart during exercise

▶ The difference between exercise and physical activity

▶ How to get started on an exercise program that is right for you

▶ How to stay with an exercise program

▶ What medicines interact with exercise

▶ What symptoms to worry about

. . . .

An active lifestyle is a healthy lifestyle. Inactivity is hazardous to your health. That's a pretty simple concept. And guess what? Almost everyone agrees with it. Then why are only 20 percent of the population active enough to obtain health benefits? We have turned into a nation of couch potatoes, and it is killing us.

This chapter looks first at the cardiac risk involved in an inactive lifestyle. Then I show you how easy it is to get started and stay with a comfortable program of regular physical activity that can:

⮕ Lower your risk of heart disease.

⮕ Improve your quality of life.

⮕ Reduce anxiety and tension and elevate your mood.

⮕ Improve your risk factors for other diseases such as cancer or diabetes.

⮕ Help you achieve and maintain a healthy body weight.

Why Exercise?

There are literally hundreds of scientific and medical studies that document the cardiac benefits of regular exercise. These were recently summarized in the *Surgeon General's Report on Physical Activity and Health.* There is no longer any question among physicians that regular physical activity is one of the very best things you can do to lower your risk of heart disease or help treat heart disease if it is already present.

Most of us are couch potatoes!

In one major summary study combining the results of 43 previous studies, for example, scientists from the Centers for Disease Control concluded that inactive people doubled their risk of heart disease compared to active people. By CDC criteria, over 60 percent of the adult population in the United States fall into the *inactive* category. By lounging on their recliners and couches, over

---

Cashing in on the benefits of physical activity

Although this chapter focuses largely on the cardiovascular benefits of regular physical activity, the simple decision to be physically active confers many other health benefits. Here are a few:

✔ **Decreasing cancer risks.** There is rapidly accumulating and strong evidence that regular physical activity cuts down your risk of cancer. In particular, the risk for those cancers which seem to have a hormonal component, such as breast cancer for women and prostate cancer for men, seems to be lowered by regular physical activity. Colon cancer has also been shown to be decreased in individuals who are physically active. A recent study from Stanford University indicted that women who were physically active for 2 to 4 hours per week decreased their risk of breast cancer by 50 percent.

✔ **Preventing diabetes.** Physical activity is a great way to lower your risk of diabetes. Studies have shown that physically active individuals reduce their risk of adult onset diabetes between 24 and 100 percent.

✔ **Achieving and maintaining a healthy body weight.** Individuals who are inactive are much more likely to gain weight during their lives than individuals who are physically active. The expenditure of calories on a regular basis also tends to preserve lean muscle mass and make individuals capable of increased levels of functioning throughout their lives.

✔ **Improving mental and emotional states.** Numerous studies have shown that physical activity reduces anxiety and tension and can improve mood and decrease the likelihood of depression.

half of all adults in the United States have chosen a lifestyle that doubles the likelihood that they will develop heart disease at some point in their lives. To put this in perspective, these individuals have **increased their risk of developing heart disease as much as if they smoked one pack of cigarettes per day!** And inactive adults outnumber pack-a-day smokers six to one.

But there's good news: With just a moderate activity or exercise program, you can reverse this risk factor. Greater activity also has a positive impact on blood cholesterol and blood pressure levels, to name just two other risk factors for heart disease.

Some simple concepts will spur you up and out the front door, walking toward a life of reduced cardiac risk.

What's in it for me?

After even a very brief period of two or three months, you may experience several positive changes:

- ✔ Tasks that previously made you short of breath are easier to perform.

- ✔ Your heart rate when you're resting is lower. Because a more efficient heart pumps more blood on each beat, it requires fewer beats per minute to supply your body with oxygen when you are simply sitting still. Some people believe that this lower heart rate is one of the reasons why fit people live longer. The famous cardiologist Dr. Paul Dudley White, who was former President Dwight Eisenhower's physician, once said, "The heart is programmed at birth for a certain number of beats. I'd rather take mine at 50 beats per minute than 75!"

- ✔ Your heart as a muscle is stronger. Over a lifetime of moderate physical activity, the heart, as a muscle, maintains better condition than the heart of the individual who remains or becomes inactive.

- ✔ The coronary arteries, which supply blood to the heart, are more likely to stay large and relatively clean in individuals who exercise on a regular basis. Remember that clean coronary arteries prevent heart attacks (see Chapter 3).

Isn't exercise more important for young people than old people?

Physical activity has been shown to be beneficial for people of all ages. Remember that if you reach the age of 65, you have an 80 percent chance of reaching the age of 80! Reducing your risk of heart disease is important at any age and keeping the heart and muscles in tune is particularly important for older individuals.

The Difference between Physical Activity and Exercise

Once when I was giving a speech about the importance of regular physical activity for heart health, a woman stood up and said, "That may be important, but I had my fill of wearing gym shorts back in grade school. I will never do it again!"

This woman was expressing the classic confusion between *exercise* and *physical activity*. While there is considerable overlap between the two, they are not exactly the same.

- ✔ **Physical activity** is a much broader concept than exercise. Physical activity can be defined as any muscular movement that utilizes energy. Sitting on your couch, for example, is not physical activity. Getting your butt off of that couch is!

- ✔ **Exercise** is a *type* of physical activity that is typically defined more narrowly as a planned and structured activity where bodily movements are repeated to achieve various aspects of fitness. We usually think of exercise as activities such as aerobic dance or jogging or swimming laps.

Drawing a distinction between physical activity and exercise may seem like nit-picking, but from a practical standpoint, the distinction is very important. Many people don't realize that simply getting out of their easy chairs and raking the leaves on a brisk autumn day or spending an hour gardening classifies as physical activity and such physical activity over a lifetime has been shown to lower the risk of heart disease.

How Much Physical Activity Is Enough?

Many people are confused about how much physical activity is required to lower their risk of heart disease and how hard they need to work at it. Recent guidelines from the Centers for Disease Control (CDC) and the American College of Sports Medicine (ACSM) recommend that every adult try to accumulate at least 30 minutes of moderate intensity physical activity on most if not all days.

The two keys: Accumulate and moderate

Accumulate means that short bursts of physical activity throughout your day are as good as going to the gym for 30 minutes (an impossibly short trip). So look for ways in your daily life to accumulate physical activity. Take the stairs instead of the elevator. Park farther away from the store and walk to your destination. Take a simple fitness walk for 10 minutes at lunchtime. They all count.

Moderate, as the word suggests, means a level of exertion that is between light and heavy. In other words the type of activity that you choose should be intense enough that you know you are exerting yourself, but not so intense that you are out of breath with sweat running down your brow.

Here are some examples of moderate activity:

✔ Sweeping	✔ Bowling
✔ Washing the car	✔ Leisurely cycling
✔ Gardening	✔ Slow swimming
✔ Mowing the lawn	✔ Table Tennis
✔ Raking Leaves	✔ Horseback riding
✔ Mopping	✔ Walking
✔ Painting walls	✔ No-load hiking
✔ Vacuuming	✔ Recreational Tennis
✔ Cleaning	✔ Shooting baskets

I will never forget when my laboratory first started performing walking research. Jay Leno joked on the *Tonight Show,* "Now they tell us that walking is good for us — the next thing they'll be saying is that sitting is good for us!" While the audience laughed, he was really stating a common myth that you need to exert yourself to a high level in order to achieve cardiac benefits. Research has clearly shown that walking is adequate to achieve almost all cardiac benefits. Most important, walking (and other regular, moderate intensity activities) will significantly lower your risk of developing heart disease.

No pain, no gain? No way!

Many people have the misconception that exercise needs to be painful in order to be beneficial. Nothing could be further from the truth. In fact, if exercise is painful it probably isn't good for you. And for heart patients, pain, particularly chest pain, is typically a warning sign that you are exerting yourself too hard. Slow down.

Ease on down the road — for a great start

If you charge into heavy exercise, you'll wear yourself out at best and injure yourself at worst. Here are four basic ways to make sure that you stay within the "moderate" exertion zone — and stay with it.

- **The Talk Test.** Make sure that you can carry on a normal conversation with a companion while you are engaged in a bout of physical activity.

- **Perceived Exertion**. Pay attention to your body. Ask yourself, "Am I exerting myself at a moderate level or am I really exerting myself at a light level or heavy level?" Be honest with yourself. (Nobody but you is going to blab.) Using this subjective gauge, believe it or not, most people can accurately determine if they are working at a moderate intensity level of exertion.

- **Your Pulse.** The pulse is found on the thumb side of the inside of the wrist. With a little practice, most people can find it. Count your pulse for 10 seconds and multiply by six to find out your heart rate in beats per minute during exertion. Moderate exertion takes place between 60 percent and 70 percent of your predicted maximum heart rate.

  To estimate your maximum heart rate subtract your age in years from 220 beats per minute. Thus, for a 40-year-old individual, the predicted maximum heart rate is 220 beats minus 40 beats — 180 beats per minute. The moderate exertion level of 60 to 70 percent of 180 beats equals 108 to 126 beats per minute.

- **Heart Rate Monitor**. There are inexpensive heart rate monitors on the market that will accurately keep track of your heartbeat during exercise and will take the hassle out of accurately determining your exertion level.

The Right Way to Get Started

Most people have trouble getting started with regular activity or exercise for one simple reason: They make it too complex. To increase your chance of selecting the right activity program, ask yourself these three questions. And answer them honestly. (No daydreams of making the next Olympic team.)

- What do I like to do?
- What is convenient for me?
- What have I successfully done in the past?

For many people, the answer to these questions will be the physical activity of walking. For others it may be jogging, aerobic dance, in-line skating, or other forms of regular exertion.

Avoid the deadly home-gym syndrome. You have an *acute* case of home-gym syndrome the first time that you buy a piece of exercise equipment and take it home only to hang clothes on it. You have a *chronic* case of home-gym syndrome when you buy the second piece of home fitness equipment and now have a matched pair of expensive clothes racks.

Don't get me wrong, I am not against fitness equipment. In fact, I have three to four pieces of home fitness equipment in both my workout areas. But be realistic and pick forms of exercise that are simple, enjoyable, and convenient.

What's the Best Activity?

People often ask me what is the best activity or exercise. My answer never changes: It is the form of exercise that you will do! Look at *all* the things you like to do because somewhere in that list is an activity that will get you started.

Start your program with aerobic exercise

Every beginning exerciser should build his or her program around a core of what are called *aerobic* exercises. A*erobic* literally means "in the presence of air." So aerobic exercises are those that require your muscles to burn more oxygen (and you to breathe faster). The hard-working, air-hungry muscles demand more oxygen-rich blood from the heart. The heart in turn works a little harder and grows stronger. In this way aerobic exercise helps lower the risk of heart disease.

Mix and match activities

Many different kinds of aerobic activities and exercises exist. All of them are good for the heart. Pick the one that you think may be most convenient for you, or, better yet, mix and match. I should also emphasize that daily forms of physical activity such as leaf raking, lawn work, gardening, even brisk house-work, all qualify as *moderate* physical activity and all are equally beneficial for the heart. Make them part of your overall plan.

Here are some aerobic activities you might enjoy:

✔ Aerobic dance	✔ Jumping rope
✔ Cross-country skiing	✔ Rowing
✔ Cycling, outdoors 9.4 mph	✔ Running/jogging

- ✔ Cycling, stationary (50-60 rmp)
- ✔ Dancing, jazz, modern, tap
- ✔ In-line skating

- ✔ Stair climbing
- ✔ Swimming
- ✔ Walking, 3-4+ mph

Involve Your Physician

Preventing heart disease requires teamwork. It is always best if you can establish open communication and a collaborative relationship with your physician. Let your physician know of your desire to participate in a program of regular physical activity and seek his or her guidance. Most physicians will welcome the opportunity to talk about lifestyle measures with you and can help you fine-tune your physical activity program to account for your unique personal circumstances such as current medications, current level of physical activity, and current physical conditions, including existing heart disease. You may consider having an exercise tolerance test before starting to exercise. See Chapter 13.

Older people, people who have one or more risk factors for heart disease (see Chapter 3), and individuals who have been very inactive may benefit from taking an exercise tolerance test prior to starting a program of physical activity. The American Heart Association and the American College of Sports Medicine both recommend that men over the age of 50 and women over the age of 55 who have been previously very sedentary have a physician-supervised exercise tolerance test prior to starting a new exercise program.

Develop a Personal Plan for Physical Activity

Remember that when it comes to physical activity, people usually falter on simple issues rather than complex issues. In addition to choosing an activity (or activities) that is enjoyable, convenient, and successful for you in the past, you must remember that achieving the goal of a healthier heart through physical activity is a race that is won by the tortoise and not the hare.

Adopt the following watch words for planning your personal program. You might even want to post them on your mirror or tape them to your sweatband.

- ✔ Start slow
- ✔ Progress slowly
- ✔ Use common sense to avoid dangerous symptoms

Gearing up for success

One of the easiest ways to increase the likelihood that you will stick with your exercise program is to obtain proper gear. In the case of walking or running, this can be very simple. The most important gear for walkers and runners is proper footwear and proper clothing.

Choosing proper shoes. Any good shoe store, either a regular shoe store or an athletic shoe store, should be able to offer you good advice about walking or running shoes appropriate for your level of fitness, the terrain that you walk or run on, and climatic conditions that you exercise in. Finding proper, well-fitting footwear will increase your comfort during your walk or run and thereby encourage you to stick with your program. One tip is to buy walking or running shoes in the afternoon since your feet tend to swell a little bit in the day and you will get a better fit if you try them on in the afternoon.

Exercise Clothing. Most regular exercisers understand the value of *layering*. Select good athletic clothes all the way from running or walking shorts and tee shirts on up to a jogging or walking suit. If you exercise in cold, rainy, or snowy weather, don't forget the value of some of the newer products such as water-resistant running suits which will increase the likelihood that you will exercise during foul weather. A hat and gloves are also very important and often neglected aspects of athletic clothing.

If you have been previously very inactive, starting out at a low level of moderate intensity, such as walking 5 minutes per day, represents a good beginning. Once you are comfortable with this level of exertion, you can increase it slowly. Try building up your walk or other activity by approximately one minute per week until you reach 30 minutes on most, if not all, days.

Of course, don't leave your common sense at home! If you have any symptoms such as chest discomfort during a walk, you should slow down or stop and discuss the symptom at the earliest possible time with your physician Remember that the most important heart benefits from regular physical activity accrue to individuals who find ways of remaining physically active throughout their lives.

Five Tips for Sticking with It

1. Set a time and place.

Most people find that routines are helpful. Try to establish at least one time and place for physical activity each day. Other activities then tend to take care of themselves. How about walking the dog in the morning? Or taking a 10-minute, mind-clearing walk at lunch?

2. **Be prepared.**

   Always be on the lookout for unexpected opportunities to insert a little activity into the nooks and crannies of your life. Adopt a mindset that emphasizes more physical activity.

3. **Include family and friends.**

   Undertaking activities with family and friends makes them more social and enjoyable. This practice also increases the likelihood that you will carve out time for physical activity each day.

4. **Have fun.**

   If your activity isn't fun, you aren't going to do it. Choose things you look forward to.

5. **Prioritize.**

   If you don't make physical activity a priority, you are highly unlikely to stay with it day in and day out, week in and week out, month in and month out.

If You Already Have Heart Disease, What Then?

The good news is that regular physical activity not only helps prevent heart disease, but it also plays very important role in the therapy for individuals who already have various cardiac conditions. Anyone who has heart disease, however, will need to modify any physical activity program appropriately for his or her condition.

I want to emphasize very clearly that any individual who has existing heart disease *must carefully discuss physical activity with his or her personal physician* and make sure that his or her exercise program is modified to be safe and effective for his or her particular situation. With this caution in mind, you can achieve many important benefits from physical activity even if you already have existing heart disease.

✔ **Coronary artery disease.** Individuals with coronary artery disease (CAD) should undertake physical activity programs both to increase their ability to perform activities of daily life as well as to lower their risk of having additional problems for their coronary artery disease.

If you have suffered a heart attack, your program of physical activity should take place in a supervised cardiac rehabilitation program under the guidance of a trained cardiologist (see also Chapter 16).

If you have angina, your physical activity program should take place at a slightly lower level — at least 15 beats per minute below the level at which you experience chest pain.

What about strength training?

Recently there has been a lot of talk about the health benefits of strength training. Although strength training has multiple overall benefits, it should not be the core exercise for people who want to prevent heart disease or, in particular, who already have heart disease.

Virtually all the medical literature supporting the link between exercise and reducing the risk of heart disease comes from studies of aerobic exercise. In fact, strength training may be contraindicated in patients who have coronary artery disease or who have high blood pressure. The problem with strength training in these individuals is that it can cause dramatic increases in blood pressure. These increases in blood pressure in turn cause the heart to work harder. This can be a particular problem in individuals who already have narrowing of the coronary arteries. Individuals who have hypertension also can experience very significant and even dangerous increases in their blood pressure if they do any heavy lifting during strength training.

This is not to say that strength training has no place or benefit either in the reduction of risk for heart disease or in treatment for heart disease. Strength training can benefit the heart patient by increasing the efficiency of muscles, thus allowing an individual to carry out either leisure-time or work activities at a lower percentage of their maximal capacity. Regular strength training can also help individuals prevent weight gain, which is of significant benefit for patients with heart disease.

If you have heart disease and want to start strength training or want to use this modality to lower your risk of heart disease, the best advice is to find a skilled health professional with knowledge and background in cardiac rehabilitation. This individual will help you establish the best routine for you. These routines will typically be based on high repetition, low weight strength training. This approach allows the muscles to become more efficient without risking the danger of dramatic elevations in blood pressure.

✔ **Hypertension.** (See also Chapter 9.) Regular physical activity not only reduces the risk of developing hypertension, but is also very effective as a treatment for hypertension. In this instance, you will need to reduce your level of exertion about 10 percent below individuals who do not have high blood pressure. If you are using *perceived exertion* to monitor your level of activity, aim for "light moderate" rather than "moderate" activity. If you are using heart rate to gauge your exercise, aim for 50 to 60 percent of predicted maximum heart rate rather than 60 to 70 percent.

✔ **After a heart attack.** (See also Chapter 15.) In the normal heart, approximately 70 to 80 percent of the blood that is returned to the heart is pumped out with each beat. In an individual who has heart failure, less than 40 percent, and in some instances as low as 15 to 20 percent, of the blood that is returned to the heart is pumped out in each beat. If you have heart failure, you can still benefit from physical activity but you *must* use a much lower level of exertion. The goal in this situation is to increase the efficiency of muscles so that they require less blood flow from the heart. In this instance, if you are gauging your exercise program by *perceived exertion*, you should aim for "light" rather than "moderate." If you are using a percentage of predicted maximum heart rate, aim for 40 to 50 percent of your predicted maximum heart rate.

How do medicines affect exercise?

Individuals who have heart disease or risk factors for heart disease (such as hypertension or elevated blood cholesterol) often take medicines which may interact with exercise. It is important to understand which medicines may affect your exercise program.

✔ **Beta blockers.** Individuals with heart disease and/or hypertension are often on a class of medicines known as beta blockers. These medicines lower blood pressure and decrease the work of the heart. They also lower the heart rate response to exercise. If you are on a beta blocker medicine, you should gauge the intensity of your exercise by perceived exertion rather than by heart rate. Remember to gauge your exercise to achieve "moderate" levels of exertion. Individuals on beta blockers can achieve the same cardiac benefits as individuals who are not.

✔ **Calcium Channel Blockers.** Calcium channel blockers are also common among individuals who have heart disease or hypertension. Some of these medications can also lower the heart rate response to exercise. Once again, the good news is that they do not prohibit you from achieving the multiple cardiac and other health benefits from regular physical activity.

✔ **Diuretics.** Diuretics are common for individuals who have high blood pressure or heart failure. These will not reduce the benefit of physical activity for the heart; however, it is important that you pay particular attention to adequate hydration if you are on a diuretic. Drink plenty of water before, during, and after activity. If you are on fluid restriction, consult your physician about water intake and be sure to monitor your weight daily.

Chapter 7

Planning Your Personal Heart Healthy Exercise Program

- -

In This Chapter

▶ Why walking may be the best form of heart healthy exercise

▶ How to determine your level of fitness

▶ Who needs a medical evaluation and who doesn't

▶ How to plan an exercise program that fits your level of fitness

▶ Five specific walking programs

▶ Six key signs of over exercising

▶ What symptoms to worry about when you are exercising

▶ What form of physical activity is best for weight management

▶ How to overcome the most common excuses for not exercising

- -

*I*t's time to bridge the gap between intention and action. In this chapter, I discuss how to get off that couch, into those walking (or running, if you insist) shoes, out that front door, and down the road toward a happier lifestyle and lowered risk of heart disease.

Choosing Your Exercise Activity

When it comes to picking the right exercise to get you started on the road toward improved cardiovascular health, honesty is the best policy. And being honest with yourself starts by asking yourself those three questions I discussed in Chapter 6:

✔ What do I like to do?

✔ What is convenient?

✔ In what form of exercise have I successfully participated in the past?

Walk On By

If you are honest, many of you will conclude you've enjoyed walking most often and most conveniently. Yes, walking — that simple skill you've been competent in since you were one year old. Most people, however, totally underestimate the power of regular fitness walking. In fact, many 50 and 60 year olds enrolled in walking studies in my research laboratory have asserted that "walking would only be good for someone like my parents" — who must be in their 80s or 90s! Of course, walking is good for their parents, but it is also good for them.

A fish tale with a moral

Talking so often to people like these about cardiovascular health reminds me of the two sofa jockeys who decided to go on a weekend fishing trip. After they packed up all their camping gear and fishing tackle, one man also packed his running shoes because he thought he might get back into a little physical activity. Well, as the men were tramping across a meadow on the way to their campsite, a ferocious grizzly bear suddenly broke into the open on the far side of the meadow and started running toward them. They froze with terror. Then one man began to run for the nearest tree. The other, however, dropped his pack, grabbed his running shoes, and calmly began to lace them up. His fleeing companion yelled over his shoulder, "You're the stupidest man I ever met. No one can outrun a grizzly bear!" "Who said anything about the bear, my friend?" the first replied, rising to his feet. "I simply intend to outrun you!"

What's the point? Most people, when it comes to exercise, think that they need to outrun the ferocious grizzly bear of their inactive past. In fact, all they need to do in order to get most of the cardiovascular benefits is to outrun (or as I hope I will be able to convince you, out*walk*) their previously sedentary selves.

Why walking is the best heart healthy exercise

Extensive research conducted by my laboratory and others has demonstrated some simple facts about walking:

- ✔ Virtually everyone can get aerobic benefit from walking.
- ✔ Walking is usually the simplest and most convenient form of physical activity for the vast majority of people.
- ✔ Walking can accommodate people of all ages and backgrounds because the intensity is very flexible.

✔ Walking is simple. It is as easy as putting one foot in front of the other, opening your front door, and setting off down the road.

✔ Most of the research that has shown that regular physical activity lowers the risk of heart disease has focused on walking.

✔ For most people, I recommend walking as the best form of regular exercise to lower the risk of cardiovascular disease — and so do 90 percent of my fellow physicians.

✔ Still need more convincing? There are three times as many fitness walkers in the United States as joggers. Currently inactive individuals who say they want to start an exercise program choose walking 6 times as frequently as jogging and 18 times more often than aerobic dance.

With all these facts, it should be no surprise that the Healthy Heart Walking Program is the focus for this chapter. The total Healthy Heart Walking Program features five separate 12-week programs designed to benefit every level of physical fitness from poor to excellent.

If you prefer a different form of physical activity and/or aerobic exercise, however, don't be dismayed. Almost everything I say about walking applies to other forms of aerobic exercise as well. All aerobic activities are equally good in terms of their cardiovascular benefits.

Getting Started

Before jumping into your walking shoes and heading out the door, you must prepare to succeed. That means taking several steps that will help you choose and carry out the walking program that is right for you:

✔ Testing your current level of physical fitness

✔ Planning your individual program

✔ Reviewing the essential elements of an exercise session.

Testing, testing, testing — determine your current level of fitness

If you want to get started on a walking program, or any other program of increased physical activity or exercise, it is highly desirable to test your level of readiness. If you have been previously sedentary, this is absolutely imperative so that you can perform your exercise program safely. In other instances, such testing assures that your program is comfortable and at the right level for you.

The Physical Activity Readiness Questionnaire (PAR-Q) and the *One Mile Walk Test* that I present here are self-administered tests to help you determine whether you need to have a medical evaluation before starting any activity program and what your current level of physical fitness is.

Who needs a medical evaluation?

If you have been inactive, and/or are a man over the age of 50 or a woman over the age of 55, and/or have one or more risk factors for heart disease, you should definitely have a medical evaluation (as I discuss in Chapter 6). In some instances, this may mean only a phone call to your physician. In other instances, your physician may want to give you an exercise tolerance test.

How do you know if you have a condition which may make even moderate exercise unsafe or uncomfortable? First, ask yourself the seven questions outlined in Table 7-1. If you answer *yes* to any of these questions — even one — it's mandatory that you fully discuss your walking or any other activity program with your physician *before* you start.

Table 7-1		Physical Activity Readiness Questionnaire (PAR-Q)
Yes	**No**	
❑	❑	1. Has your doctor ever said you have heart trouble?
❑	❑	2. Do you frequently have pains in your heart and chest?
❑	❑	3. Do you often feel faint or have spells of severe dizziness?
❑	❑	4. Has a doctor ever said your blood pressure was too high?
❑	❑	5. Has your doctor ever told you that you have a bone or joint problem such as arthritis that has been aggravated by exercise or might be made worse with exercise?
❑	❑	6. Is there a good physical reason not mentioned here why you should not follow an activity program even if you wanted to?
❑	❑	7. Are you over age 65 and not accustomed to vigorous exercise?

Used with permission. Canadian Society for Exercise Physiology.

How active are you?

You, or you and your physician, should also consider your current level of physical activity when deciding which exercise program is best for you. Table 7-2 provides a quick test to help you estimate this factor.

Table 7-2	Physical Activity Questionnaire

What statement best describes your general activity level for the previous month? Simply circle the level that applies to you.

I do not participate in regularly programmed recreation, sports, or heavy physical activity.

I avoid walking or exertion — for example, always use an elevator, drive whenever possible instead of walking.	0
I walk for pleasure, routinely use stairs and/or occasionally exercise sufficiently to cause heavy breathing or perspiration.	1

I participate regularly in recreation or work requiring modest physical activity such as walking, golf, horse-back riding, calisthenics, gymnastics, table tennis, bowling, weight lifting, or yard work.

Ten to 30 minutes per week.	2
Thirty to 45 minutes per week.	3

I participate regularly in heavy physical exercise, such as brisk walking, running or jogging, swimming, cycling, rowing, skipping rope, or running in place. I engage in vigorous aerobic activity such as tennis, basketball, or handball.

I run or briskly walk two to three miles per week or spend 45 minutes to an hour per week in comparable physical activity.	4
I run or briskly walk three to five miles per week or spend 60 to 90 minutes per week in comparable physical activity.	5
I run or briskly walk five to 10 miles per week or spend 90 to 180 minutes per week in comparable physical activity.	6
I run or briskly walk over 10 miles per week or spend over 180 minutes per week in comparable physical activity.	7

This test is adapted and used with permission of the authors R.M. Ross and A.S. Jackson, "Exercise Concepts, Calculations and Computer Applications" (Dubuque: Brown and Benchmark, 1990).

Please note the number that you choose because it helps guide you in selecting the walking program that is appropriate for you.

Testing your level of physical fitness using the One-Mile Walk Test

Some years ago my laboratory and I developed the first walking test ever used to estimate a person's cardiovascular fitness. We called it *The One-Mile Walk Test*. And we soon knew we were on to something big. It was featured on the *Today Show* and *Good Morning America*. Ultimately, over one million individuals wrote for the brochure describing the test. The One-Mile Walk Test teaches you a great deal about your level of cardiovascular fitness as well as establishes the correct walking program for you. Here's how to take the test:

1. **Be sure to wear a watch with either a sweep second hand or a digital second hand and either find a quarter-mile track or other measured track at a local high school or college or measure a one-mile distance on a flat uninterrupted stretch of road. Take along a paper and pencil to make notes.**

2. **Warm up and stretch for four to five minutes. It is particularly important to stretch the major muscles of your legs. You should also warm up a bit by first walking slowly, and then gradually building up your speed until you are walking briskly. This also warms up the muscles of your legs.**

3. **Note your start time and walk the mile as briskly as possible, maintaining a steady pace.**

4. **At the end of the mile, note your time in minutes and seconds on your score card.**

5. **Estimate your relative cardiovascular fitness by comparing your results to the data presented in the Table 7-3.**

Table 7-3   One-Mile Walk Cardiovascular Fitness Standards

Females (All Times Are in Minutes and Seconds)

	20-29	30-39	40-49	50-59	60-69	70+
Excellent	<13:12	<13:42	<14:12	<14:42	<15:06	<18:18
Good	13:12-14:06	13:42-14:36	14:12-15:06	14:42-15:36	15:06-16:18	18:18-20:00
Average	14:07-15:06	14:37-15:36	15:07-16:06	15:37-17:00	16:19-17:30	20:01-21:48
Fair	15:07-16:30	15:37-17:00	16:07-17:30	17:01-18:06	17:31-19:12	21:49-24:06
Poor	>16:30	>17:00	>17:30	>18:06	>19:12	>24:06

Males (All Times Are in Minutes and Seconds)

	20-29	30-39	40-49	50-59	60-69	70+
Excellent	<11:54	<12:24	<12:54	<13:24	<14:06	<15:06
Good	11:54-13:00	12:24-13:30	12:54-14:00	13:24-14:24	14:06-15:12	15:06-15:48
Average	13:01-13:42	13:31-14:12	14:01-14:42	14:25-15:12	15:13-16:18	15:49-18:48
Fair	13:43-14:30	14:13-15:00	14:43-15:30	15:13-16:30	16:19-17:18	18:49-20:18
Poor	>14:30	>15:00	>15:30	>16:30	>17:18	>20:18

Using the time it took you to complete the One-Mile Walk Test, note whether you fall into the Poor, Fair, Average, Good, or Excellent category. (Yes, write that on your paper.) In a moment you'll use this information, coupled with your age, to determine which level of the Healthy Heart Walking Program is best for you.

Get the right gear for walking

Having the appropriate equipment increases the likelihood that you will get started, stay with your program, enjoy (rather than fight) the elements, and avoid injury. For walking (and running), spending a few extra dollars on well designed, appropriate footwear is worth the cost. The purchase of an all-weather exercise suit is also a must. All too often I see patients who start off well during the warm weather and stay with their exercise program until autumn. Then, since they have no proper exercise suit, all their good intentions blow away with the wind (or actually with the snow, rain, sleet, or hail!). So make sure you're ready for the demands of the climate you live in. (For further information on gear, see Chapter 6.)

Develop an exercise plan that fits your lifestyle

Would you go off on a journey to a new location without taking a road map or some other plan of how to get there? Taking a short time to develop a simple exercise plan is just as smart. It will increase enjoyment of your exercise program and the likelihood that you will stick with it. Plan for these three essential elements.

- ✔ **Time.** Choose a time of day that is convenient for you. Some people prefer to walk in the morning before they get involved in their daily activities. Others find that lunchtime or late afternoon is better. Some can only find time in the evening (but beware since evening exercise tends to get disrupted by family, other obligations, or fatigue). Following a regular schedule makes exercise a habit. Most successful exercisers actually block off time in their future schedules on a daily or weekly basis to assure that they accomplish this important task.

- ✔ **Location.** If you are walking, find a convenient outdoor route for good weather. Look for a route that is relatively flat and has few interruptions such as traffic lights. When the weather is bad, shopping malls or fitness centers provide excellent alternative locations.

- ✔ **Partners.** Exercising with friends or with a "walking buddy" can make sessions more enjoyable and provide a little extra push to get out and do it. It's hard to let that friend down after you arrange to walk together.

Some people prefer listening to the radio or music tapes while they walk. If you do listen to music, make sure you walk on sidewalks or other areas away from traffic because you won't be able to hear approaching vehicles over hip hop, rock, or even Bach.

Step by Step through a Session of the Healthy Heart Walking Program

To achieve the most cardiovascular benefits safely and efficiently, every exercise session of the Healthy Heart Walking Program (or any alternative aerobic activity) should contain these six key elements:

- **Warm up.** Warm up with both pre-walk stretches and a gradually progressive walking period of two to three minutes until you get up to the pace that you intend to maintain during the aerobic portion of your exercise. This is important to prevent injury and work on flexibility as well as to settle emotionally into your workout. Use a general stretching program which emphasizes lower body stretches particularly of the large muscles in the front of the leg (the quadriceps muscles) and in the back of the leg (hamstring and calf muscles).

- **Distance.** Each program gives the recommended distance to walk in each session in miles. If you are walking on a track or using a treadmill, these distances are easy to determine. If you are walking outside in your neighborhood, drive your car along your favorite route and record appropriate distances to various landmarks. Record the distances along several different routes to add variety.

- **Pace.** Each program gives the speed at which you should walk in miles per hour. If you are just getting started, for example, the starter Blue program recommends a fairly leisurely pace of 2.5 miles per hour. By the time you reach the advanced Red program, the pace starts at 3.0 miles per hour and by week 12 it has advanced to 4.0 miles per hour, which is a good brisk pace for virtually anyone.

- **Time walked.** Each program tells you how many minutes it will take you to walk the recommended distance at the recommended pace.

- **Target intensity level/target heart rate** (Percentage of maximum). The walking programs are designed so that if you walk each session's distance at the indicated pace, you are likely to achieve the proper intensity for each session. If you have any questions about this, use your heart rate as the deciding factor.

The proper intensity for your walk is determined by maintaining your heart rate in the target heart training zone that represents an exertion level given as a percentage of your maximum heart rate. The target heart rates for the five walking programs generally range from 60 to 70 percent of your predicted maximum depending on your fitness level.

To estimate your maximum heart rate, subtract your age in years from 220 beats per minute. Thus, for a 40-year-old individual, the predicted maximum heart rate is 220 beats minus 40 beats — 180 beats per minute. The moderate exertion level of 60 to 70 percent of 180 beats equals 108 to 126 beats per minute.

Exceptions to these intensity levels. Certain individuals may need to moderate the intensity of their walks.

- If you already suffer from coronary artery disease, and have either angina, have suffered a heart attack, or have undergone bypass surgery or angioplasty, it is important that you walk at least 10-15 beats below the exercise heart rate where you experience symptoms. If you have questions about this, you should discuss them with your doctor.

- If you take beta blocker medicines either because you have coronary artery disease or hypertension, your maximum heart rate will be slowed down. In that situation you should regulate your exercise session by "perceived exertion" rather than target heart rate. You should try to exercise at a moderate level.

✔ **Cooldown.** Toward the end of your walk, slow your pace down and begin your cooldown. Conclude your cooldown with the same stretches that you used before your walk.

✔ **Frequency.** To foster heart health, aerobic activity must be regular. Each program indicates how many times per week you should walk (or perform an alternative form of aerobic activity) to achieve benefits.

The Healthy Heart Walking Programs

For ease of use, the five 12-week programs of the Healthy Heart Walking Program are color-coded to correspond to the colors of the spectrum. The colors are Blue, Green, Yellow, Orange, and Red. Actually, the full color spectrum also contains *indigo* and *violet*, but I have only five walking programs. Besides, who knows what color *indigo* is anyway?

The least intense program is Blue, followed by the Green program, which is slightly more intense, and so on up to Red — the most intense of the programs. If you like, think of these color levels as belts (*a la* karate) marking your achievement. The only shame is to have no belt at all.

Selecting the right walking program

Using your results on either the activity scale or the One-Mile Walk Test, use Table 7-4 or Table 7-5 to determine which program is right for you.

If you used the Physical Activity Questionnaire

Table 7-4	All Walkers of All Ages
Score	*Program*
0, 1, 2	Blue
3, 4	Green
5	Yellow
6	Orange
7	Red

If you used the One-Mile Walk Test

Table 7-5	Walking Program Selection Charts					
Women (by Age)						
Test Result	*20-29*	*30-39*	*40-49*	*50-59*	*60-69*	*70+*
Excellent	Red	Red	Red	Red	Orange	Yellow
Good	Red	Red	Orange	Orange	Yellow	Green
Average	Orange	Orange	Yellow	Yellow	Green	Blue
Fair	Orange	Yellow	Green	Green	Blue	Blue
Poor	Yellow	Green	Blue	Blue	Blue	Blue
Men (by Age)						
Test Result	*20-29*	*30-39*	*40-49*	*50-59*	*60-69*	*70+*
Excellent	Red	Red	Red	Red	Red	Orange
Good	Red	Red	Red	Red	Orange	Yellow
Average	Red	Orange	Orange	Orange	Yellow	Green
Fair	Orange	Orange	Yellow	Yellow	Green	Blue
Poor	Orange	Yellow	Green	Green	Blue	Blue

Getting started with the appropriate program

Start with week 1 of the appropriate program and progress through week 12. At the end of twelve weeks, retest yourself using either the activity scale or the One-Mile Walk Test and initiate the next fitness walking program or maintain your activity at its current level. Remember, the point is to get started on a program that you can continue throughout your life, so don't be too concerned if the programs seem very mild to start. These programs are intended to get you started on the enjoyable habit of physical activity rather than to provide maximum stress from day one.

Conversely, if you start your walking program and find that it seems too difficult, drop back a level. For example, if your estimate using PAR-Q indicates that you could start at the Yellow Program level, but that seems overly strenuous, drop back to the Green Program. Progress and enjoyment, not pain, is your goal.

Tables 7-6 through 7-10 describe each Healthy Heart Walking Program.

Table 7-6				Blue Program			
Week	**1-2**	**3-4**	**5-6**	**7**	**8-9**	**10-12**	**Maintenance**
Warm-up (min)*	5-7	5-7	5-7	5-7	5-7	5-7	5-7
Mileage	.75	.8	1.0	1.0	1.25	1.5	1.5
Pace (mph)+	2.5	2.5	2.5	3.0	3.0	3.0	3.0
Time Walked (min)	18	20	24	20	25	30	30
Heart Rate (% of max)	50-60	60	60-70	60-70	60-70	60-70	60-70
Cool down (min)*	5-7	5-7	5-7	5-7	5-7	5-7	5-7
Frequency (times per week)	3	3	4	4	5	5	5

*Warm-up and cool down should be slow walking that you gradually increase to your training pace.

+ The pace listed is only an approximation. The actual pace that you should use should keep your heart rate at the level the program recommends.

Table 7-7				Green Program			
Week	**1-2**	**3-4**	**5**	**6-8**	**9-10**	**11-12**	**Maintenance**
Warm-up (min)*	5-7	5-7	5-7	5-7	5-7	5-7	5-7
Mileage	1.0	1.1	1.25	1.5	1.5	1.75	1.75
Pace (mph)+	2.5	2.5	2.5	2.5	3.0	3.0	3.0
Time Walked (min)	24	27	30	36	30	30	35
Heart Rate (% of max)	60-70	60-70	60-70	60-70	60-70	60-70	70
Cool down (min)*	5-7	5-7	5-7	5-7	5-7	5-7	5-7
Frequency (times per week)	3	3	4	4	5	5	5

*Warm-up and cool down should be slow walking that you gradually increase to your training pace.
+ The pace listed is only an approximation. The actual pace that you should use should keep your heart rate at the level the program recommends.

Table 7-8					Yellow Program				
Week	**1-2**	**3-4**	**5**	**6**	**7**	**8**	**9-10**	**11-12**	**Maintenance**
Warm-up (min)*	5-7	5-7	5-7	5-7	5-7	5-7	5-7	5-7	5-7
Mileage	1.25	1.5	1.5	1.6	1.6	1.75	1.75	2.0	2.0
Pace (mph)+	2.5	3.0	3.0	3.0	3.5	3.5	3.5	3.5	3.5
Time Walked (min)	30	30	30	32	27	30	30	34	34
Heart Rate (% of max)	60-70	60-70	60-70	60-70	60-70	60-70	60-70	60-70	60-70
Cool down (min)*	5-7	5-7	5-7	5-7	5-7	5-7	5-7	5-7	5-7
Frequency (times per week)	4	4	4	5	5	5	5	5	5

*Warm-up and cool down should be slow walking that you gradually increase to your training pace.
+ The pace listed is only an approximation. The actual pace that you should use should keep your heart rate at the level the program recommends.

Table 7-9	Orange Program						
Week	*1-2*	*3-4*	*5*	*6-8*	*9-10*	*11-12*	*Maintenance*
Warm-up (min)*	5-7	5-7	5-7	5-7	5-7	5-7	5-7
Mileage	1.5	1.6	1.75	1.75	2.0	2.25	2.25
Pace (mph)+	2.75	2.75	3.0	3.25	3.25	3.5	3.75
Time Walked (min)	33	35	34	32	37	38	36
Heart Rate (% of max)	60-70	60-70	60-70	60-70	60-70	60-70	0-70
Cool down (min)*	5-7	5-7	5-7	5-7	5-7	5-7	5-7
Frequency (times per week)	4	4	5	5	5	5	5

*Warm-up and cool down should be slow walking that you gradually increase to your training pace.
+ The pace listed is only an approximation. The actual pace that you should use should keep your heart rate at the level the program recommends.

Table 7-10	Red Program								
Week	*1-2*	*3-4*	*5*	*6*	*7*	*8*	*9-10*	*11-12*	*Maintenance*
Warm-up (min)*	5-7	5-7	5-7	5-7	5-7	5-7	5-7	5-7	5-7
Mileage	1.75	1.75	2.0	2.0	2.25	2.25	2.25	2.5	2.5
Pace (mph)+	3.0	3.0	3.25	3.5	3.5	4.0	4.0	4.0	4.0
Time Walked (min)	35	35	37	34	39	34	34	38	38
Heart Rate (% of max)	60-70	60-70	60-70	60-70	60-70	60-70	60-70	60-70	60-70
Cool down (min)*	5-7	5-7	5-7	5-7	5-7	5-7	5-7	5-7	5-7
Frequency (times per week)	5	5	5	5	5	5	5	5	5

*Warm-up and cool down should be slow walking that you gradually increase to your training pace.
+ The pace listed is only an approximation. The actual pace that you should use should keep your heart rate at the level the program recommends.

Other Forms of Physical Activity

Other forms of aerobic activity (such as swimming, cycling, jogging, or aerobic dance) can also fit into an overall approach to increasing your cardiovascular health. If you choose another aerobic activity as the core of your program or use it in a mix-and-match fashion to vary day-to-day or week-to-week activity, you can easily adapt the guidelines given for the five Healthy Heart Walking Programs. The key considerations are *time* and *intensity (pace)*.

Please note that each of the walking programs gradually increases in distance and pace. If you decide to substitute another form of aerobic activity for walking, use the minutes of exercise and percentage of your predicted maximum heart rate as your guideline. For example, if your walking program calls for 25 minutes of walking at 60 percent of your predicted maximum heart rate, and on a given day you decide to swim or bike, use the guidelines to perform this alternative activity for 25 minutes at 60 percent of your predicted maximum heart rate. Following this procedure, it is easy to substitute one aerobic activity for another on a daily, weekly or seasonal basis.

Staying with it — overcoming excuses

Everyone, even the most regular exerciser, has periods when it is more difficult to exercise than others. Oftentimes we are our own worst enemy because we make up excuses for why we don't stick with our exercise program. Here are some common excuses and how to overcome them.

Excuse 1: I am busy. I don't have time.

Solution: Find a specific time to exercise and write it on your calendar or appointment book. Keep your appointment to exercise just as you would keep any other appointment.

Excuse 2: The weather is bad.

Solution: Have a number of different alternative locations for your walking program such as shopping mall or a fitness facility when the weather is bad. Better yet, buy a treadmill and walk at home. Anticipate change of season (for example fall to winter) and make a plan for walk-ing during the winter months before the weather turns bitterly cold.

Excuse 3: I am too tired.

Solution: You may be exercising too hard if it makes you tired. Also, consider exercising ear-lier in the day. Your walk should invigorate you and if it is not doing this, you should adjust your schedule or the intensity of your walk.

Excuse 4: Walking is boring! I don't look forward to it and enjoy it.

Solution: Vary your walking route. Employ dif-ferent strategies such as walking with family and friends. Join a group such as the mall walk-ing group; walk with a radio or tape player.

Excuse 5: Walking cuts into family time.

Solution: Ask your family members to join in your walking program. It benefits all of you!

Six Signs of Over-Exercising

Many individuals starting an exercise program don't realize how easy it is to over-exercise. Watch out for these warning signals:

- **Difficulty finishing.** If you can't complete your exercise program with energy to spare, decrease your walking pace and/or your distance.

- **Inability to carry on a normal conversation during walking.** If this happens, you are going too fast. Slow down!

- **Faintness or nausea after exercising**. If your walking is too intense or if you stop walking too abruptly, you can feel faint. This happens because increased blood flow to the legs during walking may cause blood to pool temporarily in the veins and make it difficult for the heart to maintain an adequate output. Decrease your walking pace and increase the time of your cool down.

- **Chronic fatigue.** If during the remainder of the day or evening after exercise you feel tired rather than stimulated, you are exercising too hard. If you feel very fatigued or have chest pain after exercise, decrease the pace and/or distance of your workout.

- **Sleeplessness.** A proper exercise program should make it easier, not more difficult, to get a good night's sleep. If you are having more difficulty sleeping normally, decrease the amount of exercise until your symptoms subside.

- **Increased aches and pains in your joints**. Some muscle discomfort is inevitable when you start exercising after being very inactive. However, your joints should not hurt or continue to feel stiff. Make sure that you are doing your warm up correctly. Muscle cramping and back discomfort may also indicate poor warm-up technique. If symptoms persist, consult your physician.

Medic Alert: Symptoms to Watch for During Exercise

The key to safe exercise is to never leave your common sense at home. It is important to stay tuned to any symptoms that you have during an exercise session in order to achieve maximum benefit and at the same time exercise safely. This is particularly true if you are at risk for heart disease or already have established signs or symptoms or manifestations of heart disease. If the following symptoms occur, contact your physician before continuing your walking routine or any other form of physical activity.

✔ **Discomfort in the chest, arm, upper body, neck, or jaw during exercise.** This may very well be angina. If you have any questions about it, you should discuss them with your physician. This type of discomfort may be of any intensity and may be experienced as aching, burning, a sensation of fullness, or tightness.

✔ **Faintness or lightheadedness during exercise.** These symptoms may occur after exercise if the cooldown is too brief. Usually this is not serious and can be managed by extending the cooldown. However, if a "fainting spell" or feeling that you are about to faint occurs during exercise, immediately discontinue the activity and consult your physician.

✔ **Excessive shortness of breath during exercise.** While you are walking or performing any other form of aerobic exercise, the rate and depth of your breathing should increase but it should not be uncomfortable. A good rule to follow is that breathing should not be so difficult that talking is an effort. It is also important to consult your physician if wheezing develops or if recovery from shortness of breath takes more than five minutes at the conclusion of an exercise session.

✔ **Irregular Pulse.** If your pulse is irregular or skips or races, either during or after exercise, such that it differs from your normal pulse, it is important to consult your physician.

✔ **Change in usual symptoms.** If your usual symptoms change, such as an increase in angina or shortness of breath or if pain from an arthritic joint or the site of a previous orthopedic injury occurs or becomes more severe or persistent, you should consult with your physician.

✔ **Any other symptoms.** Finally, you should always discuss any other symptoms that cause you concern with your physician. Exercise should be a pleasure, not a chore. Pain is a warning sign that you should not ignore.

Remember that medications can also affect your exercise program's intensity but not its effectiveness. See Chapter 6 for details.

Coping with the Environment

Conditions in the environment can affect your body's response to exercise. As conditions change, you may need to adjust your program.

✔ **Heat.** High humidity and elevated temperatures increase stress on your heart. Whenever the temperature is above 75° F, decrease your walking speed, drink plenty of water, and check your heart rate more frequently to make sure that you are not exceeding your prescribed heart rate. Anytime the temperature is above 75° F and the humidity is more than 75 percent, it's a good idea to exercise indoors.

✔ **Cold.** Exposure to the cold can also increase the work of your heart and potentially trigger an attack of angina. Whenever the temperature or wind chill is below 20° F, limit your walk to 30 minutes and avoid windy areas. Wearing layers of clothing also helps. Wearing a scarf over your mouth can make breathing dry, cold air more comfortable. If the temperature or wind chill is below 0° F, exercise indoors.

✔ **Air Pollution.** High levels of carbon monoxide can trigger shortness of breath or angina. If you have to walk in areas where air pollution is high, perform your exercise session early in the morning before the carbon monoxide and oxidant levels are high and decrease your walking pace and duration. During periods of very high pollution levels, you may want to walk indoors.

✔ **Terrain.** Avoid walking in hilly areas. If you can't avoid hills, decrease your pace when walking uphill so that you do not exceed your recommended heart rate.

✔ **Altitude.** If you live or travel to high altitude places, be aware that altitude can affect your walking or other exercise program. You can obtain specific recommendations from your physician. You should limit your activity level for the first 24 to 48 hours in altitudes above 6,000 feet.

Health Considerations

Although certain health conditions may have an impact on your walking or other exercise program, the good news is that walking can benefit a wide variety of acute and chronic conditions and illnesses. It is always important to discuss your own particular health background and current circumstances with your personal physician to determine how you may need to modify your exercise program.

Walking and weight management

Walking is an excellent adjunct to a program to manage your weight properly. Walking and other forms of physical activity not only burn calories, but also help maintain a lower weight over the long haul.

Walking consistently can make an enormous difference in terms of weight control. For example, if you weigh 175 pounds and walk two miles every day, you can lose up to 20 pounds in one year as long as you don't increase your caloric intake.

Most people underestimate how many calories you can burn during a walking session. The table that follows shows calories burned per mile based on your walking pace and body weight.

Caloric Cost of Walking (Calories/Mile)

Walking Pace		Body Weight					
(mph)	(min/mile)	100	125	150	175	200	225
		Calories Burned					
2.0	30	60	75	90	105	120	136
2.2	27	58	72	87	101	116	130
2.4	25	56	70	84	98	113	127
2.7	22	53	66	79	92	105	118
3.0	20	53	66	79	92	105	118
3.3	18	53	67	79	92	105	118
3.5	17	54	67	81	94	108	121
3.75	16	56	69	83	97	111	125
4.0	15	58	73	87	102	116	131
4.3	14	62	77	92	108	123	139

Chapter 8

Heart and Soul: Mind/Body Connections, Stress Reduction, and Cardiac Health

• •

In This Chapter

▶ Links between emotions and the heart

▶ Why stress harms cardiac health

▶ The link between stress and high blood pressure

▶ Why anger kills

▶ How emotional states can mimic heart disease

▶ The healing power of love

▶ A four-part plan for stress reduction for a healthy heart

▶ Five simple strategies for controlling anger

• •

The mind, the emotions, and the heart have long been linked in the human imagination. From prehistoric times, we have identified the heart as the seat of love and other emotions.

✔ We "give our hearts" to those we love.

✔ And when they "break" them, we suffer "heartache," which the dictionary defines as "anguish of mind."

✔ Like medieval knights swearing allegiance to their king, we still place hands over our physical hearts to pledge loyalty to our nations.

✔ A close call "makes our hearts stop" and "scares us to death."

✔ If we fight bravely to the end in any cause, we "never lose heart," but if we give up easily, we are "fainthearted."

✔ Anger makes our "blood boil," but a positive, cheerful outlook makes us "lighthearted."

Our prehistoric ancestors undoubtedly used the same telling expressions linking the mind and heart as they told stories around the fire in the family cave or confronted the woolly mammoth outside in the wilderness.

Even though it has taken a long time for modern science to begin to catch up with folklore and language, we are beginning to understand that there are powerful, very real links between mind and body. While it appears that emotional states and psychological health can impact virtually every organ system, the links between the mind and heart have probably been the most fully studied and understood. In this chapter, I review the links between stress, anger, love, friendship, intimacy, fear, and many other physiological states and cardiac health. I also review some simple strategies for controlling stress and anger and opening up your heart to promote cardiac health.

Stress and the Heart

High stress levels constitute one of the cardiac health risks (and general health risks) that each of us faces daily. In fact, a growing body of scientific and medical evidence links stress to a variety of illnesses ranging from heart disease and cancer to the common cold. Unfortunately, stress is endemic in our modern, fast-paced society. One study from the National Institute of Mental Health found that over 30 percent of adults experience enough stress in their daily lives to impair performance at work or at home.

What is stress?

Despite literally hundreds of studies about stress, a precise definition is frustratingly difficult to come up with. Perhaps the best simple definition came from Canadian scientist Hans Selye, who in 1956 defined stress as "the nonspecific response of the body to any demands made on it" in his pioneering book *The Stress of Life*. This simple definition incorporates both key components of stress, namely the demand (typically external) and the response (typically internal). This general definition makes it easy to see that we face multiple demands (stressors) each day. How we respond is up to us. The way that we respond can contribute either to improved cardiac health or to increased cardiac risk.

Positive versus negative stress

Many people don't realize that it is possible to have positive stress. But a certain amount of stress in our lives may be necessary for optimal performance. For instance, outstanding athletes often perform at their best in the "big game." And you may one of the many who feel they work best when faced with a deadline. However, when the stress becomes excessive or, more important, when your *response* to the stress becomes negative, it may harm your health in general and your cardiac health in particular.

Stress and heart disease

When it comes to the heart, stress can do the following:

- ✔ Increase the likelihood of developing coronary artery disease.
- ✔ Create chest discomfort that can mimic heart disease.
- ✔ Cause palpitations or even very serious arrythmias.
- ✔ Contribute to the development of high blood pressure.

Numerous scientific studies have linked job-related stress to the increased likelihood of developing coronary artery disease. Some of these studies have shown that heart attacks occur more often in the six months following negative life changes, such as divorce, financial set back, or the death of a spouse or close relative than in the six months before these negative life changes. While this evidence is not as strong as the evidence that links other established major risk factors such as elevated cholesterol, cigarette smoking, and physical inactivity to heart disease, it is still strong enough to make stress a risk factor for heart disease (see Chapter 3).

Stress and high blood pressure

The link between stress and high blood pressure has been well established. Many years ago, Dr. Walter Cannon, a famous physiologist, coined the phrase *Fight or Flight* to describe the physiological changes that occur during stress and linked this response to our genetic makeup as human beings. When confronted with a dangerous and frightening saber toothed tiger, for example, our ancient ancestors needed to make an immediate decision to stand and fight, freeze with fear, or immediately take flight. One physiological response to this stress was elevated blood pressure.

Unfortunately, we still have the genetic makeup that causes our blood pressure to rise in emotionally stressful situations. For example, studies show that air traffic controllers whose jobs place them under continual high stress are more likely to have high blood pressure than individuals in many other professions.

Constant pressure over things and situations that we feel we have minimal control is a particularly dangerous form of stress. For example, blood pressure rises in soldiers during time of war, in civilians faced with natural disasters such as floods or explosions and in whole societies where social order is unstable.

Are you Type A?

About 40 years ago, Dr. Ray Rosenman and Dr. Meyer Friedman developed the concept of *Type A Personality,* which linked certain kinds of behavior and personality traits with an increased incidence of heart attack. Unfortunately, the concept of Type A behavior has often been loosely and incorrectly applied to any hard-driving, busy worker.

Type A behavior, however, originally described individuals' response to a highly specific, structured interview in which they exhibited excessive aggression, competitiveness, and hostility. Individuals who have true Type A behavior are likely to have a sense of incredible urgency as they attempt to accomplish poorly defined goals in the shortest period of time. They also are often angry when confronted with unexpected delays. Both *frustration* and *anger* are essential to manifest the cardiac danger associated with a Type A personality. Hard workers who are happy in their work, even if they are "workaholics," are more likely to fall into what Rosenman and Friedman characterized as "Type B" personalities who are not at increased risk of heart disease.

Why anger kills

Recent work from a variety of investigators, most prominently Dr. Redford Williams at Duke University, has shown that it is specifically the hostility component of Type A behavior that accounts for almost all the increased risk of cardiac disease. Using one of the subscales on the psychological inventories administered to many individuals in large heart health trials, Dr. Williams and colleagues identified cynical mistrust of others, frequent experience of angry feelings, and the overt expression of this cynicism and anger in aggressive behavior as the keys for the psychological profile that increases the risk for heart disease. We know that anger kills when we let it control our behavior — think road rage — but now we know it may also kill by damaging our hearts.

Friendship, Intimacy, and Cardiac Health

Difficulties in connecting with others and in experiencing and creating intimacy appear to increase the risk of developing heart disease and suffering its consequences. Conversely, the ability to create positive connections, experience friendship, and develop intimacy appear important to cardiac health.

The lonely heart

Maybe poets are absolutely correct when they write about "dying of a broken heart." Numerous studies have shown that individuals who feel isolated and alone are much more likely to experience health problems, including heart disease and cancer, than individuals who experience intimacy, love, and a sense of being connected.

✔ In one study of over 2,300 men who had survived a heart attack, published in the prestigious *New England Journal of Medicine,* those who were classified as socially isolated and having a high degree of stress had over four times the risk of death compared to those with low levels of stress and isolation. These relationships held up even when controlling for other cardiac risk factors, such as smoking, diet, exercise, and weight.

✔ In another study conducted at Duke University of 1,400 men and women who had at least one blockage of a coronary artery (determined by coronary angiography), those individuals who were not married and did not have at least one close confidant were over three times as likely to have died at follow up, as were those who were married and/or had a confidant.

✔ In a third study, individuals who had recently suffered a heart attack and lived alone experienced twice the risk of dying after a heart attack, as compared with those who lived with one or more other individuals and described their relationships as close.

✔ In many other studies, conducted in diverse cultures, social isolation has increased the risk of heart disease, sudden death, and cancer.

The healing power of love

Numerous studies have shown that individuals who give and receive love decrease their risk of heart disease and other diseases.

✔ In one famous study conducted among Harvard undergraduates in the early 1950s, individuals were asked to describe their relationship with their parents. When their medical records were examined in the 1980s, the results were astounding. Ninety-one percent of these former students who felt they did not have a loving relationship with their parents had serious diagnosed diseases by midlife, most prominently coronary artery disease and high blood pressure. However, less than fifty percent of those who had warm and loving relationships with their parents had developed these chronic diseases in adult life.

✔ A similar study conducted at John Hopkins Medical School showed that physicians who ultimately developed severe medical problems were much less likely to have described close loving relationships earlier in life than were individuals who did not suffer such medical problems.

> ✔ In another study of elderly individuals with heart disease, those who were able to reach out for help had one-third the risk of dying from heart disease compared to older individuals who tried to "go it alone."

Make the connection

As you can see, the ability to connect with other individuals appears to carry significant cardiac benefit. If you feel isolated or lonely, it may be time to make some connections.

✔ Invest time and thought in friends and/or family as seriously as in your work.

✔ Join an interest group. From chess clubs to gardening clubs, from book clubs to folkdance societies, from running clubs to writing classes, there's an activity-related group that matches your interests.

✔ Find a third place. Beyond home and work, people have long benefited from a close connection to a *third place* in their communities. For many this is their church, synagogue, mosque, or temple. For others it may be a social group, community organization, or other activity or group that is meaningful for them. The identity of your third place is not as important as the fact that you have one.

Can You Be "Scared to Death"? The Psychological Bases of Arrythmias and Sudden Death

We all have experienced our hearts "racing" after a bad scare or when something angers us, for instance. But strong emotion can also produce serious rhythm disturbances. (See also Chapter 17.)

Hardwired: The psychological-physiological link

Although the feelings of joy, anger, or depression may be complex functions, the body has only a very limited vocabulary of physiological responses to them. Most of these responses are mediated through the nervous system, which controls all the body's functions.

The nervous system is divided into two major branches: The sympathetic nervous system and the parasympathetic nervous system.

- ✔ If the sympathetic nervous system is stimulated (the part of the nervous system that results in the Fight or Flight Response), various rhythm disturbances caused by rapid heart beat or extra beats may occur. Fear or anger are two stimuli that trigger this system. Stress may also cause palpitations, typically experienced by individuals as "skipped" heartbeats or irregular heartbeats.

- ✔ If the parasympathetic nervous system is stimulated (the part of the nervous system that is responsible for maintenance of routine body function, also called "rest and digest" functions) a slow heart rate can result. The most common result of an excessively slow heartbeat is fainting. Typically any condition that would produce a faint — crowded room, hot day, having blood drawn — triggers this system.

Who's most at risk?

Individuals who are most susceptible to rhythm abnormalities provoked by emotion are those with underlying cardiac disease, particularly coronary artery disease. But occasionally people with normal coronary arteries will develop severe cardiac arrhythmias in stressful settings.

But can you "drop dead" from stress?

There is certainly plenty of anecdotal evidence that individuals may collapse and die when faced with sudden overwhelming emotional stress. Dr. George Engel reviewed a number of cases in which psychological stress appeared to cause sudden death. He found that the common setting for the occurrence of sudden death included one of the following:

- ✔ Hearing of the death of a friend or relative.
- ✔ An acute episode of grief.
- ✔ Mourning or the anniversary of a sad event.
- ✔ Loss of status or self esteem.
- ✔ Personal threat or danger.
- ✔ Reunion or triumph.

Specific evidence is often lacking in these situations, but experts believe that in most of these instances the sudden death results from a severe form of cardiac arrhythmia called _ventricular tacchycardia_, which ultimately degenerates into a fatal cardiac arrhythmia called _ventricular fibrillation_ where the heart ineffectively quivers and is unable to pump out blood.

What About Stress Caused by Heart Problems?

Just as psychological stress can result in either acute or chronic heart problems, the flip side is also true — heart disease can result in psychological problems.

We probably know most about what happens after a heart attack. (See also Chapter 15.) Many people go through a three-part psychological response to having a heart attack.

- ✔ Initially, the individual experiences great anxiety, produced by the physical event of heart attack and by fears of dying.

- ✔ In the second stage, the individual typically denies that they have had a heart attack or that anything is seriously wrong with them.

- ✔ The third phase has been called *home-coming depression*. In this situation, the individual may become depressed and worried about the long-term consequences of their heart attack or be remorseful about lifestyle practices that may have contributed to their cardiac problem.

During and after a heart attack, psychological stress can be diminished when the individual is surrounded by caring, supportive health care workers and family. Studies have shown that individuals who have such a strong support system are much more likely to recover from a heart attack than individuals who do not.

The Heart Attack That Isn't: Emotional Disorders That Mimic Heart Disease

Studies have shown that 10 to 20 percent of cardiac patients may have symptoms caused not by their heart disease, but by underlying emotional disorders. Perhaps an equal number of individuals who do not have heart disease visit their physicians with manifestations of underlying emotional problems that may initially be confused with heart disease. The three most common emotional disorders that may mimic heart disease are anxiety states, panic disorder, and depression.

✔ **Anxiety states.** The spectrum of anxiety states extends from chronic anxiety through attacks of anxiety in specific settings. Such anxiety states may often be accompanied by symptoms such as rapid heart beat, palpitations, chest pain, or tightness or shortness of breath. While these symptoms should be taken seriously, a physician typically can rule out serious cardiac disease. After serious cardiac disease has been ruled out, anxiety states typically respond well to support and reassurance, including psychological counseling and therapy if necessary.

✔ **Panic disorder.** Although panic disorder is one of the anxiety states, its presentation may be so dramatic and so similar to cardiovascular disease that it deserves separate consideration. Individuals with panic disorder can experience a sudden outpouring of feelings of terror and impending doom. These may be accompanied by symptoms such as chest pain, severe shortness of breath, and irregular heartbeat, which may resemble serious cardiac disease. These attacks often occur in predictable settings such as crowded rooms, theaters, or other public places where the exit may be restricted. Once again, a physician can typically distinguish between a panic disorder and serious heart disease. In this situation, a careful history is very important to making the right diagnosis.

✔ **Depression.** Considerable overlap exists between depression and heart disease. Sometimes individuals who have heart disease become depressed, and in other instances the medicines used to treat high blood pressure or coronary artery disease may cause a tendency towards depression. Treatment of the underlying depression typically resolves all symptoms in such an individual.

Psychotropic Medications and the Heart

Psychotropic medications are those that act on the mind, such as medications prescribed for anxiety or for depression. (*Psyche*= mind; *tropic*= influencing.) Since the increasing development of such medications has increased the ability to manage these disorders effectively, they are used by a large number of individuals in our society. But many of these medications that work on the brain may also affect the heart. For example, some of the medicines for treating depression may contribute to rapid heart beat and palpitations.

Taking your medication if you suffer from depression is very important and most antidepressant medications are very safe. But if you also have heart disease, you may want to discuss any potential effects on the heart with your physician.

A Four-Part Plan for Controlling Stress

Stress may be dangerous to the heart, but the good news is that some simple strategies may significantly lower stress and thereby improve cardiac health. Here are four ways to lower stress in your life and contribute to cardiac health.

✔ **Modify or eliminate circumstances that contribute to stress and cardiac symptoms.**

Often people do not realize that aspects of their daily lives can compound problems with stress. Cutting back on caffeine-containing beverages, such as coffee and tea, for example, may make a substantial difference to stress levels and manifestations such as cardiac palpitations. Be aware that many soft drinks also contain substantial amounts of caffeine and consumption of these beverages should also be reduced if stress and cardiac symptoms are a problem. Fatigue and insomnia may also contribute to stress. Be sure to get plenty of rest and a good night's sleep if you are experiencing symptoms of stress. Avoid the temptation to use alcohol as a way to relax; it may seem to offer temporary stress release but usually leads to greater problems.

✔ **Live in the present.**

The basis for all effective stress reduction is to live in the present. It may sound simple, but many people spend an inordinate amount of time either regretting the past or fearing the future. Strategies such as biofeedback, visualization, and medication can help you live in the present and substantially lower stress.

✔ **Get out of your own way.**

Many people compound the inevitable stresses of daily life by layering on negative feelings concerning these stresses. It is important to recognize that no one can live a life that is completely free of stress and not to compound the problem by allowing feelings of negativity or low self-worth to make this stress worse.

✔ **Develop a personal plan for stress.**

Developing a personal plan to alleviate stress is one of the most effective ways to handle it on an ongoing basis, rather than allowing it to become free-floating anxiety. Many people find that daily exercise, meditation, "time out" either alone or with family, and other such strategies provide effective ways to control the stresses of daily life.

10-minute time outs against stress

"Stepping away for ten a day" can lower your stress dramatically. Try one of these techniques.

Go outside. The right short break outside can ease the tension.

Do: Stroll. Clear your mind. Smell the flowers. People watch.

Don't: Think about your schedule. Outline that memo. Pick at a worry.

Tune into calm. You can also get away right in your office or easy chair. Find a quiet, comfortable spot. Allow no interruptions. Sit quietly and focus on calm. Consciously clear your mind, gently pushing away any intruding thoughts of work or problems. It may help to listen to quiet music, visualize peaceful scenes, or focus on deep, slow breathing. A nice stretch at the end of your ten minutes can be a nice transition back to activity.

Listen to your body. Using biofeedback techniques can help foster a relaxed state. In research conducted in my laboratory, we found that individuals who took ten minutes each day to focus on relaxing using a heart rate monitor were able to dramatically reduce their stress levels. They used the same techniques that I describe earlier, but used the heart rate monitor as their point of focus. Sitting quietly, you focus on your heart rate, picturing it going lower. Using the other visualization techniques in combination with the biofeedback can enhance the time out.

Meditate. Practicing any of several formal types of meditation can be very useful to persons who find it congenial.

Catnap. If you are one of those lucky souls who can drop instantly to sleep and wake refreshed in 10 or 15 minutes, you can experience the 10-minute time out in one of its most satisfying forms (at least, so say its devotees).

Five Simple Steps for Controlling Anger

The hostility or anger component of the Type A personality poses the most significant cardiac risk. Here are five simple strategies to help control anger:

- ✔ **Learn how to trust other people.** An open heart is a healthy heart. Individuals who are isolated and fearful of other people increase their risk of cardiac disease. By making an effort to open yourself up to trusting other individuals, you can substantially lower your risk of heart disease.

- ✔ **Plant a garden and care for a pet.** The Irish poet, William Butler Yeats, said that the definition of a civilized human being was one who planted a garden and cared for a domestic pet. This is not only a prescription for a civilized human being, but also a prescription for a heart healthy life.

- ✔ **Practice asserting yourself.** Many people keep their emotions bottled up inside. They are often pleasantly surprised to see that by standing up for what they believe in a pleasant way, they can not only control unwarranted stress in their life, but also lead a happier daily existence.

✔ **Become a volunteer.** There is a wonderful body of literature that suggests that volunteers not only do good for other people, but they also improve their own health. Somehow, the act of giving of yourself to other people results in improved health for yourself.

✔ **Practice forgiveness.** Many people keep themselves in a constant state of anger for wrongs or supposed slights from other people or from the environment at large. Learning how to forgive others is doing one of the very best things that you can do to improve your own cardiac health. While you're at it, forgive yourself, too, for past shortcomings — imagined or real.

Part III
Preventing Heart Disease: The Big Four

ATTEMPTING TO REDUCE THE STRESS IN HIS LIFE, WALDO "WHIP" GUNSCHOTT GOES FROM BEING A WILD ANIMAL TRAINER TO A WILD BALLOON ANIMAL TRAINER.

In this part . . .

In this part, you cut right to the heart of what you need to know to control four conditions that are major contributing causes of heart disease: high blood pressure, elevated cholesterol, smoking, and being overweight. By understanding and controlling each of these conditions, on your own and with the help of your physician and other experts as necessary or advisable, you can do a lot to prevent heart disease. You get the facts and tips you need to corral high blood pressure (hypertension), tackle cholesterol, stamp out smoking, and weigh in on healthy weight loss and management.

Chapter 9

Combating High Blood Pressure to Reduce Your Cardiac Risk

· ·

In This Chapter

▶ High blood pressure, normal blood pressure, and optimal blood pressure

▶ The link between high blood pressure, heart disease, and stroke

▶ High blood pressure's link to five other lifestyle-related issues

▶ Six simple steps to lower your blood pressure

▶ How to work with your physician in a partnership against high blood pressure

▶ The main classes of medicines used to treat high blood pressure

▶ Ten steps for a lifetime approach to high blood pressure

· ·

High blood pressure, or *hypertension,* is quite common in the United States. Over one-fourth of the adult population, over 50 million people, suffer from high blood pressure. Furthermore, as we grow older, we are more likely to have high blood pressure. At some point in our lives, almost all of us will develop high blood pressure. But don't despair. Fortunately, in partnership with your physician, you can do a lot to prevent high blood pressure in the first place and to control it if you get it. By doing so, you can lower your risk of heart disease, kidney failure, stroke, and many other serious conditions associated with poorly controlled hypertension. An added bonus — enhanced physical well-being and probably your enjoyment of life.

Hypertension: The Silent Killer

Hypertension is called the "silent killer" because high blood pressure itself does not typically cause any noticeable symptoms. The result:

✔ Many people are not even aware that they have high blood pressure. In fact, over 25 percent of individuals with hypertension don't know it.

✔ Many more know they have high blood pressure and aren't being treated.

✔ Others are being treated but still don't have their blood pressure under good control. Among persons being treated, only 20 percent have their blood pressure effectively controlled.

✔ Over 50 percent of individuals with high blood pressure are not being treated at all.

But it doesn't have to be this way. We have enormous room to improve in combatting hypertension. The place to start is with a little education.

What Is Blood Pressure?

As the heart pumps blood through the circulatory system, the pumped blood exerts pressure against the interior walls of the blood vessels. Your *blood pressure* reading consists of two measurements of the pressure exerted on the walls of the arteries. These measurements are expressed in millimeters (mm) of Mercury (Hg). For example: 110/70 mm Hg or 120/80 mm Hg are two typical readings for "normal" blood pressure. The top or higher number, called *systolic pressure*, expresses the pressure exerted as the heart contracts or "beats," pumping blood through the circulatory system. The bottom or lower number, called *diastolic pressure*, expresses the pressure exerted when the heart is at rest between beats.

What Is High Blood Pressure, or Hypertension?

Many people mistakenly think that you either have hypertension or you don't. In fact, blood pressure readings span a continuum all the way from *optimum* to *severely elevated*. Experiencing one elevated reading does not mean that you have hypertension. Everyone's blood pressure tends to spike up in situations that produce anger, pain, fear, or high stress. For example, your blood pressure probably rises when you have a shouting match with a family member or give a speech or interview for a new position — maybe even when you visit your friendly doctor!

Having *hypertension* means that your blood pressure is consistently elevated above the normal ranges. (It doesn't mean that you are super tense. Even the calmest, most laid-back individuals can have high blood pressure.) This is no do-it-yourself diagnosis, either. You need to have your blood pressure checked regularly, ideally as part of a regular periodic checkup. If you happen to check your blood pressure at a health fair, for example, and it's elevated, be sure to see your physician. Your physician will take blood pressure readings on several occasions to determine if your blood pressure is consistently elevated and, if it is, how severe the elevation is.

Categories of blood pressure

For many years, until the mid 1980s, hypertension was typically defined as readings higher than 140/90 mm Hg. This rather arbitrary cutoff was chosen to define high blood pressure because the risk of cardiovascular complication becomes very significant at this point. Based on the review of the larger body of more recent research, however, a recent national medical commission formed a more sophisticated classification of high blood pressure, which you can review in Table 9-1.

Table 9-1 Classification of Blood Pressure for Adults 18 and Older*

Category	Systolic (mm Hg)	Diastolic (mm Hg)
Optimal	<120	and <80
Normal	<130	and <85
High-Normal	130-139	or 85-89
Hypertension		
Stage 1	140-159	or 90-99
Stage 2	160-179	or 100-109
Stage 3	≥ 180	or ≥110

Key: < less than; ≥ greater than or equal to

*Reprinted from The Sixth Report of the Joint National Committee on Prevention, Detection, Evaluation and Treatment of High Blood Pressure. National Institute of Health. National Heart, Lung and Blood Institute. National High Blood Pressure Education Program. NIH Publication No. 98-4090. November 1997.

High blood pressure

These new classifications put blood pressure in appropriate perspective. As Table 9-1 illustrates, individuals with a systolic blood pressure greater than 140 mm Hg or a diastolic blood pressure greater than 90 mm Hg are considered to have *hypertension*. Hypertension is then further divided into three stages of increasing severity.

However, even individuals who have slightly lower blood pressure than these readings may be considered to have *high/normal* blood pressure. This distinction is made because individuals in this category have a greater risk of ultimately developing hypertension.

Optimal blood pressure

The other important category in this new classification is that of *optimal blood pressure*. Individuals with a systolic blood pressure of less than 120 mm Hg and a diastolic blood pressure of less than 80 mm Hg are considered to have optimal blood pressure because blood pressure below these levels lowers the risk of heart disease to the very lowest possible level.

Is it possible to have blood pressure that is too low?

Yes. But you have to have a very low blood pressure indeed before this becomes a problem. Individuals who have systolic blood pressure less than 90 and diastolic pressure of less than 60 (less than 90/60 mm Hg) may actually have blood pressures that are too low. For the vast majority of people, however, the range of optimal blood pressure is so great that *optimal* remains a very important distinction.

How Dangerous Is Hypertension?

Well, it's not called a killer for nothing. High blood pressure is a significant risk factor for coronary heart disease (the leading cause of death in the United States) as well as a very significant risk for stroke, heart failure, and kidney failure. An individual with poorly treated hypertension at least doubles his or her risk of all of these conditions. Thus, even individuals who have no symptoms when initially diagnosed with hypertension should work hard to control blood pressure to prevent these potentially devastating potential complications.

What Causes Hypertension?

In the vast majority (over 90 percent) of individuals with high blood pressure, physicians are not able to determine its exact cause. In medicine, this is known as *idiopathic* hypertension. That's not to say that physicians are idiots, just that we have not yet figured out the precise mechanisms, functions, or agents that cause hypertension. In these individuals, the condition is also termed *essential* high blood pressure. Just like *idiopathic* does not mean that doctors are idiots, *essential* does not mean that it is essential to have it. Quite the contrary! What is *essential* is to treat it! Look at some of the factors that appear to contribute to hypertension.

- **Salt intake.** Among the theories about what causes essential high blood pressure, most relate to problems that our kidneys appear to have handling excess salt. Population studies have shown that societies with a high salt consumption (such as the United States) have a correspondingly high incidence of high blood pressure. But in cultures where salt intake is low, the incidence of high blood pressure is extremely low. Other studies have shown that for most individuals with hypertension, restricting salt intake helps to lower high blood pressure.

- **Inherited predisposition.** Hypertension also seems to have a genetic component. Some people may be genetically predisposed to have high blood pressure. But while hypertension does indeed run in some families, this tendency may result as much from a shared lifestyle as from a shared genetic background. We certainly know that lifestyle factors, such as obesity (and abdominal obesity in particular), inactivity, cigarette smoking, and high alcohol consumption are all associated with increased risk of hypertension.

- **Known causal conditions.** In approximately 10 percent of individuals, the specific underlying cause for hypertension can be discovered. This condition is known as *secondary hypertension* (meaning it's a secondary result of a separate primary condition). If the underlying condition can be treated and corrected, then secondary hypertension is usually corrected, too. Conditions known to cause secondary high blood pressure include:

  - Narrowing of the arteries that supply the kidneys

  - Some other diseases of kidneys

  - Some abnormalities in the endocrine system, such as overactive adrenal glands

  - Some transient conditions such as pregnancy for certain women

  - Certain medications can also increase the risk of high blood pressure, such as oral contraceptives or estrogen replacement therapy following menopause.

If you have been diagnosed with high blood pressure, your doctor will have explored any of these potential underlying causes for hypertension at the time that the diagnosis is made.

Ganging Up — Other Conditions That Contribute to Hypertension

Though we may not know the exact mechanisms causing essential hypertension, a number of conditions are strongly associated with an increase in high blood pressure. Arresting any one of this gang of probable causes usually leads to lower blood pressure. For many people, controlling these conditions actually returns their blood pressure to normal levels.

✔ **Obesity:** Hypertension is most clearly associated with obesity (weighing more than 20 percent over desirable body weight). Obesity contributes to an estimated 40 percent or more of all high blood pressure in the United States. While not all individuals who are overweight have high blood pressure, the association remains very clear.

✔ **Cigarette smoking:** Cigarette smoking and other tobacco products increase blood pressure, both short-term while you are smoking or chewing and long-term, because components in the smoke or chewing tobacco such as nicotine cause your arteries to constrict. Childhood experiments with the nozzle on the garden hose have probably shown you what happens when you force the same volume of liquid through a smaller opening. That higher pressure is not a happy thing for your arteries.

✔ **Alcohol intake:** Drinking small to moderate amounts of alcohol (less than two beers, two glasses of wine, or one shot of distilled spirits) per day has been shown in a number of studies to reduce mortality in coronary heart disease. Higher consumption of alcohol (three or more alcoholic drinks per day), however, is clearly associated with increased blood pressure, not to mention an increased risk of dying from heart disease.

✔ **Physical inactivity:** People who are physically inactive increase their likelihood of developing high blood pressure. In one large study of over 16,000 individuals, inactive people were 35 percent more likely to develop hypertension than were active people, whether or not they had a family history of high blood pressure or a personal history of being overweight.

Hypertension in Specific Groups of People

Having high blood pressure raises some special issues for certain groups of people.

Children and adolescents

Children and adolescents who have blood pressures in the top 5 percent for their age group are considered to have elevated blood pressure. It is mandatory to seek potential underlying causes in all children and adolescents who have high blood pressure. In most instances, treatment for these children and adolescents involves lifestyle measures such as increased physical activity and, if the child is overweight, weight loss. Medicines are used only as a last resort and, even then, usually only in children who have extremely high blood pressure. A child or adolescent with high blood pressure should be treated by a pediatric cardiologist or a pediatrician who is knowledgeable in the particular demands of treating high blood pressure in young people.

The elderly

As already indicated, the older we grow, the more likely we are to have high blood pressure. And if you are over 60 and African American, you have an even greater risk (about 15 percent higher) than older people overall of having hypertension.

Because high blood pressure is so common in older individuals, both men and women, if you are over 60 it's mandatory that you have your blood pressure checked frequently by your physician and pay particular attention to positive lifestyle measures, such as maintenance of normal body weight and regular physical activity.

African Americans

In all age groups (not just those over 60), adults of African-American decent have a higher prevalence of high blood pressure than do Americans of other ethnic groups. Furthermore, the condition appears more dangerous in African Americans. Compared to the general U.S. population, African Americans experience three times as much hypertension-related kidney failure, 80 percent more stroke-related deaths, and a 50 percent higher mortality rate from heart disease. African Americans have also been shown to suffer more damage to their kidneys than whites at comparable levels of blood pressure.

Although the causes underlying this difference, like the underlying causes for most hypertension, remain unknown, ongoing research suggests several possibilities:

> ✔ **Later diagnosis and treatment.** Many African Americans may not receive treatment for high blood pressure until they've had the condition for some time and damage has occurred.

✔ **Greater sensitivity to salt.** Recent research suggests that some African Americans have a genetic trait that increases salt sensitivity and its corresponding effect on elevating blood pressure.

✔ **High salt and low potassium intake.** Many African Americans eat a diet that is high in salt and low in potassium, both factors associated with elevated blood pressure.

Fortunately, research shows that when African Americans receive appropriate treatment using current therapies, their success in controlling blood pressure equals that of whites receiving identical treatment. Because of the prevalence of high blood pressure and earlier onset, if you are African American you should be sure to have your blood pressure checked regularly. Starting as a child or a teen is not too early.

Persons with diabetes mellitus

High blood pressure is much more common in individuals with diabetes than the general population and is particularly dangerous for them because it carries a high risk of cardiovascular complications. Individuals who have high blood pressure and diabetes are really susceptible to "double trouble" because of the increased risk of suffering damage to their kidneys, which in turn increases the risk of high blood pressure. For all these reasons, individuals with diabetes need to be carefully monitored for high blood pressure, and this condition needs to be treated aggressively. The latest recommendations are that persons with diabetes maintain a blood pressure of less than 130/85 mm Hg.

Pregnancy

Some women develop high blood pressure during the third trimester of pregnancy. This condition, called *gestational hypertension*, should be treated cautiously by a physician who is familiar with this condition. Gestational hypertension must also be carefully distinguished by the physician from preeclampsia, which is a potentially lethal condition. Fortunately, women who develop gestational hypertension have no apparent increased risk of hypertension following the pregnancy as compared with the general population.

If a pregnant woman has had hypertension before she becomes pregnant or develops it before the 20th week of pregnancy, she is described as having *chronic hypertension*. This condition, too, should be treated by a physician experienced with treating high blood pressure during pregnancy.

The goal of treating high blood pressure during pregnancy, whether it is gestational or chronic, is to lower any health risk to both the pregnant woman and the baby. For these reasons and many others, prenatal care is very important for all pregnant women.

Take Charge of Controlling Your Blood Pressure

Many of our daily habits and practices can help prevent high blood pressure or help control existing hypertension. These lifestyle measures can also be an important adjunct to treatment even if you require medicines to control your blood pressure.

Manage your weight

For overweight individuals — even those "just" 15 or 20 pounds overweight — weight reduction is a highly reliable way of lowering blood pressure. In most studies, individuals lose approximately 1 mm Hg from both their systolic and diastolic blood pressure for every two pounds that they lose. Thus, even small amounts of weight loss can make a profound difference in blood pressure control. Individuals who lose 10 pounds can anticipate a 5 to 7 mm Hg reduction in both their systolic and diastolic blood pressure. For this reason, your doctor may first recommend weight reduction if you are overweight and have high blood pressure.

Get regular physical activity

Use it (your body) and lose it (your high blood pressure). Physically active individuals reduce their risk of developing hypertension by 20 to 50 percent over their couch potato peers. Individuals who already have hypertension can often lower their blood pressure by 5 to 10 mm Hg simply by participating in moderately intense aerobic activity 30 to 45 minutes on most days of the week.

  ✔ If you have hypertension, you must conduct this physical activity at a *moderate level*. That means reducing the intensity of your exercise to a level slightly less than that recommended for individuals your age without hypertension (see Chapters 6 and 7 for more details of moderate exercise).

  ✔ Your 30 to 45 minutes of physical activity need not take place all at one time but may be accumulated over the course of the day.

  ✔ The benefits of regular physical activity for blood pressure control are additive to those of weight loss.

Eat a low-sodium, heart-healthy diet

Many aspects of proper nutrition play significant roles in blood pressure control, so it's wise to adopt a heart-healthy way of eating as I outline in Chapter 4. Perhaps most important, however, individuals with high blood pressure need to consume a diet that is low in sodium. The American Heart Association recommends a diet that contains no more than 2 grams of sodium a day.

The best ways to lower sodium in your diet:

- Remove the salt shaker from the table.
- Don't add extra salt to food.
- Emphasize fresh fruits and vegetables and grains.
- Avoid salty snacks and processed foods.

Your physician, often working in conjunction with a registered dietitian, can help you build such a diet. There may also be a role for increasing potassium in your diet to lower your blood pressure. Fresh fruits and vegetables are often high in potassium.

Avoid tobacco use

Cigarette smoking and other use of tobacco, such as chewing tobacco, have been repeatedly shown to raise blood pressure. The good news is that within a few months after quitting cigarette smoking, individuals will experience significant reduction in their blood pressure.

Limit alcohol intake

If you consume alcoholic beverages, do so only in moderation (no more than two alcoholic drinks a day max). If having a few drinks with friends is the way you unwind at the end of the day, try some alternative ways of relaxing — join a gym or aerobics class, check out the local coffee shops, or play a team sport.

Chill out — reduce stress

If you are in a stressful environment, finding ways to reduce this stress often helps lower your blood pressure. Check out the suggestions in Chapter 8.

Working with Your Doctor to Control Your Blood Pressure

If you want to succeed in combating high blood pressure, which has no immediate symptoms and lasts for many years, you need to develop a long-term partnership with your physician. This typically involves three stages.

Medical evaluation

The diagnosis of high blood pressure requires at least two or three different blood pressure readings on separate visits to your doctor's office to show that your blood pressure is consistently greater than 140/90 mm Hg.

If your blood pressure is elevated to just under 140/90 mm Hg, you may have *high/normal* blood pressure (also called *labile* blood pressure). In this situation, your doctor may ask you to help in the diagnosis by monitoring your blood pressure at home. A number of excellent home monitoring devices are available that can provide accurate readings at home, and your doctor may recommend one. Don't be surprised if your blood pressure is slightly lower at home than in the doctor's office. This phenomenon is called the *white coat syndrome* because a number of people get nervous in their doctor's office and being nervous is one of the emotional states that may elevate blood pressure temporarily.

Treatment

The second phase in combating hypertension is treatment. Depending upon the severity of your hypertension, your physician may first ask you to make some of the lifestyle changes I discuss earlier to help control your blood pressure. Your doctor may also prescribe medications in conjunction with these lifestyle measures to provide further blood pressure control. I discuss more about medications later in this chapter.

Self-monitoring

After diagnosing your high blood pressure, your doctor normally asks you to participate as a partner in your own care. What does this entail?

Selecting a home blood pressure monitor

Many brands and types of home blood pressure monitors are available for purchase. Three basic types are available, any one of which may work well for you.

Mercury-based monitor, also called a *sphygmomanometer.* This is the gold standard of monitors against which all others are measured. Your doctor's office probably uses one. It has a long glass gauge displaying the column of mercury, a cuff, and inflator bulb and is used with a stethoscope. Because mercury is poisonous and because they are a little clumsy to use, mercury monitors are not usually recommended for home use. But they do give accurate, consistent measurements over the long-term because they don't need periodic readjustment.

Electronic or digital monitor. Recent advances in the sensitivity and reliability of the electronic monitoring devices have made these monitors much more accurate. Because they are easy-to-use, have clear displays, work with one hand, and don't require the use of a stethoscope, many people prefer them. They come in versions that have either manually inflated or automatically inflated cuffs. There are also reliable digital wrist monitors.

Warning: Avoid small digital finger monitors and the like (often sold in cheap mail order catalogs); most of these so-called "monitors" are highly inaccurate and a waste of your money.

Aneroid monitors. These monitors are similar to mercury equipment except that they have a dial-type gauge (rather than mercury), and they can get out of whack and need readjustment. These monitors have a gauge, cuff, inflator bulb, and stethoscope. If you choose one of these, you may want to make sure that the cuff has a D-ring for easy one-handed use and a self-bleeding deflation valve so that you can concentrate on measuring accurately (rather than on trying to let the air out properly).

Whatever monitor you select, be sure that you follow the manufacturer's instructions to the letter. If you need help, ask your doctor's staff for some basic instruction.

- Your doctor may ask you to monitor and keep a log of your blood pressure.

- You must follow the lifestyle modifications with commitment.

- If medication is prescribed, you must be faithful about taking it as directed. Astonishingly, over 50 percent of all medicines prescribed are either not taken at all or not taken correctly. It is virtually impossible to control your blood pressure if you don't meticulously follow prescribed lifestyle measures and medication regimens.

- The final, often crucial key to success: You must share honestly any problems or side effects you're having with either lifestyle modifications or medications with your doctor so that adjustments can be made. Don't worry that you'll be a bother — doctors know that it can take some time to fine-tune a treatment to work best for you. If your doctor seems too rushed or reluctant to work with you, find one who isn't.

To Medicate or Not to Medicate? That Is the Question

When Hamlet raised his famous question, "To be or not to be," he was voicing a philosophical dilemma. Your physician also often faces the dilemma of whether or not you need medication in addition to lifestyle measures. Medicines are definitely indicated if positive lifestyle measures have not succeeded in adequately reducing your blood pressure. In this situation, your physician has many excellent medications to choose from.

Different medications also work differently for different individuals, so it may take a period of adjustment to find just which medication or combination of medications works best for you. In most instances, your physician will be able to control your blood pressure with one medicine. However, in some instances, your doctor may combine several medications, often in different classes.

Classes of medications for hypertension

There are three general classes of medications typically used in controlling high blood pressure.

- ✔ **Diuretics:** Diuretics, the first choice of many physicians, lower blood pressure by lowering blood volume through increasing the amount of sodium and water passed through the kidneys. With regular diuretic therapy, blood pressure often falls 10 mm Hg.

- ✔ **Alpha and beta blockers:** These medications inhibit various portions of the nervous system, particularly receptors called "alpha" and "beta" receptors. They help lower blood pressure by slowing the heart rate and decreasing the force with which the heart pumps or by helping arteries to relax or dilate, thus lowering the pressure required to pump blood through the arteries. Among physicians, beta blockers are another popular first choice as treatment for high blood pressure.

- ✔ **Vasodilators:** These drugs act directly on the walls of the arteries and cause them to relax, thereby reducing the amount of pressure needed to pump blood through the arteries. There are two major types of vasodilators in use.

  - • **ACE inhibitors:** These drugs help reduce blood pressure by decreasing substances in the blood which cause vessels to constrict. The ACE stands for angiotensin converting enzyme. Both short-acting (taken several times a day) and long-acting (typically taken once a day) ACE inhibitors are available for treatment of high blood pressure. Your physician may want to monitor kidney function and potassium levels closely when starting or increasing this medication.

- **Calcium antagonists:** Also called *calcium channel blockers,* calcium antagonists inhibit the inward flow of calcium into cardiac and blood vessel tissue, thereby reducing the tension of the heart and the constriction of blood vessels.

Ten Tips for Controlling Your Blood Pressure for a Lifetime

Because the complications of high blood pressure result from years of increased pressure pounding on the blood vessels walls, it is important to adopt a lifelong approach to controlling hypertension. Remember that the goal is not simply to lower blood pressure in the short-term but to reduce the long-term devastating complications of hypertension.

To achieve that goal, adopt these ten steps:

1. **Remember that the goal of treatment is to reduce blood pressure and complications of poorly controlled hypertension.**

2. **Become knowledgeable about hypertension.**

3. **Make a commitment to helping your physician control your blood pressure by actively joining in a partnership to assist in your therapy.**

4. **Maintain regular contact with your physician.**

5. **Routinely monitor your blood pressure at home.**

6. **Take your medicines as your doctor prescribes.**

7. **Integrate medicine-taking into routines of daily living.**

8. **Adopt positive lifestyle behaviors to help lower your blood pressure.**

9. **Monitor side effects and report any troublesome ones to your physician.**

10. **Maintain a positive attitude about achieving the goal of life-long blood pressure control.**

What If Hypertension Doesn't Respond to Treatment?

Some individuals have a condition called *resistant hypertension*. These individuals often require a combination of lifestyle measures coupled with two or three medications to control their high blood pressure. If you experience this situation, keep working closely with your physician. Blood pressure can almost always be controlled, even if you have resistant hypertension, provided that you meticulously follow the regimens that are developed in partnership with your physician.

Chapter 10

Controlling Cholesterol

. . . .

In This Chapter

▶ How elevated cholesterol multiplies the risk of coronary heart disease

▶ Lipoproteins — the good, the bad and the ugly!

▶ The trying problem of elevated triglycerides

▶ Three key steps you can take to help lower your cholesterol

▶ The four main classes of drugs which help lower cholesterol

▶ Women, cholesterol, and the role of Estrogen Replacement Therapy

▶ Elevated cholesterol and hypertension: controlling the deadly duo

. . . .

Cholesterol always seems to be in the news. For a while, Americans were so obsessed with lowering blood cholesterol that other important risk factors for heart disease were almost ignored. Then the pendulum swung the other way as revisionists began to underestimate the danger of an elevated cholesterol level. The truth lies somewhere in between.

There is no question that elevated blood cholesterol significantly increases — doubles, in fact — the risk of coronary artery disease. And in combination with other risk factors, cholesterol helps multiply the risk many times over. So controlling cholesterol is vital to lowering the risk of heart disease. For most people, achieving that goal is usually not hard: Some simple daily steps can make a great difference (even if you also have to take medication and even if you already have heart disease).

Good News/Bad News About Cholesterol

The good news is that between 1960 and 1991, the average cholesterol level in the United States decreased from 220 mg/dl to 205 mg/dl. This drop no doubt contributed to the 50 percent decline over the past 25 years in the incidence of death from heart disease. The bad news is that elevated blood cholesterol remains extremely common and heart disease is still the leading killer in the U.S. An estimated 32 percent of American men and 27 percent of

American women have elevated blood cholesterol levels which put them at increased risk for heart disease. An even greater percentage of men and women over age 50 have elevated cholesterol levels. We still have a long way to go.

The relationship between cholesterol level and risk of heart disease does not function like a light bulb — either on or off. It's more like the gradual acceleration your car experiences entering a freeway. As cholesterol in the blood gradually rises to a level of about 200 mg/dl, the risk of heart disease also gradually increases. Once you are above that level, the risk of heart disease and of dying from heart disease increases much more rapidly, as Figure 10-1 shows. By the time that your cholesterol level has reached 250, you have more than twice the risk of dying from heart disease compared to individuals whose cholesterol is below 200.

Figure 10-1:
A little change in cholesterol levels makes a difference in mortality rate.

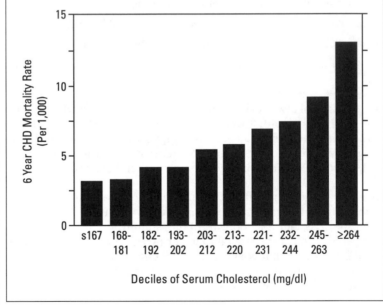

Multiple Risk Factor Intervention Trial (MRFIT). Used with permission.

But good news! The reverse is also true. Lowering your blood cholesterol level even a smidgen can make a positive difference. And the more you lower it, the greater the benefit. It is estimated that for every *one* point that your cholesterol drops, your risk of heart disease drops *two* percent. Thus, a drop in your cholesterol of 10 points can decrease your risk of heart disease by 20 percent! (Wouldn't you love returns like that on your IRA?)

What Is Cholesterol Anyway?
The Lowdown on Lipids

Cholesterol is a naturally occurring waxy substance present in human beings and all other animals. It is an important component of the body's cell walls. The body also requires cholesterol to produce many hormones (including sex hormones) as well as the bile acids that help to digest food. Since cholesterol plays such important biological roles, having adequate amounts of cholesterol is absolutely essential for life itself.

Humans get cholesterol from two sources. Our livers manufacture a great deal, and we consume a considerable amount from animal products such as meat, eggs, and dairy products. However, we get into trouble when we have too much cholesterol in our blood. Our level of blood cholesterol (sometimes called *serum* cholesterol) gets too high usually because we eat too much saturated fat (which encourages the liver to manufacture cholesterol) and too many foods that contain cholesterol (dietary cholesterol). Actually, we don't need to consume foods with cholesterol because our bodies always make enough. In fact, in years of research, there's never been a known cholesterol deficiency in a human being.

To get to where it needs to go in our bodies, cholesterol is carried around the blood stream attached to complicated structures called *lipoproteins.* When cholesterol levels in the blood are too high, excess cholesterol deposits on the inside walls of the arteries in the form of *plaque*, causing the arteries to narrow. The result is the condition called *atherosclerosis*, which is the basis of coronary heart disease, angina, and heart attacks.

Lipoproteins: The good, the bad, and the ugly

And just what is a lipoprotein? It's a cross between a protein and a lipid such as cholesterol or triglycerides. There, don't you know a lot more. Would it help if I told you that *lipid* comes from the Greek word for *fat*? (Yes, *fat* as in *lipo*suction.) Although it's a little more complex than that, it's enough to know that the lipoprotein serves as the mode of transportation through the blood stream for cholesterol and other lipids (fats) such as triglycerides. It is sort of like a cruise ship steaming across the Atlantic Ocean. View the ship as the proteins and all the passengers (including the Family Cholesterol) on board as the lipids. Not a perfect analogy, but you get the point.

Lipoproteins can be separated and measured according to their weight and density. They range all the way from very low density to high density. One particularly dangerous form is called *LDL* or *low density lipoprotein*. LDL is dangerous because it contains more fat and less protein, making it fairly unstable. Because it is unstable, LDL tends to fall apart, easily adhering to artery walls. On the other hand, a beneficial type of lipoprotein called *HDL*, or *high density lipoprotein*, can actually help protect your heart from heart disease. HDL is stable and does not adhere to artery walls but instead actually helps carry cholesterol away from the artery walls. This is particularly important for the coronary arteries.

When you have a check up, your doctor may look at the results of your blood tests and say, "Well, you need to work on raising your 'good' cholesterol and lowering your 'bad' cholesterol." That can be a little confusing until you realize that their names offer you a tip for keeping track of which is which. You want to keep your high density lipoproteins (HDLs) *high* and your low density lipoproteins (LDLs) *low*. Repeat after me: High, HIGH! Low, LOW! Forgetting this mantra can result in ugly consequences for your arteries.

Don't hang these plaques on your walls

As I noted a moment ago, when cholesterol levels in the blood are too high, excess cholesterol is deposited on the inside walls of arteries, where special cells latch on to them. The process creates a cholesterol-rich "bump" in the wall that is then covered with scar tissue that creates a hard, shell-like covering. This buildup of matter is called *plaque*. And as bad as that more familiar but different plaque on your teeth is, this is worse. Figure 10-2 compares a healthy artery to one narrowed by plaque.

Figure 10-2:
A healthy artery compared to one narrowed by plaque.

Healthy artery

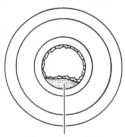

Plaque forming

The more excess cholesterol you have in your blood, the more plaques of various sizes build up on your artery walls, narrowing the arteries and decreasing the flow of blood. Decreasing blood flow means decreased oxygen and nutrients reach the heart muscle which may respond with pain called *angina.* Plaques can also be very unstable and apt to break off, triggering a blood clot in an artery. The result can be a heart attack (if the clot occurs in a blood vessel to the heart) or a stroke (blocked blood vessel in the brain) or other serious condition.

Lowering the level of cholesterol in your blood can slow down, stop, or even reverse the buildup of harmful plaque in your arteries, lowering your risk of heart disease and heart attack.

The trying problem of elevated blood triglycerides

Another way that fats are carried through the blood stream is in a form called *triglycerides.* Although triglycerides, like cholesterol, are lipids, they have a different makeup. As the name suggests, these are chemicals made up of three (hence *tri*) fat molecules (fatty acids) carried through the blood stream on a glycerol backbone. Much like cholesterol, the triglycerides are ferried around the blood stream by being joined together with proteins in the form of lipoproteins. Although the link between elevated blood triglycerides and heart disease is not as strong as the link between LDL cholesterol and heart disease, having elevated blood triglycerides also puts you at increased risk for coronary artery disease.

Testing Your Cholesterol and Other Lipid Levels

In the fight to lower cholesterol, to be at your best, you have to test. It is as simple as that. Every adult (and most children) should know his or her cholesterol level. A simple finger-prick blood test is all that is required for testing cholesterol. You should have such a test at least every five years, or more often if your cholesterol level is elevated or if you have other risk factors for heart disease.

If the simple test shows your cholesterol level is elevated, your physician may recommend that you have a fasting blood test performed so that a determination can be made of your LDL, HDL, and triglycerides. This is called a complete *lipid profile* or *lipid analysis.* Physicians often include this more extensive test as a routine part of a regular physical checkup.

If you take a simple test outside your doctor's office, perhaps at a health fair, and your cholesterol level measures 200 mm/dl or higher, be sure to share this information with your physician so you get proper follow-up.

What are those mystery numbers? Decoding the test results

Your overall cholesterol level is expressed as a number of milligrams (mg) per deciliter (dl — ⅒ of a liter) of blood: 200 mg/dl or 220 mg/dl, for example. If you have a fasting blood test to obtain a complete lipid profile, the level of LDL and HDL will also be expressed as milligrams per deciliter (mg/dl). The results may also compare the level of HDL (the good guys, remember) to your total cholesterol level. This comparison is usually expressed as a ratio; for example, 3:1 or 4.5:1 means that there is one unit of HDL for every 3 or 4.5 equal units of total cholesterol. (Sometimes just the first number appears on the test report; the one is implied.) The most exciting thing about this arcane knowledge, however, is that you don't need the foggiest idea of what a milligram or a deciliter is to understand how to use these numbers effectively.

What do my cholesterol levels mean in terms of risk of heart disease?

Here are some general guidelines for interpreting the results of your cholesterol measurement.

- If you do not already have existing coronary artery disease, a total cholesterol of below 200 mg/dl is considered a *desirable blood cholesterol*. But please remember that within a broad range of values, lower is better. Thus, a cholesterol of 170 mg/dl is better than a cholesterol of 190 mg/dl.

- If your cholesterol is between 200 and 239 mg/dl, this is considered *borderline high blood cholesterol*.

- Individuals who have a blood cholesterol of 240 mg/dl or above are classified as having *high blood cholesterol*.

- A *low* HDL cholesterol level is also considered an independent risk factor for heart disease over and above total cholesterol and LDL levels. Individuals whose HDL is below 35 mg/dl are considered to have *low HDL cholesterol*. A ratio of 3:1 or better for HDL is considered good.

- If your triglycerides are below 200 mg/dl, they are considered to be *normal*. Between 200 and 400 mg/dl is considered *borderline/high* for triglycerides. At a level between 400 and 1,000 mg/dl, you are considered to have *high* triglycerides and at a level greater than 1,000 mg/dl, you are considered to have *very high* triglyceride levels. In addition to increasing your risk of coronary artery disease, very high levels of triglycerides may also injure a vital organ, the pancreas, which is responsible for producing insulin in the body.

Cholesterol in Context: Managing Your Cholesterol

Here is a riddle for you: How is cholesterol control different from spandex? When it comes to controlling cholesterol, one size definitely does not fit all. In determining how best to control your cholesterol, your physician will take into account not only your cholesterol level and personal history but also a number of other factors such as your age and gender and whether you already have coronary heart disease. The intensity and components of a plan will vary depending on these factors, but in all cases treatment will focus on positive lifestyle factors such as proper nutrition, increased physical activity, and optimal weight management. Let's take an overview of how cholesterol is usually controlled and then look at some specific individual situations.

Overview of typical cholesterol treatment

✔ **If your cholesterol level is at or below 200 mg/dl** and you have no evidence of coronary heart disease or no other major risk factors, then no treatment is necessary. Just keep eating sensibly and staying active.

✔ **If your cholesterol is elevated (higher than 200 mg/dl) but you have few other risk factors and no evidence of coronary heart disease,** then you may receive relatively less intensive therapy. The goal of reducing your cholesterol level is to reduce your risk of ever developing coronary heart disease, a practice called *primary prevention.* Proper nutrition and increased physical activity is the primary approach to lowering your cholesterol and raising your HDL level. If your cholesterol level is very high, your physician may recommend medication.

✔ **If your cholesterol is elevated (higher than 200 mg/dl) and you have other risk factors,** then you may receive a moderately intensive treatment program that focuses on positive lifestyle changes such as proper nutrition, weight management, and increased physical activities. If your cholesterol level is very high, your physician may also prescribe medication.

✔ **If your cholesterol is elevated (higher than 200 mg/dl) and you already have established coronary heart disease** and/or are at high risk to suffer from its complications such as angina or heart attack, then you may receive the most intensive therapy. This most likely will include substantial lifestyle modifications and medication.

Individual situations that affect cholesterol treatment plans

✔ **If you have risk factors other than elevated cholesterol,** the approach that you and your physician take to help you manage elevated blood cholesterol should take into account not just your cholesterol and lipid levels, but also the other risk factors which you possess (see Chapter 3). Some risk factors such as hypertension or low HDL influences therapy for elevated blood cholesterol.

✔ **If you already have coronary heart disease and may have suffered a complication of it, such as angina or heart attack** (see also Chapters 14 and 15), the goal of treatment is to prevent further complications. In medicine we call this *secondary prevention,* indicating that the goal is to prevent second and third events, or complications, in people who already have an established problem. If you fall into this category, your physician may want to dramatically lower your LDL cholesterol, probably to below 100 mg/dl. The rationale for lowering your LDL cholesterol to this degree is that many studies have shown that such a dramatic lowering of LDL cholesterol may reduce the likelihood of further complications of heart disease and may even contribute to reversing heart disease.

✔ **If you have low HDL cholesterol,** remember that this represents an independent increased risk of heart disease over and above a high level of LDL or total cholesterol. While there are not many therapeutic options available to raise HDL, your physician may certainly recommend that you increase your physical activity which has been shown to help raise HDL. Certain lipid lowering medications, in particular the fibric acids and niacin, have also been shown to raise HDL.

✔ **If you are younger,** such as a young adult, premenopausal woman, or man below age 35, you have an increased long-term risk of coronary artery disease if you have an elevated cholesterol level but you are still at moderately low risk. Thus, if you have no other risk factors for heart disease, your physician may certainly recommend improved nutritional practices and weight management (if you are overweight) coupled with increased physical activity (if you are currently sedentary). Medications to lower your cholesterol may be recommended only if your cholesterol is extremely high or if you have other significant risk factors for coronary artery disease.

✔ **If you are older,** remember that age is an independent risk factor for heart disease. The older we get, the greater our risk for coronary artery disease. But, if you reach the age of 65, you have a greater than 80 percent chance of reaching the age of 80! Thus, prevention is important — and possible — at any age. Because many older individuals who have elevated cholesterol also have other chronic illnesses, it is particularly important to seek your physician's advice in this situation because some of the medications for lowering cholesterol interact with medications for other chronic or acute conditions.

✔ **If you are a woman,** you may underestimate the dangers of coronary artery disease — like too many women — and therefore tend to underestimate the importance of controlling cholesterol as well. Remember that heart disease is the leading cause of death in women, as well as in men. This is particularly true for post-menopausal women. Blood cholesterol levels among American women increase sharply around age 40 and continue to rise until more than half of women over age 55 need to lower their cholesterol levels.

Manage Your Cholesterol with Three Key Steps Daily

How you choose to conduct your daily life in three important areas can help you lower elevated blood cholesterol. The key lifestyle decisions involve committing yourself to proper nutrition, including low-fat and low cholesterol consumption, increased physical activity, and maintaining a healthy weight.

Eat "heart smart" to control cholesterol

The overall goals of proper nutrition in individuals with elevated blood cholesterol are to help lower cholesterol levels while still maintaining a balanced and nutritionally adequate eating pattern. Guidelines for two diets to accomplish this have been developed by the American Heart Association and the National Cholesterol Education Program from The National Institute of Health. These are called the *Step I Diet* and the *Step II Diet*. As the names suggest, you start with the Step I Diet and if it doesn't bring your cholesterol down, you move on to the more restrictive Step II Diet.

Table 10-1	AHA Diet Recommendations
AHA Step I Diet Recommendations	
Restrict total fat to less than 30% calories of total calories	
Restrict saturated fat to less than 10% calories of total calories	
Restrict dietary cholesterol intake to less than 300 mg per day	
Restrict sodium intake to less than 2400 mg per day	

(continued)

Table 10-1 (continued)

AHA Step II Diet Recommendations

Restrict total fat to less than 30% calories of total calories
Restrict saturated fat to less than 7% calories of total calories
Restrict dietary cholesterol intake to less than 200 mg per day
Restrict sodium intake to less than 2400 mg per day

Source: National Cholesterol Education Program: Circulation, Vol. 89, p.1329, 1994, American Heart Association.

As shown in Table 10-1, the principles of the Step I Diet follow the general eating patterns recommended for good health by essentially every major health organization in America. To see what this approach to heart-healthy eating means in terms of real food, read Chapter 4. Even if you do not have heart disease, the principles of this diet constitute the best thinking for overall good nutrition for every adult. In reality, these eating principles also constitute proper eating for any child over the age of two as well. (A somewhat higher fat intake is recommended for babies and infants under the age of two in order to promote brain development.)

When the Step I Diet is not sufficient to lower blood cholesterol below 200 mg/dl, the Step II Diet calls for greater reductions in consumption of saturated fat and dietary cholesterol. Because the dietary guidelines for the Step II Diet are somewhat more restrictive than the Step I Diet, it is best to undertake this plan with the advice and counsel of a registered dietitian to make sure that you maintain nutritional adequacy in your overall eating plan.

Many individuals suffer from the misconception that food cannot be enjoyable and tasty as part of a Step I or Step II Diet. All the recipes found in *The Healthy Heart For Dummies* are compatible with the Step I Diet and many are compatible with the Step II Diet. These recipes, which are found in the Appendix, have been contributed by top American chefs and show that heart-healthy eating can also be satisfying and delicious.

Get at least 30 minutes of physical activity daily

As I discuss in great detail in Chapters 6 and 7, a sedentary lifestyle is a strong and established risk factor for coronary artery disease. The good news is that increased physical activity not only lowers an individual's overall risk for coronary artery disease, but also helps with cholesterol problems.

Regular aerobic activity has been clearly shown to increase HDL cholesterol which, in turn, is associated with decreased risk of heart disease. Even moderately intense physical activity, such as brisk walking, can raise HDL cholesterol. Of course, if you have been very sedentary or already have established coronary artery disease, it is essential to check with your physician before starting a program of increased physical activity.

Maintain a healthy weight

Next to proper nutritional practices, the most important lifestyle intervention to lower elevated cholesterol in overweight individuals is weight loss. Weight reduction helps lower LDL cholesterol, lower triglycerides, and raise HDL cholesterol. People usually underestimate the benefit of weight reduction for correcting lipid problems. Even 15 or 20 pounds over your optimal weight can contribute to elevated cholesterol.

Drug Treatment for High Cholesterol

In some instances, lipid-lowering medications are required to manage high cholesterol. This is particularly true if your blood cholesterol is extremely high, if you have other major risk factors for heart disease, or if you already have established coronary artery disease. In these instances, your physician will probably recommend drug therapy, in addition to lifestyle measures, to lower elevated blood cholesterol.

Medications used to treat high cholesterol

While there is a bewildering variety of cholesterol medications available, the major ones fall into one of four categories:

- **Statins.** Numerous statin medications are available to help lower blood cholesterol. All these medications act on an enzyme that is essential for the body's production of cholesterol. Their action is to slow down, or inhibit, this enzyme, which rejoices in the name "HMG-CoA reductase." (Remember that tongue twister and you'll probably be one up on your doctor!) Many studies have shown that these medications powerfully reduce cholesterol and lower the risk of coronary artery disease. Statin medicines are particularly useful in lowering high levels of LDL cholesterol.

- **Bile Acid Sequestrants.** These medications lower blood cholesterol by binding with cholesterol-containing bile acids in the intestines where they are then eliminated in the stool. Bile acid sequestrants have a long history of safe and effective use for lowering blood cholesterol. These medications are particularly valuable in individuals who have elevated LDL cholesterol.

✔ **Fibric Acids.** Fibric acids are particularly effective in lowering triglycerides and have also been demonstrated to modestly lower LDL cholesterol. They are particularly appropriate in individuals who have high triglyceride levels and elevated LDL cholesterol. Some of these medications also have been shown to raise HDL cholesterol.

✔ **Nicotinic Acid.** Nicotinic acid, which is a form of the B vitamin called niacin, is effective in lowering triglycerides and total blood cholesterol, as well as raising HDL cholesterol. Despite these benefits, some individuals may have difficulty tolerating this medication because of its side effects, which include itching of the skin and flushing, as well as gastrointestinal distress.

Although niacin is inexpensive and available over the counter, never self-medicate for cholesterol control; you must be monitored by a physician because of potential for major dangerous side effects.

Estrogen Replacement Therapy as cholesterol therapy

Estrogen Replacement Therapy (ERT) may be a very valuable therapy for post-menopausal women with high blood cholesterol. Estrogen has been shown to lower LDL cholesterol and raise HDL cholesterol. Some studies have suggested that ERT in post-menopausal women reduces the risk of coronary artery disease. However, the recent HERS study indicates that starting ERT is not advisable for women with established coronary artery disease. Estrogen Replacement Therapy may also help retard osteoporosis, which is the bone loss that is particularly common in older women. It should be noted, however, that these drugs may slightly increase the risk of breast cancer and uterine cancer. If you are contemplating Estrogen Replacement Therapy, it is essential to have a full discussion of the pros and cons of this approach with your physician.

General considerations regarding drug therapy

If your physician starts you on medication to help lower cholesterol, it is important to have a repeat cholesterol level test in four to six weeks after the initiation of therapy. If adequate blood cholesterol lowering is not achieved, it may be necessary to increase the dose of medication or add a second medication.

As already indicated, lipid-lowering medications should always be used in conjunction with positive lifestyle measures, such as proper nutrition, increased physical activity, and weight management if you are overweight.

Special Issues in Controlling Cholesterol

Some special issues are important, as you and your physician work together to lower blood cholesterol.

Lowering triglyceride levels

Many steps that you take in your daily life can effectively help lower blood triglycerides. These include increasing your physical activity, weight reduction if you are overweight, and restricting alcohol and simple sugars in the diet. (Does this begin to sound familiar?) If your triglycerides are elevated in addition to cholesterol, various medications, in particular the fibric acids and nicotinic acid may be added to lifestyle measures to help control both high triglycerides and high LDL.

High blood cholesterol and hypertension

Both elevated blood cholesterol and elevated blood pressure (hypertension) are very common in the United States. Unfortunately, they frequently occur together and that spells double trouble. Because each risk factor for heart disease multiplies other risk factors, an individual who has both elevated blood cholesterol and hypertension quadruples their risk of heart disease. Unfortunately, high cholesterol and high blood pressure occur together in 40 to 50 percent of individuals who have one or the other condition. This deadly combination is particularly common in overweight individuals.

If you have both elevated cholesterol and high blood pressure, you must work with your physician to simultaneously lower both conditions. Controlling the combination of high blood pressure and elevated cholesterol represents a real challenge because some of the medications used to treat either elevated blood cholesterol or hypertension may react adversely with the other. Once again, the first line of treatment in an overweight individual is weight reduction. Other lifestyle measures, such as proper nutrition, including the principles espoused in the Step I Diet, and increased physical activity have all been shown to simultaneously lower both blood pressure and elevated blood cholesterol. (See also Chapter 9 for additional information about the treatment of hypertension.)

Elevated blood cholesterol accompanied by diabetes

After hypertension, the other dangerous condition most frequently associated with elevated blood cholesterol is probably Type 2 diabetes (also called *adult-onset diabetes* or *non-insulin dependent diabetes*). The lipid problems which accompany diabetes are typically elevated blood triglycerides, slightly elevated LDL cholesterol and low HDL cholesterol.

Since Type 2 diabetes is a clear and strong independent risk factor for coronary artery disease, it is particularly important for individuals with diabetes to have their blood lipids checked frequently. If lipid abnormalities are present, people with diabetes need to receive aggressive treatment to correct these problems.

There is also a common association between Type 2 diabetes and obesity. While not all these people have diabetes, over 80 percent of all adult-onset diabetics are overweight. If you have adult-onset diabetes and are overweight, the first and most important line of defense is to lose weight.

Other conditions associated with cholesterol

Other medical conditions that may cause blood lipid abnormalities include certain diseases of the kidney and liver and low thyroid levels. If you have any of these conditions, it is important that your blood cholesterol and other lipid levels be checked frequently and that you discuss these issues in detail with your physician.

Severe and/or hereditary forms of elevated blood cholesterol

Approximately one to two percent of the population in the United States have an inherited tendency for severely elevated blood cholesterol. Their condition is typically the result of genetic problems which affect how the body handles cholesterol. The best advice is that if any member of your family has been shown to have a severely elevated cholesterol, you, and all other family members, should consult with your physician, be screened, and put on proper therapy if you have one of these genetic conditions.

Chapter 11

Stamp Out Smoking!

● ●

In This Chapter

▶ The cardiac risks of cigarette smoking

▶ Nicotine addiction: Why it's so hard to break free

▶ How you can stop smoking

▶ How your doctor can help

▶ Aids to help you stop

▶ Why relapse is not collapse

▶ Living smoke-free for a lifetime

● ●

*T*here is only one good thing that can be said about cigarette smoking — it's good when you stop! In the United States, cigarette smoking is responsible for an enormous amount of unnecessary suffering and death every year.

✔ Cigarette smoking is the leading cause of preventable death in the United States, claiming over 400,000 lives per year.

✔ Depending on the level you smoke, cigarette smoking increases your risk of heart disease between 200 percent and 400 percent.

✔ Smoking increases your risk of lung cancer 20 to 30 times.

✔ Smoking harms those around you through second-hand smoke, which can lead to angina attacks in individuals who have coronary artery disease and may result in chronic bronchitis for children who live with smokers.

But guess what? None of this information is news to people who smoke cigarettes. As a friend once said, "Everyone who doesn't exercise knows that they should, and everyone who smokes cigarettes knows they shouldn't!" So I'm not going to rattle off too many statistics on why you should stop smoking.

I'll simply review enough of how smoking relates to coronary heart disease to give your will power extra ammunition against the urges of your nicotine habit or to reinforce your commitment to supporting someone who's trying to quit. Then I consider some specific recommendations for *how* to stop smoking. For the good of your heart and overall health, it's never too late to quit.

Why Stop Smoking?

Cigarette smoke harms virtually every vital organ, but it is particularly dangerous to the heart and lungs. (Incidentally, anyone who thinks that they are safe with smokeless tobacco, cigars, or pipes should think again. More on that later.)

Cigarette smoking and heart disease

It is astounding to me, as a cardiologist, that many people still do not appreciate how serious the link is between cigarette smoking and heart disease.

- Cigarette smokers, depending on how much they smoke, increase their risk of heart disease from two to four times over nonsmokers.
- Every cigarette you light increases your blood pressure.
- Cigarette smoking increases the bad cholesterol (LDL) and decreases the good cholesterol (HDL) in your blood stream.
- Each time you light a cigarette, the nicotine causes the coronary arteries to mildly constrict. This is bad enough in a normal individual, but can bring on significant symptoms for an individual with angina.

Cigarette smoking and other diseases

Smoking accounts for one-fourth of all cancer deaths in the United States, including 87 percent of lung cancers. Smoking has also been associated with cancers of the mouth and throat (all structures), esophagus (food tube), pancreas, cervix, kidney, and bladder. Want more bad news? Cigarette smoking is also associated with such annoying, chronic conditions as the common cold, stomach ulcers, chronic bronchitis, many other lung diseases, and with such catastrophic events as stroke.

Smoking and women

For reasons that are not completely clear, cigarette smoking seems to be particularly dangerous in women. In fact, some studies have suggested that the risk of heart attack in women who smoke is approximately 50 percent greater than the risk in male smokers. (One possible explanation for this increase is the interaction between the chemicals in cigarette smoke and female hormones.) In addition, lung cancer is now the leading cause of cancer death in women, having surpassed breast cancer in 1987.

Smoking and children and youth

Over 90 percent of current smokers started when they were children. Sadly, an estimated 3,000 children under age 18 start smoking every day. Over 71 percent of high school students have tried cigarette smoking and a third of high school students currently smoke cigarettes. If you don't start smoking as a child, however, you are unlikely to start smoking at all. If you are a young smoker, the best thing you can ever do for your long-term good health is kick the tobacco habit now.

Smoking and African Americans

Cigarette smoking appears particularly dangerous for African Americans. They have been found to have higher levels of the breakdown products of nicotine in their blood than Caucasian smokers, and for reasons that are not completely clear, African Americans who smoke appear more susceptible to heart disease than Caucasians.

Second-hand smoke

People who live or work with active cigarette smokers are susceptible to second-hand smoke (also called passive smoke, environmental tobacco smoke, or ETS). Each year, between 35,000 and 45,000 deaths from heart disease are attributed to second-hand smoke as are 3,000 deaths from cancer. Second-hand smoke is also responsible yearly for between 150,000 and 300,000 respiratory tract infections.

The Good News About Quitting Smoking

Before we get too depressed about all the bad news associated with cigarette smoking, let's look at the bright side.

✔ Each year, about 1.2 million smokers are able to quit successfully. After only one year off cigarettes, the excess cardiac risk from smoking is cut in half. Fifteen years after you stop smoking, your risk is similar to that of a person who never smoked.

✔ Male smokers who quit between the ages of 35 and 40 add an average of five years to their lives. Female smokers add three years to their lives. And it is never too late. Even men and women who quit between the ages of 65 and 69 can increase their life expectancy.

✔ Quitting smoking is truly possible. With modern smoking cessation programs, 20 to 40 percent of participants will successfully stop smoking. The new aids to help people quit smoking now on the marketplace may help this success rate climb even higher.

Nicotine Addiction: The Chain That Binds

Nicotine is a powerfully addictive drug. Using nicotine causes changes in the brain that compel people to use it more and more. In addition, attempting to stop using nicotine causes unpleasant physical and emotional side effects. Good feelings when the drug is present combined with bad feelings when the drug is not present are the hallmarks of addiction. And nicotine is judged to be more addicting than heroin.

What does nicotine do to the body?

When you smoke a cigarette, the chemical nicotine causes a number of immediate responses in the body. In the short-term, blood pressure and heart rate rise and the arteries supplying the heart narrow. When these arteries narrow, the combination of nicotine and carbon monoxide spell double trouble to the heart since carbon monoxide reduces the amount of oxygen that the blood can carry. In addition, smoking causes abnormalities in the way that the body handles various fats (causing a rise in the bad cholesterol LDL and a decrease in the good cholesterol HDL). It also affects various hormones in the body, as well as the handling of blood sugar.

What are the effects of nicotine on the heart?

Cigarette smoking harms both the heart and the arteries. The carbon monoxide in cigarette smoke appears to damage the walls of arteries and encourages the buildup of fat inside these walls. Nicotine may also contribute to this process. In addition, chemicals in cigarette smoke make platelets more sticky and thereby increase the likelihood that the blood will clot. All these effects combined increase the risk of heart disease significantly.

What's the difference between nicotine in smoke and in nicotine patches and gum?

To help them quit, many smokers are turning to such nicotine products as nicotine transdermal patches and nicotine gum, which have been shown to help smokers quit when they are used as part of an overall comprehensive program to quit smoking. Of course, nicotine is still nicotine — and still addictive. But nicotine replacement has at least two important physical differences from smoking. First, with the nicotine patch, you avoid inhaling the carbon monoxide, tars, and other toxins in smoke that are harmful. Second, when you smoke, nicotine is delivered to the brain in a sudden rush, then tapers off over a couple of hours. Nicotine patches or gum deliver the nicotine to the body at a steadier rate without the "hit" of a cigarette. Getting away from the nicotine hit may make it easier to quit. At any rate, such nicotine substitutions appear to help ease some of the psychological and physiological problems associated with withdrawal from nicotine. In the optimal situation, a physician is involved in such programs.

Are Other Forms of Tobacco as Dangerous?

Even though this chapter focuses on cigarette smoking, no form of tobacco is safe. Let's take a look.

Smokeless tobacco

Recently, there has been an increase in the use of all forms of smokeless tobacco including plug, leaf, and snuff. Perhaps the greatest cause of concern is the practice of "dipping snuff." In this practice, tobacco (either moist leaf snuff or dry powdered snuff) is placed between the cheek and the gum where nicotine and other cancer-causing agents are absorbed through the gum tissues. This practice is highly addictive and exposes the body to levels of nicotine equal to those of cigarettes.

Cigars

What price glitter — and phoney sophistication? Since 1993, the consumption of cigars and cigarillos has increased 45 percent. Expensive cigars (those costing more than $10.00 each) have increased in sales by 250 percent in the same time. Perhaps this is God's warning to us that there is too much money in the stock market.

Regardless of the elite, stylish image hyped in slick magazines, cigar smoking is extremely hazardous to your health. Almost all the same cancer-causing agents found in cigarettes are found in cigars. Overall death rate is increased by almost 40 percent in individuals who smoke cigars, compared to nonsmokers. The increased risk of mouth cancers is between 500 percent and 1,000 percent. Oh, you don't inhale the smoke? Then, just what is that blue haze hanging about in that trendy bar or in your living room?

Pipes

While there is less data available on pipes than cigars, there is no reason to doubt that they are just as dangerous as cigars. Certainly pipe smokers experience increased cancers of the lip and mouth.

What You Can Do to Stop Smoking

First, set the foundation for a successful campaign by considering the following guidelines which are based on a synthesis of lots of research and recommended by the Agency for Health Care Policy.

✔ **Be committed**. Breaking the nicotine addiction is not easy and takes an enormous individual effort. But be encouraged by the fact that half the people who have ever smoked cigarettes have quit.

✔ **Talk to your doctor.** Ask your physician about nicotine replacement therapy and available programs to help you quit smoking. This type of communication helps maximize the chance of success.

✔ **Set a quit date.** Studies have shown that you are more likely to stop if you set a specific date rather than try to "taper off."

✔ **Build on past mistakes.** The average cigarette smoker usually tries from six to ten times before he or she successfully stops smoking. Review what has worked and what has not worked for you in past efforts.

✔ **Seek the support of family and friends.** Let your family and friends know that you are trying to stop smoking and enlist them in your efforts to stop. If they are truly your friends, they will be supportive.

✔ **Learn how to cope**. Most cigarette smoking is triggered by other cues. Try to minimize the cues in your life that stimulate you to smoke.

✔ **Take the focus off of weight gain.** It is true that many people who stop smoking gain some weight, but the vast majority gain fewer than ten pounds. The health benefits of quitting smoking far outweigh the risks of the small weight gain that comes to some people when they stop.

✔ **Avoid dieting while trying to stop smoking.** Remember that famous slogan for success: KISS (keep it simple, stupid). Trying to change too many things at once is an invitation for failure.

Aids to Help You Stop Smoking

A number of different options are available to help you stop smoking. Recent research has shown that three particular program elements are particularly effective when used either alone or together to help smokers quit:

- **Nicotine replacement therapy.** Using either nicotine patches or nicotine gum doubles the likelihood of successfully quitting. Both nicotine patches and gum can now be obtained without a prescription. Nicotine nasal sprays and inhalers have also now been approved and may be helpful for some individuals. Talk to your physician about some of the newly available prescription medications.

- **Social support.** It is important to receive encouragement and support both from your physician and your family. Support from others trying to quit smoking may also be helpful. There are sure to be various smoking cessation groups in your area (both community-based and commercial). You may also want to try an online support group such as that provided by QuitNet (www.quitnet.org). For other online groups and resources enter "smoking cessation" as the search term on your Web browser. (Sure the term's a bit stiff and technical, but you'll usually get the best results with it.)

- **Skills training/problem solving.** Practical advice and techniques which physicians and other health care workers or smoking cessation specialists can discuss with you are extremely helpful in quitting.

    It has also been shown that group counseling and individual counseling can help. If counseling is employed, it is important that it be intensive and last for at least two weeks and preferably up to eight weeks.

Other techniques which may be helpful include acupuncture and hypnosis. In all instances, these aids should be used in conjunction with an overall comprehensive program prescribed by your physician and/or smoking cessation specialist.

Developing a Specific Plan to Quit

A variety of sources offer excellent information to help smokers break the habit. One particularly comprehensive pamphlet has been developed by the National Cancer Institute (your tax dollars at work in a good cause). You can get it free of charge from the NCI by calling 1-800-4-CANCER (1-800-422-6237) and asking for the booklet, "Clearing the Air; How to quit smoking and quit for keeps." Alternatively, you can read it online. (The easiest way to find it: Go to www.nih.gov and do a title search for "Clearing the Air.")

Here are the key recommendations made by the National Cancer Institute:

✔ **Prepare yourself to quit.** After you make the decision to quit, list all the reasons why you want to quit and get yourself ready. Set a target date for quitting, perhaps a special day such as a birthday or anniversary or the Great American Smoke Out.

✔ **Know what to expect.** Be realistic, you are going to have some withdrawal symptoms, but they usually will last only one to two weeks.

✔ **Involve someone else.** Get the support of family, friends, and physician. Maybe even ask another smoker to quit with you.

✔ **Before you quit, prepare yourself with these techniques**.

  • Switch brands. Find a brand that you find distasteful.

  • Cut down the number of cigarettes that you smoke, but remember, after you are down to about seven cigarettes a day, it is time to set a specific quit date.

  • Try not to smoke automatically.

  • Make smoking inconvenient (go outside to smoke when it's cold or raining, use malls or movies where smoking is prohibited, and so on).

  • Practice going without cigarettes one day at a time.

  • Clean your clothes and get rid of the cigarette smell.

✔ **On the day you quit, use these strategies.**

  • Throw away all your cigarettes, matches, and lighters; if you can't stand to throw away your collection of ashtrays, store them in the most inaccessible corner of your attic.

  • Visit the dentist and have your teeth cleaned to get rid of tobacco stains.

  • Think of things that you would like to buy for yourself. Estimate their cost in terms of packs of cigarettes and put the money aside to buy these presents.

  • Keep very busy on the big quit day and remind your family and friends so they can support you.

  • At the end of the day, buy yourself a treat or celebrate.

✔ **Immediately after you quit, adopt these techniques:**

  • Develop a clean fresh non-smoking environment. Buy flowers now that you can enjoy their scent.

  • Drink large quantities of water and fruit juice.

  • If you miss the sensation of having a cigarette in your hand, find something else to keep your hands and fingers occupied.

- Look for ways to minimize your temptation and develop new habits, such as exercise. (This decreases yet another risk factor for heart disease.)

- Don't worry about gaining a small amount of weight, but do make sure that you have a well balanced diet. As the appetite depressing affect of nicotine disappears, avoid replacing cigarettes with calorie-dense candy, cookies and snack foods. Try sugarfree gum or fresh fruit instead. This will help you deal with the common experience of gaining some weight after stopping cigarette smoking.

Relapse Is Not Collapse

If you slip and start to smoke again, don't be discouraged or give up. Remember, most smokers have to try several times before they finally succeed. Don't be too hard on yourself, and get back on your nonsmoking track as quickly as possible.

Quitting for Keeps

As you keep the faith — and fight the good fight — not smoking will eventually become a part of you. You will develop your own techniques and strategies for sustaining the positive feeling and pride that stopping smoking gives you. It is important to be vigilant for a long time about triggers for your smoking urge. When the urge kicks in, make a mental note about what was going on when it happened. What were you doing? Where were you? Who were you with? What were you thinking? Check off those things that might trigger you to smoke and try to counteract them with specific strategies. Never give up — you can do it!

Resources

Many different resources are available to help you in the fight to stop smoking. Here are a few organizations:

The National Cancer Institute/The National Institutes of Health

Toll-free: 1-800-4-CANCER (1-800-422-6237).

Website: (www.nci.nih.gov)

✔ **The American Cancer Society**

404-320-3333

Website (www.cancer.org)

✔ **The American Heart Association**

1-800-242-8721

Website (www.americanheart.org)

✔ **The American Lung Association**

212-315-8700

Website (www.lungusa.org)

Chapter 12

Overcoming Obesity: Healthy Weight Loss

● ●

In This Chapter

▶ The link between obesity and heart disease

▶ The latest information on the causes of obesity

▶ Double and triple trouble — obesity and clustering of risk factors

▶ Why it is worse to be an "apple" than a "pear"

▶ Why middle-age weight gain (even small amounts) is so dangerous

▶ Lose less than you think to lower your risk of heart disease

▶ Five proven strategies for safe and effective weight loss

▶ An eating plan for weight loss

▶ Tips for lifelong maintenance of weight loss

● ●

Americans are just too darn fat — and it is killing us. How is it killing us? The final common pathway is invariably heart disease!

From your heart's point of view, there is no such thing as pleasingly plump. Even small amounts of weight gain substantially increase your risk of heart disease. By the time that you are 20 percent overweight (the medical definition for *obese*) you have doubled your risk of heart disease.

Obesity also strongly and negatively interacts with almost every other risk factor for heart disease. In the United States, obesity accounts for:

✔ Over 50 percent of the cases of high blood pressure (see Chapter 9)

✔ At least 50 percent of all cholesterol and lipid problems (see Chapter 10)

✔ Over 85 percent of all adult-onset diabetes

By any standard then, obesity is a major cardiovascular disease risk factor. And because people underestimate its impact, that makes obesity particularly dangerous to your heart.

A Look in the Mirror

So how are we doing on the battle of the bulge? Lousy. Obesity has reached epidemic portions in the United States and continues to grow at an alarming rate. Over one out of three adults in the United States is currently obese and this percentage *grew* over 40 percent during the last decade.

Half of the adult population is overweight (defined as being 5 percent to 20 percent over appropriate body weight). Being overweight is so common in this country that we tend see individuals who are mildly or moderately over-weight as being "normal" weight; consequently, some individuals who are at a healthy weight may even appear "too thin." While it is possible to be too thin, as media attention to the psychological disorders of anorexia and bulimia has alerted us, only a very few American adults have problems with being significantly underweight. By far, the bigger health problem, in terms of your cardiovascular system is to be too fat.

The next generation at risk

Unfortunately, the problem does not stop with adults. Many children and adolescents weigh far too much. Obesity in children has more than doubled in the past twenty years. Over 20 percent of adolescents are now considered obese. If obesity in children continues to grow so rapidly, the current epidemic of obesity and its health related risks will turn out to be small potatoes indeed compared to what the next generation of Americans will be facing.

It's about health! Not looking good

Before you soothe your blues with some chips and dip, let's look at the positive side: Just a little change can help a lot. Losing even small amounts of weight, as I discuss in this chapter, can substantially lower the risks of obesity-related heart disease.

No matter what the latest discovery from the get-rich-quick fad diet promoters, the principles of safe and effective weight loss are simple, clear, and well-proven, as you learn in this chapter. To lay the bedrock foundation of change, you must begin by adopting a new mindset — you must stop thinking about obesity as a *vanity* issue. It's a *health* issue. Until all of us make this very important distinction, obesity will linger as the last great untreated risk factor for heart disease. So let's get started.

Establishing the Link between Obesity and Heart Disease

Although the links between obesity and other risk factors for heart disease, such as hypertension, cholesterol and lipid problems, and diabetes, have long been known (as discussed in previous chapters), obesity by itself was not conclusively established as a major independent risk factor for heart disease until the mid-1990s.

This conclusion was based on the results of a number of large population-based studies, including the Framingham Heart Study, the Nurses Health Study (which has studied over 100,000 nurses for over twenty years) and the Physicians Health Study (which has studied over 25,000 male health professionals). All of these studies indicate that being 20 percent (or more) over the appropriate weight at least doubles the risk of heart disease. And unfortunately, obesity also has a "dose response" curve — that is, the more overweight you become, the more your risk of heart disease increases. In response to this cumulative data, the American Heart Association (AHA) in 1998 listed obesity as a major risk factor for heart disease.

What Causes Obesity?

There is no simple answer. Like most chronic conditions, obesity has multiple causes that interact with each other. The following sections look at some major factors.

Do your genes make you fat?

The genetic contribution to obesity has been a hot research topic for the past decade. Numerous studies have shown that many different genes and gene products, such as particular proteins and enzymes, play a role in various animal models of obesity as well as in human obesity. Just how they play that role and how that will help us treat human obesity is less clear. But here are a couple of the more interesting findings-in-progress.

Leptin

The possible function of the protein *leptin* in obesity was first discovered in a particular inbred group of mice that had a gene defect that caused them to produce inactive forms of leptin and that also caused them to become massively obese. In mouse (and human) metabolism, leptin appears to work as messenger from the fat cells to the brain. As normal mice (and humans) eat, the fat cells become full and then send a chemical signal via leptin to the brain to say, "Stop eating." If the leptin is defective, the brain does not get the message. In effect, the phone keeps ringing but no one answers. So the mouse (or human) continues to eat, blissfully unaware that the fat cells are full. The only way the fat cells can accommodate excess of a good thing is to keep expanding. Result: obesity.

While there is a great deal of scientific evidence that leptin plays a role in obesity in mice and even some reasonable evidence in human beings, we must be careful not to jump to faulty conclusions. To date, the initial trials of synthetic leptin as an anti-obesity medication have been very disappointing.

In addition to the gene associated with leptin, numerous other genes have been discovered that are thought to be potentially defective in individuals who are obese. Research continues apace.

Obesity in twins

Further evidence of a genetic component for obesity comes from very well-designed experiments in identical twins. In one experiment, 10 sets of identical twins were put on identical diets designed to cause them to gain weight. While some pairs of twins gained a tremendous amount of weight, other pairs of twins gained almost no weight. In all ten pairs of twins, both members of the pairs gained almost the same amount of weight.

Promise, not payoff

All this genetic research carries tremendous promise, but almost none is likely to bear fruit in the next decade. Meanwhile, the obesity epidemic continues to rage. If obesity is linked to genetics, are people helpless against it? When all the evidence is taken together, most experts believe that a genetic background plays about a 60 to 70 percent role in obesity. Although that may seem like a lot, that still leaves a 30 to 40 percent role for an individual's own actions — ample power to make positive changes.

What about our social environment?

In the United States, we sit (and sit we do) in an environment that skillfully and inexorably promotes obesity. The food industry produces far too many calories for every man, woman, and child every year and packs them in good-tasting, calorie-dense foods, advertised with billions of dollars.

We also live in a mechanized, computerized society where physical activity is the exception, rather than the rule. The over-consumption of calories coupled with the lack of physical activity is a recipe for weight disaster — a recipe that too many of us have chowed down on.

So what's the solution? Change our actions that interact with the gene pool to cause obesity. By paying attention to proper nutrition and portion size and by looking for the nooks and crannies in our physical lives where we can be more physically active, we can turn the richness of our environment into friend, rather than foe.

Why Is Obesity So Dangerous to the Heart?

The scientific jury is still working on that problem, but the evidence suggests some compelling theories. The strongest evidence implicates the metabolic activity of the fat cells. Having an excessive number of fat cells appears to impair the body's ability to use insulin, and consequently to handle glucose, a problem that, in the extreme, leads to diabetes. To try to overcome this problem, the body produces excessive insulin, which contributes to high blood pressure. In addition, the fat cells cause the liver and muscles to handle the fats we consume in an abnormal way and increase levels of cholesterol in the blood, as well as causing other lipid abnormalities such as elevated triglycerides and depressed HDL (the good form of cholesterol). In this vicious cycle, all of these abnormalities are related to each other.

In addition to these relationships to diabetes, hypertension, and lipid problems, obesity has a direct and negative effect on the heart. Once again, there are many theories for why this is so. One particularly compelling theory is that obesity forces the heart to work harder and that the heart muscle itself may be damaged by infiltration of some of the fat cells. While the total story is still unfolding, the evidence strongly argues that having an excessive number of fat cells in general, and particularly in the abdominal area, spells a metabolic disaster, raising multiple cardiac risk factors for the obese individual.

How Do You Know If You Are Obese?

If you are 20 percent or more above a desirable body weight, by definition, you are *obese*. If you are 5 percent to 20 percent above desirable weight, you are *overweight*. The following tests can help you judge.

Mirror, mirror on the wall

For most people, a good look in the mirror with your clothes off, coupled with an honest appraisal, will give you a rough estimate of whether or not you are obese. If you are over thirty, also check your closet. If you no longer fit the clothes you were wearing ten years ago, beware of creeping middle-age weight gain. For confirmation of your estimate, use the following tool.

Body mass index

Body mass index is the way that most scientists estimate whether or not individuals are obese. Body mass index is a more sophisticated way of comparing your weight to your height than the height/weight tables with which you may be familiar. To use the body mass index table shown in Figure 12-1, find your height on the vertical axis and then run your finger across the horizontal table until you reach your weight, and then look up to the top of the column to determine your body mass index number. Anyone with a body mass index number of 25 or greater is considered overweight, and with a body mass index number of 30 or greater is considered obese.

Body Mass Index Chart

Height (inches)	19	20	21	22	23	24	25	26	27	28	29	30	31	32	33	34	35
							Body Weight (pounds)										
58	91	96	100	105	110	115	119	124	129	134	138	143	148	153	158	162	167
59	94	99	104	109	114	119	124	128	133	138	143	148	153	158	163	168	173
60	97	102	107	112	118	123	128	133	138	143	148	153	158	163	168	174	179
61	100	106	111	116	122	127	132	137	143	148	153	158	164	169	174	180	185
62	104	109	115	120	126	131	136	142	147	153	158	164	169	175	180	186	191
63	107	113	118	124	130	135	141	146	152	158	163	169	175	180	186	191	197
64	110	116	122	128	134	140	145	151	157	163	169	174	180	186	192	197	204
65	114	120	126	132	138	144	150	156	162	168	174	180	186	192	198	204	210
66	118	124	130	136	142	148	155	161	167	173	179	186	192	198	204	210	216
67	121	127	134	140	146	153	159	166	172	178	185	191	198	204	211	217	223
68	125	131	138	144	151	158	164	171	177	184	190	197	203	210	216	223	230
69	128	135	142	149	155	162	169	176	182	189	196	203	209	216	223	230	236
70	132	139	146	153	160	167	174	181	188	195	202	209	216	222	229	236	243
71	136	143	150	157	165	172	179	186	193	200	208	215	222	229	236	243	250
72	140	147	154	162	169	177	184	191	199	206	213	221	228	235	242	250	258
73	144	151	159	166	174	182	189	197	204	212	219	227	235	242	250	257	265
74	148	155	163	171	179	186	194	202	210	218	225	233	241	249	256	264	272
75	152	160	168	176	184	192	200	208	216	224	232	240	248	256	264	272	279
76	156	164	172	180	189	197	205	213	221	230	238	246	254	263	271	279	287

Figure 12-1:
Body mass index table.

Direct measure of body fat

The limitation of the body mass index is that it does not account for the difference between lean muscle mass and fat. Excess body fat is what's so dangerous to your health and heart. The best way to determine your exact status is to have your percentage of body fat measured in a hospital setting or at a health club by an individual who is skilled in this procedure.

This can be particularly useful for the few individuals who are heavy but muscular. On a body mass index table, they may be classified as "obese" while in reality they are simply muscular. For example, some body builders or NFL football players might fit into this category. But don't seize on this idea as an excuse. For every one individual who is misclassified on the body mass index table, there are a thousand individuals who are correctly classified as being obese.

Double and Triple Trouble: Obesity's Cluster Effect on Risk Factors

In addition to obesity's association for other risk factors such as hypertension, high cholesterol, and diabetes, obesity also tends to cause other risk factors for heart disease to cluster. Being obese gives an individual

- A greater than 70 percent chance of having at least one additional risk factor
- A slightly greater than 50 percent chance of having two additional risk factors
- Almost a 25 percent chance of having three additional risk factors

Make no mistake about it, it is the people who have multiple risk factors for heart disease who die of heart disease. In fact, over 55 percent of all individuals who have heart disease in the United States have at least two risk factors for heart disease.

But this scenario of double and triple threat can have a sunny ending. By effectively treating obesity — losing weight and adding physical activity — an individual can knock off two or three birds of risk with one stone.

Why It Is Worse to Be an "Apple" Than a "Pear"

The pattern of where fat is distributed in the body also contributes to the risk of obesity. Individuals who accumulate excess fat in their abdominal region (*apple-shaped* people) are at higher risk than individuals who accumulate excess fat tissue in their thighs and hips (*pear-shaped* people). Generally, men tend to accumulate abdominal obesity and women tend to accumulate more fat tissue on their hips and thighs. But there are plenty of apple-shaped women and pear-shaped men. The bottom line is, if you tend to accumulate fat in the abdominal area, you have an increased risk of heart disease.

Middle-Aged Weight Gain: Time for the Yellow Caution Flag

When a problem occurs in an automobile race, hoisting a yellow caution flag alerts drivers to slow down to avoid danger. Once the problem is cleared up, they can continue racing safely. Weight gain as an adult should raise a similar yellow caution flag for you because it has been clearly and independently associated with increased risk of heart disease.

And it doesn't take many extra pounds. Gaining just 10 to 15 extra pounds significantly increases your risk of heart disease and diabetes. The average American man or woman gains a pound a year after the age of twenty.

What does this mean for you? If you've gained ten pounds or more, heed the yellow caution flag. Make a concerted effort, at the very minimum, to prevent further weight gain and, at best, to lose the small amount that you have gained. It is much easier to prevent weight gain than to lose it.

Will Losing Weight Lower the Risk of Heart Disease?

If you are overweight, yes! Definitely. Numerous studies now show that weight loss of just 10 to 20 pounds can significantly lower high blood pressure. Weight loss of 5 percent to 10 percent of body weight can dramatically improve the control of diabetes and/or significantly improve cholesterol and lipid abnormalities.

For these reasons, every major medical organization in the United States associated with either the treatment of heart disease or diabetes advocates lifestyle measures in general and weight loss in particular as key components for their overall treatment plan for overweight individuals.

How much weight loss is enough? Anything you can lose and maintain helps. Don't forget that idea, no matter what your ideal goal. In our society, we have spent so much time glorifying thin body types and castigating overweight individuals that it is very hard to divorce our feelings and perceptions from such false values. In one study, for example, overweight women, when asked how they would feel about various percentages of weight loss, responded that they would be "very disappointed" if they only lost 10 percent of their body weight. "Elated" would be a more appropriate response because of the health benefits that a 5 to 10 percent loss represents. Let's start taking off our vanity hats and putting on our health hats. We'll look pretty good in them, too.

What Is the Best Way to Treat Obesity?

Fads come and go, but the basic principles of safe and effective treatment of obesity are continually reinforced by new research. While we will likely have more new medications available to assist in the management of obesity and will continue to learn new supportive techniques, these basic tenants of weight management always apply.

✔ **Eat a healthy diet with fewer calories than your body burns.**

Following the same good nutritional practices that form the cornerstone for good heart-healthy eating will provide the basis for most individuals to lose weight. In addition, individuals must consume fewer calories than their bodies burn. A good caloric deficit to aim for each day is about 500 calories. Three healthful calorie-cutting strategies for most people include:

- Cutting back on the amount of fat in the diet

- Substituting fruit and vegetables, not calorie-dense foods containing sugar, for the fat

- Controlling portion size and numbers

Chapters 4 and 5 and the heart-healthy recipes found in the Appendix provide lots more information on the role of nutrition in weight management.

✔ **Increase physical activity**

Increased physical activity aids initial weight loss by helping you burn more calories. Here, the trick is not to increase the amount you eat when you increase your physical activity. Physical activity is also particularly important in the long-term maintenance of weight loss. Most studies support the concept that you need to perform brisk walking, or its equivalent, for 20 to 45 minutes on most, if not all, days to maintain weight loss. You probably need to get even a little more activity during the initial phases of weight loss.

✔ **Combine proper nutrition and regular physical activity**

The most effective way to lose weight in the short-term and maintain weight loss in the long-term is to combine proper eating habits and regular physical activity. In fact, in one study of individuals who lost at least 30 pounds and kept the weight off for at least 5 years, over 90 percent paid daily attention to both sound nutrition and regular physical activity.

✔ **Adopt a long-term mindset for a long-term challenge**

For virtually every individual who is obese, weight management has been a long-term or lifelong problem. People simply do not go to bed one night at a normal weight and then wake up obese the next morning. So why do we try to treat obesity with short-term fixes? Probably because we are a nation of impatient optimists. So we try to remedy lifelong weight gain by short-term dieting. That simply doesn't work. An attitude adjustment is just as important as adjustments to how we eat and exercise. You need to think long-term. The goal is to internalize principles and practices that you can *enjoy* and follow day in and day out for life.

Are Any Good Medical Treatments for Obesity Available?

No magic bullet will ever replace appropriate lifestyle practices, but it's likely that various new medicines will become available in the next five to ten years that could help individuals with both short-term weight loss and long-term weight maintenance. In addition, some surgical procedures may be appropriate for some individuals.

Anti-obesity medicines

Weight loss medicines have a checkered history that frightens many people. Early disastrous problems with amphetamines followed by the dangerous combination of phentermine and fenfluramine (phen-fen), for example, caused appropriate concern and caution about using medicines to treat obesity for both the public and the medical profession. However, several medicines now available have great promise for helping treat obesity.

> ✔ **Sibutramine** (trade name Meridia). This medication helps an individual feel full by slightly altering brain chemistry. While it is somewhat analogous to *fenfluramine* (which is the fen part of the phen-fen combo that was such a problem), sibutramine appears to carry less of the danger and side effects, such as serious heart valve damage.
>
> ✔ **Orlistat** (trade name Xenical). Introduced in 1999, this medicine partially blocks fat intake, eliminating some calories from the diet.
>
> ✔ **Genetically engineered products.** Products, such as leptin, are likely to become more and more available in the future.

Any medications such as these should be used only in consultation with a physician trained in obesity treatment and only in conjunction with proper lifestyle measures.

Surgery

For some individuals who are *morbidly obese* (at least double ideal body weight), a surgical option such as stomach stapling may prove highly effective in lowering health risks. If you fall into this category of being severely overweight, you should seek the advice of a physician who is highly trained and experienced in this particular kind of surgery. Such surgery should be only a last resort for individuals whose obesity is so far out of control that they are running an unacceptably high risk of heart disease and other medical problems.

Be very wary of surgical procedures such as *liposuction* where doctors surgically remove body fat. Not only can liposuction be potentially very dangerous, but there are no long-term studies to show that it is effective in the treatment of obesity.

What About Those "Miracle" Diets?

If something sounds too good to be true, it probably is! Fad diets come and go. Some are just useless; others are particularly dangerous to your heart. For example, a "high-fat diet" that drastically cuts carbohydrates can create or worsen cholesterol/lipid problems. High-protein diets and diets that claim to eliminate all sugar products should also be viewed with suspicion.

In the short-term, any diet that restricts certain food groups will probably result in short-term weight loss. After all, we have the history of the grapefruit diet, the cabbage soup diet, and so on to show that, in the short-term, almost any kind of crazy diet will work. But they don't help people tackle the root causes of weight gain. So back come the pounds.

Obesity and children

When it comes to your children and weight management, it can truly be said that "an ounce of prevention is worth a pound of cure"! As already indicated, the problem of childhood obesity is growing in the United States. We also know that if you and/or your spouse are obese, your children are of particularly high risk to become obese. The longer that obesity is carried through childhood, the greater the likelihood that it will carry on into adulthood.

If you have an obese child who remains obese by the age of 10 or 11, it is time to seek a consultation with a pediatrician skilled in obesity treatment. The options for treating obesity in children are very limited and almost always should start with encouraging the child to be more physically active. Here, you need to be a good role model. Studies clearly show that parents' physical activity patterns (whether good or bad) directly influence their children's activity. Thus, if you are physically active, your child is likely to be physically active. But, if you are sedentary yourself, no matter how hard you exhort your child to be physically active, your expectations are likely to fall on deaf ears.

If you are a parent who is not obese, then engaging as a family in those simple daily steps of regular physical activity and proper nutrition can help prevent obesity for your children as well as yourself. This is one of the greatest gifts you can give your children. Just ask anyone who has struggled throughout their life with an obesity problem if you have any doubt.

No major nutritional or medical organization (and particularly the American Heart Association, American Diabetes Association, and American Dietetic Association) has supported any of the current fad diets and is unlikely to do so because they ignore the nutritional principles for safe and effective weight loss:

- ✔ Variety
- ✔ Moderation
- ✔ Portion control
- ✔ Cutting down on the number of calories consumed

Developing an Eating Plan for Weight Loss

To lose weight, you will need to develop an eating plan than enables you to consume fewer calories than your body needs to maintain its current weight while also ensuring that you get all the nutrients you need. The eating plan should also help you develop the healthy eating habits that will serve you well for the long-term.

Setting weight loss goals

Before you plan your goals, you may want to read Chapters 4 and 5, which help give you a foundation for planning. Then conduct a self-evaluation as described in Chapter 5 and set your weight loss goals. Remember that many of the modifications for eating in a more heart-healthy way also cut calories. Isn't that nice?

- **How fast should you lose?** You didn't gain weight in a week or two, and you can't lose it safely in that time either. A pound a week is a good goal. More than two or three is too much. Because it takes 3,500 extra calories to add a pound, cutting 500 calories a day from your current intake (if your weight is stable) will enable you to lose a pound a week.

- **What about physical activity?** I'm glad you asked. Physical activity is a must. Use Chapters 6 and 7 to help you add the right kind of activity and exercise to your eating plan.

Using food exchange systems for a weight loss plan that works

If you need a way to organize and keep track of your weight loss program without counting calories or carrying around a pocket calculator, the food exchange system can work for you. The original approach was developed for diabetics and others with chronic conditions who need to be able to comfortably balance and maintain a specific diet over the long-term. A food exchange system is very flexible, allowing you to fit your schedule, tastes, and lifestyle.

How the system works

Like a food pyramid, a food exchange system groups food into categories that are balanced for nutrition per serving. Vegetables, fruits, starches/breads, proteins/meats, milk, and fats are typical categories. Each food serving within an exchange group then contains approximately the same calories and nutrient values, allowing you to substitute any food for another in the category in any way you like. A set number of exchanges/servings per category per day enables you to control your daily intake at your target level of calories.

Because the categories are simple, a little practice soon makes using the exchanges second nature. (Most people can ditch the exchange guide after a couple of weeks.) How do I know? In my medical practice and in the research laboratory I head, the Center for Clinical and Lifestyle Research, hundreds have used the food exchange system with great success. Thousands of others have used the exchange programs I have published in previous books, *The Exercise Exchange Program* and *Fit Over Forty*.

What you need to get started

To use the food exchange approach to accomplish your goals for heart-healthy modifications and calorie reduction, you need three things:

- **Meal plans with daily exchanges/servings for various levels**. Remember, to lose weight you will need to consume about 500 calories less than you need to maintain your current weight. Your self-evaluation will tell the approximate calorie level of your current intake. If you currently eat about 2,300 calories a day, a meal plan providing 1,800 calories a day should help you lose weight. You'll find exchanges/servings for 1,200-, 1,500-, and 1,800-calorie meal plans in the accompanying sidebar, "Exchanges for meal plans for weight loss." In order to have an adequate balance of nutrients in your diet, you should usually not eat less than 1,200 calories a day.

- **A list of the food exchanges.** Though the standard food exchange list was developed by the American Dietetic Association and American Diabetes Association for use by diabetics, it is an excellent resource for anyone. *Exchange Lists for Meal Planning* (ADA Item #0734) may be purchased from the American Dietetic Association online (www.eatright.org) or ordered by phone (1-800-877-1600, Ext. 5000). Various versions of this type food exchange list are available in bookstores and online at various Web sites. The National Heart, Lung, and Blood Institute, as part of its "Achieve Your Healthy Weight" Web site provides a number of resources including an exchange list (www.nhlbi.nih.gov/nhlbi/cardio/obes/gp/lose_wt/fd_exch.htm).

- **A daily/weekly exchange record.** This you can make for yourself. On an index card, notebook page, or computer file, list each category and place the number of exchanges/servings allowed for the day beside it. Carry it with you and check them off as you consume them. Here's a sample:

Daily Exchange Checklist

Sample for the 1,500-Calorie Daily Meal Plan

Food Group	*Exchanges/Servings*
Vegetable	1 2 3
Fruit	1 2 3 4
Starch/bread	1 2 3 4 5
Meat/protein	1 2 3 4 5
Milk/dairy	1 2
Fat	1 2 3

Open calories: 200 (My choice)

Exchanges for meal plans for weight loss

These tables show the number of servings, called *exchanges,* you should consume in each food group to consume the given level of calories. For a full listing of what entails an exchange/serving, you'll want to consult one of the guides mentioned in the text. But here's a quick rule of thumb for one serving/exchange in each group:

Vegetable exchange = ½ cup cooked, 1 cup raw

Fruit exchange = 1 medium apple, orange, pear; 1 small banana

Starch/bread exchange = ½ cup cereal, cooked pasta/grain, starchy vegetable such as potato or beans

Meat/protein exchange = 1 oz lean meat/fish, 1 egg, 4 oz tofu

Dairy product exchange = 8 oz skim milk or nonfat yogurt, 1 oz hard cheese

Fat exchange/serving = 1 teaspoon oil, margarine, butter

Daily Exchanges/Servings for 1,200-Calorie Meal Plan

3 Vegetable

3 Fruit

4 Starch/bread

4 Meat (1 oz)/protein

2 Milk/dairy

3 Fat

80 Open calories (your choice)

Daily Exchanges/Servings for 1,500-Calorie Meal Plan

3 Vegetable

4 Fruit

5 Starch/bread

5 Meat (1 oz)/protein

2 Milk/dairy

3 Fat

200 Open calories (your choice)

Daily Exchanges/Servings for 1,800-Calorie Meal Plan

4 Vegetable

4 Fruit

6 Starch/bread

6 Meat (1 oz)/protein

2 Milk/dairy

4 Fat

300 Open calories (your choice)

Make peace with yourself — the final key

The final ingredient in a successful plan for managing your weight for life is to make peace with yourself. Quit beating up on yourself for being fat. When you slip off your plan, don't slip into the Slough of Despondency and then use the blues as an excuse to keep eating. A slip is just that — a slip. Face forward and take the next positive step. Check out the suggestions in Chapter 8 for using the mind-body connection to reduce stress and foster a relaxed attitude.

Tips for Lifelong Maintenance of Weight Loss

To lower your risk of heart disease, you must maintain the lower body weight you've achieved throughout a lifetime. And that's the big challenge. These tips can help keep you on track.

- **Adopt a lifelong strategy.** Most people have a long-term or lifelong battle with obesity. In order to defeat this enemy, you need a lifelong strategy for overcoming weight gain.

- **Go natural.** Natural products, such as fruits, vegetables, and grains tend to be low fat and relatively low calorie. Emphasize fruits and vegetables and other natural products in your diet. Avoid too many prepared foods, which are typically high in fat and sodium and contribute to weight gain and obesity.

- **Seek support of family and friends.** Food is a communal experience. Family and friends can help you meet your goals if you tell them how to help.

- **Look for nooks and crannies for physical activity**. Take the stairs at work, park further from stores, walk the dog, and so on. Pretty soon, you will find that every day presents multiple ways to be more physically active. Weight control will be a great byproduct of this mindset.

- **Accept plateaus.** When losing weight, you will inevitably experience some plateaus. This is simply the way that the body consolidates its gains. So expect it. Be patient. Don't feel that you have to lose weight every day or every week. If you get stuck at a plateau for several weeks, go back to record keeping and pay much more attention to what you are eating and how much physical activity you are accumulating.

- **Reward yourself.** Weight loss and weight management are tough jobs. Don't forget to be kind to yourself and reward yourself for accomplishments and a job well done. It's smart to make that treat something other than food!

Part IV

Understanding and Controlling Heart Disease

The 5th Wave   By Rich Tennant

"Be just a minute, folks. We got a hole between the atria and both ventricles, and a tricuspid valve that looks deformed. Once we get it patched up, you'll be on your way."

In this part . . .

In this part, you get some basic information to help you
understand coronary heart disease and its manifestations, including angina and heart attack. I look at the
many strategies that modern science and medicine offer
to prevent, diagnose, control, and manage the most
common heart conditions experienced by Americans.
These include coronary artery disease and its manifestations of angina and heart attack, heart rhythm problems,
heart failure, and other conditions. I'll also share the
importance of cardiac rehabilitation for many conditions.
You also look at the merits of various alternative therapies. Finally, I'll share tips for choosing and forming an
effective partnership with your physician.

Chapter 13

Tests and Procedures: When Each Is Used and What They Tell Us

*I*n the war on heart disease, the cardiologist has available a number of amazing tools, both simple and high-tech. Thousands of times a day, patients undergo various forms of cardiac testing in every major medical setting and cardiologist's office in the United States. The results of these tests yield significant information to help physicians work with people to maintain healthy hearts or diagnose and heal ailing hearts.

But cardiac testing and procedures can also be very frightening and intimidating. Physicians often speak a lingo all their own and forget to explain adequately to the patient the reason for each test. In addition, the strange machinery and equipment itself can jangle already tense nerves.

This chapter briefly explains most common cardiac tests and procedures and demystifies the reasons and indications for each. Although I refer to these tests in various chapters as appropriate, use this chapter as your introductory glossary. To make it easy to follow, I group them as

✔ Diagnostic tests

✔ Emergency procedures

✔ Medical and surgical procedures

Diagnostic Tests

From a physical exam to the latest high-tech procedure, diagnostic tests provide information about what's going right and what's going wrong with your heart.

Hands before scans: The history and physical examination

A seasoned cardiologist knows that carefully observing and listening to the patient can often provide more information than even the most advanced tests. There is no substitute for an excellent history and comprehensive physical exam. Being ready to share your history and proactive about doing so can aid in your evaluation and diagnosis.

What does a history include?

With any patient, I always begin by asking, "What brought you here?" The purpose in taking a patient's history is to find out as much as possible about the illness or symptoms that brought the individual to the doctor and about other factors in the patient's life that may affect his or her health. Here's the type of information a thorough history includes:

- History of the current illness, condition, and symptoms
- Current medications and dosages
- Past health history
- Family health history
- Social history, any factor that has bearing on physical and mental health, previous access to care, and so on, such as employment or economic status

What's in a physical exam?

Although we often don't think of the physical examination of the heart and vascular system as being a major test, it certainly is. For thousands of years, this venerable test has provided physicians with enormously important information to guide in further evaluation of your heart.

It has been said that a good cardiologist must have the observational skills of Sherlock Holmes, the fine feeling in the hands of an expert safe-cracker, and the ears of a rabbit. Even if your cardiologist doesn't achieve these levels of expertise, the skills of *observation*, *palpation,* and *auscultation* remain the core of physical examination.

✔ **Observation.** When you take your shirt off at the start of the cardiac physical examination, the astute physician begins with a series of observations.

- Your physician may look at the veins in your neck which give an accurate estimate of the pressures of the venous system of the heart. A little fluttering actually occurs within the vein that can further provide information concerning how the heart's booster pumps (the *atria*) are functioning.

- Your physician may also look for any abnormal motions visible on the chest wall, which can suggest a variety of different cardiac conditions.

✔ **Palpation.** After observation, it's time for the laying on of hands — literally. Here the physician *palpates*, actually *feels* with the fingertips, various cardiac structures, including:

- The strength and characteristics of the pulse of the *carotid arteries*, the two large arteries on either side of the neck that supply the brain, provide lots of useful information. A normal carotid pulse suggests that the heart is pumping strongly and that there is no narrowing of either of these important conduits of "brain food." A weak or delayed pulse (in medicine *parvus* and *tardus* — ain't Latin great?) can suggest an obstruction to the outflow of blood from the heart, such as narrowing of the aortic valve or other obstructive condition. An abnormal pulse (a *pulsus paradoxis*) can suggest that fluid has gathered in the sac around the heart or that very severe lung disease may be present.

- Palpating the front of the chest helps determine the character of the left ventricle, the main pumping chamber. A normal left ventricle rises to meet the hand, rather like a firm handshake, and then rapidly falls away as it contracts. Any difference in the feel of the left ventricle, such as a sustained grinding motion or a double impulse, can indicate either a very thickened heart muscle or one that has been damaged.

✔ **Auscultation.** Perhaps the most important part of the physical examination is *auscultation* — a fancy word that means the physician dons the stethoscope and listens to various heart sounds, such as these:

- **"Lub-dub":** The sound of a normal heart. The first heart sound (affectionately known as *lub* and medically as S1) is caused by the closure of the valves between the ventricles and the atria to prevent blood from flowing backward into areas that it should not go. The second heart sound (*dub* or S2) occurs at the end of the heart's contraction when the valves between the ventricles into the arteries close to prevent blood from flowing back into the heart. During the intervals between these two sounds, the cardiologist listens for murmurs.

- **Swoosh.** Swoosh is not just the logo for a shoe manufacturer but one sound made by abnormal blood flow. Other abnormal heart sounds also have inventive descriptions. The typical murmur that occurs when the heart contracts (systole) is often characterized as the "chug" of an engine as it climbs a hill. The murmur that occurs when the heart is resting (diastole) is often described as the whine of the whistle of the train as it climbs the hill. (No, cardiologists are not graded on creativity.)

- **Extra heart sounds.** The cardiologist also listens for abnormal extra heart sounds known in cardiology as *gallops*. These can occur as either a third heart sound (called S3) or a fourth heart sound (called S4). S3 comes after the lub-dub and has the timing of the *y* in *Kentucky* (thus the heart's rhythm goes S1=Ken, S2=tuck, S3=y). S4 comes before the lub-dub, with timing a bit like the *a* in the word *appendix*. Repeat these words quickly (that is, Kentucky, Kentucky, Kentucky) and you can tell why these sounds are called gallops. Cardiac abnormalities may also produce various *snaps* and *clicks*. For example, a mitral valve commonly produces a click when the valve prolapses (balloons backwards).

Sir, what ails you?

How important is taking a patient's history to making a good diagnosis? A story that was part of the lore of Harvard Medical School when I was a student makes a telling answer:

Some years ago, a brilliant young woman med student — who was top of the class, a future Nobel laureate — was about to graduate with highest honors. Unheard of! Highest honors were rarely awarded; the faculty hated the idea that it was even possible. But with only the written and oral finals to complete, this woman was about to do it. But if she did not do well in her orals, the faculty thought, she would not earn that *summa cum laude*.

And they had just the case in the medical center — a patient with a very rare, esoteric condition that had baffled the best faculty minds and taken batteries of tests to finally diagnose. His condition was *paroxysmal nocturnal hematuria*, PNH, which is sudden attacks in the night of blood in the urine. "We'll stump her," the faculty said. "We'll give her ten minutes with the patient and charts and ask her to diagnose the condition. She'll never do it, and we won't be able to award highest honors."

So they sent the young woman into the patient's room. In two minutes she was back in front of the surprised faculty. "Gentlemen," she said, "this patient can have only one thing, paroxysmal nocturnal hematuria." They were flabbergasted. "How did you do it? It took us weeks."

"Well," said this gifted student, "I went in and sat on the edge of his bed, took his hand in mine, and said, 'Sir, what ails you?' and he said, 'Paroxysmal nocturnal hematuria.'"

A good history is the only place to start. Be prepared to share yours.

As simple as they seem (not a single digital display anywhere), these basic tools of observation, palpation, and auscultation of the heart often lead quickly toward an appropriate diagnosis and suggest which of the array of other cardiac tests should be used to pinpoint a problem.

Electrocardiogram

Invented over 100 years ago, the *electrocardiogram* (also called *ECG* or *EKG*) represents cardiology's first "high-tech" tool. But this graphic recording of the heart's electrical impulses remains one of the most useful tests. Many physicians include it as part of a routine annual physical exam to assess any potential heart problems. More importantly, it is an early diagnostic step taken when an individual has symptoms that may represent heart disease.

How an ECG is taken

To measure the heart's electrical impulses, twelve electrical sensors (leads) are placed in specific positions on the chest, arms, and legs. Because this test is taken while the heart is at rest, the individual is asked to lie down and then electrical information from the twelve leads is gathered simultaneously. The data is recorded as a graph. The whole process is very easy and comfortable.

What an ECG can show

To the astute clinician, the graphic tracings of the heart's electrical activity can reveal

- Evidence of a heart attack
- Occurrence of angina or unstable angina during the test
- Information about the entire electrical conduction system and rhythm of the heart
- Evidence of thickening to the heart wall
- Problems in the pericardium (the sac around the heart)

Exercise tolerance test

The *exercise tolerance test* (also called *ETT* or *exercise stress test*) is an electrocardiogram taken while the heart is beating fast during exercise rather than at rest. After an individual is properly "wired up," he or she is asked to walk and/or run at progressively higher speeds on a motorized treadmill or pedal against steadily increasing resistance on a stationary cycle. These exercise activities cause the heart to speed up.

The two basic types of exercise tolerance tests are

- A *maximal* exercise tolerance test, where the individual is asked to exercise to the maximum degree possible
- A *submaximal* exercise tolerance test, where the test is stopped before the individual achieves maximal exercise

Among the clinical information revealed by this test, the most important finding may be whether there is adequate blood flow to the heart during exercise. Thus, the exercise tolerance test is extremely useful in making the diagnosis of coronary artery disease, angina, and in some instances, unstable angina. As an added bonus, your physician can estimate your cardiovascular fitness (also called your *aerobic capacity*) based on the amount of exercise that you are able to do on the exercise tolerance test.

Holter monitoring

When an individual complains of significant *palpitations,* the cardiologist often orders a 24-hour monitor to record every heartbeat for the entire 24-hour period to determine whether serious rhythm problems are occurring. This form of electrocardiogram is called *Holter monitoring*. The individual is asked to wear a small device attached to a belt around the waist and attached to electrical leads on the chest.

Echocardiography

For cardiac medicine, as for the Navy, an echo is often just the thing! (As in *sonar*, you know?) In fact, except for the ECG, echocardiography is perhaps the most widely used noninvasive procedure in cardiovascular medicine.

Invasive versus noninvasive testing

If you hear a member of your medical team mutter something about an invasive procedure, don't panic. You will not need the nearest emergency bunker. Tests and procedures in cardiac medicine are broadly classified as *noninvasive* and *invasive*. As the names suggest, noninvasive tests, such as electrocardiograms, echocardiograms, or CT scans, are ones where the body is literally "not invaded," while invasive procedures, such as cardiac catheterization, angioplasty, or electrophysiology, involve actually putting instruments inside the body or "invading" it. Thanks to modern anesthesia, these procedures have little or no discomfort.

How it works

In an *echocardiogram*, also called a *cardiac sonogram* or *cardiac ultrasound*, sound waves are bounced off the various structures of the heart. As the sound waves return to the transducer, they are measured to obtain pictures of all the structures of the heart. In some cases, a cardiologist will order a *transesophageal echocardiogram* (*TEE*), a test in which the transducer is passed into the esophagus near the heart, a position that produces extremely clear pictures of the heart's structures.

What it shows

Among its many uses, echocardiography is used for evaluating

- Whether any of the heart's four valves is narrowed (*stenosed*) or leaking (*regurgitation*) and how well replacement valves are working after surgery

- How well the heart is pumping

- Whether or not there is any major damage either to the heart muscles or the structures around the heart

- The existence of congenital heart disease

Nuclear medicine

Invasive cardiologists (who spend most of their time doing heart catheterization and angioplasty) used to joke that *nuclear* medicine was really *unclear* medicine. In fact, various nuclear techniques provide extremely valuable information about both the functioning of the heart and adequacy of blood flow. They are often used either after or in conjunction with echocardiography. Here are two of the most common nuclear techniques:

- **Gated Blood Pool Scanning.** In this test, which is also called *RVG* or *MUGA* scanning, a radioactive tracer is placed in the blood and circulates through the heart while pictures of the heart are taken. This test allows cardiologists to estimate how well the heart is pumping.

- **Thallium Stress Test**. In this test, a radioactive material, thallium, is injected into a vein. This radioactive tracer travels to the coronary arteries and ultimately is carried by the blood to the heart tissue. The test is done in two stages, with images obtained first while the individual is at rest and then while the individual is exercising or after medications are given to dilate the coronary arteries. The degree to which the tracer reaches various parts of the heart provides a good estimate of how blood is flowing through the coronary arteries.

Alphabet soup — other noninvasive tests

In the last decade, a number of sophisticated noninvasive tests (often called by their initials) have provided increasing promise and capability of precisely visualizing cardiac structures and assessing their function. Here are four that are already making contributions to cardiac diagnosis and are likely to contribute even more in the future.

✔ **Positron Emission Tomography.** This test (also called *PET testing* or *PET scan*) can provide very precise information about blood flow to cardiac structures. A computerized tomograph also displays the data as a three-dimensional image. In a PET scan, radioactive material, called a *tracer,* is injected into the patient; as the tracer reaches the heart, a series of exposures are recorded as an image. To enable the images to be taken from all sides, the patient lies on a platform that can be positioned inside a large, circular X-ray machine (looks a bit like a huge donut). Because the technique and the equipment to perform PET testing is quite expensive and sophisticated, it is available in only a limited number of centers in the United States. PET scans are useful in the diagnosis of coronary artery disease as well as the functioning of the heart muscle.

✔ **Computerized Tomography of the heart**. Also called a *CT scan,* this test combines the power of X-ray images with computer processing to present a variety of cardiac structures in a cross-sectional format. With the advent of new, ultra-fast CT scanners, it is now possible to determine the amount of calcium in the coronary arteries, which may lead to early, precise diagnosis of coronary artery disease. This potential benefit of ultra-fast CT is under active exploration. Like the PET scan, CT scans use radioactive tracers and circular (or tunnel) X-ray equipment.

✔ **Magnetic Resonance Imaging.** Often called an *MRI,* this test, which uses a powerful magnetic field rather than X-rays to form its images, offers the possibility of collecting both pictorial and metabolic information about the heart and other structures without the need for additional tests that use radiation. Recent evidence suggests the MRI may be extremely useful in determining the composition of fatty plaques in coronary arteries, which may lead to early, precise diagnosis of coronary artery disease. Most MRI equipment uses a moving platform that is positioned within a circular or enclosed tunnel in the equipment that houses the magnets that create (noisily, I might add) the magnetic field. New, open MRI equipment has been developed, however — an innovation welcomed by the claustrophobic.

✔ **High resolution carotid ultrasound**. This test can provide useful information about the walls of the carotid arteries. Certain characteristics of the walls of these major vessels of the neck have been strongly associated with coronary artery disease. Thus, carotid ultrasound has gained an increasing following as a noninvasive way of estimating the risk of coronary artery disease.

Plumbing 101: Heart catheterization and angiography

Cardiac or *heart catheterization* (*cath*) is an invasive procedure in which the cardiologist inserts a small plastic tube called a *catheter* into a vein or artery in the leg or arm and guides it into the heart or coronary arteries. It can be used to perform various diagnostic tests and treatment procedures. When a contrast material (often called a *dye*) is injected through the catheter to make the arteries or other structures of the heart visible to X-rays, the procedure is called *angiography*. An advanced procedure, it is usually performed in a heart catherization laboratory by a cardiologist specializing in the field.

It may give you a chuckle to know that in the profession, these invasive cardiologists (of which I am one) are called *plumbers* because they work on the pipes (the coronary arteries) and the pump (the heart).

Patients undergo heart catheterization both to determine pressures in the heart and also to provide definitive evidence of any abnormalities that may be present, either in the pumping chamber itself or the arteries that supply it. As a practical matter, cardiologists can either catheterize the left heart or the right heart.

Left heart catheterization. The cardiologist typically enters the arterial circulation in the groin (the *femoral artery*) and threads the catheter up either into the left heart pumping chamber itself or individually into each of the three arteries that supply the heart. Then, contrast material is injected and pictures are taken. Patients usually undergo a left heart catheterization to determine pressures and to take pictures of the left heart and the coronary arteries that supply it to determine the amount of blockage or coronary artery disease present. Virtually all patients who undergo *coronary artery bypass grafting* and all patients who undergo *angioplasty* undergo heart catheterization. (For more information regarding these procedures, see "Medical and Surgical Procedures," later in this chapter.)

Right heart catheterization. The cardiologist enters the large vein in the leg (the *femoral vein*) and threads a catheter up into the right atrium and from there into the right ventricle and then out into the pulmonary artery, taking pressures along the way as shown in Figure 13-1. This is typically done to see how the right heart, which pumps blood to the lungs, is functioning. Occasionally it is also done to see if there is any congenital abnormality such as a hole in the muscular walls (the septa) that separate the right and left atria and right and left ventricles. Such holes (called an atrial septal defect [*ASD*] and a ventricular septal defect [*VSD*]) are relatively rare conditions that usually must be repaired surgically.

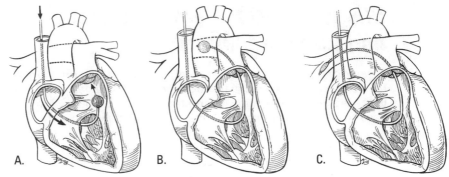

Figure 13-1:
Right heart
catheteriza-
tion.

A. B. C.

Emergency Procedures

Here are two common emergency procedures used when an individual experiences a sudden stoppage of the heart or rhythm problems.

Cardiopulmonary resuscitation (CPR)

Cardiopulmonary resuscitation, commonly called CPR, is required when an individual experiences sudden heart stoppage. CPR techniques were introduced approximately 25 to 30 years ago and have evolved since.

There are two main branches of CPR:

- Basic cardiac life support (BCLS)
- Advanced cardiac life support (ACLS)

Although advanced cardiac life support requires training in skills and equipment found in an ambulance or hospital setting, basic cardiac life support can be learned by every individual. Studies have shown that BCLS procedures can be life saving.

If a family member has serious heart disease, I strongly urge you to learn the techniques of BCLS. These are based on the *ABCs* of CPR:

- Establishing an adequate **Airway**
- Helping the individual **Breathe**
- Establishing **Circulation** by putting pressure on the chest

BCLS courses are taught in every major metropolitan area in the United States and you can obtain information from the American Red Cross, a local branch of The American Heart Association, or your local healthcare institution. Prompt administration of BCLS can be life saving. I strongly urge you to learn these techniques.

Defibrillation

Everyone who's ever watched a doctor show on TV has seen the defibrillation equipment's paddles whipped out and applied to some poor soul on the gurney. What screenwriter or director could resist such drama? And in truth, no matter how exaggerated the TV scenarios, something pretty dramatic is going on in the heart of any one who needs this emergency procedure called *defibrillation*.

The heart depends on a system of electric impulses to maintain its rhythm and contract properly. Nothing good happens when this electrical system goes awry. At worst, rather than contracting, the heart simply quivers, or *fibrillates* (in cardiology this is called *fibrillation*). Because a heart experiencing ventricular fibrillation generates no blood flow and quickly leads to death, emergency action is required. Using the paddles you're familiar with and an adjustable source of electricity, an electrical current is directed to the heart to try to jumpstart it.

After CPR, the American Heart Association rates access to early defibrillation as vital to the chances of survival of a victim of sudden cardiac arrest (sudden ventricular fibrillation). The continuing development of *automated external defibrillators* (*AEDs*) that weigh only a few pounds, use long-lasting batteries, and can be operated by lay people with some basic training (such as firefighters, police, flight attendants, safety officers) should make this life-saving procedure more widely available.

While I'm on the topic of defibrillators, I should mention that the technology has advanced to the point that tiny defibrillators (about the size of a pacemaker) can be implanted in the chest wall and deliver a shock directly to the heart. These are increasingly used in individuals with serious arrhythmias who have survived an episode of sudden cardiac death (yes, it's called that because, without resuscitation, that is the outcome). These implantable defribrillators are used by electrophysiologists and can be life saving.

Medical and Surgical Procedures

After a diagnosis has been made, treatment options for certain conditions may include various medical and surgical procedures.

The electric company

Because the complex electrical impulses that control the heart's rhythm and contraction are so critical, a whole branch of cardiology has grown to detect rhythm abnormalities and also correct underlying electrical problems in the heart. In addition to some of the diagnostic tests that I discussed earlier, here are the most commonly used medical or surgical "electric" procedures involving the heart.

- ✔ **Cardioversion**. This procedure, which applies a small amount of electrical current to the heart, can be used to treat certain rhythm abnormalities, such as these:

  - Irregular beating of the heart's atria, or booster pumps *(atrial fibrillation)*

  - A rapid heartbeat, originating in the booster pumps *(atrial tacchycardia)*

  - A rapid heartbeat, originating in the ventricles *(ventricular tacchycardia)*

  The equipment used is the same as for defibrillation but smaller amounts of electricity are used.

- ✔ **Pacemakers.** These devices are used, either temporarily or permanently, to speed up a heart that is beating too slow, a condition called *bradycardia* (brady=slow; cardia=heartbeat). Pacemakers actually "pace" the heartbeat by delivering electrical impulses which are very similar to the heart's own electrical system. The typical pacemaker employed now has one electrical beat that goes into the atrium, and one that goes into the ventricle. These are called *A-V pacemakers*. They are powered by batteries that can last for many years.

  Pacemakers are typically placed in the front of the chest using a minor surgical procedure to create a "pocket" under the skin. The electrodes are then threaded into the right atrium and ventricle.

- ✔ **Cardiac electrophysiology**. The most advanced form of electrical work on the heart, electrophysiology takes place in specialized laboratories, very similar to heart catheterization labs. Specialized electrical catheters are placed into various portions of the heart where either monitoring or corrective electrical work can be performed either to diagnose or correct rhythm problems or other electrical abnormalities. This procedure is typically performed in large hospital centers by specially trained cardiologists whose field is electrophysiology.

Angioplasty

When the narrowing or blockage of coronary arteries becomes very severe, *coronary angioplasty* (also called *balloon angioplasty*) is one of the procedures that is used to relieve the problem.

How it works

Using the technique of heart catheterization, the cardiologist enters the narrowed or blocked coronary artery or arteries with a specialized catheter that has a high-pressure balloon near the tip. Once in the narrowed section of the artery, the balloon is inflated. The inflated balloon stretches the artery and literally squashes the plaque up against the side of the blood vessel, as illustrated in Figure 13-2. This procedure opens up the artery and allows a greater blood flow.

Limitations

One drawback of angioplasty is that in 25 to 40 percent of cases, the narrowing will recur in the artery, a condition called *restenosis*. In this case, another angioplasty may be necessary or even bypass surgery.

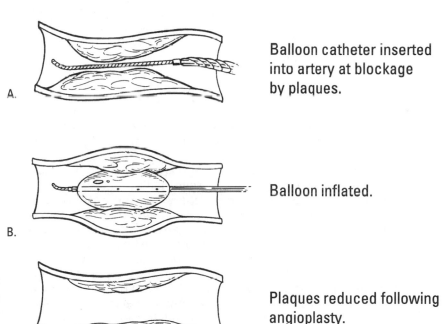

A.

Balloon catheter inserted into artery at blockage by plaques.

B.

Balloon inflated.

Figure 13-2:
Balloon
angioplasty.
C.

Plaques reduced following angioplasty.

Use of stents

In certain cases where it appears likely that this narrowing process will recur, the cardiologist may place a device called a stent in the area where the angioplasty has occurred. These mechanical devices, which look a little like coiled springs, are designed to hold the blood vessels open.

Related procedures

Other procedures similar to angioplasty have been developed:

- ✔ **Laser angioplasty** uses a laser on the end of the catheter to incinerate the fatty plaque deposits that cause the narrowing.

- ✔ **Atherectomy** literally removes the fatty plaque in a process similar to Roto-Rooting. (One more reason why invasive cardiologists are called plumbers.)

Cardiac surgery

Certain problems with severely blocked arteries, damaged heart valves, and various other structures of the heart may require surgery. Such surgery is performed by cardiac surgeons, who train first as general surgeons and then specialize in cardiac surgery. Although they belong to different specialties, cardiologists and cardiac surgeons work closely together. Here are some of the most common types of cardiac surgery.

Coronary Artery Bypass Grafting (CABG)

In coronary artery bypass grafting (CABG, often pronounced "cabbage" in the lingo of physicians), a piece of vein from the leg or artery from the chest is used to "bypass" the blockage in a coronary artery and restore blood flow.

Different techniques for doing CABG are possible. In the traditional form, an incision is made through the sternum and the chest is opened to reach the heart (hence the term *open heart surgery*). At the same time, a donor vein for the bypass graft is surgically removed (*harvested,* a surgeon would say) from the leg. In most cases, the patient is also placed on a heart-lung machine (pump oxygenator) that takes over for the heart, which is stopped for the surgery. The surgeon then attaches one end of the bypass vein to the aorta and the other to the blocked coronary artery below the blockage (called *occlusion),* as shown in Figure 13-3. When all the grafts to be performed are complete, the patient is removed from the heart-lung machine and the heart is restarted. After the surgery is complete, CABG patients are carefully monitored in the Intensive Cardiac Care Unit (ICCU).

Instead of or in addition to using donor veins for the bypass, the surgeon in some instances may use a mammary artery from the chest. In this case, just one end of the graft artery is brought over and attached to the coronary artery below the blockage and blood then flows from the mammary artery to the coronary artery.

More recent techniques have involved using miniature instruments from the surface of the body through small incisions. This "minimally invasive" cardiac surgery may have the advantage of a more rapid recovery; however, certain forms of cardiac surgery, such as valvular heart surgery or very complicated forms of CABG, are not possible with this new technique.

Valvular heart surgery

When any of the four cardiac valves become so damaged that it cannot function properly, the damaged valve needs to be replaced with a *prosthetic* valve. This may either be a *mechanical valve* or a valve that has been specially cultured from a pig called a *porcine valve*. Each of these different valves has particular advantages and disadvantages. Surgeons will always discuss with patients the pros and cons of each type of valve. As in coronary artery bypass surgery, valve repair requires open heart surgery and the use of a heart-lung machine.

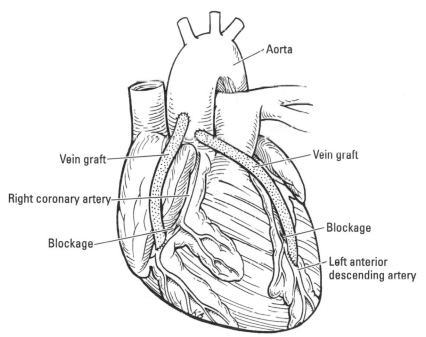

Aorta

Vein graft

Vein graft

Right coronary artery

Blockage

Blockage

Left anterior descending artery

Figure 13-3:
Heart bypass with two grafts.

Other forms of cardiac surgery

Cardiac surgeons also perform operations on other aspects of the heart and also on any other structure in the chest; thus, these surgeons may remove cardiac tumors, repair congenital heart disease, or perform various pieces of surgery on the lungs.

Monitoring heart performance and pressure in hospital

The heart function of almost every patient in the coronary care unit (CCU) with a medical heart problem or after heart surgery receives constant monitoring. Here are some of the procedures that monitor heart performance and pressure.

- ✔ **Arterial catheterization.** A small tube (catheter) is placed into a branch of the arterial system to monitor very accurately both the blood pressure and the level of oxygenation in the arterial circulation. While such *arterial catheters* (also called *arterial lines* or *A lines*) may be put in any artery, the most common is the artery on the thumb side of the wrist.

- ✔ **Central venous catheterization.** Often, in order to deliver potent medications, it is necessary to have access to the deep venous system. This venous system may be entered either through the neck, the groin, or the arm. Then a long catheter is threaded up near the right side of the heart so that medications can be delivered efficiently and pressures within the venous system can be accurately measured. This procedure of measuring the *central venous pressure* (also called *CVP*) happens frequently in the coronary care unit.

- ✔ **Pulmonary artery catheterization.** The pulmonary artery is the main vessel leading out from the right ventricle that carries deoxygenated blood to the lungs where it is reoxygenated. Often the pressures in pulmonary arterial circulation are extremely useful in helping to determine therapies for the patient. Thus, a thin catheter is often inserted into a vein and threaded into the right atrium, through the right ventricle, and out into the pulmonary artery. This allows accurate pressure measurements in both the right and left side of the heart. (Refer to Figure 13-1.)

Chapter 14

Coronary Artery Disease, Angina, and Unstable Angina

Coronary artery disease. Over 12 million people alive today in the United States suffer from some form of it. Every 29 seconds, an American will suffer a complication of CAD; every minute, another will die from it. It's the most significant chronic condition and the leading cause of death for all segments of our society.

But Americans have been fighting back. Over the last decade, the death rate from coronary artery disease has declined over 25 percent. We can make this number decline even further if we understand how coronary disease develops and what we can do to prevent and to control it in order to get the most out of life.

If you or a loved one has been diagnosed with coronary artery disease or if you simply want to work on prevention, empowerment starts with learning the facts about coronary artery disease, its manifestations of angina and unstable angina, and how to work with your physician to make best use of the many treatments available.

What Is Coronary Artery Disease?

Coronary artery disease (also known as *CAD, coronary heart disease [CHD], coronary atherosclerosis,* or *coronary arteriosclerosis*) is the slow, progressive narrowing of the three main arteries (and their branches) that supply the heart. This narrowing of the arteries gradually starves the heart muscle of the high level of oxygenated blood it needs to function properly. Lack of adequate blood supply to the heart typically produces symptoms that range from angina and unstable angina to heart attack or sudden death.

A blood cell's view of the causes and progression of CAD

Imagine your blood as the river of life coursing through your body, reaching every last cell. This stream delivers the oxygen-rich red blood cells, disease-fighting white blood cells, and all other necessary substances to every body cell and carries away waste matter. Among these substances in the blood are various fats, or lipids, including those nefarious fellows — LDL cholesterol. As I describe in Chapter 10, when too many of these fatty foes swim along in your bloodstream, they deposit themselves as fatty plaque on artery walls. These plaques keep growing and often become *calcified* (hardened). The clotting elements of the blood, such as platelets, also get into the act making those plaque deposits (sometimes called *lesions*) bigger and narrowing the arteries further.

This is not good for any artery and the organs or tissues it serves, but it's really bad for your heart. Every second of your life, your heart willingly works hard to meet every demand. To do this, the heart depends totally upon a high level of oxygenated blood flow through its three main coronary arteries (as I discuss in Chapter 2). As these fatty plaques become progressively more severe, no matter how hard those good red blood cells fight to get oxygen to your heart, enough of them can't get through the narrowed channels. Such progressively diminishing blood flow tends to trigger increasingly severe symptoms of coronary artery disease. Figure 14-1 illustrates the progressive development of CAD.

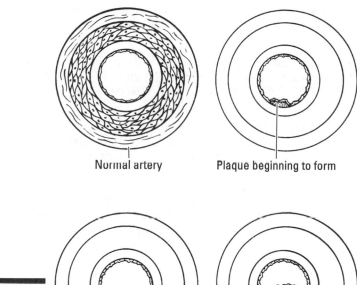

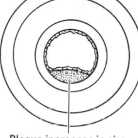

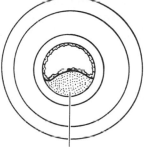

Normal artery   Plaque beginning to form

Figure 14-1:
The process
of coronary
artery
disease.

Plaque increases in size   Large plaque has formed

What are the symptoms, or manifestations, of CAD?

Because every person is an individual, physical responses to progressive coronary artery disease vary. Not every individual with CAD has every manifestation and symptom of the condition. Plus individuals experience specific symptoms in different ways. But these manifestations are typical:

- **Nothing.** Many people can have significant CAD but experience no discomfort or other sign of the disease. That's why in medicine, this condition is called *silent ischemia*. (*Ischemia* means "lack of blood flow.") People with diabetes are particularly susceptible to silent ischemia, but others can have it, too.

- **Angina.** More formally known as *angina pectoris*, angina is typified by temporary chest pain usually during exertion. It may have other manifestations as well.

🖊 **Unstable angina.** Chest pain that is new, occurs when you're at rest, or suddenly grows more severe is called *unstable angina*. It's a medical emergency.

🖊 **Heart attack.** When blood flow to a coronary artery is cut off completely it causes an acute heart attack, or myocardial infarction, the most severe result of CAD. The closure can be gradual or result from a clot. (See also Chapter 15.)

🖊 **Sudden death.** Although the cause of sudden death from CAD is often ventricular tachycardia or ventricular fibrillation in the setting of an acute heart attack, I have listed it separately to make the point that the first indication or symptom for many people that they have CAD is a fatal heart attack. How many people? It's hard to say exactly, but there are 250,000 sudden cardiac deaths each year, and the American Heart Association indicates that about half of all deaths caused by coronary artery disease are sudden and unexpected. Many of these deaths happen to younger people in their fifties, forties, or younger.

What Is Angina?

When coronary artery disease progresses enough to significantly diminish the blood flow to the heart tissue it produces *angina pectoris*, commonly called *angina*. Angina is typically a discomfort felt in the chest, typically beneath the breast bone (or sternum) or in nearby areas such as the neck, jaw, back, or arms.

🖊 Individuals often describe the chest discomfort as a "squeezing sensa-tion," "vice-like," or "constricting," or " a heavy pressure on the chest." (In fact, our term *angina* comes from a Greek word that means "strangling" — a strangling pain.)

🖊 Angina is often brought on by physical exertion or strong emotions and is typically relieved within several minutes by resting or using nitroglycerin.

🖊 Some individuals may experience angina as a different symptom than chest discomfort (or in addition to it). Shortness of breath, faintness, or fatigue may also be manifestations of angina, although if chest pain is absent they may be called *anginal equivalents*.

🖊 When chest pain occurs at rest, it is usually classified as *unstable angina*.

And just how do you pronounce the word? Some people say *an-ji'-nuh* and others say *an'-juh-nuh*. Either is correct. Some cardiologists may be a little snobby about their preference (who, us?), but pay them no mind.

What causes angina?

You know how your muscles begin to scream when you run faster than your blood can carry adequate oxygen to them. The same thing may happen when the coronary arteries become so narrowed that the oxygen supplied to the heart muscle by the blood can't meet the demands of the heart. The temporary chest discomfort called *angina* is your heart's way of getting your attention. It occurs when you ask your heart to work harder and it demands more blood — for instance, when you are walking briskly or running, climbing a hill or stairs, having sex, or doing house or yard work. Strong emotions such as fear or anger can also trigger an episode.

Does angina damage the heart?

Angina does not usually damage the heart. Angina is a temporary condition — the usual episode lasts only 5 to 10 minutes. The chest discomfort makes you stop and rest, slowing the heart and lessening its demand for blood. Alternatively, most people with angina know to take a nitroglycerin tablet under the tongue when they have an angina attack. The nitroglycerin dilates the coronary arteries allowing increased blood flow to the heart.

Any discomfort that lasts longer or does not stop with rest may be a heart attack and should be treated as an emergency.

How is angina diagnosed?

The individual's own description of the discomfort he or she experiences provides the most important information leading to the diagnosis of angina. However, a number of tests are also used. (See also Chapter 13.) Some of these can be conducted in your physician's office, and some require the resources of a hospital.

- **Electrocardiogram (ECG or EKG).** The tracings of an ECG taken during an episode of chest pain can show a number of characteristic changes that can help a physician make the diagnosis of angina.

- **Exercise Tolerance Testing (Exercise Stress Test).** The tracings of an ECG taken continuously as an individual exercises at increasing levels of exertion and as his/her heart rate increases can show changes that provide evidence of coronary artery disease and angina.

✔ **Thallium Stress Testing.** In some instances, either for individuals who are not able to exercise or for those whose initial exercise tolerance test is equivocal, a thallium stress test may be required. Radioactive material (thallium) is injected through a vein and special cameras take pictures of the heart to assess the adequacy of blood flow.

✔ **Stress Echocardiogram.** An echocardiogram taken at rest and then during exercise can provide evidence of inadequate blood flow to the heart by showing images of the normal or abnormal motion of the heart muscle as it contracts.

✔ **Cardiac Catheterization**. Cardiac catheterization, also called *cath* (slang) or *angiography*, is often used to make the final diagnosis of coronary artery disease when other tests have suggested that CAD is present. By injecting contrast material into the coronary arteries to take actual pictures of the arteries, cardiac catheterization provides direct evidence of whether narrowings are present and also provides the physician with a "road map" that helps guide patient and physician in determining the next steps in the treatment of coronary artery disease if it is present.

Are there other types of angina?

Although the most common form of angina results from the slow, progressive narrowing of the coronary arteries from coronary artery disease, two other rare forms of angina may also occur:

✔ **Variant angina,** or *Prinzmetal's angina* (named after the cardiologist who first described this condition), occurs when the coronary arteries actually spasm, or contract suddenly. While this may occur in a normal coronary artery, spasm is most likely to occur where there is already fatty plaque present. Treatment for this condition is similar to that for the more common form of angina, although a greater emphasis may be placed on medicines that decrease spasm (for example, calcium channel blockers).

✔ **Microvascular angina,** recently discovered, results from narrowing of tiny vessels in the heart while the major coronary arteries remain largely free of plaque. It is usually treated medically with common angina medications.

Are there other causes of chest pain?

All chest pain is not angina and does not involve the heart. Various conditions involving other structures in the chest can occasionally cause chest discomfort:

- Spasm of the esophagus
- Reflux of acid from the stomach
- Hiatal hernia
- Inflammation of the bones or cartilage of the chest wall or sternum
- Muscular pain from muscles of the chest wall, back, shoulders, or arms

In many of these instances, the characteristics of the pain will distinguish it from angina. Pain is typically not coming from the heart if it is

- Extremely short in duration (lasting less than 10 seconds)
- Feels like it is on the surface of the chest wall rather than deep inside or is sharp, stabbing pain
- Is not associated with exertion

When is chest pain an emergency?

People with coronary artery disease and angina typically live with this problem for many years and learn how to manage it effectively with appropriate medicines and advice from their physicians. When angina pain changes in character, however, it can signal unstable angina or even heart attack. If you experience any of the following characteristics of chest discomfort, *you should call 911 and be taken to a hospital immediately.*

- Pain or discomfort that is worse than you have ever experienced before

- Pain or discomfort that is not relieved by three nitroglycerin tablets in succession, each taken five minutes apart

- Pain or discomfort that is accompanied by fainting or lightheadedness, nausea, and/or cool clammy skin

- Pain or discomfort lasting longer than 20 minutes or that is very bad or worse than you have experienced before

If any of these symptoms occur, you should call an ambulance and be taken immediately to a hospital. Under no circumstances should you drive yourself to the hospital. (See also Chapter 15.)

How is angina treated?

Typically, people who have angina can live comfortably for many years with this condition by learning to manage the symptom and lower their risk factors for complications.

All patients with angina and underlying coronary artery disease should be treated with risk-factor reduction and lifestyle modification to decrease the likelihood of complications from progressive narrowing of the coronary arteries. In addition, medication or surgery may be used as appropriate.

Risk factor reduction

No matter what other strategies your doctor employs, risk-factor reduction will play a critical role in the management of symptoms of angina and the underlying coronary artery disease. If you are reading this book from cover to cover, the critical factors should be a familiar litany by now:

- ✔ Controlling high blood pressure
- ✔ Managing your cholesterol through improved nutrition and, in some instances, medication
- ✔ Managing your weight, if you are overweight
- ✔ Increasing the amount of physical activity in your life
- ✔ Ceasing smoking, if you currently smoke

These factors, which are important for an overall heart-healthy lifestyle, are discussed fully in Parts II and III of this book.

Lifestyle modifications

Developing angina can be a big blow emotionally. So big that patients often adopt an unrealistically gloomy perception of their prognosis. Actually, there's a lot you can do to adapt. Start with an open, frank discussion with your physician about how to use the following lifestyle modifications:

- ✔ Adjusting your approach to physical activity, leisure time pursuits, vacation plans, eating habits, and other practices can help control and even reduce the symptom of angina.
- ✔ Modifying strenuous activities that consistently and repeatedly produce angina can often be done by simple measures such as slowing your walking pace, strolling (not sprinting) to the car through the rain, vacuuming or raking more slowly, and so on.
- ✔ Avoiding strenuous activities that require heavy lifting, such as snow shoveling, unless you discuss it with your physician, is desirable.

✔ Adding slowly progressive exercise training, under your physician's supervision, can dramatically increase your ability to carry out enjoyable activities of daily living.

✔ Considering with your physician other interventions such as medication or surgery if/when your angina causes unacceptably severe modifications of your lifestyle can help. Quality of life is important!

Medical management

In conjunction with reducing risk factors and modifying certain activities, a variety of medicines can control the symptoms of angina. The medical management of angina is typically designed *to diminish the demand for blood flow* to the heart. The common medications include nitrates, particularly nitroglycerin; beta blockers; aspirin; and calcium antagonists.

Because all these medications are also used in the treatment of unstable angina, I discuss each class of medications in detail in the next section on unstable angina.

Angioplasty and bypass surgery

Borrowing a concept from economics, the treatment of both angina and unstable angina can be explained by the laws of supply and demand. Where medical management typically seeks to lower the heart's *demand* for blood flow, angioplasty and bypass surgery are designed to *increase the **supply** of blood flow* to the heart.

✔ In angioplasty, a balloon advanced by a catheter into the narrowed coronary artery is inflated to help open the artery.

✔ In bypass surgery, a vein or artery from another part of the body is surgically grafted to a coronary artery to literally "bypass" a narrowing and restore blood flow.

For more information regarding these procedures, please see Chapter 13.

What Is Unstable Angina?

Unstable angina, while it typically results from underlying coronary artery disease and is often related to angina, represents a very significant turn for the worse. It is usually a medical emergency.

As the name suggests, *unstable* angina results when angina gets out of control. In unstable angina, the lack of blood flow and oxygen to the heart becomes acute and, therefore, very dangerous because the risk of complications such as heart attack is much greater.

Where stable angina has typical characteristics and predictable triggers such as exertion or strong emotion, unstable angina is characterized by one or more of the following symptoms:

- ✔ Anginal discomfort at rest or awakening from sleep
- ✔ A significant change in pattern of the angina where it occurs with less exertion or is more severe than before
- ✔ A significant increase in the severity or frequency of angina
- ✔ New onset, or first experience, of anginal chest pain

If you have any one of these characteristics, you must seek immediate medical attention.

What causes unstable angina?

The basic underlying coronary artery disease that causes angina also causes unstable angina. However, several additional elements also appear to contribute to turning angina into unstable angina.

- ✔ The plaque narrowing a coronary artery can crack open or rupture. When the body tries to heal the crack by forming a blood clot, this sudden narrowing can trigger a change from angina to unstable angina. If the clot blocks the artery entirely, a heart attack ensues. This process is depicted in Figure 14-2.
- ✔ In addition to the mechanical narrowing from the clot, substances released from the platelets may trigger the coronary artery to go into spasm causing further narrowing and complications of the blockage and resulting in unstable angina.

How is unstable angina treated?

If you have any of the symptoms described for unstable angina, you must be evaluated at the hospital.

If you have known coronary artery disease, your previous experience should be your guide as to whether you have experienced a sudden worsening of your symptoms. You should call your physician if there is any change in the circumstances related to your chest discomfort, the pattern of the chest discomfort, or the severity of the symptom.

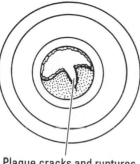
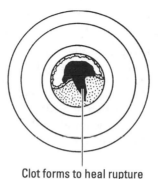

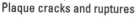

Figure 14-2: When the plaque narrowing a coronary artery cracks open or ruptures, a clot forms, which can block the artery entirely, causing a heart attack.

Plaque cracks and ruptures

Clot forms to heal rupture

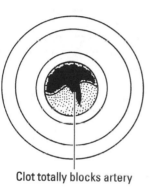

Clot totally blocks artery

How is unstable angina treated in the emergency room?

Because, in its early manifestations, unstable angina may be very difficult to distinguish from an acute heart attack, the procedures for treating both are very similar in the emergency room. (See Chapter 15 on heart attacks.)

- ✔ After you arrive at the hospital emergency room, the physicians and nurses will evaluate you for signs of unstable angina.

- ✔ If a diagnosis of unstable angina seems probable, a number of medications may be administered to prevent blood clots from forming in the coronary arteries, to increase the oxygen supply to your heart, and to relieve pressure on the heart.

- ✔ It is very important that you communicate with the physicians in the emergency room to let them know whether or not your chest discomfort has been relieved.

✔ Your physician will also take an electrocardiogram to help to determine whether or not your heart is receiving adequate blood flow.

✔ Based on your past medical history, the nature of your chest discomfort, the electrocardiogram, and in some instances blood tests, a decision will be made in the emergency room about whether or not to keep you in the hospital. Even if your chest discomfort has gone away, if your history is strongly suggestive of unstable angina, it is imperative that you be admitted to the hospital so that therapy is readily available and, if further chest discomfort occurs, medical staff can administer such procedures as an electrocardiogram taken during an episode of chest discomfort to secure the diagnosis of unstable angina.

✔ If you are discharged home, your personal physician will typically follow up in a day or two to evaluate you and perhaps order additional tests. It is important to note that if you are discharged to home and your pain recurs, it is imperative that you call the ambulance and return to the hospital. Don't be embarrassed or worried that you're being a "bother."

Because angina can be difficult to diagnose in many instances, it may take your physicians or the emergency room physicians several visits to be certain whether or not you have angina, and if so, whether it is stable or unstable.

Tests for unstable angina

In addition to the ECG, the tests helpful both in the diagnosis and in the eventual treatment of unstable angina are the same as those discussed for angina: exercise tolerance test, stress echocardiogram, nuclear stress test, and cardiac catheterization.

How is unstable angina treated?

If tests reveal that you have narrowing of one, two, or three of the coronary arteries, your physician will develop a plan for how best to treat your unstable angina. This plan may include the use of medicines, angioplasty (PTCA), or coronary artery bypass surgery (CABG).

Medical therapy

A variety of medications that decrease the work of the heart or decrease the propensity of the blood to clot at the sites of fatty plaques may be used to treat both stable and unstable angina. These are the most common:

✔ **Nitrates.** Nitrates, particularly nitroglycerin, are very valuable mainstays for treatment of both angina and unstable angina. They relieve pressure on the heart and may also increase blood flow to the heart by causing the coronary arteries to dilate. Nitroglycerin often relieves discomfort very quickly. Nitroglycerin/nitrates may come in the form of tablets or sprays that you put under the tongue, a pill that you take by mouth, a cream that you apply to your skin, or a patch that you wear on your skin.

✔ **Beta blockers.** These medications, another mainstay of treatment, decrease how hard the heart must work by lowering blood pressure and decreasing heart rate. In about 10 percent of individuals, side effects such as tiredness, dizziness, or depression may occur.

✔ **Calcium antagonists.** This class of medicines block calcium flow into the muscle cells of arteries and allow the arteries to dilate. (These medicines are also called *calcium channel blockers.*) These medications are typically less effective than nitrates and beta blockers in angina treatment, although they may be used in conjunction with nitrates and beta blockers. They are particularly useful if any significant degree of spasm of the coronary arteries is present.

✔ **Aspirin.** That's right, good old aspirin. Many people know that aspirin can relieve a minor pain or fever. However, aspirin is also important in treating angina and unstable angina because it helps prevent platelets from sticking to the walls of vessels and contributing to the blood clot that can narrow or block off a coronary artery. Aspirin should be part of therapy for individuals with known or suspected coronary artery disease, who have not experienced any problems with bleeding.

✔ **Platelet receptor inhibitors.** This new category of drugs can enhance aspirin therapy by blocking the ability of platelets to stick to each other. These medicines, which are typically delivered by vein in the hospital, may further help in the acute setting of unstable angina. Forms of these drugs that can be taken by mouth are currently being researched.

Angioplasty

An alternative to medical therapy, which may be more appropriate to some patients with unstable angina, is called *angioplasty,* or *PTCA (percutaneous transluminal coronary angioplasty).* This procedure uses the technique of heart catheterization. (See also Chapter 13.) In angioplasty, a catheter is inserted into an artery that is narrowed. Near the tip of this catheter is a small balloon that is inflated by a physician when the catheter reaches the blockage. When the balloon is subsequently deflated, the blockage is often dilated enough for more blood to pass through and decrease anginal discomfort. A stent may also be inserted to keep the artery open.

Coronary artery bypass surgery

When there is severe blockage of multiple coronary arteries or severe blockage of the main branch of the left coronary artery, *coronary artery bypass surgery* (also called *coronary artery bypass grafting* or in medical slang, *CABG*) may be recommended as the most effective therapy. Surgery is also recommended when medical therapy and angioplasty do not control the symptoms of angina. During coronary artery bypass surgery, a piece of vein from the leg or an artery from the chest is used to "bypass" areas of blockage of the coronary arteries. (See also Chapter 13.)

Fighting the Good Fight

While coronary artery disease and angina represent a significant health challenge to anyone diagnosed with them, there is no reason to surrender. A patient I'll call Mark sure didn't.

A driven, successful vice president of sales, Mark pushed himself hard — long days, snatched meals and snacks, lots of smokes, no activity. At 48, he had a sudden heart attack. When he came to my office three weeks later, he was still badly shaken but also felt lucky to be alive. What could he do to turn his life around? Could he continue to prosper in his work without killing himself? As we worked together on a plan, he made a commitment to change. He quit smoking — hard, but he did it. He cut excessive fat and calories out of his diet — at first because he had to, then because he liked what he was eating and how he felt and looked. He started a walking program and worked up to jogging. He was such a changed man that a number of his salesmen began to tease him about his newfound commitment to health and fitness. One called him a narcissist. "That made me mad," said Mark, "but then I thought, whoa. What's so bad about that? When I think about my life before, I remind myself of my dad — he dropped dead at 45 of a massive heart attack. So what's wrong with putting my health first? That way I'll be around to take care of my family, to excel in my work, and to enjoy my life!"

Working in an effective partnership with your physician, you too can combat, control, and tame this chronic condition.

Chapter 15

Heart Attack!

The very thought of a heart attack scares most people. With good reason. Each year in the United States alone, nearly 1.5 million individuals suffer an acute heart attack — about one individual every 20 seconds. Of these, one third die. And about one half of these deaths occur within one hour of the event and are usually a result of cardiac rhythm problems associated with the heart attack.

The problem of heart attack is all the more tragic because it often strikes individuals in their peak productive years. About 45 percent of heart attacks occur in individuals under the age of 65. Furthermore, of those Americans who die of coronary artery disease, the underlying condition that causes heart attacks, 29 percent of the women and 37 percent of the men are under the age of 55.

In an otherwise grim picture, however, there is cause for some hope. The death rate from heart attacks has decreased about 30 percent over the last decade and recent studies have shown that heart attacks are being diagnosed earlier and treated more effectively than ever before. And we can do even better.

In this chapter, I show you how to fight back against heart attacks, starting with educating yourself.

What Is a Heart Attack?

A heart attack, known medically as a *myocardial infarction (MI)*, occurs when one of the three coronary arteries that supply oxygen-rich blood to the heart muscle (myocardium) becomes severely or totally blocked, usually from a blood clot. When the heart muscle does not receive oxygenated blood, it begins to die. The severity of the heart attack depends on how much of the heart is injured or dies during the heart attack.

That is why it is so critical, if you think you are having a heart attack, to get immediately to a hospital where therapy can be instituted. New clot busting medicines can often dissolve a clot that caused the heart attack, open the blood vessel, and save some or all of the heart muscle at risk. While some of the heart muscle usually dies during a heart attack, the remaining heart muscle continues to function and can often compensate, to a very large degree, for the heart muscle that has died.

What complications are associated with heart attacks?

Damage to the heart caused by a heart attack can result in a number of complications, depending on the location and severity of the damage:

- Irregular heartbeats (also called *arrhythmia)*
- Damage to the heart valves or the structures that support the heart valves
- Heart failure resulting from an inability of the weakened muscle to pump enough blood to the rest of the body
- Rupture in the heart — a catastrophic complication

All these problems associated with heart attack can be diminished if the individual who is suffering the heart attack receives prompt medical therapy. I discuss them in detail later in the chapter.

Are a heart attack and sudden cardiac arrest the same thing?

Although we often call sudden cardiac arrest "a massive heart attack," they are not technically the same thing. A heart attack (myocardial infarction) results from a blockage of the coronary arteries. *Sudden cardiac arrest* is caused by ventricular fibrillation, the electrical malfunction in which the heart begins to quiver rapidly, rather than contracting and pumping blood regularly. Cardiac arrest strikes without warning. Because blood flow essentially stops, its victim loses consciousness and dies within minutes unless emergency help is available.

Many but not all victims of sudden cardiac arrest have underlying coronary artery disease. Sudden cardiac arrest often occurs in the setting of an acute heart attack, but not always. It can also occur from electrical malfunction when a heart attack is not involved.

What Causes a Heart Attack?

Almost always, heart attack is caused when a blood clot forms in the site of an already existing fatty plaque, which has narrowed the coronary artery. Thus, individuals who have a history of coronary artery disease, who have experienced previous angina (see also Chapter 14), or have had a previous heart attack are at much higher risk for heart attack than individuals who do not have this history.

✔ The blockage that triggers the heart attack is usually caused by an acute blood clot. Most acute blood clots occur when one of the plaques or fatty deposits on the artery walls cracks or ruptures, causing the sticky, blood clotting elements (platelets and other substances) in the blood to stick to the plaque and form an acute blood clot, cutting off blood flow in the coronary artery.

✔ Other, much more rare causes of acute blockage of an artery supplying the heart, include:

- Inflammation of the artery

- Spasm

- Certain blood clotting abnormalities

- Severe spasm, acute blood clot, or other problem caused by cocaine use

What Are the Symptoms of a Heart Attack?

Different people may experience the symptoms of a heart attack in different ways. However, the typical symptoms include some or all of the following:

✔ A heavy chest pain or tightness, usually experienced in the front of the chest, beneath the sternum and often radiating to the left arm, left shoulder, or jaw

- Shortness of breath
- Nausea
- Sweating
- Clamminess, cool skin, pallor
- A feeling of general weakness or tiredness

In an individual who has underlying angina, the symptoms may be particularly difficult to differentiate from the chest discomfort of angina. (See Chapter 14.) However, when a heart attack is occurring, chest discomfort is usually more severe and may occur at rest or with less activity than usual.

The signs of a heart attack may often be subtle. This is particularly true in individuals who have diabetes who may not have the classic symptoms of chest, shoulder, or arm discomfort.

About two-thirds of individuals who experience an acute heart attack have had some warning symptoms in the weeks or days preceding the acute event. Often they realize this after the event — hindsight. Work on your foresight — know and take the warning signs of heart attack seriously. (See the nearby sidebar, "Heart attack warning signs? Call 911!")

Timing Is Everything

Unfortunately, many people who are experiencing a heart attack either don't recognize symptoms or deny them. Don't let this happen to you; it can be deadly.

Heart attack warning signs? Call 911!

Coronary artery disease is extremely common in both men and women in the United States, particularly in individuals who are in their forties and beyond. Even you've never had a single sign of trouble, call 911 and go straight to the hospital for prompt evaluation if you have any of these warning signs as described by the American Heart Association. (Do not take a meeting, do not put it off for an hour, just *go!*)

- Uncomfortable pressure, fullness, squeezing, or pain in the center of the chest lasting more than a few minutes
- Pain spreading to the shoulders, neck, or arms
- Chest discomfort with lightheadedness, fainting, sweating, nausea, or shortness of breath

✔ About one half of all heart attack victims delay two hours or longer before deciding to get help. This can be a serious or even fatal mistake.

✔ Delay, in the early phases of a heart attack, significantly increases the risk of sudden death from rhythm problems.

✔ Delay also increases the likelihood that a significant amount of heart muscle will die, thus raising the increase of disability, even if the individual survives.

Timing is everything! If you or a loved one experiences any symptoms or warning signs of a heart attack, use the survival plan outlined in the next section and go immediately to a medical facility. Don't delay!

What to Do If You Think You Are Having a Heart Attack

The following six-point survival plan, adapted from recommendations from the American Medical Association, can save your life. Take these steps if you or a loved one is experiencing the symptoms of a possible heart attack:

1. **Stop what you are doing, and sit or lie down.**

2. **If symptoms persist for more than two minutes, call your local emergency number or 911 and say that you may be having a heart attack. *Leave the phone off the hook* so that medical personnel can locate your address in the event that you become unconscious.**

3. **Take nitroglycerin if possible. If you have nitroglycerin tablets, take up to three pills under your tongue, one at a time, every five minutes, if your chest pain persists. If you don't have nitroglycerin, take two aspirin.**

4. **Do not drive yourself (or a loved one) to the hospital if you think you are having a heart attack. Ambulances have equipment and personnel who are trained to deal with individuals who are having a heart attack. Driving yourself or a loved one to the hospital is an invitation for a disaster.**

5. **If the person's pulse or breathing stops, any individual trained in cardiopulmonary resuscitation (CPR) should immediately begin to administer it. Call 911 immediately, but do not delay instituting CPR.**

6. **When you arrive at the emergency room at the hospital, announce clearly that you (or your loved one) may be having a heart attack and that you must be seen immediately. Do not be shy about this.**

Deadly excuses for delay

You've probably heard that getting treatment during the first "golden hour" after an accident gives trauma victims the best chance of survival and full recovery. The same is true of victims of those biological accidents — heart attacks. Using any of these common excuses for delay can be deadly:

✔ **How embarrassing if it's just heartburn.** And what if it's not? Don't let a little embarrassment cost your life or health.

✔ **I'm not sure if my pain fits the warning signs.** The symptoms of heart attack vary from individual and can be very vague. Let the physicians decide. It's our job and we want to do it for you.

✔ **I'm too young to have a heart attack.** Heart attacks can and do happen at any age.

✔ **The pain's not that bad; I'll wait awhile and see if it goes away.** Don't. Delay significantly increases your risk of disabling damage and death.

✔ **Only men get heart attacks.** Absolutely not. Women also suffer heart attacks and their survival rate is not as good, in part because they delay getting medical attention.

✔ **I'm healthy as a horse — I can't be having a heart attack.** Denial won't stop a heart attack. For many victims, particularly younger people, heart attacks happen suddenly without any noticeable warning signs.

What Medical Treatment Occurs in the Emergency Room?

Modern emergency rooms have medical teams as well as equipment to take immediate steps to determine whether or not you are having an acute heart attack and, if so, to immediately start therapy that can reduce the severity of the heart attack and may save your life.

When you arrive at the emergency room, a team of doctors and nurses take care of you immediately.

✔ They will ask you questions about the nature of your symptoms while they are placing electrodes on your chest, arms, and legs so that they can perform an electrocardiogram (ECG).

✔ If the ECG shows the characteristic patterns associated with acute heart attack, the medical team performs certain procedures immediately, such as administering clot busting medicines to attempt to alleviate the blockage of the artery that is causing the heart attack.

✔ While this is going on, the physician conducts a brief history to determine exactly the symptoms that you either have experienced or are currently experiencing, the duration of these symptoms, severity of these symptoms, past medical history, and so on.

✔ This is followed in a rapid fashion by a brief physical examination that focuses on the heart and lungs.

✔ Almost simultaneously, blood is drawn and sent to the laboratory to look for the presence of chemical markers that indicate damage to the heart.

✔ An intravenous line is inserted into a vein of the arm to enable prompt and efficient administration of medicines.

✔ If the heart is experiencing abnormal rhythm patterns, the physician may need to use electric current through a defibrillator to restore a normal heart rhythm.

✔ Medical staff will continue to ask you about chest discomfort that you may be experiencing. Always answer as accurately as you can. (This is no time for silent bravery!)

✔ Medicines to diminish this discomfort and to start treatment are typically administered, such as aspirin (to decrease the clotting ability of platelets) and beta blockers (to slow the heart rate and lower the blood pressure). Both of these medications have been shown to decrease the complications of acute heart attack. Treatment with *thrombolytic therapy* (thrombus = clot, lyse = break up) is also started with intravenous clot busting medicines.

All of these procedures take place in rapid fashion, but will be conducted calmly by the trained professionals who are caring for you and reassuring you. Their goal is to create a calm atmosphere to diminish your anxiety.

What Medical Treatment Occurs When You Are Admitted to the Hospital?

If the initial evaluation in the emergency room either confirms the diagnosis of acute heart attack or raises a strong suspicion, you will be admitted to the hospital or observed for 24 hours in the emergency department's *Chest Pain Unit*.

In the hospital, you will be admitted to a specialized unit within the hospital called a *Coronary Care Unit (CCU)*. These Coronary Care Units have specialized equipment and specially trained staff who are able to continue your treatment and to diagnose and quickly treat any complications that may occur from the acute heart attack. Your treatment typically will contain a number of elements.

✔ Continuing medical treatment to stabilize your condition, limit damage, and prevent complications.

✔ Continuous monitoring for potential complications such as heart rhythm problems, fall in blood pressure, heart valve problems, or any other continuing chest pain or other symptom.

✔ Additional testing to confirm or rule out the diagnosis of acute heart attack and to determine the location and extent of the blockage.

✔ Depending on the outcome of the tests, further procedures such as angioplasty or coronary artery bypass surgery may be performed to restore or maximize blood flow to the heart muscle and minimize the amount of muscle that is damaged or dies.

Typical medical treatments used in the CCU

Any or all of the following treatment measures are often used to treat the early stages of a heart attack:

Prevention of additional blood clots

In persons who have just had a heart attack, additional blood clots are a dangerous possibility. These medications can help prevent this happening:

✔ **Aspirin**, as I mentioned earlier, is used to decrease the "stickiness" of platelets and thus lessen their ability to continue to build blood clots within the coronary arteries.

✔ **Anticoagulants**, or blood thinners, also protect against the tendency of additional blood clots forming either in the coronary arteries or within one of the heart's chambers near the damaged area of muscle.

✔ **Platelet receptor inhibitors**, new medicines that act in conjunction with aspirin to further reduce platelets sticking together, may also be given.

Control of cardiac pain

Pain management is important in treating an acute heart attack because cardiac pain is a marker for continued damage to the fragile cells of the heart muscle. Pain management is typically accomplished with a combination of medicines such as pain relievers, nitrates, and beta blockers.

✔ **Pain relievers**, also called _analgesics,_ can be used during the acute phase of a heart attack. Morphine is probably the most commonly used.

✔ **Nitrates**, such as nitroglycerin, increase blood flow through the coronary arteries and decrease the work of the heart.

- **Beta blockers** decrease pressure on the heart and slow the heart rate, both of which decrease the demand from the heart muscle for oxygen.

- **Oxygen** improves the supply of oxygenated blood to the heart muscle. This is typically delivered through a oxygen mask or through an oxygen tube that is placed in the nose.

Typical tests given in the CCU

While continuous monitoring is ongoing and medications are being given to decrease pain and limit the size of the heart attack, additional tests will be conducted in the CCU. These may include the following:

- **Electrocardiograms (ECG)** are typically taken at least every eight hours in the CCU to look for evidence of the extent of the heart attack and also to provide an early warning for some of the potential complications of a heart attack. You will also have continuous ECG monitoring to assess the electrical activity of the heart.

- **Physical examinations** are usually performed at least every six hours in the CCU to check for complications of the heart attack and also assess your lungs to see if any fluid buildup has occurred, which can decrease the oxygen supply to the heart and further complicate the heart attack.

- **Echocardiograms**, ultrasound tests, are performed in some patients to assess how well their heart is working and also look for any complications of a heart attack that may have occurred.

- **Coronary angiography**, or **heart catheterization**, is often conducted within the first two or three days following an acute heart attack. This procedure helps assess the degree of narrowing in the coronary arteries and the effectiveness of the clot busting medicine, if this has been administered. Heart catheterization helps to determine whether or not other acute interventions will be necessary to maintain blood flow to the vessel that had been acutely clotted off and opened up temporarily through the clot busting medicine.

Other procedures that may be needed

Depending upon the severity of the narrowing of the coronary arteries, not just in the area affected by the heart attack but throughout the coronary arterial system, your physicians may recommend angioplasty or bypass surgery to help maintain or restore adequate blood flow to the heart for the longer term.

What Are the Possible Complications of a Heart Attack?

One of the key reasons to seek medical therapy as early as possible for an acute heart attack is to decrease possible complications such as the following.

✔ **Recurrent chest pain:** Recurrent or continued chest pain is one of the most dangerous aspects of an acute heart attack because, as noted earlier, it indicates inadequate blood flow to the heart and often further damage to the heart. If, once in the hospital, your chest pain continues or recurs it is very important to tell the healthcare workers so that they can take additional measures to alleviate chest pain and prevent further damage to the heart.

✔ **Arrythmias:** An acute heart attack often damages the electrical system of the heart, which controls the heart's normal rhythm. This can result in rhythm problems, also called *arrythmias* or *dysrhythmias*. When the electrical system goes entirely haywire it may result in a very dangerous condition called *ventricular tacchycardia* where an abnormal electrical impulse causes the heart to beat so very fast that it cannot pump out adequate blood. This condition can rapidly degenerate to *ventricular fibrillation*, where the heart simply quivers and produces no blood flow. Ventricular fibrillation must be immediately terminated by an electrical shock, *defibrillation*, delivered by a medical professional. (See Chapter 17 for more on rhythm disturbances.)

✔ **Heart failure:** When a heart attack damages the heart severely, either acute heart failure or *chronic heart failure* (also called *congestive heart failure*) can ensue. Where the normal heart pumps out with each beat 75 to 80 percent of the blood in the chamber, a heart damaged by a severe heart attack may pump only 15 to 20 percent, a condition that leads to heart failure. A number of medicines are available to treat both acute and chronic heart failure. (Chapter 18 discusses heart failure fully.)

✔ **Low blood pressure:** The reduced capacity of a heart damaged by an acute heart attack may result in low blood pressure, a condition called *hypotension*. In this setting, blood pressure can get dangerously low, preventing adequate blood flow to the coronary arteries, as well as to the rest of the body. Various medications and other interventions can be given in the hospital to reverse the problem.

✔ **Disruption of a cardiac valve:** The four heart valves that control blood flow in and out of the heart are operated by a series of muscles that may be damaged by an acute heart attack. When this happens, one or more valves may be unable to function normally. In this situation, torrential amounts of blood may flow back through a valve that normally would be closed. This condition, called *valvular regurgitation*, can cause a serious problem during an acute heart attack.

- **A rupture of the heart muscle:** When the part of the heart muscle that dies as a result of the heart attack is large or very weak, it is possible that this dead heart tissue can actually rupture or break open. This is a catastrophic complication. In many instances, the rupture is fatal. In other instances, a small hole in the heart can be repaired on an emergency basis by cardiac surgery.

- **Bleeding:** While the modern clot buster medicines have revolutionized the treatment of heart attacks and saved many lives, they do have one very serious side effect: The same mechanism that allows them to dissolve clots in the coronary arteries can cause acute bleeding episodes elsewhere in the body. In the CCU, the medical team is always on the lookout for any evidence of bleeding, which could cause serious problems such as a stroke.

How Long Will You Stay in the Hospital?

A typical stay in a Coronary Care Unit (CCU) will be two to three days for an uncomplicated heart attack. If the heart attack has been ruled out, a stay in the CCU may be only 24 hours. If complications occur, the stay in the CCU may be extended to four or five days or even longer.

Once you have been stabilized and the acute events surrounding your heart attack have been treated, you will enter what most hospitals call a "Step Down Unit." You will stay there for the next four to six days while you complete your recovery and begin your rehabilitation from the heart attack.

What to Expect During Recuperation

The rehabilitation process is started in the hospital and then takes place over the next few months after discharge from the hospital. The steps you take in the hospital include

- Changing over to medications that can be taken orally.

- Working with your physician and the trained cardiac rehabilitation specialists to assess and start treatment of risk factors for heart disease that may be present. (Yes, it's back to school for you.)

- Beginning a progressive increase in physical activity, starting with slow walking initially in your room, followed by walking in the hospital hallway.

Prior to discharge, many individuals may also undergo a low level exercise tolerance test on the treadmill to determine their degree of functional recovery as well as to guide the physicians in prescribing additional, necessary procedures.

Others may instead take a symptom-limited exercise tolerance test a few weeks later.

In addition to the physical and medical issues related to acute heart attack, almost every patient undergoes a spectrum of emotional responses to acute heart attack. These may vary from extreme anxiety during the actual event to depression and remorse following the heart attack. The good news is that the vast majority of individuals who survive a heart attack go on to lead long and productive lives. In fact, 88 percent of heart attack survivors under the age of 65 can return to work within three months. The entire process of cardiac rehabilitation is so important that I have devoted Chapter 16 to it.

Chapter 16

Cardiac Rehabilitation

· ·

· ·

*W*ould it surprise you that only 25 percent of individuals who could benefit from cardiac rehabilitation programs participate in them? What an enormous and tragic waste that 75 percent of eligible people miss the following benefits of cardiac rehabilitation programs:

- Improvement in exercise tolerance and ability to carry out activities of daily living.

- Improvement in symptoms such as angina or shortness of breath.

- Improvement in cholesterol and blood lipid levels.

- Reduction in cigarette smoking.

- Reduction of stress and improvement in sense of well-being.

- Reduction in mortality. For example, heart attack victims who participate in rehabilitation programs experience a 25 percent reduction in mortality during the three years after as compared to those who do not participate.

What Is Cardiac Rehabilitation?

Cardiac rehabilitation is a long-term program, with several therapeutic components, that is designed to help individuals get better after a variety of heart problems, angioplasty, or cardiac surgery.

Specific plans and components for a cardiac rehabilitation program are usually tailored for the specific conditions and needs of each patient, but all cardiac rehabilitation programs should contain at least these four areas:

- Education about your cardiac condition and treatment
- Exercise training and physical activity prescription
- Lifestyle modifications to reduce risk factors for heart disease
- Counseling and support

I look at each of these components in more detail in a moment.

What Are the Goals and Benefits of Cardiac Rehabilitation?

While individual prescriptions for cardiac rehabilitation may vary according to each individual and his or her condition, the goals and benefits always remain the same:

- Educate a person about how to control his or her cardiac condition
- Reduce disability and improve functional capacity, including the ability to carry out life's daily activities effectively and independently
- Decrease the likelihood of further problems from the cardiac condition, perhaps even decreasing the need for heart medicines
- Identify and provide ways to modify risk factors that may result in continued problems from various forms of heart disease
- Increase the likelihood that an individual will return to work and a full, happy, and long life following a cardiac event

Who should receive cardiac rehabilitation?

Modern cardiac rehabilitation programs should be an important component of an overall care plan for many patients with heart disease, including these seven conditions.

✔ Coronary artery disease/angina

✔ Following a heart attack

✔ Following coronary artery bypass surgery

✔ Following coronary angioplasty

✔ Following heart surgery on the valves

✔ Before and following heart transplantation

✔ Heart failure

As can be seen from the conditions listed, the vast majority of individuals with heart disease can benefit from cardiac rehabilitation.

Where Does Cardiac Rehabilitation Take Place?

Formal, medically supervised cardiac rehabilitation programs can take place either in the hospital or in the community. These programs offer the great advantage that everything you need to improve your cardiac health can be found in one place and knowledgeable medical staff is on hand at all times to provide not only education but also ensure safety and keep you motivated.

✔ If you have been hospitalized for a heart attack, cardiac surgery, or other problem, your rehabilitation program starts while you are in the hospital. After you are discharged, you typically continue your program on an outpatient basis at either a hospital or community cardiac rehabilitation program.

✔ Unfortunately, some people are unable to participate in formal cardiac rehab programs because they live so far away from the centers where the programs are provided. With advancing communications technology, many hospitals and cardiologists are beginning to offer new home-based rehabilitation programs that use telephone-based supervision and communication with participants. Such home-based programs are intended only for persons who have stable cardiac conditions and who are at low or moderate risk for further problems.

What Does a Cardiac Rehabilitation Program Include and How Long Does It Last?

Ideally, you should continue to work on your "rehab" for the rest of your life because the information, strategies, and techniques you learn give you excellent tools for living long and well overall (not just for retooling the ticker). But that said, formal cardiac rehabilitation programs usually have three phases:

1. **Rehabilitation during hospitalization**
2. **Formal supervised rehabilitation program during recovery**
3. **Maintenance program**

Rehabilitation while you're in the hospital

After hospitalization for a cardiac problem or surgery, your rehabilitation begins while you are in the hospital.

✔ Members of the rehabilitation team begin to counsel you on your cardiac condition and how to manage it. Topics may include nutrition, weight reduction (if necessary), stress reduction, stopping smoking, and other life-style modifications. You also begin supervised physical therapy and physical activity.

✔ When you are ready to go home, the team makes sure that you have received instructions for what you should do at home to continue your progress. Your physician also usually recommends when you should begin a medically supervised cardiac rehabilitation program. The timing will depend on your particular situation and condition, but generally you'll be ready to start in one to three weeks.

✔ In the meantime, you're not idle at home. You need to continue with the physical activities, exercise, and diet your physician has recommended to continue your recovery. In some instances, your physician may prescribe home visits from persons like a social worker or physical therapist to assist you.

Rehabilitation during recovery

After your initial recovery, you will begin to participate in a medically supervised cardiac rehabilitation program.

What the program contains

Typical cardiac rehabilitation programs feature group and individual exercise, along with a variety of educational programs to help lower risk factors for heart disease.

- Your physical activity usually includes aerobic exercise, either on a treadmill, stationary cycle, or a walking track. There are also equipment and activities to enable persons with walking difficulties to build their aerobic capacity. (Plus enhancing mobility is a goal.)

- The physical activity starts slowly to ensure safety but gradually builds to a more intensive program.

- During your exercise program, your heart rate, blood pressure, and, at least in the early stages, your electrocardiogram (to measure the electrical impulses and rhythm of the heart) are all monitored by a nurse or other healthcare professional to make sure that you have no problems.

- Strength training, in some instances, may be included. Proper instruction and supervision are crucial, and strength training is not advised for all cardiac conditions.

- Most programs include classes in nutrition, risk factor reductions, weight management (if necessary), smoking cessation programs, and stress management education.

- Access to counseling should also be available.

    • Job and vocational guidance to help in returning to work

    • Education about physical capabilities and limitations, including, but not limited to, when sexual relations can be started again, how much exertion can be taken in daily life, and so on

    • Psychological counseling and emotional support

How long the program lasts

Although your physician recommends the length of time you should participate, six to twelve weeks is usually the minimum. A number of studies, however, indicate even greater improvement for persons who participate for periods of three to six months to a year.

Maintenance

To maintain and increase the gains you achieve during your formal rehab program, it's very important that you continue your physical activity program as well as sustain and strengthen your new ways of eating and other lifestyle practices. In fact, "keeping on keeping on" is the key to unlocking the lasting benefits of cardiac rehabilitation.

The Role of Education in Cardiac Rehabilitation

Just the idea of heart disease is scary to us. Actually having a heart attack or needing angioplasty or bypass surgery is even scarier: So scary you may try to avoid thinking about your condition — you just want to get over it and get back to your old life. Or so scary it's hard to think positively about the future. Fear, denial, anger, and all the other emotional reactions to heart disease or a "cardiac event" are normal. The first tool for dealing with them is knowledge.

Knowing as much as you can about your condition, how to manage it, how to reduce any limitations, and how to enhance abilities can unlock the door to a new freedom and a new discovery of what it means to have a good life. That's why education is the first component of a cardiac rehabilitation program. A knowledgeable, educated patient is also a person empowered to become an equal partner in his or her recovery and rehabilitation.

The Role of Exercise Training and Physical Activity

Slowly progressive exercise training and physical activity programs and prescriptions represent the cornerstone of all modern cardiac rehabilitation programs.

Understanding the benefits of exercise training

Progressive exercise training can yield a variety of benefits for individuals with heart disease.

- ✔ Exercise can increase the efficiency and performance of the heart muscle itself, as well as increase the efficiency of the exercising muscles, thereby reducing the workload that the heart must perform.

- ✔ Regular progressive exercise programs can reduce the likelihood of further cardiac problems. This is particularly true when such exercise programs are combined with risk factor reduction and psychological support.

- ✔ Increased exercise capacity can significantly improve your quality of life and result in a variety of other psychological benefits.

- ✔ Regular exercise can help you feel that you are playing an active role in your recovery from heart disease.

- ✔ As functional capacity increases, the likelihood of returning to work and favorite activities increases.

- ✔ Progressive exercise programs may also interact in a positive way with other risk factors for heart disease. For example, regular physical activity can significantly increase high density lipoprotein (HDL) which is associated with decreased cardiac problems. In addition, regular physical activity can help with weight loss and may also lower low density lipoprotein (LDL), thereby further lowering the risk of future cardiac problems.

Getting started on an exercise program and cardiac rehabilitation

In most instances, your physician will want you to undergo some form of exercise tolerance test as part of the early process in cardiac rehabilitation. During the test, your physician is looking for evidence of inadequate blood flow to the heart, abnormal heart rhythms, or inadequate pumping action of the heart during exercise. Armed with this information, the physician and other healthcare workers can then develop an individualized exercise program that allows you to achieve the maximum benefits of exercise, while ensuring maximum safety.

To ensure your safety as you begin exercise after suffering a cardiac event, a number of exercise factors are carefully monitored including the following:

- ✔ Duration of exercise
- ✔ Intensity of exercise
- ✔ Frequency of exercise

Using these factors, your exercise program follows a slow progression to help maximize your functional capacity and encourage you to adopt a safe program which can be carried on for the rest of your lifetime.

Rehabilitative exercise training for specific conditions

While the basic principles of exercise training apply across all cardiac rehabilitation, some people with specific conditions require various modifications in the actual practice of exercise training.

Patients with heart failure

Exercise programs in cardiac rehabilitation can be extremely helpful in individuals who have heart failure. Some studies have shown that individuals with heart failure may improve their exercise capacity between 25 and 30 percent through controlled exercise programs. Quality of life has also been shown to increase and symptoms typically decrease. The exercise prescription, however, needs to be modified in such individuals because of their limited endurance. Lower target heart rates are used and intermittent rest periods are also employed to allow individuals to slowly increase their endurance. Typically, heart rates during exercise sessions are set at 10 beats per minute below the level at which any evidence of shortness of breath occurs. (For a complete discussion of heart failure, see Chapter 18.)

The elderly

Individuals over the age of 65 who have cardiac problems and participate in cardiac rehabilitation can achieve significant improvements in their capacity to conduct activities of daily living. In one study, the functional capacity increased by 50 percent. Although exercise programs may need to be modified to accommodate limited endurance, elderly individuals stand to gain the most from cardiac rehabilitation.

Patients with heart rhythm problems

Individuals who have been hospitalized with heart rhythm problems may benefit from cardiac rehabilitation programs. Because these individuals may be at particularly high risk for problems during cardiac rehabilitation, however, it is mandatory that they receive supervision by physicians who are knowledgeable about their specific rhythm problems and that they have appropriate medical therapy to suppress the rhythm disturbance. These individuals also require longer periods of continuous monitoring using electrocardiograms than individuals who have not had problems with cardiac rhythm.

Women

Although women experience the same benefits of exercise training as men during cardiac rehabilitation, women are significantly less likely to be referred for cardiac rehabilitation. This is particularly unfortunate since more than half of all deaths from coronary artery disease now occur in women. Plus the likelihood of problems, including death following heart attack, is higher among women than it is among men. Thus, cardiac rehabilitation is particularly important for women. So, women, insist on it or know the reason why not.

Cardiac transplantation patients

Cardiac rehabilitation has been shown to be highly effective in cardiac transplantation patients, helping to increase both endurance and the capacity to perform activities of daily living. A number of changes occur in the cardiovascular system following cardiac transplantation, however, which require modifications of typical cardiac rehabilitation programs. For example, the heart rate response to exercise in a heart that has been transplanted is very different than in a non-transplanted heart, because during the transplantation process, all the nerves that supply the normal heart are severed, resulting in a difference in the nervous supply. Therefore, cardiac transplantation patients need to be involved in programs with an experienced rehabilitation team whose members are skilled in the particular exercise prescription for cardiac transplantation.

Following coronary artery bypass surgery or heart attack

Astonishingly, only 15 percent of eligible patients who could benefit from cardiac rehabilitation following heart attack or coronary artery bypass surgery are estimated to be involved in formal cardiac rehabilitation programs. This low rate of participation is probably a result of a combination of inadequate referrals from physicians, poor patient motivation, financial considerations, and other logistical issues, such as distance from major cardiac rehabilitation centers or inconvenience.

If you or a loved one are in this situation, it is important to make that extra effort to get involved in a cardiac rehabilitation program so that you can derive the multiple benefits.

The Role of Lifestyle Modifications to Reduce Risk Factors for Heart Disease

Risk factor reduction is particularly important in individuals who have heart disease and/or who have undergone a cardiac procedure. Cardiac rehabilitation programs should place particular emphasis on blood pressure control, proper nutritional counseling, weight reduction (if the individual is overweight), and smoking cessation.

- **Blood pressure control.** Managing your blood pressure to keep it at normal levels can help reduce your risk of further problems and complications from your heart disease. Taking a multifaceted approach of education, modifying your diet, following a physical activity program, reducing stress, and taking prescribed medications is important. (See also Chapter 9 on hypertension.)

- **Nutritional counseling**. Strong evidence exists that lowering blood cholesterol and improving lipoprotein profiles are extremely beneficial for individuals who have coronary artery disease. The principles behind the Step I and Step II American Heart Association Diet (see Chapter 10) form the foundation for nutritional counseling in cardiac rehabilitation programs. It is important that a registered dietitian provide such instructions. In addition, sodium restricted diets are appropriate for individuals who have high blood pressure or heart failure.

✔ **Weight control**. Studies show that losing weight and maintaining weight at an appropriate level can help persons with heart disease control high blood pressure, improve and even normalize their cholesterol levels, and control the risk of diabetes. Weight loss can also contribute to better ability to comfortably carry out your daily activities. (See also Chapter 12.)

✔ **Smoking cessation.** There is no doubt that continued smoking in patients with coronary artery disease increases the likelihood of further complications and even death. The converse is also true. Individuals who stop smoking following a heart attack benefit greatly by reducing their risk of further cardiac events. (See also Chapter 11.)

The Role of Counseling and Support

The majority of individuals who have suffered an acute problem from heart disease experience one or more psychological problems. It's normal.

✔ Moderate to severe depression occurs in up to 20 percent of people following a heart attack, and significant anxiety disorders requiring therapy are present in up to 10 percent.

✔ Almost 25 percent of individuals never resume sexual activity following a heart attack and over 50 percent decrease their sexual activity following a heart attack.

✔ Family, marital problems, and social isolation are also common sequels to heart disease.

It is also common for people with severe heart disease to go through a cycle of fear, often leading to anger, and ultimately leading to depression. Here are some of the most common feelings:

✔ Fear that you're dying

✔ Fear that chest pains will recur

✔ Fear of never returning to work

✔ Fear of never having sex again

✔ Anger that a heart problem happened to you

✔ Anger at yourself for conditions that resulted in the heart problem that may or may not have been under your control

✔ Anger with family and friends

✔ Depression at the thought that "life is over" or will never be the same again

✔ Depression at the idea that others may think you're weak or "damaged goods"

In all of these situations, psychological counseling can help, particularly in the early phases of recovery, and therefore should be part of all cardiac rehabilitation programs.

The support of the counselors can also help you establish positive interactive links with your family and friends. A number of rehab programs have support groups and education classes for family members that can be really helpful in enhancing the recovery of the whole family. (Yes, heart problems do affect more than the physical "victim.") You may also enjoy participating in a support group with persons with similiar conditions — there are even some online. Ask your cardiologist or staff at your rehabilitation center if they know of groups in your area.

Returning to Work

One of the benefits of cardiac rehabilitation is that trained professionals can help guide someone who has suffered from a heart problem in important decisions, such as when and if to return to work, whether to change the type of work one does, and the risks involved for having further problems if one returns to work.

Often your physician is guided by the results of objective tests, such as the treadmill exercise test. This information, in conjunction with the physical demands that you have to perform as part of your job, can help guide the decision about when and if to return to work. The exact nature of the work, whether or not it involves strenuous labor, and particularly whether or not it involves work with the arms and chest, are all important issues to discuss with your physician.

The good news is that most people can return to work following most acute heart problems, and cardiac rehab helps that happen sooner.

Forming a Partnership with Your Physician

If you feel that you or a loved one are eligible for cardiac rehabilitation and could benefit from such a program, *discuss this with your physician.* If your physician is not willing to consider cardiac rehabilitation for you and you feel you are eligible, it may be worth obtaining a second opinion.

Some questions to discuss with your physician include:

- ✔ Am I eligible for cardiac rehabilitation?
- ✔ Is it covered by my health insurance?
- ✔ Where is the nearest cardiac rehabilitation program?
- ✔ How often should I go to cardiac rehabilitation?
- ✔ How long should I remain in a cardiac rehabilitation program?
- ✔ What benefits can I expect from a cardiac rehabilitation program?

Strategies for Long-Term Success

How successfully any rehabilitation program helps to lower your risk of future cardiac events relates directly to how conscientiously you follow the program.

It is important to assess in your own mind and heart and also discuss with your family and physician all the potential benefits of cardiac rehabilitation and develop a strategy for sticking with it in the long run (or long walk!).

Cardiac rehabilitation has many benefits, minimal risk. Comprehensive cardiac rehabilitation programs can help you or a loved one fight back against heart disease. The biggest risk is to not participate at all. Make sure that you know if cardiac rehabilitation is appropriate for you, and if it is, take advantage of this potentially life saving part of modern cardiac care.

Further Resources and Information

If you think that you or a loved one may be eligible for cardiac rehabilitation, talk to your physician, nurse, or healthcare professional. You can also obtain information from your local chapter of the American Heart Association by calling 1-800-242-8721, and you can read more about cardiac rehabilitation on their Web site (www.americanheart.org).

Chapter 17

I Got Rhythm: The Heart's Electrical System

- -

In This Chapter

▶ The heart's electrical system, in and out of synch

▶ Palpitations, we've all got them, even if we're not in love

▶ Symptoms — when to worry

▶ How rhythm problems are diagnosed

▶ No juice — problems with conduction

▶ Measures to treat arrhythmias — from the simple to the profound

▶ Charging up the cardiac electrical company

- -

Day in, day out, the beat goes on — the heartbeat — and it all depends on the heart's electrical system. Infinitely subtle and wonderfully specialized, the heart's electrical system allows the heart to smoothly accelerate from 40 to 50 beats up to 200 beats per minute and then decelerate back with nary a hitch. But when this electrical system suffers from some insult, such as lack of blood flow to the heart, it can start causing us problems.

In this chapter, I sort through the seemingly bewildering causes and conditions that can result in cardiac rhythm problems and tell you when to worry and when not to.

What Are Arrhythmias?

Cardiac *arrhythmias,* also called cardiac *dysrhythmias*, are irregularities or abnormalities in the beating of the heart. Arrhythmias are surprisingly common. They can arise in a wide variety of settings and can range from the totally insignificant to the life-threatening.

The insignificant. If each of us were hooked up to a 24-hour, continuous electrocardiogram (such as the Holter monitor that I discuss in Chapter 13), we would find that all of us have a few "extra" heartbeats and a few "skipped" heartbeats. Technically, all these are cardiac arrhythmias. Yet, for the vast majority of us, these minor irregularities carry absolutely no health consequences.

The life-threatening. More severe cardiac arrhythmias, however, can be deadly.

- Over 40,000 individuals die each year from a primary rhythm problem.

- Rhythm problems are a contributing cause of death in about 25 percent of all deaths each year in the United States.

- Over 4 million individuals are admitted to hospitals every year with a rhythm problem as at least part of their initial symptoms.

What's Electricity Got to Do with the Causes of Arrhythmia?

Everything. In the final analysis, all cardiac rhythm problems relate to the underlying electrical activity that drives the heart and tells it when to beat and to the interaction between this electrical activity and the heart's anatomy. But before getting into what causes the problems, it's necessary to review and expand the understanding of the heart's electric company.

The heart's electric company at work

As I first discuss in Chapter 2, the cardiac electrical system is an exquisite grouping of cells and fibers that uses electrical impulses to tell the heart when to contract. You can follow the route of these electrical impulses, using the schematic drawing of this system in Figure 17-1. (Don't worry, it's lots easier to follow than the wiring schematic in your car manual.)

A small group of cells high up in the right atrium controls the rhythm of the heart. This group of cells is called the *sinus node,* or *sinoatrial node*. Acting as the heart's pacemaker, these cells spontaneously discharge an electrical impulse that is carried through the atrium and down, to another node, located at the intersection of the atria and the ventricles. Not surprisingly, this second node is called the *atrioventricular node,* or *AV node*.

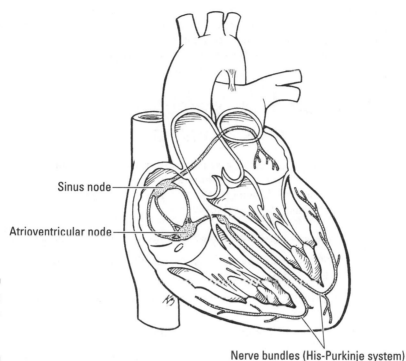

Figure 17-1:
The heart's
electrical
system.

Sinus node

Atrioventricular node

Nerve bundles (His-Purkinje system)

Behaving as a traffic cop, the AV node receives the electrical signals from the sinus node, slows them down, and makes sure that the proper number reach the ventricles to alert them to contract.

Below the AV node are two more specialized bundles of nerve tissue located in the *septum,* the muscular wall that separates the two ventricles. These nerve bundles function as pathways carrying the electrical signal to contract to all of the cells in both ventricles. (If you've just got to know, these pathways are called the *His-Purkinje system.)*

Should this primary electrical system have problems, the heart does have an emergency backup system. If the sinus node doesn't fire, other cells in the electrical system such as the AV node or the bundles below can send a spontaneous signal to the heart muscle cells to contract. But there's a catch. At each lower lever of "command," the rate of the electrical impulse is slower, so the heart beats or contracts more and more slowly.

In addition to its own internal electrical system, the heart is also influenced by the body's ultimate electrical system, the brain and central nervous system. You might say that the cardiac electrical system is *networked,* to use a modern concept. Working at its best, this network creates the ultimate flexibility for changes in cardiac rhythm to respond to particular needs. It's the central nervous system, for example, that orders the heart to speed up when you start to run and slow down when you rest or sleep.

When the heart's electric company goes haywire

When anything happens to disturb or interrupt the normal functioning of the heart's electrical system, problems with cardiac rhythm result. A variety of underlying conditions, which are often interrelated, can cause cardiac rhythm problems. These include:

- **Problems related to the electrical system itself,** such as:
    - The sinus node may lose the ability to trigger the electrical impulse or do so erratically.
    - Cells that normally depolarize by themselves lose their ability to do so.
    - The AV node may lose its ability to direct the signal.
    - The signal to beat may originate in a site other than the sinus node.

- **Lack of blood flow to the living tissues of the electrical system,** such as that produced by coronary artery disease, can cause:
    - Arrhythmias, abnormal rhythm patterns
    - Conduction blocks or heart blocks, in which there's difficulty even getting the signal through

- **Congenital abnormalities, problems that people are born with,** such as:
    - Certain valve abnormalities
    - Calcium growth around electrical system cells

- **The effect of underlying disease states or conditions,** such as:
    - Coronary artery disease
    - Coronary valve disease or heart failure
    - Stress
    - Flu — ever wonder why your heart beats fast when you have a fever?

✔ **The result of things we do to ourselves**

- Caffeine (Did you really need that extra cup of coffee that caused your heart to "race"?)

- Tobacco

- Alcohol

- Diet pills

- Cough and cold medicines

What Are the Symptoms of Cardiac Arrhythmias?

The symptoms of cardiac rhythm problems are just as diverse as the problems themselves. They also range from inconsequential to life-threatening.

✔ **Palpitations.** Probably the least worrisome of symptoms, palpitations describe a variety of uncomfortable sensations of one's heartbeat, such as the sensation that your heart is missing a beat or skipping a beat. To some people, palpitations may feel like a fluttering in the chest. In and of themselves, these skipped or missed beats are not terribly worrisome. However, when multiple skipped beats occur in succession, this can lead to serious problems.

✔ **A racing or pounding heart.** Although these symptoms can arise from strong emotion or exercise, if they occur at rest, they may indicate a significant rhythm problem.

✔ **Lightheadedness or dizziness.** Though many conditions can cause these symptoms, they can also be associated with arrhythmia. If this symptom is not a one-time passing event, you should have your doctor check out the possible causes.

✔ **Passing out.** Unlike a fainting spell where the faintness may come on a bit gradually with the world "graying out" and with your body going sweaty or clammy, the passing out caused by rhythm problems tends to be sudden. Anyone experiencing a sudden fainting spell or more than one episode of what seems to be an "ordinary" fainting spell should seek medical attention to determine the underlying problem.

✔ **Cardiac collapse and sudden death.** This is the most severe rhythm problem. While in some instances cardiac collapse (cardiac arrest) can be treated effectively with cardiopulmonary resuscitation (CPR), it is certainly a life-threatening emergency. Anyone who survives such an episode requires advanced electrical diagnostic techniques in the hands of a skilled cardiologist trained in the field of electrophysiology.

How Are Cardiac Rhythm Problems Diagnosed?

Cardiologists have a wide variety of techniques, ranging from very simple to extremely complex, to help diagnose underlying rhythm disturbances. I describe these techniques more fully in Chapter 13, but here are some of the ways they are used to diagnose rhythm problems.

✔ **History.** A detailed history of exactly what symptoms occur and under what circumstances is extremely valuable in diagnosing an underlying cardiac rhythm problem. As already indicated, symptoms may range from palpitations to fainting or cardiac collapse.

If you are experiencing minor rhythm problems such as palpitations, it is a good idea to take your own pulse during an episode to try to further characterize what is happening to the heart rate. Often, your physician may ask you to tap out the rhythm during an office visit.

✔ **Physical examination.** Your physician will conduct a complete physical examination with an emphasis on the cardiovascular system. In addition to listening to your heart, your physician may perform extra procedures, such as pressing on one of the arteries in your neck. This technique often slows down the heart and may provoke a rhythm problem that may have caused fainting. Your physician may also ask you to perform a little mild exercise in his or her office.

✔ **Electrocardiogram (ECG).** The next step after the history and physical examination is invariably an electrocardiogram. Because the ECG traces the electrical impulses of the heart, it gives an excellent indication of many underlying problems that can result in rhythm disturbances. An ECG can also pick up abnormalities in the conduction of the electrical impulses that have not caused any symptoms. These abnormalities, which usually require no treatment, may be insignificant or subtle indicators of possible future problems that your physician may want to keep an eye on.

✔ **Exercise Tolerance Testing.** Sometimes arrhythmias that are provoked when the heart is going faster can be determined by performing Exercise Tolerance Testing. In this situation, your physician will be looking either for rhythm problems that are stimulated by the heart going faster or by inadequate blood flow to the heart when exercise is making your heart work at faster speeds.

✔ **Long-term electrocardiographic monitoring.** Doctors often ask individuals to wear an electrocardiographic monitoring system in order to detect and record an underlying heart rhythm problem. This may be an event monitor that you activate or that activates automatically only when a rhythm disturbance occurs. Or it may be a 24-hour Holter monitor, as I describe in Chapter 13. Both allow you to function normally during monitoring.

✔ **Electrophysiologic studies.** Electrophysiologic studies, also called *EPS*, have grown in sophistication and popularity over the last 25 years. This procedure is very similar to a cardiac catheterization. In this case, catheters with electrical monitoring sensors are passed into various chambers of the heart in an attempt either to monitor a rhythm problem or stimulate one so that precise treatment can be determined. Electrophysiologic studies are absolutely necessary if an individual has been resuscitated from a cardiac collapse. EPS studies may also be highly relevant if an individual has fainted and the underlying cause may be cardiac. In addition, EPS studies may be useful if an individual is having persistent and dangerous rhythm problems that cannot be managed with medications.

Specific Rhythm Problems

Just like people, rhythm problems come in all different shapes and sizes. In an attempt to lend some order to this complex field, cardiologists typically classify rhythms according to their anatomic point of origin. Very broadly, rhythm problems can be characterized as those arising:

✔ From structures in the atria (including the sinus node and the AV node, located between the right atrium and ventricle).

✔ From structures in the ventricles.

Rhythms that arise in the atria are usually less dangerous than rhythms that arise in the ventricles because the atria act as booster pumps, while the ventricles are the main power source for the body. As a consequence, any rhythm problem that impedes the ventricles' ability to do their work can lead to serious trouble.

Rhythm problems arising in the atria

These rhythm problems are typically a result of the electrical system causing the heart to beat too fast, called *tacchycardia*; too slow, *bradycardia*; or chaotically, *fibrillation*.

Sinus Tacchycardia

Although the heart must be able to beat fast when you exercise or exert yourself, a fast heartbeat when you're at rest can cause problems, particularly if you have any narrowing of your coronary arteries. Among the variety of situations that can lead to sinus tacchycardia are fever, certain endocrine abnormalities (such as an elevated thyroid level), anxiety, and pain.

Bradycardia

To some degree, a slow heartbeat may actually be desirable. For example, a trained athlete often has a heart rate in the high forties or low fifties when at rest. However, in cardiology, any resting heart rate of less than 60 is called bradycardia. Bradycardia becomes dangerous when the electrical signal generated by the sinus node is so slow that the heart does not beat often enough to pump adequate blood. In this case, it may be necessary to treat the slow heart rate either with medication or in some instances with a pacemaker.

Atrial flutter

When lovers say that their hearts are fluttering, they are describing a pleasing sensation. However, it's not so great when the atrium starts to flutter. In an atrial flutter, a very rapid, regular electrical signal (which is not effectively transmitted to the ventricles) causes a very rapid heartbeat. Correcting this condition requires either medication or *cardioversion*, the therapy that uses a carefully controlled electrical current to shock the atrium back into better behavior. (For more details on cardioversion, see Chapter 13.)

Atrial fibrillation

Atrial fibrillation occurs when the electrical signals are chaotic and the muscles of the atria quiver rather than contract. The electrical impulses also reach the ventricles very erratically, producing an erratic heartbeat. The condition is very common in individuals who have heart disease and can be caused by a variety of conditions including coronary artery disease, hypertension and an elevated thyroid level.

Atrial fibrillation by itself is not immediately life-threatening. But because the atria are not contracting effectively, they can gather clots that can pass through the heart and into either the brain or the lungs. If a clot travels to the brain, it typically results in a *stroke*. A clot in the lungs can cause a very serious condition called *pulmonary embolism*. (For more information on these conditions, see Chapter 19.)

Because of the possible outcomes, it is very important to treat atrial fibrillation aggressively. Treatment may include medications and/or cardioversion. In addition to medicines to control the heart rate, all patients who have atrial fibrillation must take blood thinning medicines (anticoagulants) to lower the risk of blood clots generated in the atria being thrown to the brain or lungs.

Rhythm disturbances arising in the ventricles

Similar rhythm disturbances originate in the ventricles. However, as already indicated, because these rhythm problems affect the main pumping chambers of the heart, they are usually more significant or dangerous than those affecting the atria. Here are some of the common rhythm problems that can arise in the ventricles.

Ventricular premature contractions

Ventricular premature contractions (also called *VPCs* or *VPVs*) can occur when a small grouping of cells in the ventricle generates an abnormal electrical signal. This extraneous signal causes the heart to beat prematurely and takes one or more beats out of the normal sequence. Often, individuals do not even recognize these premature beats. But if they do, they usually have the sensation of a skipped or extra beat.

VPCs can occur in anyone but are more common in individuals who have underlying coronary artery disease. Occasional VPCs are not typically worrisome. But VPCs pose a danger when they start to group together or occur very frequently because they may stimulate or trigger much more serious cardiac problems, such as ventricular tacchycardia or ventricular fibrillation.

Ventricular tacchycardia

Ventricular tacchycardia occurs when continuous extra heartbeats originate from an abnormal group of cells in the ventricle. If sustained for any length of time, this condition is very dangerous because the ventricles in this racing rhythm cannot pump adequate blood. When the onset is sudden or acute, ventricular tacchycardia requires an electrical shock to the heart using a defibrillator to convert it back into a normal rhythm. To prevent further episodes of this dangerous rhythm, individuals either are placed on antiarrhythmic medicines or have a permanent defibrillator implanted in the chest to deliver a small electric shock directly to the heart if ventricular taccycardia occurs.

Ventricular fibrillation

This is the most dangerous cardiac arrhythmia. Ventricular fibrillation occurs following an episode of ventricular tacchycardia and, in fact, is usually triggered by it. In ventricular fibrillation, the ventricle *fibrillates*, or quivers, and does not adequately contract to generate oxygenated blood flow to the working heart or other organs. This is a medical emergency that requires immediate electrical shock to try to jolt the heart back into a normal rhythm.

Passing the Beat on — Conduction Problems

In addition to the rhythm problems I discuss, abnormalities can occur in the actual conduction of electrical impulses throughout the heart. These conduction problems can affect not only the various components of the heart's specialized electrical system but also individual cardiac cells.

- ✔ The most severe of these conditions are called *heart blocks,* or *conduction blocks.* Heart blocks prevent the electrical impulses from getting down to the ventricles in a timely fashion and result in inadequate blood flow. Heart blocks can delay each signal, block part of the signals, or block all signals from reaching the ventricles. In this last case, the ventricles' backup system initiates the heartbeat, but the rate is very slow and insufficient. The most effective treatment for a severe heart block condition is a temporary or permanent cardiac pacemaker.

- ✔ In other conduction abnormalities, the electrical impulses speed through the conduction system at a faster pace than they should. These syndromes can result in very fast *tacchycardias* that can also be dangerous. A variety of treatments for these is available, ranging from medication to defibrillation or other electrical procedures to interrupt the abnormal conduction patterns that are allowing impulses to reach the pumping chamber too rapidly.

How Are Rhythm Problems Treated?

As I hint in the discussion of types of problems, a wide variety of treatments are available. As you look over the following summary, remember that in all the therapies, your active participation and commitment is critical to success.

Lifestyle measures

As I note earlier, palpitations, the most common symptom of arrhythmia, may be caused by or made worse by practices such as drinking too many caffeinated beverages (coffee, tea, and many soft drinks), consuming too much alcohol, not effectively treating stress, or not obtaining adequate rest. Changing any or all of these lifestyle measures can often make palpitations disappear.

Treating underlying illnesses

If an underlying illness, such as a fever, pain, anxiety, or endocrine problem, causes a rhythm problem, it is essential to treat the underlying condition in order to treat the rhythm problem. Thus, it is important for your physician to explore and treat any underlying conditions as part of the therapy for your cardiac rhythm problems.

Medications

A bewildering variety of medications are available to treat cardiac arrhythmias. Plus the use of these medications can be very complex. So if you have a serious rhythm problem, your personal physician will probably have consulted with a cardiologist who is skilled in the use of these medications.

To give you a brief overview, the medications fall into four major classifications, depending on their mechanism of action and exactly how they work within the cardiac electrical system. Not surprisingly, a number system denotes these four classes. If you are taking an anti-arrhythmic drug, you will be taking a Class 1, Class 2, Class 3, or Class 4 medication. Even though your physician is unlikely to have told you where your particular medication fits within the classifications, he or she is guided by this broad scheme in selecting, from the 30 to 40 anti-arrhythmic drugs available, the proper medication to treat your specific cardiac rhythm problem.

Electrical therapy

Just as cardiologists specializing in heart catheterization are known as "plumbers" within the profession, cardiologists who specialize in treating cardiac rhythm problems with electrical therapy are known as "electricians." This is a term of endearment for the rest of the profession, because these men and women have highly specialized knowledge that can be lifesaving for many cardiac patients. Basically three different kinds of electrical therapy are used to correct cardiac rhythm problems.

Cardioversion

It takes one to fix one. Because the heart is an electrical system, the skilled application of an external source of electricity can jolt the heart back into its normal rhythm. This process is called *cardioversion*.

During cardioversion therapy, the patient is usually mildly sedated (of course, in an emergency, time is not taken for sedation). Then two electrical paddles are applied to the chest wall at the level of the heart (usually one is placed on the front of the chest and the other on the side of the chest) and an electrical current is passed through the heart. This shock causes the electrical system to "reboot" itself and often pop back into the normal sinus rhythm, which is desirable.

Cardioversion can very effectively treat various cardiac arrhythmias, including atrial fibrillation, atrial flutter, ventricular tacchycardia, and ventricular fibrillation. Cardioversion, also called *defibrillation*, is literally a lifesaver in emergencies when acute ventricular tacchycardia and ventricular fibrillation threaten immediate death because the heart is not putting out any oxygenated blood. Modern cardioversion or defibrillation equipment is capable of sensing underlying cardiac rhythm and applying exactly the right amount of shock at exactly the right time to maximize the likelihood of converting the heart back into its normal rhythm.

Pacemaker therapy

Pacemakers are typically used when the heart has very slow rhythm, particularly as a result of conduction blocks. Modern cardiac pacemakers can sequentially pace both the atria and the ventricles to generate a very effective cardiac output. These pacemakers are able to sense the heart's own rhythm and only kick into action when the rhythm slows to a certain point. Advances in electronic design and battery power have also enabled pacemakers to become very small and last for ten or more years between battery changes. And, to the delight of those who rely on them, modern pacemakers are not sensitive to microwave ovens and the like.

Surgical therapy

Surgical procedures to treat cardiac arrythmias vary from techniques to destroy abnormal electrical cells to prevent them from making the heart beat too fast to implantable defibrillators that can sense a dangerous cardiac arrhythmia and fire an internal electrical impulse to terminate it.

Most advanced surgical procedures require either an operating room and surgeons skilled in cardiac rhythm problems and/or a specialized catheterization laboratory devoted to electrical abnormalities and their correction. This latter laboratory is called an *electrophysiology* laboratory, and the cardiologists who specialize in this area are called *electrophysiologists*.

Electrophysiology techniques can be used to evaluate and diagnose a wide variety of rhythm problems and to administer electrical activity to treat them. Such techniques can also be used to assess the efficacy of various drugs in suppressing dangerous cardiac rhythms.

Chapter 18

Heart Failure

*I*f you're like lots of folks, *heart failure* conjures up an image of a heart that suddenly stops or a heart that's totally ruined. Relax. Neither image is accurate. Heart failure (also often called *congestive heart failure* or *CHF*) is the term cardiologists use to describe the condition of a heart that is no longer able to adequately pump blood to meet the body's needs. You can have varying degrees of heart failure, and many factors contribute to this condition. Heart failure is always very serious but not instantly fatal. There is a lot you can do to maximize the quality and length of life if you or a loved one has heart failure and more you can do to prevent developing it in the first place. That's what this chapter is about.

What Is Heart Failure?

Heart failure occurs when the heart can no longer adequately pump blood to the lungs and throughout the body. Usually, heart failure occurs slowly, often over a period of years, and is caused by an underlying condition such as coronary artery disease, leakage of one of the heart valves, or various diseases of the heart muscle itself. At first the heart compensates for small decreases in its ability to pump with a number of mechanisms:

✔ It enlarges (*dilatation*) to allow more blood into the pumping chambers.

✔ The heart muscle walls may thicken (*hypertrophy*) to strengthen the pump and allow it to exert more force during contraction to move more blood.

✔ It may beat faster (like trying to pitch more pails of water on a fire).

These compensations can develop for years before an individual notices any symptoms. But ultimately, when even these mechanisms fail, significant heart failure occurs. By then, these compensatory mechanisms have often also become part of the problem.

How serious heart failure is depends on how much pumping capacity the heart has lost. As I discuss in Chapter 2, a normal heart discharges about three-quarters of the blood in the main pumping chambers with each contraction, or beat. Heart failure often occurs if the amount of blood ejected per beat, called the *ejection fraction,* drops below 50 percent. Certainly below 40 percent, heart failure ensues. However, many people can survive for many years with ejection fractions of 20 to 30 percent or sometimes even 15 percent.

However, the greater the loss of pumping capacity, the more likely the individual may suffer a number of complications. All forms of heart failure are serious health problems that require medical treatment. In order to improve your chance of living longer, it is important to take care of yourself if you have heart failure, see your physician regularly, and pay scrupulous attention to recommended treatments. Fortunately, significant advances have occurred in our knowledge of heart failure and the available treatments in the last five years.

Are there different types of heart failure?

Heart failure is not just one "disease." It's actually a way of describing a group of conditions and symptoms that occur when any of a number of problems keeps the heart from pumping enough blood. There are, therefore, several ways to look at heart failure, the most common being 1) which side of the heart is most affected or 2) which part of the cardiac cycle is most affected.

- ✔ **Left heart failure.** When the left ventricle of the heart cannot adequately pump blood out to the body, the blood begins to back up into the lungs. This form of heart failure, as a consequence, is usually called *congestive heart failure,* because fluid seeps out of the backed up blood vessels and into the small airways of the lungs making them "congested." That's why shortness of breath is the most pronounced symptom of this condition. Several underlying conditions, which I discuss in a moment, can contribute to left heart failure.

- ✔ **Right heart failure.** In this case the right ventricle is not pumping adequately. The most obvious symptom is a buildup of fluid in the legs and ankles, a condition of swelling called *edema*. Right heart failure usually occurs as an ultimate result of left heart failure. However, people with very severe lung disease can also have right heart failure, because the right heart is not able to generate adequate pressure to pump blood through a diseased pair of lungs. (This last condition called *cor pulmonale* is in Chapter 19.)

✔ **Systolic heart failure.** This classification refers to the heart's inability to eject adequate amounts of blood during its contraction, or its *systole*. Symptoms of systolic heart failure are typically lung congestion.

✔ **Diastolic heart failure.** This classification refers to the heart's inability to relax between contractions, or its *diastole*, and allow enough blood to enter the pumping chamber. The gathering of fluid, called *edema*, in the abdomen and legs is typical of diastolic heart failure.

Does heart failure affect some groups of people more than others?

While heart failure is a very serious medical condition for any individual, certain groups tend to suffer more complications from heart failure than others.

✔ Most commonly, the prevalence of heart failure increases with age. Both men and women over the age of 70 who have heart failure are significantly more likely to die from it than younger individuals.

✔ Although men and women tend to get heart failure in comparable numbers, men tend to suffer more problems and do not survive as long after diagnosis as women. The reasons for this are not totally understood.

✔ African Americans (both men and women) have a greater prevalence (about 25 percent more) and higher death rates from heart failure than do Caucasians. Although the reasons for this are again unclear, factors such as the greater incidence among African Americans of hypertension and diabetes, which often underlie heart failure, and a pattern of less timely access to health care undoubtedly contribute.

What Causes Heart Failure?

Anatomy is destiny, as I often say. Anatomically, the heart is a pump. Any condition that significantly compromises the heart's ability to function as a pump, overloads the pump, or restricts its filling leads to heart failure.

Direct damage to the heart muscle

By far, the most common causes of heart failure are those events or conditions that damage the muscle of the heart itself, the *myocardium*. And what cardiac culprits most frequently damage the heart muscle?

- ✔ **Heart attack.** The muscle damage and scarring caused by heart attack can weaken the heart's pumping strength.

- ✔ **Myocarditis**. This condition is an acute inflammation of the heart muscle (*myo* = heart, *card* = muscle, *itis* = inflammation or infection).

- ✔ **Cardiomyopathy**. This is the name used for diseases of the heart muscle. Cardiomyopathies are characterized by whether they 1) enlarge and weaken the heart muscle, 2) thicken and stiffen the heart muscle, or 3) stiffen the heart muscle without thickening. I discuss cardiomyopathies in detail in Chapter 19.

Overloading the heart

The heart as pump may also be compromised by being overloaded.

- ✔ **Volume overloads** occur when the heart is asked to pump too great a quantity of blood. These overloads typically result from leaking heart valves that cause torrential volumes of blood to leak back into the heart. This condition can overwhelm the heart, producing heart failure.

- ✔ **Pressure overloads** occur when the heart is asked to pump against pressures that it cannot adequately pump against. This can occur either when a heart valve is narrowed (*stenosed*) or when the blood vessels have an increased resistance, such as occurs in hypertension.

Inability of the heart to fill adequately

The heart's pumping ability is also compromised when it cannot take in adequate blood to pump out. Inadequate filling can occur when the valves leading into the heart become narrowed, when the sac around the heart (the *pericardium)* becomes scarred and constricts the heart *(constrictive periocarditis)* or fills with fluid *(cardiac tamponade)* and presses down on the heart, or in certain instances when the heart muscle itself becomes so damaged that it becomes "stiff" and cannot adequately relax enough to fill.

Underlying conditions that stress the heart

In addition to these three classifications, a variety of underlying noncardiac illnesses and conditions may cause a heart that is functioning marginally well to be tipped over into heart failure. Such conditions may include an overactive thyroid gland, a systemic infection, a blood clot to the lungs, a low blood count, or any other condition that can increase the demands on the heart or decrease its ability to perform to the point that the pump fails.

What Are the Symptoms of Heart Failure?

Because heart failure produces a lack of blood flow to vital organs (including the heart) and muscles, the symptoms of heart failure are typically shortness of breath, fatigue, and/or edema and coughing.

Shortness of breath

Because how much of the heart's pumping ability has been compromised affects how short of breath an individual is, this symptom has been classified on a scale of 1 to 4. At grade 1, the individual has shortness of breath only with vigorous exertion. At Grade 4, the individual is short of breath at rest.

The symptoms of shortness of breath can further be divided into a triad of complaints that involve when and where the shortness of breath occurs. (In typical medical fashion, each of these has a Latin name.)

- **Dyspnea,** which is simply shortness of breath, is the most prevalent and earliest symptom of heart failure. Usually, this dyspnea progresses slowly so that the individual begins to subtly restrict activities to avoid this unpleasant sensation.

- **Orthopnea** describes the inability to breathe comfortably while lying flat. Individuals with heart failure, particularly as it progresses, find they breathe more comfortably when the upper part of the body is elevated (on pillows or sitting) rather than recumbent.

- **Paroxysmal nocturnal dyspnea (PND)** is somewhat similar to orthopnea but describes transient episodes of severe shortness of breath that typically occur at night when the individual is lying down and that may not be relieved by sitting upright.

Fatigue

In addition to the triad of respiratory symptoms, fatigue is a typical symptom of congestive heart failure. This is caused by inadequate blood flow to the muscles and other tissues, which makes it difficult to accomplish any level of significant exertion or even the activities of daily living.

Edema and coughing

As I mention earlier, when the heart fails to pump adequately, fluid can accumulate in the feet, ankles, legs and sometimes the abdomen — the swelling called *edema*. Fluid can also accumulate in the lungs, producing the congestion that gives congestive heart failure its name. For some individuals, this lung congestion may result in persistent coughing or in wheezy or raspy breathing.

Can other conditions mimic the symptoms of heart failure?

Conditions that cause either shortness of breath or edema may mimic heart failure. Typically, the conditions that cause shortness of breath are conditions of the lung, such as chronic obstructive pulmonary disease, asthma, or pulmonary infections. Conditions that cause edema include problems with either the liver or the kidneys or problems with the veins. In each of these instances, a shrewd physician who takes a good history, performs a good physical examination, and judiciously orders the proper tests can distinguish between cardiac causes of shortness of breath and edema versus other conditions that may mimic congestive heart failure.

How Is Heart Failure Diagnosed?

The diagnosis of heart failure is made through a combination of a careful history, a thorough physical examination, and a number of cardiac tests. (For more details about each, check out Chapter 13.)

- ✔ **History.** The history of any of the pulmonary symptoms (such as those just described), coupled with a history of heart disease and/or a recent illness that might have tripped a previously compensated heart over into heart failure, all point in the direction of heart failure as the diagnosis.

- ✔ **Physical examination.** In a physical examination, a physician may observe some more common signs:

  - An extra heart sound (also called a *gallop)*

  - Fluid in the lungs, which can be detected with the stethoscope

  - An abnormal motion of the heart that indicates to the physician's touch an increase in size or abnormal contraction pattern

  - Abnormal pressures in the neck veins

- Pitting edema, or fluid accumulation in the legs. When the physician presses down on the ankle, the impression left by the finger persists.

✔ **Laboratory tests.** Although there is no specific laboratory test for congestive heart failure, a number of tests are useful.

- A complete blood chemical analysis and blood count can indicate abnormalities in liver function, in kidney function, and in electrolytes (indicators of fluid retention).

- An electrocardiogram will often show abnormalities of underlying heart disease that may have led to the heart failure.

- A chest X-ray may show accumulation of fluid in the lungs.

- Advanced cardiac tests, such as an echocardiogram or a nuclear test, may indicate whether the heart is enlarged and provide an estimate of the ejection fraction. If the ejection fraction is 40 percent or less, the diagnosis of heart failure is highly likely.

- Heart catheterization and angiography may occasionally be helpful in the diagnosis of heart failure, particularly if any of the heart valves are leaking, causing fluid overload in the heart.

How Is Heart Failure Treated?

Treatments for heart failure generally attempt to counteract the negative effects of the heart's own compensatory mechanisms, such as retention of fluids or to strengthen the pumping ability of a weakened or damaged heart directly. These treatments range from lifestyle modifications to a variety of medicines and procedures.

Here are some of the treatment modalities that you can take or that will be instituted by your doctor to help treat heart failure.

Steps you can take

Modifying certain lifestyle practices, as your doctor may direct, can assist in treating congestive heart failure and can enhance the comfort and quality of your life as you live with the condition.

✔ **Weigh yourself.** You should weigh yourself every morning at the same time, typically after you have used the toilet, but before you have had breakfast. Typically, physicians recommend that if you rapidly gain more than two pounds you should contact your physician because it may mean that your body is retaining fluid and if so you may require an adjustment in your medication.

✔ **Restrict sodium.** Because sodium causes the body to retain fluid, you should try to restrict your sodium. Even a small increase in sodium in an individual who has heart failure can tip that person over into a very serious bout of lung congestion.

✔ **Limit fluids and alcohol.** Alcohol can further depress the pumping ability of the heart, and increased fluids can increase the fluid buildup, both in the lungs and the rest of the body. Heavy, long-term consumption of alcohol is a contributing factor in developing heart failure.

✔ **Perform light or moderate exercise.** It was once thought that people with heart failure shouldn't exercise. However, recent studies have shown that moderate exercise can help the heart pump more efficiently and also help the muscles work more efficiently. More efficient pumping and working reduces demands on the heart. Of course, if you have heart failure, you won't be training for a marathon or triathlon — easy does it. Very carefully, too. *Before undertaking any exercise, you absolutely must talk to your doctor about the best type and amount of exercise for you and also discuss warning signs of over exercising.*

Medical treatment of heart failure

A variety of medicines, including several newly developed types, are useful in the treatment of heart failure. Not all of these drugs are right for all patients, and often combinations of drugs are used to address individual situations. Here are some of the medicines that your physician may use.

✔ **Diuretics.** Often called *fluid pills* or *water pills* by the people who take them, diuretics help reduce the amount of fluid in the body and are very useful in individuals who have heart failure and fluid retention. (As I discuss in Chapter 9, diuretics are also very useful in the treatment of hypertension.)

✔ **Digitalis.** Digitalis (digoxin) helps the heart contract more vigorously. Digitalis was one of the very first medicines available for the treatment of heart failure. It was initially made from the foxglove plant, whose Latin name *digitalis* gives the drug its name. (Deposit that in your trivia bank!) Though one of the first, it's still one of the best medicines for stimulating the heart to pump more effectively and for reducing the symptoms of heart failure.

✔ **Angiotensin Converting Enzyme Inhibitors (ACE inhibitors).** Although they were originally developed for treating high blood pressure, ACE inhibitors have been shown to reduce the work of the heart by decreasing the pressure in the blood vessels that the heart has to pump against. This effect, studies indicate, may slow the loss of the heart's pumping ability and improve the quality of life and survival in individuals with heart failure. Of note, several studies have now shown that many physi-cians underuse these drugs. They have become a very important part of the standard treatment of heart failure. Feel free to ask your physician more about them.

✔ **Beta Blockers.** Because beta blockers (another drug developed to treat hypertension) slow the heart's contraction rate, thus reducing its pump-ing action, beta blockers for a long time were not considered appropri-ate for individuals with heart failure. Recent studies, however, have suggested that certain beta blockers may be very valuable in individuals with heart failure. This is probably because they reduce the likelihood that these individuals will suffer from significant rhythm problems of the heart.

✔ **Inotropes.** Inotropes are a series of powerful medicines that make the heart contract more powerfully. They must be delivered intravenously. Individuals who have very significant heart failure often can benefit from entering the hospital and being given 24 to 48 hours of these powerful intravenous medicines.

✔ **Spironolactone.** This medicine (often known by its brand name Aldactone) blocks a hormone that causes the heart to retain fluid in heart failure. A recent study showed that using this drug for heart-failure patients signif-icantly improves outcomes.

✔ **Surgical Treatment of Heart Failure.** If medicines are no longer effec-tive as an individual progressively slips into further heart failure, surgi-cal techniques may be used. There are several different surgical options.

 • **Procedures to shrink the size of the heart.** Such procedures are still considered experimental and only used in very severe cases of heart failure and even then, only by some surgeons who are partic-ularly skilled in their application. Two active experiments that have received press attention are 1) **cardiomyoplasty,** in which the end of a muscle is detached from the back and attached to the heart, then stimulated to contract using an implanted electric stim-ulator and 2) the **Batista procedure,** in which a triangular section of left ventricle muscle tissue is removed from an enlarged, weak-ened heart to reduce the size of the pumping chamber and increase its effectiveness. Note that both are experimental and not approved for wide use yet.

 • **Inserting a mechanical device to assist the heart.** In some cases, a mechanical pump called a *left ventricular assist device (LVAD)* may be sewn into the pumping chamber to assist in pumping. LVADs have typically been reserved for use only as transitional devices in place for days or weeks while a patient is waiting for cardiac transplant. However, in the future as the design is refined, these devices may be available for long-term treatment.

- **Heart transplants.** The treatment of last resort for certain very severe, life-threatening cases of heart failure is a cardiac transplant. Replacing the entire heart in appropriate candidates has proven highly effective. This can be lifesaving treatment for advanced heart failure. But donor hearts are scarce, and there are other concerns that limit this option, including organ rejection. Candidates for heart transplants are usually under 65 and have healthy vital organs (other than the heart) and no other life-threatening conditions/diseases.

How to Work with Your Doctor to Fight Heart Failure

Because the therapy of heart failure requires a great deal of precision and consistency, it is very important that patients work very carefully with their physicians to maximize the efficacy of their therapies. Here are some steps you can take that can help control your heart failure:

✔ See your physician regularly, and don't be afraid to ask questions.

✔ Closely follow your physician's instructions.

✔ Take medication consistently and according to instructions.

✔ Follow recommended lifestyle practices.

✔ Immediately report to your physician any change in your condition, such as increased weight, shortness of breath, or swollen feet.

Chapter 19

Other Cardiac Conditions

*I*n this chapter, I look at a variety of conditions in which the heart plays a major role — but usually not the only role. In a sense, this chapter is a kind of grab bag. Although each condition covered in this chapter generally affects fewer Americans than coronary artery disease and its major risk factors, these conditions are hardly minor — particularly if you or a family member has one. So, buckle your seatbelts for a quick tour of other important cardiac conditions. I describe each condition, hit the highlights of treatment, and tell you where you can find more information if you need it.

Stroke

Stroke is very common in the United States — in fact, it's the third leading cause of death in the U.S. behind heart disease and cancer. A stroke is also called a *cerebral vascular accident (CVA)* or, with increasing frequency these days, a *brain attack*. Although it involves the cardiovascular system, stroke is considered a separate condition from other cardiovascular diseases.

✔ Because of new treatments, many more people now survive strokes than in the past. In fact, more than 4 million American stroke survivors are alive today.

✔ Stroke affects men and women equally, although men are somewhat more likely to have strokes at an earlier age than women.

✔ Stroke is the leading cause of serious long-term disability in the United States and is responsible for over one half of all hospitalizations for neurologic disease.

What is a stroke?

There are basically three different kinds of stroke:

✔ A **cerebral embolism** occurs when a blood clot travels from somewhere else in the body to the brain. When the blood clot lodges in a vessel in the brain, it cuts off blood flow to the portion of the brain supplied by that vessel. Without adequate oxygen, that portion of the brain suffers damage or even "dies," resulting in such typical stroke symptoms as paralysis or problems with speech, vision, or comprehension (depending on which portion of the brain was damaged). This type stroke is also called an *ischemic stroke* because it's caused by lack of blood flow (ischemia).

The blood clots causing the stroke may travel from a number of different locations in the body.

• These blood clots often occur in the major arteries in the neck which supply the brain (the carotid arteries). This is why your doctor often listens with a stethoscope over your neck, to hear if there is a narrowing of one of these arteries, which leads to turbulence that can be heard by the physician.

• Blood clots also commonly form in the heart, particularly in people with atrial fibrillation. In this case, when the left atrium fibrillates rather than contracting normally, blood clots can form in the blood and travel directly up to the brain.

✔ A **cerebral thrombosis** describes a form of stroke that comes from progressive narrowing of the arteries in the brain, or sometimes in the carotid arteries in the neck. It is also a type of ischemic stroke. The difference between a thrombosis and an embolism is that in a thrombosis the plaque (cholesterol again) that narrows the artery and any clot that may form on it don't move. The typical underlying causes for this type of blockage are atherosclerosis and high blood pressure. Before having a major stroke, many people may experience a temporary lack of blood flow to the brain called a *transient ischemic attack* (TIA), which is really a small stroke in which the effects (such as those listed in the next section) usually last for only a few minutes or hours. Never ignore these; treat them as a serious warning and consult your physician.

 A **hemorrhagic stroke** comes from bleeding in the brain. (Yes, the same Greek root word as hemorrhage: *hemo* = blood, *rhage* = to break.) This bleeding may be caused by congenital abnormalities, such as *aneurysms,* or may also come from fragile blood vessels, often in the setting of high blood pressure. Occasionally, this type stroke can occur in the setting of pregnancy because the blood vessels are made fragile from the extra estrogen in the blood stream.

What are the symptoms of a stroke?

If you see or have one or more of these symptoms, don't wait — call 911 right away!

 Sudden numbness or weakness of the face, arm, or leg, especially on one side of the body

 Sudden confusion or trouble speaking or understanding speech

 Sudden trouble seeing in one or both eyes

 Sudden trouble walking, dizziness, or loss of balance or coordination

 Sudden severe headache with no known cause

Treatment can be more effective if given directly. Every minute counts!

Source: National Institute of Neurological Disorders and Stroke and the Brain Attack Coalition.

How is stroke treated?

Prevention is the most important treatment in stroke. The more effective treatment of hypertension in the last twenty years, for example, has lowered the prevalence of stroke in the U.S. — a major breakthrough. And following the lifestyle practices that reduce your risk of developing coronary artery disease also helps you lower your risk of stroke.

Five tips to lower your risk of stroke

 Treat high blood pressure.

 Quit smoking.

 Manage heart disease.

 Control diabetes.

 Seek help for transient ischemic attacks (TIAs).

New medicines work to treat stroke and prevent stoke. Typically administered immediately after a stroke or TIA has occurred, new clot-busting medicines have been shown to lessen the serious problems that result from strokes. Other useful medicines include anti-platelet agents (which reduce the clotting function of platelets), blood-thinning medicines (anticoagulants), and neuroprotectants (which help protect the brain against secondary damage).

Individuals who have underlying predisposition to stroke, such as individuals with atrial fibrillation, or individuals who have had surgery to treat narrowed or malformed arteries should also have long-term blood thinning medications (anticoagulants) to decrease their risk of stroke.

Surgery is used to treat and prevent some types of strokes. Here are just a few examples:

- ✔ Where not too risky, persons whose stroke results from a cerebral aneurysm will usually have surgery to repair or "clip" the ruptured aneurysm and reduce the risk of new or continued bleeding.

- ✔ Surgically cleaning plaque out of the narrowed carotid arteries (carotid endarterectomy) is widely and safely used as stroke prevention therapy.

- ✔ Some congenital vascular malformations that pose a higher risk for stroke (such as the tangle of blood vessels called *arteriovenous malformation*) can be treated surgically.

Rehabilitation therapy helps stroke patients regain better function. The leading cause of serious disability for American adults is stroke. No contest. Once stroke has damaged a portion of the brain, physical therapy, occupational therapy, speech therapy, and psychological therapy can help patients regain as much functional ability as possible. The good news is that the brain is wonderfully *plastic* — which means that it has the ability to learn and change with healthy parts taking over for injured parts. As a consequence, some stroke patients are able to regain full or satisfactory function. The tragic news, however, is that severe strokes can be permanently debilitating. The best treatment is still prevention.

For more information on stroke

The National Institute of Neurological Disorders and Stroke provides lots of useful information on its Web site (www.ninds.nih.gov), including an informative 23-page booklet, "Stroke: Hope Through Research." You may also reach their public information office at the following address:

NIH Neurological Institute
P.O. Box 5801
Bethesda, MD 20892
1-800-352-9424

National Stroke Association
96 Inverness Drive East, Suite 1
Englewood, CO 80112-5112
1-800-787-6537
Web site: www.stroke.org

Provides education, information, research, and referrals, and sponsors nationwide chapters and support groups.

National Rehabilitation Information Center
1010 Wayne Avenue, Suite 800
Silver Spring, MD 20910-5633
1-800-346-2742
Web site: www.naric.com

Provides excellent access to online databases and resources.

Peripheral Vascular Disease

When disease narrows the arteries of the heart, it's called *coronary artery disease*. When that same disease process affects other arteries, particularly in the arms and legs, it's called *peripheral vascular disease*. And don't think peripheral means unimportant.

What causes peripheral vascular disease?

The narrowing of arteries in the body's extremities happens the same way as it does in the coronary arteries. Fatty plaques composed of cholesterol, other lipids, and proteins build up on the artery walls to produce atherosclerosis. This condition affects about 12 percent of individuals 65 to 70 and 20 percent of those over 70. It's particularly common in cigarette smokers. The most common arteries involved are those of the legs.

Although many people with peripheral vascular disease never experience symptoms, the most common symptom is pain in the leg muscles during exertion such as fast walking or climbing a hill or stairs. In medicine, this leg discomfort is called *claudication*. This discomfort or pain usually goes away when at rest *(intermittent claudication),* but if the arteries are totally or nearly blocked, the pain can persist during rest. Severe blockage may lead to severe complications.

How is peripheral vascular disease treated?

A number of treatments are available to relieve the lack of blood flow to the legs caused by peripheral vascular disease.

- ✔ **Slowly progressive physical activity** is usually the first recommendation for individuals who have intermittent pain. Directed by your physician, a daily program of moderate and slowly progressive exercise can improve physical fitness and help develop alternate circulation through smaller blood vessels (called *collateral circulation).*

  Because circulation is often poor in the lower leg, taking good care of the feet is very important. That includes not wearing tight socks and avoiding injury. Poor circulation in the feet makes even small injuries such as blisters potentially dangerous because the injury is slow to heal and any infection is difficult to treat. So if you have peripheral vascular disease, be sure you understand and carry out your doctor's instructions for proper foot care religiously.

- ✔ **Modifying lifestyle behaviors to lower the risk of developing atherosclerosis** can help slow or even stop the process of narrowing in the peripheral arteries. Quitting smoking is particularly helpful.

- ✔ **Surgical and nonsurgical treatments can be used to restore blood flow** when the narrowing is very severe. These treatments can include balloon angioplasty, a technique very similar to the procedure used to open coronary arteries (see Chapter 13). However, in this case, the balloon-tipped catheter is threaded down into the narrowed artery of the leg and expanded to open up the artery and allow more blood flow to occur.

Valvular Heart Disease

As I discuss in Chapter 2, the four heart valves serve as the traffic cops of the heart, directing blood flow in the proper direction and preventing it from backing up improperly.

As long as these valves open fully and shut tightly, all is well. But if any disease or injury causes any valve to leak (have *regurgitation)* or to narrow (have *stenosis),* then major problems can result. Significant valve leakage can overload the heart because extra blood flowing back into the heart requires an extra strong beat to eject it. A narrowed valve can cause the heart to thicken because it is being asked to pump against a much higher pressure.

What are some common valve malfunctions and their causes?

Regurgitation and *stenosis* are the two most common malfunctions, or conditions that cause malfunctions. Although either condition can affect any or all valves, the mitral and aortic valves in the left heart, the main pumping chamber, are those usually affected. Both conditions can, and often do, exist simultaneously in either the same valve or different valves. A number of different conditions can cause valves to leak or narrow, including:

- Congenital valvular problems (a condition you're born with).

- Damage to valve structures, such as when the structures that anchor the flaps of the mitral valve break.

- Progressive problems, including those which may come through the aging process, such as calcification, or those that come through an infection, such as rheumatic fever or endocarditis. If the problem becomes very severe, it may require open heart surgery and valve replacement.

Because valve problems produce broad rather than specific symptoms, your physician will use the symptoms and physical exam to consider whether your problem may be valvular and to order further tests as necessary.

A couple of conditions need an extra word:

- **Mitral valve prolapse:** This condition is a "ballooning" back of the mitral valve when the heart contracts. During physical examination, it produces a murmur and "click" heard through the stethoscope. This condition is particularly common in adolescents and young adults, particularly women. Six to ten percent of young women have the condition of mitral valve prolapse. (For reasons that are totally unclear, these are mostly *thin* young women.)

  In any event, it is important to know if you have mitral valve prolapse because this condition makes you more susceptible to infections of the heart valve. Such infections can damage the valve enough to require surgical replacement.

- **Infectious endocarditis:** Heart valves can be infected with bacteria that have been introduced into the blood stream in various ways. This condition is called *infectious endocarditis*. While normal heart valves may contract endocarditis, it is much more common in individuals who have an underlying valve problem. Bacteria spilled into the blood stream from dental work is one common cause of endocarditis. An infection elsewhere in the body may also cause bacteria to enter the blood stream.

There are no symptoms specific to endocarditis that would allow you to identify it, but the possibility is another reason to take a persistent high fever and other symptoms of infection to the doctor.

Although these infections of the heart valve can be very serious, usually they can be effectively treated with intravenous antibiotics lasting anywhere from two to six weeks. However, in some instances the infection can become so destructive that one or more valves may need to be replaced.

The best advice, if you have any mitral prolapse or any underlying valve abnormality, is to make sure that you take antibiotics, both prior to and after any procedure where there may be the potential for bacteria to enter the blood stream — even if it's "just" a dental procedure or very minor surgery. Ask your physician which antibiotics are right for you and why.

How are valve problems treated?

If a valve abnormality is not progressing rapidly or causing any serious problem, your physician may simply keep a close eye on it so that treatment can be initiated when and if necessary. Also taking preventive antibiotics as necessary if you have an underlying valve abnormality is a good idea.

Various nonsurgical and surgical techniques can also be used:

✔ Balloon catheter procedures (balloon valvuloplasty) can be used in certain situations to widen a narrowed valve.

✔ Surgical modification and repair can be used to correct other valve problems.

✔ Valve replacement with either a pig's valve (porcine valve) or mechanical valve offers very effective treatment when a diseased valve cannot be repaired. Because blood clots may form on the "foreign" surfaces of any mechanical valve, individuals who have these replacements must take anticoagulants for as long as they have the mechanical valve, usually the rest of their lives. Porcine valves do not require anticoagulation but they typically don't last as long before needing replacement.

Diseases of the Aorta

View the aorta as the major superhighway leading out of the heart. For every organ in the body, including the heart, blood must first flow into and through the aorta before being efficiently distributed to all of the working tissues. (See Figure 19-1.)

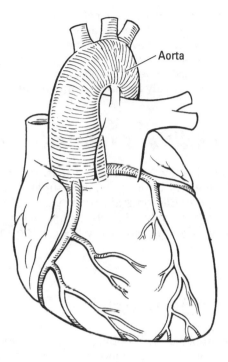

A healthy aorta can take the pounding of being right next to the heart and the regular thrusts of large volumes of blood being ejected into it with each heart beat. However, various conditions can cause the aorta to malfunction. *Catastrophic* doesn't begin to describe what that means.

What causes aorta problems?

The most common problems of the aorta arise from the same disease process that affects the coronary arteries, mainly atherosclerosis.

When the aorta becomes hardened from atherosclerosis, it can leak or even break apart. This is called an *aortic dissection*. It may also be provoked by high blood pressure, pregnancy (presumably because the aorta is weakened by the extra estrogen floating around the body), or in certain abnormalities of the connective tissue. One such connective tissue abnormality is called Marfan's syndrome. A number of professional athletes have actually died from aortic dissections caused by Marfan's.

The aorta may also have *aneurysms* — weaknesses in the artery wall where it actually balloons out. Although these aneurysms may occur adjacent to the heart, they more commonly occur in the section of the aorta that travels down the middle of the body. In this latter case, they are called *abdominal aortic aneurysms* (AAAs). Your doctor can often feel such aneurysms by placing his or her hands on the abdomen. Because a developing aneurysm has no symptoms, the potential is another reason to have a thorough physical regularly. After diagnosis, such aneurysms need to be carefully examined because as they continue to expand, they can actually rupture, a catastrophic outcome.

How are these conditions treated?

A leaking aorta is a medical emergency. A ruptured aorta is frequently fatal. An aorta that leaks or is in danger of rupturing requires surgery to replace the weakened section with a woven Dacron graft. Such surgery should only be performed by a surgeon highly skilled in this procedure, because the potential for problems with the coronary arteries, as well as the aorta, is very high.

Diseases of the Pericardium

Normally the *pericardium,* the thin sac surrounding the heart, is lubricated from bodily fluids, allowing the heart to freely move around as it contracts. When the pericardium becomes inflamed or infected — a condition called *pericarditis* — it can threaten the heart's health rather than protect it.

What causes pericarditis?

A wide variety of conditions can cause pericarditis, including bacterial or viral infections, inflammation, diseases of the connective tissue, or even cancer. In a sense, many of these conditions result from the fact that the pericardium is doing its job as the last defense against invasion of the heart. However, when these conditions occur, they can cause the pericardium to malfunction. Fluid can build up in the pericardial sac or fibrous tissue can infiltrate the pericardial sac after an infection and in these instances, the function of the heart can be impeded.

Individuals with pericarditis often have chest discomfort when they breathe in deeply or change positions, and this discomfort is often relieved when they change positions. There may also be a buildup of excess fluid between the pericardium and the heart, a condition called *pericardial effusion.*

How is pericarditis treated?

Treating pericarditis requires treating the underlying condition. If pericarditis is caused by an infection, treatment of that infection typically causes the pericarditis to resolve. In some cases, it is necessary to drain the effusion away from the heart through a needle *(pericardiocentesis)* or through surgery. On rare occasions, the pericardium may have to be removed surgically, but one can get along very well without it. Often, however, pericarditis gets better without any treatment other than the use of a nonsteroid anti-inflammatory drug (NSAID) such as ibuprofen.

Diseases of the Heart Muscle

As I discuss in Chapter 18, certain conditions called *cardiomyopathies* can actually harm the heart muscle itself. About 50,000 Americans suffer from a cardiomyopathy. And these conditions are the leading reason for heart transplants.

What are cardiomyopathies?

The term *cardiomyopathy* literally means "disease of the heart muscle" (*cardio*= heart; *myo* = muscle; *pathy* = disease), and we speak of *cardiomyopathies* because the term covers a number of conditions. These conditions are typically classified according to the three basic ways that they affect the heart muscle and its function. Each of these types of cardiomyopathy may have many different causes.

- ✔ **Congestive cardiomyopathy.** In this type, the heart becomes *dilated,* or enlarged, and heart muscle ceases to be able to contract well. A virus often causes this type of damage but other conditions can also cause congestive cardiomyopathy, such as damage from chronic, excessive alcohol consumption. In many cases the cause is *idiopathic,* or unidentified.

- ✔ **Hypertrophic cardiomyopathy.** In this type, the heart muscle becomes thickened, or *hypertrophied*, although it continues to contract well. The thickening of the muscle makes the pumping chamber smaller and also keeps the heart muscle from relaxing properly between contractions.

- ✔ **Restrictive cardiomyopathy.** In this type, which is rare in the U.S., abnormal tissue may be deposited or grow within the heart muscle itself which causes it to become stiff. This happens in certain conditions such as radiation to the chest (which may occur if there is a tumor elsewhere in the chest) or in certain connective tissue diseases.

How are cardiomyopathies treated?

The therapy for cardiomyopathies depends on the underlying condition and the type of cardiomyopathy. If an infection causes it, treatment of the infection is very important. In addition, treatments including medicine and surgery to help the heart contract more properly may also be employed. Because advanced cardiomyopathies generally lead to heart failure, you may find the discussion of the treatment of heart failure in Chapter 18 helpful.

Pulmonary Embolism

A blood clot to the lungs is called a *pulmonary embolus*. Unfortunately, over one half million Americans have an episode of blood clot to the lungs every year and about 200,000 of these individuals die as a result.

What causes pulmonary embolism?

Typically, pulmonary embolism is the result of an underlying disease. For example, individuals with certain types of cancer may have blood that is particularly likely to clot and cause pulmonary blood clots to the lungs. Pulmonary embolisms are also a danger for individuals who experience prolonged bed rest or inactivity. Other risk factors include certain medications (such as birth control pills) and inherited clotting disorders.

There are two major sources of blood clots to the lung:

- ✔ By far, the most common type blood clot forms in the pelvic veins and deep veins of the legs. Such a clot then travels into the right side of the heart and is ejected into the lung circulation where it can block off blood flow to a portion of the lung.

- ✔ In some instances, the blood clots can actually arise in the right side of the heart itself. This is particularly true in cases of atrial fibrillation.

How is this condition treated?

Because a pulmonary embolism can be life-threatening, it's important that the condition be diagnosed and treatment started as quickly as possible. Shortness of breath can be one symptom, and certainly any sudden or rapidly developing shortness of breath should send you right to the doctor or emergency room. The most common treatment of a blood clot to the lungs is anticoagulation with blood thinners. This can be done initially with intravenous drugs (such as Heparin) followed by three to six months of anticoagulation with medicines that are taken by mouth. When blood clots are particularly dangerous or recurrent, it may also be possible to put a mechanical "filter" in the veins coming out of the legs to actually catch the blood clots before they can make it into the heart or out into the lungs.

Cor Pulmonale

I devoted an entire chapter to heart failure (Chapter 18), which is caused by problems with the heart itself. When the right heart fails because of conditions in the lungs (not the heart), it's called (in Latin, natch) *cor pulmonale* (*cor* = heart, *pulmonale* = lungs).

In cor pulmonale, disorders of the lungs, such as emphysema, cause pressures to rise in the blood circulation in the lungs. This pressure in turn causes the right side of the heart to fail in its job of pumping blood into the lungs.

Treating the underlying disorder is, by far, the most effective treatment for cor pulmonale. Certainly, stopping cigarette smoking or other irritants to the lung is very important. In addition, individuals may benefit from blood thinning medicines to prevent blood clots from traveling to the lungs. Occasionally, a surgical lung transplant is required to correct underlying lung problems which are causing the right heart to fail.

Congenital Heart Disease

Congenital heart disease in adults is quite rare. Congenital heart disease in newborns complicates about one percent of births. Treatment of the various congenital abnormalities are in the domain of the pediatric cardiologist and the pediatric cardiac surgeon. An adult patient has congenital heart disease usually only because the defect escaped detection in childhood. Why? The defect may have been very subtle, it may have been misdiagnosed as a benign condition, or inadequate medical attention may have been given.

What are common congenital defects?

Over 90 percent of adults with congenital heart disease have a one of five different conditions:

- **Atrial septal defect (ASD):** An abnormal opening between the two atria because there is a hole in the septum

- **Ventricular septal defect (VSD):** An abnormal opening between the two ventricles because there is a hole in the septum

✔ **Pulmonic stenosis (PS):** A narrowing of the valve leading from the right heart into the lungs

✔ **Patent ductus arteriosus (PDA):** An abnormal connection from the aorta to the pulmonary artery

✔ **Coarctation of the aorta (COARC):** A narrowing of the aorta occurring after the aortic valve

How are these defects treated?

Treatment typically requires surgical correction of the underlying defect, although occasionally, medicines may be used, either as a transitional phase or as part of the overall therapy.

Cardiac Tumors

Like any other organ, the heart can be susceptible to various tumor growths. Fortunately, these are quite rare. When the heart is involved with a tumor, it is three times more likely to be a metastatic tumor from another organ system than a tumor of the heart itself. Most tumors that metastasize to the heart are close anatomically. These include lung cancers, in particular, and cancers that travel in the blood stream (breast cancer, melanoma, and leukemia). Major tumors of the heart muscle itself are quite rare.

If the tumor is metastatic, it is usually treated by treating the underlying primary cancer. Tumors of the heart muscle itself are treated with chemotherapy, radiation, and/or occasionally surgery.

Cardiac Trauma

Just like any other organ in the body, the heart can be injured in various traumatic ways, including penetrating or non-penetrating chest injuries. The most common type of cardiac trauma occurs in an automobile accident where the chest slams against the steering wheel (another reason to wear your seat belt). In some instances, cardiac trauma may be overlooked because other types of trauma may be more obvious. Because the heart is defended strongly by the ribs and muscles inside the chest cavity, it is relatively protected. However, serious cardiac trauma can be fatal.

If the heart is actually penetrated (in medicine this is called a *laceration*), blood can leak into the pericardium and rapidly cause death. It is important to suspect and check for cardiac trauma anytime an individual has been in a setting where it could occur, such as motor vehicle accident. Recognition of the injury and its rapid diagnosis through techniques such as echocardiography may be lifesaving.

Typically, surgery is required if significant cardiac trauma occurs. Whenever an individual is in an automobile accident where the chest hits the steering wheel, physicians and patients alike should be alerted to the possibility that cardiac trauma has occurred.

Non-Cardiac Surgery in Patients with Heart Disease

Many people who have heart disease undergo surgery for problems that have nothing to do with their cardiovascular system. In fact, approximately one-third of surgical patients over the age of 35 have some form of cardiovascular disease, including hypertension. To ensure safe surgery in these cases, the underlying heart disease must be considered for at least two reasons:

 ✔ Surgery, in and of itself, stresses the cardiovascular system, which may be dangerous in individuals who have severe or unstable heart disease.

 ✔ Anesthesia may also interact with underlying heart disease.

It is essential that any person with heart disease have a complete medical work-up from their family physician and/or possibly a cardiologist prior to undergoing any form of non-cardiac surgery.

When It's Time for Two: Pregnancy and the Heart

Even the highly desired condition of pregnancy can have multiple interactions with the heart. Most obviously, pregnancy increases the work of the heart because it must support the circulation of both mother and fetus. In fact, cardiac output during pregnancy can increase by as much as a third. For this reason, even for an otherwise healthy woman, it is important to carefully monitor the cardiovascular system throughout the pregnancy. Particular attention should be given to blood pressure because some women may experience excessive rises in blood pressure, which can be harmful not only to the woman herself but also to her fetus.

What about pregnancy when you have heart disease?

When women with underlying heart disease get pregnant, it is very important that a cardiologist who is knowledgeable and skillful in the management of heart disease during pregnancy be included as part of prenatal care. With proper cardiac care, there are very few reasons why pregnancy, even in a woman with underlying heart disease, cannot be safely and successfully completed.

What about exercise and other heart-healthy lifestyle practices during pregnancy?

The American College of Obstetrics and Gynecology has published recommendations for exercise and other helpful practices for pregnant women. Of course, these recommendations should be carried out in conjunction with the advice and recommendations of your personal obstetrician/gynecologist.

Walking is one activity recommended to benefit mother and fetus. You should observe one caution, however: Decrease the intensity of a walking program to account for the fact that the cardiac output is raised by the pregnancy itself. Also be particularly careful during hot and humid weather or if you have an ongoing cold or other viral infection. It is very important not to experience excessive increases in body temperature, which can harm both fetus and mother. With these caveats, regular exercise can be very beneficial to the physical, emotional, and spiritual sides of pregnancy.

For More Information

For additional information about these and other diseases of the heart, you will find that the Web site of the American Heart Association (www.americanheart.org) offers an easy-to-use reference guide, "Heart and Stroke A - Z Guide." Other helpful sites include the National Heart Lung and Blood Institute (www.nhlbi.nih.gov), the Mayo Clinic (www.mayohealth.org) and Johns Hopkins Health Information (www.intelihealth.com).

Chapter 20

Reversing Heart Disease: Hope or Hype?

*W*hen Thomas Wolfe's famous novel, *You Can't Go Home Again,* came out in 1940, most people felt his title had hit on one true thing. For many years, cardiologists believed that same truth applied to coronary artery disease: Once you had this progressive, relentless condition, you might slow the process down, but you couldn't actually reverse it — you couldn't go home again.

But *mirabile dictu* (hot-diggety!), in medicine as in life, the quest goes on. We now know that *yes*, you can do a number of things that can at least halt the progression of coronary artery disease (CAD) in its tracks for most people. And 50 to 60 percent of those who adopt the strict measures may actually experience some reversal of their coronary artery disease. If you have CAD and want to make this happen, however, you are going to have to stop cold and make major changes in how you eat, exercise, work, and generally live your life. You usually have to take lipid (cholesterol) lowering medicines, too. But as long as you are willing to do your part, there is more hope than hype in the promise that you can reverse coronary artery disease.

Before we go any further, I want to emphasize three points.

✔ Most of this book is devoted to reversing your *risk factors* for heart disease so that you never get it. We are talking about something fundamentally different in this chapter — help for people who already have significant narrowing of their coronary arteries.

✔ If you're thinking that, with the news in this chapter, you can live a life of sin (sloth and gluttony of the seven deadlies come to mind) — then repent and turn the negative health effects around, forget it! It is still — and always will be — better to *prevent* heart disease than to try to reverse it.

✔ This chapter is not a do-it-yourself manual. You must work with your cardiologist. If you have CAD, you have a dangerous condition. Even in the best outcomes, only 50 to 60 percent of individuals who stringently follow the regimens outlined in this chapter actually experience some reversal of their heart disease. Some individuals experience a halt in the progression of their coronary artery disease (also a very good thing!), while 20 to 30 percent continue to experience progression of CAD, despite their best efforts. For all of these reasons, it is critically important not to try to "go it alone."

Back to the Future: Can You Turn Coronary Artery Disease Around?

The simple answer to this question is *yes*. A number of studies show that under the right circumstances, 50 to 60 percent of narrowing of coronary arteries can actually be reversed, at least to some degree.

Different approaches have been used in various studies, but the cumulative results to date support one central therapeutic strategy. These findings indicate that by diminishing the amount of lipid (cholesterol and fats) within the plaque, you can decrease the likelihood that the plaque will rupture and set in process the catastrophic sequence of events that lead to unstable angina or heart attack. (See Chapter 14 if you want to review how plaque formation takes place.)

A look at the evidence on regression of CAD

In the past decade, there have been over 20 major scientific studies that have shown that regression of coronary artery disease can occur. These can be broken down into studies of four therapeutic approaches:

✔ Either diet or diet plus other interventions

✔ Intervention with a single drug to lower lipids

✔ Combinations of drugs to lower lipids

✔ Other interventions to lower lipids

In the following sections, I look at the findings on each approach to reversing CAD.

The evidence for diet or diet plus other lifestyle interventions

There have been five major studies in the last 15 years that have used either diet alone or diet in combination with other lifestyle factors or, in several instances, low fat diet in combination with medicines. The results of these studies have been quite consistent.

✔ In cases where cholesterol has been lowered more than 25 percent and LDL cholesterol in particular has been lowered more than 30 percent, at least some degree of regression of coronary artery disease has occurred in approximately 50 percent of individuals.

✔ When total cholesterol has been lowered by between 10 and 20 percent, regression of coronary artery disease has occurred in about one-third of patients.

The evidence for single drug interventions

In the ten studies where drug therapy was used to lower lipids as a mechanism to promote regression of coronary artery disease, the results again are consistent:

If total cholesterol is lowered more than 20 percent and LDL cholesterol lowered approximately 30 percent, anywhere from 30 to 50 percent of individuals with underlying coronary artery disease experience regression of the CAD or at least a halt of progression.

The evidence for using combinations of drugs

There have been three studies that have used a combination of drug interventions to lower cholesterol. Once again, the results are quite promising.

Approximately one-half of individuals experienced either regression of CAD or a halt in progression, provided that they had significant lowering of their total cholesterol and LDL cholesterol. In some instances, HDL cholesterol has actually risen as well.

The evidence for other interventions

There was one study that used surgery to lower cholesterol in an attempt to cause regression of coronary artery disease. In this study, part of the small bowel was bypassed in order to decrease the absorption of fats. In this situation, about 50 to 60 percent of individuals experienced either regression of coronary artery disease or halt in progression.

A promising outlook and a caution

The cumulative evidence of these studies is very hopeful. And ongoing research should help us learn more about what therapies may enable us to achieve regression of CAD. But we are far from all the way there. No matter how many individuals achieved improvement in these trials, we must remember that in many of them, *20 to 30 percent of individuals actually experienced progression of their coronary artery disease, despite significant lowering of their lipids.*

How Does Coronary Artery Disease Regress?

The studies just discussed also provide evidence that these therapies work to reverse coronary artery disease by boosting and reinforcing the body's natural healing process.

Just as an injury to the vessel wall stimulates the formation of plaque that narrows the arteries, such an injury also stimulates a number of natural processes that slowly attempt to heal the injury. Dramatic changes such as a swift and significant reduction in LDL appear to speed these healing processes up, thereby promoting regression of CAD.

How therapy attacks the most dangerous plaque — the "culprit lesion"

The process of regression of coronary artery disease is particularly dramatic in attacking the type of plaques that cardiologists call *culprit lesions.* (These narrowings are called culprit lesions because they are usually the ones that crack and "commit the crime" — cause acute heart problems.) Although culprit lesions account for only about 10 to 20 percent of all plaques narrowing coronary arteries, they appear to be responsible for 80 to 90 percent of episodes of unstable angina and heart attack. They are also characterized by having a great deal of lipids in their core, which may be the central reason why they appear to be the plaque that stabilizes when you dramatically lower cholesterol and other lipids.

How do you know if regression has occurred?

In the studies of regression of coronary artery disease, of course, researchers had to find ways to positively confirm whether or not the narrowing of coronary arteries had been somewhat reversed. That meant that earlier studies required study participants to undergo repeat heart catheterizations to take actual pictures of their coronary arteries. A costly process and not much fun for the individual. More recent studies have used non-invasive techniques such as PET scanning (see Chapter 13) — still costly but less time-consuming and more pleasant for participants. You can also see why there are just dozens of important studies and not hundreds.

As a practical matter, if you are working with your doctor to try to reverse your own coronary artery disease, in all likelihood, you won't be required to go through these advanced tests. You can assume, with a reasonable degree of certainty, that you are doing everything in your power to create regression of coronary artery disease if you and your physician have undertaken the steps that I recommend in the following section to dramatically lower your cholesterol in general, and your LDL cholesterol in particular.

A Practical Approach to Regression of Coronary Artery Disease

So can you put all this cutting-edge research to work for you? Yes, you can set in motion the processes that can reverse coronary artery disease — at least to a degree. I want to emphasize that this is no magic bullet, but conscientiously taking the following four steps while working with your physician as your ally may help you overcome this foe.

1. Lower your lipids.

Lowering total cholesterol and, in particular LDL cholesterol, appears to be essential in reversing the process of atherosclerosis. Research is ongoing to settle the debate about whether the absolute level of LDL cholesterol below which regression occurs or the percentage change of cholesterol and LDL cholesterol matters the most in promoting such regression. Based on the best current evidence, I recommend that you try to lower your total cholesterol by about 20 percent and your LDL cholesterol by at least 30 percent in order to maximize your chances of setting in process regression of coronary artery disease. I also believe that achieving a total cholesterol of below 170 and an LDL cholesterol below 100 is highly desirable.

There are two main ways to do this:

- **By diet alone.** Several studies cited in this chapter use strict, low-fat, vegetarian diets. The diet advocated in the Lifestyle Heart Trial, for example, is an extremely low-fat diet with less than 10 percent of calories from fat, as well as significant reduction in saturated fat. Individuals who were able to stick with this very restricted diet lowered their total cholesterol by 24 percent and their LDL cholesterol by 37 percent. *Drawback*: This type of restricted diet is very difficult for most patients to follow.

- **By diet and medication.** As a practical matter, most of the studies support combining a diet that derives less than 30 percent of calories from fat and less than 10 percent of calories from saturated fat (the AHA Step 1 Diet described in Chapter 10) with one or more of the powerful lipid-lowering agents. Such an approach can lower lipid levels to the point where CAD regression begins. And most people may find it easier to stick with this approach than with the very low-fat diet alone. Of course, you should work with your physician on this, and a registered dietitian who is skilled in low fat diets should also be brought into the picture.

2. Get regular exercise.

I am a strong advocate of regular exercise. Moderate exercise in conjunction with other risk factor lowering has been shown to lower the risk of secondary events from coronary artery disease and should be part of any program designed to promote regression of coronary artery disease.

3. Reduce stress.

The Lifestyle Heart Program, developed and popularized by Dr. Dean Ornish, emphasizes stress reduction as part of its overall model for regression of coronary artery disease. I have long been an advocate of mind/body interaction and think that stress reduction techniques such as visualization and meditation can play a very significant role in the CAD regression. Many cardiologists, however, remain unconvinced of the value of these mind/body techniques for reversing heart disease.

4. Work to reduce all your risk factors for CAD.

Numerous studies in the cardiac rehabilitation literature (see Chapter 16) show that a comprehensive approach for lowering risk factors for coronary artery disease results in significant decrease of the likelihood of recurrent complications. It certainly is important to control blood pressure, stop cigarette smoking, and lose weight (if you are overweight) as ways to promote regression of coronary artery disease.

If you're one of the millions of Americans who suffer from coronary artery disease, there is hope that you "can go home again" or at least turn around on the path and head towards home. But you must really commit to the process — and I mean you have to be what one dignitary in a delightful slip of the tongue called *unswavering* (unswerving and unwavering). Then your body in its infinite wisdom will help you along the path toward regression.

Chapter 21

Alternative Therapies: Are They for You?

You know by now that I believe that you can do many things in your daily life to enhance both your short- and long-term quality of life. But where do alternative therapies fit in?

Let me say right from the beginning that Western medicine does not have all the answers. There are a number of aspects of alternative therapy and a number of behaviors as well as products that fall under the rubric of alternative medicine that can be beneficial. But because "alternative" can be used to cover so many areas, that old warning of *caveat emptor* — let the buyer beware — certainly applies here. If you are careful and use the *proven* alternative medicine techniques judiciously and in combination with the many benefits of the modern Western cardiovascular medicine, however, you can derive important benefits without taking unnecessary risks.

In this chapter, I look at some alternative therapies that have been proven to be beneficial in the fight against heart disease and discuss how to judge which techniques are questionable or even pure baloney.

What Is Alternative Medicine Anyway?

A number of different definitions have been offered for "alternative" medicine. In fact, the definition has changed quite a bit over the last decade. In a sense, perhaps the broadest definition defines this type of medicine by what it is *not*. Alternative medicine is, in essence, an alternative to traditional Western medicine. It has come to include a variety of behavioral techniques, such as relaxation methods or meditation and other spiritual techniques, as well as a number of different clinical approaches, such as chiropractic, massage, and herbal remedies. As a practical matter, it has come to include both mind therapy (behavioral) and body therapy (clinical). The mind therapies include mental imagery, hypnosis, relaxation, and so on. Body therapies include not only chiropractic but also acupuncture and herbal treatments.

Placebo versus Proof: Caveat Emptor

Emotions tend to run pretty high when people talk about alternative medicine. Some people believe that the techniques of alternative medicine have made enormous differences in their lives. However, many physicians point out that almost none of these techniques have been subjected to rigorous scientific testing; so there is little scientific evidence of whether or not many of these techniques are clinically effective.

In a sense, both positions are right. Thanks to the complex interdependency of the human mind and body, sometimes you can get benefits from a therapeutic action just because you believe you will. Physicians first observed this phenomenon while trying to test whether particular substances were biologically active. Part of a group of test subjects would receive a potential drug and, for control, the other half a pharmacologically inert substance called a *placebo* (often a sugar pill), but none would know exactly which substance they received. In any type experiment, some of the subjects taking the placebo would show an improvement in symptoms. This response became known as the *placebo effect*.

The placebo effect is not phony or bad, it's just a fact of human psychology. We often can, and do, use it for our benefit. Our admirable attachment to teddy bears is a case in point. What is a teddy bear? Objectively, just cloth pieced together and stuffed. Can a stuffed bear reach out and give us a hug? Can one fend off the monsters of the night? Yet as children (and beyond) have not most of us drawn immense comfort at stressful or anxious times from our teddies? At a more complex level, similar things are happening when we search for treatments for what ails us.

Finding research on alternative therapies

It's a challenge to find and understand scientific information about various alternative therapies. But the National Center for Complementary & Alternative Medicine (an institute of the National Institutes of Health) provides a number of excellent online resources, including *The Complementary and Alternative Medicine*

Citation Index, links to other databases, and tips on how to conduct searches on alternative medicine subjects.

You can consult their Web site (`nccam.nih.gov/nccam`) or call their consumer information office (1-888-644-6226).

Western medicine tests potential medicines and therapies by conducting scientific trials that are designed to control for the placebo effect. It is important to understand that very few techniques or substances in alternative medicine have been put to this type of controlled scientific trial. While this is not to say that some of these substances cannot have benefit, you should always sort through the evidence as best you can and educate yourself to determine which of these substances and techniques in alternative medicine really have proven benefit.

Positive Lifestyle: The Proven Alternative

From one perspective, this entire book has focused on helping to develop alternatives to developing coronary artery disease and to requiring invasive, complicated cardiovascular procedures. I have long advocated taking those positive steps in your daily lifestyle that lower your risk of heart disease. I call this approach to good health *lifestyle medicine.*

A certain degree of overlap exists between these positive lifestyle measures and those things that are traditionally encompassed in alternative medicine, but I think there is a very important distinction. Lifestyle medicine is about those daily habits and practices that *have been clearly proven to lower your risk of heart disease.* At the same time, each one of these proven lifestyle measures offers an *alternative* that can often prevent the need for advanced cardiac techniques or medicines used in Western medicine. These measures help put you in control of your life — that feeling of autonomy that so many persons who adopt alternative therapies are seeking. Here are six important lifestyle measures.

The big three: Exercise, sound nutrition, weight management

This book is full of information about how regular physical activity, sound nutritional practices, and weight management prove a powerful alternative to developing coronary artery disease and for aiding in the treatment of it. To review physical activity benefits, see Chapters 6 and 7; for sound nutrition, Chapters 4 and 5; and for weight management, see Chapter 12.

Mind/body connections

There is probably no organ in the body (with the possible exception of the brain) that is more affected by our emotional state than the heart. There are profound mind/body connections that impact everything from hypertension to cardiac rhythm. Using mind/body techniques such as visualization, relaxation, and biofeedback as well as other natural methods of stress reduction can clearly lower your risk of heart disease. I regard these mind/body techniques as part of a positive lifestyle, although many people consider them to be components of alternative medicine. (See also Chapter 8.)

Spirituality

It may be splitting hairs, but I separate spirituality from mind/body connections, although both are aspects of our psychological makeup. It is amazing how important spirituality is to our outlook in life and perhaps even our cardiovascular health. Two cases in point:

- ✔ **The power of prayer.** One recent study revealed that over 95 percent of people undergoing coronary artery bypass grafting engaged in prayer the evening before. I think placing more emphasis in modern cardiovascular medicine on understanding and respecting the spirituality of our patients would not only be good for us health care givers as spiritual human beings but would probably enhance the outcome of many of the procedures that we undertake.

- ✔ **The power of gardening.** Major studies have shown that individuals who garden regularly lower their risk of heart disease. Although gardeners may get a little exercise every day, it's typically not enough to account for all the benefit. I think on some profound level, gardeners are getting a dose of spirituality as they tend other living things. Gardeners are optimists who plant the seeds in the spring, confident of crops in the fall. Without a doubt, my patients who are gardeners seem to do better than individuals who don't have this connection with life and the earth.

Is natural better?

In recent years, "natural" products have developed quite a cachet. Now, I am all for natural products. Eating fruits and vegetables is the most *natural* way of getting not only fiber, but also many antioxidants and vitamins, particularly vitamin C.

Some of our most important drugs have been developed from plant sources. You may have the source of one of the first and most important medicines for heart rhythm problems — digitalis — growing in your garden now. It is known as foxglove. At first, foxglove plants were ground up to produce a powder containing digitalis. Later, scientists were able to purify and get even better results working with these same compounds in the laboratory. So the current medication we know as *digoxin* leads straight back to the foxglove and shares the same chemistry.

Which leads to my last point: Just because some product is "natural" doesn't mean that it is better than a similar product that has been synthesized. Natural is neutral. Simply describing a product as "natural" does not by itself qualify it as beneficial or ineffective, as safe or harmful. Natural products, by their nature, have not been subjected to the same purifications that other products such as approved medicines may have undergone. This not to say that all natural products should be avoided; it is simply to alert the consumer that natural does not necessarily equal better or safer. Nor does synthesized necessarily mean a product is not natural or does not have natural origins. As always, do your homework and use your common sense.

Volunteerism

In the Disney movie *The Lion King*, my favorite song has always been "The Circle of Life." This song by Elton John reminds us we are all connected to each other in the circle of life. Recent studies have shown that individuals who work as volunteers and help other people actually improve their own health. Isn't it wonderful to know that by following your natural inclination to connect with other people and do good that a totally unintended side benefit is also improving your own health?

Can Any Natural Supplements Lower Your Risk of Heart Disease?

Ten years ago, I would have joined most physicians in saying that if you eat a balanced and healthy diet and meet all of the recommended daily allowances of vitamins and minerals, then there is probably no general need for supplements. However, just within the last five years, a number of studies have persuaded me that there are situations where supplementation may be appropriate. At the same time, there are still many issues to explore. So I recommend that you consider supplementation on a case by case basis. Find out as much as you can about any given supplement and its potential role in cardiovascular health and total health before adding it to your diet.

Here are recommendations about some more popular natural supplements currently available with regard to whether there is sufficient evidence to recommend them as substances that can lower your risk of heart disease.

Phytosterols

Plant substances that are chemically related to cholesterol, called *phytosterols,* help fight heart disease by binding onto cholesterol in the intestines, thus preventing it from being absorbed. Over 50 phytosterols have currently been identified in nature, and many different foods are rich in them, including legumes such as peas and kidney beans, wheat germ, oranges, bananas, brussels sprouts, and cauliflower.

For optimal results, you should consume phytosterol-rich foods with meals, because it's the act of mechanically binding to cholesterol that gives them their cholesterol-lowering properties. Phytosterols give you one more good reason to eat at least five servings of fruits and vegetables daily. *Phytosterol* may even sound cool enough to get your kids to try a brussels sprout.

Monascus purpureus

Monascus purpureus, a red yeast that is fermented with rice, comes from the ancient Chinese herbal medicine chest and has recently been subjected to rigorous trials by Western science. The results have been very impressive.

- ✔ *Monascus purpureus* (available in the United States under the trade name Cholestin) has been shown to lower cholesterol anywhere from 15 to 20 percent.

- ✔ In individuals who have elevated triglycerides, it has also been shown to lower triglycerides about the same amount.

- ✔ It has a particularly profound effect on LDL cholesterol (the bad cholesterol) and may even increase HDL in individuals who have low levels of HDL.

The active chemicals in powdered *monascus purpureus* that appear to be most active in lowering cholesterol are kin to the class of drugs also called *statins.* For individuals who want to take a natural substance as an adjunct to cholesterol-lowering therapy, it is hard to beat *monascus purpureus.*

Garlic

Beloved in all the world's cuisines, garlic was touted for medical benefits over 5,000 years ago in Sanskrit records from ancient India. Hippocrates also wrote about garlic's use, as did the Chinese. Most recently, garlic has been promoted as a way of lowering cholesterol and triglycerides. Be careful on this one though, because the most recent studies have not shown that garlic significantly lowers cholesterol. (I say this with a certain amount of sadness, because I love garlic and use it regularly in cooking.)

Garlic may have some medicinal benefits, however. Other studies have suggested that it may contain substances that help inhibit blood clotting. This would, of course, be beneficial in terms of lowering the risk of heart attack and stroke. For now, let's just say that the jury is out on garlic as a beneficial cardiovascular supplement. However, if you enjoy the taste of garlic, it certainly can't hurt and may help — so enjoy!

Niacin

Niacin, a B vitamin, has long been known to be essential for preventing pellagra, a condition characterized by skin inflammation and gastrointestinal disturbances. More recent studies have shown that niacin also reduces total cholesterol levels while increasing HDL, the good cholesterol. Decreases in LDL of between 20 and 30 percent with increases in protective HDL of 20 percent have frequently been shown. In fact, niacin is one of the few substances that both lowers LDL and raises HDL. Cardiologists now use it as a mainstay in therapy to lower cholesterol.

Niacin tablets come in a variety of sizes, from 50 mg to 750 mg. A typical starting dose would be 100 mg three times a day. Some people will ultimately benefit by taking up to 1,000 mg a day. It is best to take niacin with meals to avoid stomach and intestinal upset. Of course, niacin is best used in conjunction with a low-fat, low-cholesterol diet. I should warn you that niacin can have some minor side effects such as flushing and itching, particularly when you first start taking it. However, these side effects usually diminish rapidly and can be treated symptomatically by taking one-half an aspirin tablet when you take the niacin.

Folate

This is another B vitamin that is thought to lower a dangerous form of amino acid in the blood called homocysteine. High homocysteine levels have been associated with increased risk of heart disease. I believe that the evidence is strong enough to recommend that every adult man and woman consume 400 micrograms of folate every day. This is very hard to achieve simply by eating fruits and vegetables, although green leafy vegetables and citrus fruits do contain high levels of folate. The best advice is to take either a multivitamin with folate or consume a fully fortified cereal such as Total every day to get your folate.

Fiber

Dietary fiber occurs in two major forms: soluble and insoluble.

Soluble fibers combine with water and fluids in the intestine to form gels that can absorb other substances and trap them. The trapped substances include bile acids that contain a lot of cholesterol. Thus, soluble fiber is particularly good as a way of lowering cholesterol because as bile acids are excreted from the body, the liver uses up cholesterol to make more bile acids.

So much strong evidence is available supporting this function of soluble fiber that the Food and Drug Administration has allowed certain foods rich in soluble fiber to make the health claim that when used in conjunction with a low-fat diet, these foods may further lower your risk of heart disease. Perhaps the most prominent among such foods that are eaten regularly are oatmeal and Cheerios and its clones.

Insoluble fiber may also carry health benefits that are not related to heart disease. For example, this type fiber helps trap water in the stools, providing more bulk and helping food move through the digestive system more quickly. This effect may help lower the risk of colon cancer.

The American Heart Association and National Cancer Institute recommend consuming 25 grams of fiber daily. Most of us consume only 12 grams. Thus, I strongly recommend that you try to increase the amount of fiber in your diet. High-fiber foods such as bran, beans, oatmeal, and many cereals are an excellent source of fiber, as are many fruits and vegetables. Some fiber supplements such as Metamucil and Citrucel may also help.

Soy protein

Some cultures have prized soy protein for its health benefits since ancient times. Modern science confirms that the type of protein found in soy beans has a very complete set of amino acids, which are the building blocks for the body's protein. Soy protein also seems to lower cholesterol and also is thought to carry antioxidants that may help prevent heart disease in ways other than simply by lowering cholesterol levels. If you enjoy the taste of soy, you can consume extra soy protein by drinking soy milk or using soy-based meat substitutes.

Fish oil

Why do certain cultures that consume large quantities of cold water fish (the Eskimo culture, for instance) have low incidences of heart disease? The reason seems related to the oils these fish contain, which are high in a substance called omega-3 fatty acids. A number of studies have shown that cholesterol levels can be lowered by as much as 10 percent when fish is substituted for red meat in the diet several times per week. What a good reason to enjoy fish. I strongly recommend it. You'll get an excellent source of high level protein that may, in addition, contain these cholesterol lowering substances. One word of caution, however: The evidence is inconclusive about the benefits of taking fish oil supplements rather than actually eating the fish.

Antioxidants

Antioxidants are thought to decrease the likelihood that LDL cholesterol will be oxidized. Should this finding be borne out by continuing research, it could prove useful because it's the oxidized form of LDL cholesterol that seems to do the most damage. Recommended antioxidants include vitamin C, vitamin E, and beta carotene. The doses that seem to be necessary to yield these potential cardiac benefits are vitamin C, 250 to 500 mg a day, and vitamin E, 200 to 400 IU (International Units) per day.

But any definite conclusions about the benefits of antioxidants remain up in the air. More recent trials of antioxidants have not shown the benefits of lowered risk of heart disease indicated by earlier trials. So what would I do? I usually tell patients that I do not object to them taking antioxidants, but that there's not yet a final answer to the role they may play in combating the risk of heart disease (or risk of any other disease).

The Wisdom of the Willow: An Aspirin a Day May Keep the Cardiologist Away

In Disney's retelling of the legend *Pocahontas,* when Pocahontas needed advice, she sought wisdom from Old Willow. In cardiovascular medicine, we too could use more wisdom from the willow. Particularly from the acetylsalicylic acid found in willow bark. You know it as *aspirin.*

Aspirin has been in our medicine cabinets for so long — over 100 years — that we may have forgotten that it is in essence a "natural" product, originally derived from willow bark. Of course, it is now synthesized in the laboratory and made commercially available as aspirin.

Aspirin is one of the true miracles of nature. Because from a cardiovascular standpoint it makes platelets less sticky, aspirin has been clearly shown to lower the risk of subsequent cardiac problems for persons who have underlying coronary artery disease.

Unless there is a strong contraindication (such as a history of significant gastrointestinal bleeding), any individual who has a history of coronary artery disease should be taking an aspirin a day. To help prevent CAD, every man over age 50 and any woman over 55 should also take one aspirin daily. Even one baby aspirin a day will bring about the anti-platelet effect.

Many people find that the potential for stomach irritation is reduced if they take enteric coated aspirin.

Commonsense checklist for evaluating alternative therapies

So how do you sort through all the claims, evidence, information, and sometimes heated rhetoric about particular alternative products or techniques? Using these questions may help you find and evaluate the information you need to make wise decisions.

✔ When researching a specific therapy (particularly a very controversial one), have you reviewed the arguments and evidence from *all sides* of the issue?

✔ What evidence supports the effectiveness of the therapy?

Scientific trials or only testimony and anecdote?

Quantifiable data or opinion?

How old, how large, and how well-designed were any scientific trials? (Good science is always pushing the envelop, reevaluating, seeking to acquire more data — and changing its mind when necessary. A few scientific trials from, say, the 1920s or 1950s that are unsupported by more recent studies or even contradicted by later studies would not be, as you can see, the best evidence of the effectiveness of a given substance or technique.)

✔ How safe is the therapy?

Is there concrete evidence (not just a provider's or recipient's opinion) that the benefits outweigh the risks?

Evidence that the product does no harm when used as directed?

Under what conditions is service or treatment delivered?

✔ What are the credentials and expertise of the practitioner of an alternative therapy or developer of a product? (A mail-order Ph.D. from a diploma mill would not inspire confidence in the developer of the "SuperWhammo Mighty-Mineral Supplement," would it?)

✔ What is the cost of the treatment or product?

✔ Have you discussed the therapy with your primary care physician? If you're actually using the therapy, have you told your doctor? Your doctor needs a complete picture to give you the best health care, plus many doctors are good sources of information.

Chapter 22

Working with Your Doctor: The Rules of Engagement

*I*n the words of comedienne Joan Rivers, "Can we talk?" Talking, of course, should be exactly what you and your doctor do. Throughout this book, one of my mantras has been "form a partnership with your physician." Fighting so serious a foe as heart disease is not a battle to take on by yourself. But finding the right physician in the mazes of the medical system is not always easy. Nor is knowing how to establish clear lines of communication and cooperation. Hence, this chapter. Think of it as a primer on partnership.

The Fundamentals of Partnership

Like all partnerships — whether business partnerships, marriages, or friendships — patient/physician partnerships must be based on open communication and trust. At its best, a partnership between you and your physician can be a long-term trusting relationship with benefits to your cardiovascular health. Discussing how to optimize your cardiovascular health with your physician should also be a pleasure that you — and your doctor — look forward to. Many doctors (it pains me to say) are not willing, able, or ready to accept this kind of a partnership with their patients. But I believe that every patient needs to be a good consumer. That means you need both realistic goals and realistically high expectations in selecting and working with a personal physician and, if you need one, a cardiologist.

Choosing a Primary Care Doctor

Almost invariably, individuals, even those who have heart disease, start out with their primary care doctor. I have always been surprised at how randomly many people choose a physician. You should regard your physician (who is, after all, a health care professional) as a consultant to you, just as you regard your accountant or your lawyer as consultants and take the same care in choosing him or her.

What traits to look for in a physician

First, look for a doctor who has superior knowledge about medicine, who listens, who asks pertinent questions and provides useful explanations and answers. Also look for a physician who displays determination to keep working on any medical problem that you have and who is also pragmatic and cost conscious. Above all, your physician needs to be someone who cares and inspires confidence, optimism, and hope in you.

To identify such candidates, most people begin by asking neighbors, family, or friends for recommendations. You can also obtain information or referrals by contacting the local hospital, local medical school, or local medical society. Many hospitals, clinics, and private practices now have Web sites where you can obtain basic information as well.

Interviewing a potential physician

Narrow your choice down to two or three physicians, and then call their offices to see if you can arrange a time to speak with them, either in person or on the phone. This important "pre-interview" allows you to find out how the physician approaches the world and his or her patients. Here are some questions that you can ask during the pre-interview:

- "Where did you go to medical school?"
- "Where did you train after medical school?"
- "What are your special areas of medical interest?"
- "Can you tell me a little bit about how you approach medicine and patient care?"

✔ If you have a cardiac condition already present, ask them about their background and knowledge concerning your particular condition. Also ask them how they feel about lifestyle factors such as exercise and nutrition. It may even be worthwhile to ask how they feel about mind/body connections and supplements. (Be careful with these questions, because some of the very best physicians may be thrown off guard by them, until they know you better.)

✔ Ask about practical matters such as, "Which insurance plans does your practice accept?" and "At which hospitals do you have admitting privileges?" This last question is particularly important because the best physicians almost inevitably have admitting privileges at the best hospitals.

Matching your needs

As you consider the answers to your questions and just how the conversation went in general, don't forget yourself. Who *you are* as an individual plays a role in which doctor is best for you. Some people like detailed and thorough explanations. Others want a more regimented approach with less specific information. Don't be embarrassed to interview a few physicians to see if they fit best with who you are as a person. Remember, you are establishing a long-term partnership here and you should not rush into it.

Choosing a Cardiologist

If you already have established heart disease, then you are best cared for by both your family doctor and a cardiologist. A cardiologist has advanced training in cardiology, a subspecialty of internal medicine. Pursuing such a subspecialty typically means anywhere from three to five years of training beyond full training in internal medicine.

Choosing a cardiologist can be a little trickier than choosing a family care doctor because the normal sources of information, such as family and friends, may be less familiar with cardiology specialists. Plus, you may belong to an insurance plan or managed care plan that requires that you select from a particular group of physicians or that you be referred by your primary care physician. So start by asking your primary care physician some questions about the cardiologists that he or she would recommend:

✔ Where did the cardiologist train?

✔ What are his or her areas of specialty within cardiology?

✔ At what hospitals does the cardiologist practice?

✔ How does the cardiologist approach his or her patients?

✔ Is the cardiologist willing to form partnerships and talk to patients, or is he or she more likely to give directions and expect that they be followed?

✔ How accessible is the cardiologist?

✔ How is the cardiologist as a human being?

On the basis of this information, you may then want to interview two or three different cardiologists in much the same way that you interviewed your primary care doctor.

Choosing and Working with a Managed Care Plan

In this day and age, almost half of Americans get their basic medical care through some form of managed care plan, whether it's an HMO (health maintenance organization), PPO (preferred provider organization), or some other member of the Alphabet City of managed care.

If you receive your insurance through your employer, as many Americans do, you may be offered a choice of plans or choices within a single plan. If so, don't make the common mistake of basing your choice solely on cost. (That's not how you chose your car, is it?) Instead, look carefully at issues such as these:

✔ Access to the physicians that you want to see

✔ The qualifications of the physicians who have chosen the plan

✔ The hospitals that are affiliated with the plan

✔ Logistical issues such as convenience of doctors and hospitals to you

✔ If you have an established cardiac condition, the availability of certain treatments through the managed care plan

Your human resources professional at work should be able to help you sort through these issues. Web sites are also available for most managed care plans so that you can search for information on each plan.

If you must provide your own health insurance, you may have a more difficult time finding an affordable plan that gives you the coverage you want. Check with friends who are self-employed and with insurance agents about possible individual plans. A group or organization to which you belong may also offer members some form of group insurance. Do an online search for possibilities. Again, be sure to get answers to the questions you need. If you have an existing condition, such as cardiovascular disease, this will affect what coverage you can obtain.

Choosing a Hospital

Choosing a hospital is a surprisingly important health care decision, particularly if you have cardiac disease. Recent studies have shown that patients at certain hospitals tend to have better outcomes. As a general rule, these hospitals are those that have programs for physicians in training. If your primary care physician or cardiologist plans to refer you to a hospital for advanced testing or a surgical procedure, don't be shy about asking about the expertise and experience of the hospital in this area. If I were facing open heart surgery, for instance, I'd surely want to be in the care of a hospital team that specialized in such surgery, performed it very frequently (like every day!), and had an outstanding record for care.

If you already have established heart disease, I advise you to choose a large hospital with experience in cardiac care and a training program, if possible. Within medicine, these hospitals are typically "tertiary care" hospitals. That means that they are specialized to care for many advanced illnesses, including severe forms of heart disease. Usually, these hospitals can be identified through local medical societies or through the local or regional medical school in your area.

Establishing a Partnership with Your Physician

Establishing an effective partnership between you and your physician requires four key elements. The first two elements are shared. The third is your domain and the fourth that of your physician.

Communication. Open communication, the foundation of partnership, is clearly a two-way street.

- You have the right to expect that your physician will fully and openly give you the information that will help you understand your condition and participate in your treatment.

- By the same token, your physician has the right to expect that you will be very frank about the symptoms that you are having, not only from your condition, but also from any medicines that you are taking.

Trust. Trust enables both communication and commitment in partnership. You must trust that your physician always has your best interest at heart and that your physician is competent, caring, and concerned about your well-being. By the same token, your physician has the right to expect that he or she can trust you to be committed to your own well-being.

Commitment to the treatment plan. Your responsibility within the partnership is to be committed to a treatment plan that you and your doctor agree upon. You should not agree to a treatment plan unless you intend to carry it out.

Commit yourself also to learning all you can about your condition and the whys and wherefores of various treatment procedures. Ask again if you don't understand something. Ask your doctor for information. Use reputable print and online resources (such as those recommended throughout this book) to educate yourself. The more informed and knowledgeable you are, the more committed and equal a partner you're likely to be.

Quality Care. Your physician bears responsibility for quality care. This is not only a function of the knowledge and integrity of the physician, but also of the total medical care system serving you. It is the physician's responsibility to ensure that any other physicians involved in your care also practice quality care. All of the facilities, including the office and the hospital and the performance of all the individuals within these settings are also ultimately the responsibility of the physician.

What do you have a right to expect of your physician?

As a consumer, you have the right to expect that your physician will

- ✔ Listen carefully and provide thorough clear explanations for procedures, conditions, and treatment options
- ✔ Answer questions
- ✔ Possess the skills and knowledge of a physician committed to ongoing medical education and at the cutting edge of medical science

If you are not getting these from your physician, it is time to look for another doctor.

What does your physician have a right to expect of you?

Yes, we docs have the right to some expectations, too. I can tell you, as a physician, there is nothing more frustrating than trying to control blood pressure in someone who intermittently takes their medicine, or trying to control blood lipids for someone who does not pay attention to even the basics of sound nutrition and decreasing the amount of fat they eat. You need to be your own best friend when it comes to your own medical care.

Your commitment is so important, that I'm going to reemphasize some points:

✔ If you have reservations or doubts about the treatment plan your doctor proposes, discuss these problems fully with your physician before you agree to the plan.

✔ After you agree upon a plan, do it — and stick to it. If any problems, symptoms, or side effects arise, tell your doctor. Pick up the phone and tell the receptionist or nurse (whoever is the gatekeeper on incoming calls) exactly why you need to talk to the doctor.

✔ Be sure to follow the lifestyle measures. Treatment is more than just taking any prescribed medication.

✔ Don't ever be ashamed to share your problems with your doctor. There is nothing shameful about having difficulty changing your life. It is hard, but it is possible. You should have the kind of relationship with your doctor that allows you to talk about this and not feel ashamed.

✔ Educate yourself about your condition.

Helping Your Primary Care Doctor and Cardiologist Communicate

This may seem like a strange topic to include. After all, shouldn't your doctors work with each other as a matter of course? Of course, they try their best to do this, but I can tell you that many times lab values and other critical information are lost, even in the best systems between the best doctors.

You can play a very important role as a fail-safe communication link between your primary care physician and your cardiologist. One way to do this is to make sure that the notes that go into your physician record are also sent to you. Such notes would include not only the impression of your progress both from your primary care doctor and your cardiologist, but also any pertinent findings and laboratory values. Your medical record, by the way, is a legal document that belongs to you.

Optimizing Office Visits: The Nuts and Bolts

Office visits to the doctor are a pain, aren't they? Particularly if you have to go out of town. So here are some tips for getting the most out of them.

✔ **Be efficient.** Respect your physician's time and expect that your physician will respect your time too. If forms need to be completed, try to arrive a little early. Bring notes that track your symptoms and, if you have been referred by a primary care physician, try to bring copies of pertinent medical records and lab tests. Bring a written list of the medications that you are taking, as well as the frequency and dosage. If you have a discharge summary from a hospitalization, that is a useful document to share with your physician, particularly a subspecialist such as a cardiologist. If you need to cancel, common courtesy mandates that you try to do this as early as possible (the same goes for the physician).

✔ **Describe your symptoms.** Be prepared to describe any symptoms that you have and when they occur, how severe they are, and how they affect you.

✔ **Bring notes.** It is always useful for a physician to see your notes about issues that you have. Write down ahead of time any questions that you might have. (That doesn't mean you can't ask new ones as they arise.)

✔ **Ask about the diagnosis.** It is important to ask specifically about what the likely diagnosis is and what tests the physician regards as important to specifically pin down the diagnosis. Don't be afraid to ask for this in layman's terms.

✔ **Take notes.** Many times, patients leave the doctor's office and forget what they discussed. Visiting the doctor is often very stressful, so don't be afraid to take notes during the discussion. Also bring someone with you — a second pair of ears helps. Or use a tape recorder. Ask for instructions in writing, if possible.

✔ **Schedule a follow-up appointment.** If a follow-up appointment is necessary, ask the doctor specifically when this should occur. It is also important to ask how to reach the physician in case an emergency arises.

Tips for asking the right questions

Here are some recommended questions that you can ask your doctor about any condition that he or she may discover during the evaluation. You may even want to copy this list to take with you.

✔ What is my diagnosis?

✔ What tests will I need to undergo?

✔ Are there any side effects or dangers to these tests?

✔ What is the recommended treatment?

✔ What are the potential side effects of the treatment?

✔ Are there any treatment choices?

✔ Are there any other questions that I should be asking?

✔ Is there any source of information that I can read about my diagnosis?

Testing Made Easier

Most of us at some time face testing either to confirm the diagnosis or to assess the efficacy of treatment. Finding yourself, chart and referral slip in hand, wandering through a maze of unfamiliar hospital halls can be frightening and confusing. Avoid such anxiety and confusion by planning ahead.

✔ Ask your primary care physician or your cardiologist exactly what tests you will be undergoing and what the potential benefit and outcome of each of the tests or procedures will be.

✔ Ask for a map and/or directions to the testing center or hospital. If your physician's office doesn't have such, call the testing center for directions (including where to park and where to check in).

✔ When you arrive at each testing or procedure area, don't be afraid to ask the technicians exactly what will happen during the test, any side effects that you might feel, and what is likely to be learned from the test. Most technicians and physicians are delighted to explain their procedures.

Special Issues in the Doctor-Patient Relationship

I have outlined some general rules of engagement for working with your physician. However, a few special circumstances may come up that you will need to consider. The following sections look at a few of them.

Research

Many physicians today are involved in clinical research. Most do this both to further knowledge and to keep up with modern medical advances. For the most part, this is a good thing. Unfortunately, a few unscrupulous physicians engage in clinical research for monetary gain and sometimes pressure patients to enter research projects that may not benefit the patient.

If your physician recommends that you enter a clinical research trial, you have the right to ask whether or not the therapy being studied has any recognized benefit. You also have the right to have a thorough explanation as to why this therapy is being recommended and how it would differ from regular therapy. While I support clinical research, I think it is important that patients not be coerced (even subtly) into participating in clinical research trials — particularly when there are currently established therapies in almost every aspect of cardiovascular disease.

What to do when you can't get your physician's attention?

Nothing is more frustrating than having your physician ignore you when you have questions, concerns, or troubling symptoms. Unfortunately, many physician's offices screen calls in such a way that it's difficult to get through to the physician. Often an assistant, such as a nurse, will take your question, confer with the doctor, and call you back. If you feel your concerns have been handled appropriately by this "physician extender," that's okay. If not, specifically request that the physician call you back to address your concern. If the physician is unwilling to do this after several phone calls, then write the physician a letter saying that you are concerned about their failure to call you back in a timely manner. If the physician ignores even the written request, then it is time to look for a new physician. After all, would you accept that kind of treatment from your lawyer or accountant?

When to get a second opinion

You have a right to obtain a second opinion about any serious diagnosis. Second opinions are deeply respected in medicine. A good physician will never be offended if you seek a second opinion. After all, in many instances, two heads are better than one. Don't be embarrassed to ask your physician for a recommendation of someone to offer a second opinion. If your physician is the kind of doctor that you want to see, he or she will have no problem with this straightforward request.

What about switching doctors?

It is also completely within your rights as a patient to switch physicians. Different patient and physician styles often do not mesh perfectly and that can hinder your ability to communicate adequately. You also need to trust that your physician has superior medical skills and knowledge. If you do not feel confident in either of these areas, it is time to start looking for another physician.

One word of caution here: As you're considering the need to switch, examine your own thinking and emotions for signs of denial. Sometimes when a physician gives a diagnosis that is difficult to accept, a patient may have the inclination to start looking around for a doctor who will give them a more comfortable, if less truthful, diagnosis. Too often, such "doctor shopping" can lead to inferior care.

Part V
The Part of Tens

The 5th Wave   By Rich Tennant

"You know, anyone who wishes he had a remote control for his exercise equipment is missing the idea of exercise equipment."

In this part . . .

In this part, you find the facts that bust the most common myths about heart disease. Then there are the heart-healthy foods you can use to fine-tune your nutrition plan. I also show you when to take ten symptoms that may signal heart disease to the doctor. I round this section off with ten secrets for long-term success in heart-healthy living.

Chapter 23

Ten Myths about Heart Disease

. . . .

In This Chapter

▶ Busting myths before they bust your heart

▶ Avoiding misconceptions that lead to unwise choices

. . . .

*I*t is not surprising that there are myths about heart disease. The heart is, after all, a truly mythic organ — the fount of all life. Throughout the world's cultures, the heroes and heroines of myth and legend are usually persons of "great heart." Often persons of great cunning as well, but it's their heart, their embodiment of the courageous life that inspires us. But while myths can inspire, myths can also kill. Particularly the many myths about heart disease. So let's bust a few.

The Myth of Modern Maturity

Heart disease is a disease of middle age and older years.

Many people think of heart disease as a problem of middle and older age, because that's when the manifestations of heart disease such as angina and heart attack strike. What a dangerous myth. Although the *manifestations* of coronary artery disease typically occur in our middle and later years, the *roots* of coronary artery disease lie in childhood. While most of this book has focused on steps that adults can take to lower their risk of heart disease or to manage it, you should also take a few simple steps to help your children. The best way to do this is by your example. See Part II for suggestions.

The Myth of the Old Boy Network

Men are much more likely to get heart disease than women.

Way too many women think that heart disease is mainly a male disease. But heart disease is by far the leading cause of death for women. Women are 6 to 10 times more likely to die of heart disease than breast cancer (which women fear more). When cardiovascular disease and stroke are combined, these two diseases claim more female lives every year than the next *16 causes of death combined.* Many of these deaths are preventable. Use the daily lifestyle measures in this book to stop this equal opportunity killer.

The Myth of Thomas Wolfe

Once you have heart disease, it is relentlessly progressive.

If you have been reading this book cover to cover, you know that Thomas Wolfe wrote the novel, *You Can't Go Home Again.* Up until the last ten years, coronary artery disease appeared to be a relentless lifelong process that resulted in increasing symptoms and, ultimately, death. Fortunately, over the last decade, we have found out that following a low-fat heart-healthy diet and regimen of physical activity, usually in conjunction with taking cholesterol-lowering medications, can often halt the process of atherosclerosis in its tracks and sometimes even reverse the process to some degree. See Chapter 20 for details on how to turn down the path heading "home" to healthier, more normal arteries.

The Eisenhower Myth

Once you have had a heart attack, your life will move inexorably downhill.

In 1954, President Dwight Eisenhower suffered a heart attack while in office — a first. His cardiologist, Dr. Paul Dudley White, from Harvard Medical School and Massachusetts General Hospital, went on national television to assure the anxious public that if President Eisenhower paid attention to what he ate and became involved in a regular walking program, he could continue to fulfill the strenuous duties of the highest office in the land. Most people were surprised to hear it. As Ike proved, there's no reason to give up after you have had a heart attack. Modern cardiac rehabilitation can help individuals who have suffered a heart attack or have other serious forms of heart disease to live full, vigorous lives for many years after the first manifestations of heart disease. See Chapter 16 for more details on modern cardiac rehabilitation.

The Myth of No Pain, No Gain

To get cardiac benefit from exercise, you need to get sweaty and out of breath.

Many sedentary individuals (and indeed, many exercisers!) share the myth that you have to exercise at a fairly intense level to achieve cardiac benefits. To some degree, this myth grew from the advice of well-intentioned exercise physiologists that improving your aerobic fitness requires at least three or four 20 to 30 minute sessions weekly of continuous vigorous exercise. Now, this advice is excellent if your only goal is to improve your aerobic capacity. However, if your goal is to lower your risk of heart disease, totally different rules apply — you need simply to get more active. By more active, I mean trying to *accumulate* 30 minutes of *moderate* physical activity on most, if not all, days. Don't let the myth that you've got to sweat like crazy for thirty minutes straight keep you and your heart declining . . . uh, reclining on the couch. See Chapters 6 and 7 for how to start.

The Myth of Marathon Monday

High-level exercisers never get heart disease.

I named this myth in honor of the elite athletes who run the Boston Marathon in my hometown in April. Lots of folks think that if you're fit enough to run a marathon, then you won't die of heart disease. An interesting concept, but unfortunately, totally false. Every year a number of individuals who are regular exercisers die of heart attacks or other acute manifestations of coronary artery disease while exercising. What happened? Many forgot that coronary heart disease has multiple risk factors. An active lifestyle certainly lowers one of those risks, but you can't ignore the others. See Chapter 3 for more on risk factors.

The Myth of Pleasingly Plump

Medicalizing obesity is a subtle form of prejudice.

This is a difficult and subtle myth. As I discuss in detail in Chapter 12, obesity is a very significant risk for heart disease. Recently, a movement has arisen in the United States promoting "fat acceptance." The basic belief in this movement is that overweight individuals have been routinely discriminated against in our country in very unfortunate ways. I agree. But some proponents also say that medicalizing obesity, by calling it a chronic disease, simply extends this prejudice into the medical profession. No one should ever tolerate in our society, and particularly within medicine, prejudice against people who are overweight. By the same token, it needs to be stated very clearly that obesity is hazardous to your cardiovascular health. All physicians should carefully counsel individuals who are obese about ways to lose weight and practice lifelong healthy weight management to lower cardiovascular disease. You can look great and you are certainly of great worth — but for your heart, there is no such thing as "pleasingly plump."

The Cave Man Myth

If you have chest pain, the best thing to do is wait and see if it goes away.

The Peanuts character Linus once asked Charlie Brown how he approached a problem. Did he tackle it right away, or think about it first? Charlie Brown responded, "I try to go into a cave and hope that it will go away." That may work in other areas of your life, but ignoring the symptoms of acute heart disease is a bad idea. The more delay before treatment of a heart attack, the greater the potential heart damage. If you are having significant chest discomfort, shortness of breath, or any other symptoms that suggest a heart attack, call 911 immediately and be transported to the emergency room. Don't hide in a cave! See Chapter 15 for more on heart attacks.

The Myth of the Stiff Upper Lip

It is not possible to die of a broken heart or be scared to death.

Folk wisdom has long suggested that people could be scared to death or die of a broken heart. Many cardiologists, however, said your emotions and your mental state could affect your behavior but not your heart. From this point of view, it doesn't matter whether you keep a stiff upper lip and bury your fears, pain, and stress or deal with them. Yet as I discuss in Chapter 8, multiple scientific studies show that important mind/body connections exist for health in general and cardiovascular health in particular. Our levels of stress, our connection to other people, our sense of giving and receiving love are all very important for our cardiovascular health. Our goal should be to use these profound linkages to promote cardiovascular health.

The Myth of Jupiter

We will all die of heart disease if we live long enough.

Jupiter, the Roman King of the Gods, you may remember, killed mere mortals by hurling thunderbolts from the sky. This myth expresses the presumption that heart disease is an act of God. Not so. Dying of heart disease is not inevitable. Instead, you must recognize that your own habits and actions play the biggest role in whether you develop heart disease. Let's take a tip from baseball great Mickey Mantle, who humorously said of his health-destructive lifestyle, "If I knew I was going to live so long, I would have taken better care of myself!" I don't know about you, but when Jupiter hurls those thunderbolts at me, I intend to step aside! And to do it, I'm using all the information I've shared in *The Healthy Heart For Dummies*.

Chapter 24

Ten Great Heart-Healthy Foods

A hearty meal is often the way to reach our hearts, isn't it? You can both affirm the pleasures of the table (no food cops!) and adopt a balanced, moderate approach to nutrition that enhances your heart health. Chapters 4 and 5 show you exactly how to do it. Then use these ten great heart-healthy foods to fine-tune your nutritional plan for improved cardiac health.

Olive Oil

Olive oil and other monounsaturated fats have enhanced the tasty food and heart health of Mediterranean people for centuries. Monounsaturated fats have the dual advantage of raising HDL (good cholesterol) without raising total cholesterol. Of note, the American Diabetes Association has also recognized the value of monounsaturated fat and recommended increasing consumption of this for most diabetics. Besides olive oil, other sources of monounsaturated fats include olives, fish, sesame seeds, avocados, peanuts, walnuts, pecans, and some other oils (peanut, walnut, canola, and sesame). The drawback? Like all oil, olive oil has 120 calories per tablespoon. So don't go wild.

Fish

I love fish! Both as a cardiologist and a food lover. Studies show substituting fish for red meat in the diet significantly lowers the amount of saturated fat in the diet and has a very positive effect on lowering cholesterol levels and the risk of heart disease. This is thought to be a result of the Omega 3 fatty acids in these fish. Omega 3 fatty acids also lower triglycerides and may make platelets less sticky and thereby less likely to clot, which reduces the risk of unstable angina or an acute heart attack. Fish, such as salmon, tuna, herring, or blue fish are all high in Omega 3 oils. But don't turn fish into a cardiac nightmare by frying it. Fish oil capsules, by the way, don't seem to have the same benefit.

Soy Foods

Soy protein can help lower LDL cholesterol (the bad cholesterol) and raise HDL (the good cholesterol). Soy also contains antioxidants called *isoflavones,* which may help prevent heart disease in other ways. Although it differs from animal protein, soy protein has a much more complete set of amino acids (the building blocks of proteins) than most vegetables, and so can be substituted for fat-rich meats. The only negatives about soy are that some people don't like the taste and that most studies suggest that you must consume 30 to 50 grams daily to get the cardiac benefits. (That's a lot of tofu.) Including plenty of soy protein can be particularly important for *vegans* (vegetarians who eat no animal products, not even milk and eggs) for many reasons beyond heart health.

Soluble Fiber

From a cardiac health point of view, I am a soluble fiber stalwart. The scientific evidence of its cholesterol-lowering benefit is so strong that the Food and Drug Administration now allows food manufacturers whose products are high in soluble fiber to state that "the consumption of soluble fiber as part of an overall low-fat diet further reduces the risk of coronary heart disease." Where can you find it? Whole oat cereals such as oatmeal or Cheerios and its clones are good. Other sources of soluble fiber include dry beans and peas, barley, whole grain oats, citrus fruits, apples, and corn. My laboratory has also done work on psyllium, another soluble fiber that significantly lowers cholesterol levels.

Whole Grains

In addition to soluble fiber, whole grains contain the other major type of fiber, insoluble fiber (which is very important for bulking of stools and decreasing the risk of colon cancer), as well as a variety of phytochemicals. By eating more whole grains, you can cut your risk of heart disease significantly, maybe as much be one-third or one-half. But you must make sure you're eating *whole grains,* not refined grains, where parts of the grains, such as the husk, have been removed. Unfortunately, most Americans eat less than half the recommended 25 grams of fiber every day. So what are high fiber foods? Cereals such as Wheaties, Cheerios, oatmeal, shredded wheat, wheat germ and bran are all excellent sources of whole grains. Look for cereals that have 3 to 6 grams of fiber per serving. Whole-grain breads with at least 2 grams of fiber per serving can be another good source.

Fruits and Vegetables

Now where is my soapbox!? I simply cannot say too much good about fruits and vegetables: Eating five servings of fruits and vegetables a day can help lower your risk of coronary artery disease, lower your blood pressure, and reduce your risk of colon cancer. They are a great source of fiber. Eating more is a great way to reduce the amount of fat in your diet. Because fresh produce is now flown in from all over the world, grocery stores are stocked year-round with high quality, fresh produce. To encourage fruit and veggie consumption, I recommend you keep at least three different kinds of fresh fruit available — in the fridge or in a bowl on the kitchen counter or table handy for snacking. Focus on what is in season.

B Vitamins — Folate and B$_6$

Okay, so these are components of many foods. But folate, also called folic acid, and B$_6$ are so important that they have to make any cardiologist's list of top ten. Both of these B vitamins help lower the blood levels of homocysteine, which at high levels has been shown to increase the risk of heart attacks. By consuming more folate- and B$_6$-containing foods (and in some instances supplementing your diet), you can lower your risk of heart disease. To remember what foods are rich in folate, think *foliage*. (They have the same root word.) That means green leafy vegetables are a good source of folate. So are dried beans, peas, and orange juice. Fully fortified whole grain cereals and a multivitamin supplement are other sources. Good sources of B$_6$ include chicken, lean beef (in moderation), whole-grain cereals, and bananas, as well as vitamin supplements.

Monascus Purpureus

Monascus purpureus is a red yeast grown on rice that has been found in the natural Chinese diet for over 1,000 years (see also Chapter 21). It's commonly known in the United States by the brand name Cholestin. Though technically a supplement rather than a food, monascus purpureus works. In a number of studies, it has been shown to reduce overall cholesterol by approximately 15 percent and LDL cholesterol (the bad form) by 20 percent in individuals who have an elevated cholesterol between 200 and 280mg/dl. In individuals who have high triglycerides, triglyceride reductions in excess of 20 percent have been achieved. For individuals who want additional cholesterol-lowering benefits from a supplement, over and above following a Step I American Heart Association Diet, Cholestin may be an excellent choice.

Tea

In one song the Rolling Stones told us that they were looking for "a little tea and sympathy." Well, from the cardiac standpoint, they might not have been too far off. Tea, whether it contains caffeine or not, appears to be beneficial to the heart. Black tea is a source of *flavinoids*, which are antioxidants thought to retard the development of atherosclerosis. In one study of 700 men and women in Boston who drank one or more cups of tea a day, the risk of suffering a heart attack was less than half of the individuals who did not follow this practice. So, even if the Rolling Stones couldn't "get no satisfaction" from a cardiac stand-point by drinking tea (not a bad idea since most of the Stones are in their mid fifties), they could at least get some "tea and sympathy."

Alcohol

For the heart, alcohol is a mixed bag. I never recommend that individuals who do not currently drink alcohol start. On the other hand, a number of studies have shown that moderate alcohol consumption lowers the risk of heart disease. This benefit of alcohol appears to come both from alcohol's ability to increase HDL cholesterol (the good form), as well as its ability to decrease the likelihood of abnormal clotting in the blood. Of all the forms of alcohol, red wine seems particularly beneficial because of the anticlotting substances and the chemicals found in the skins of grapes, which are present longer in the wine-making process of red wine than in white wine. These substances also are present in purple grape juice, although you need to drink about twice as much grape juice as wine to get the cardiac benefit.

A word of caution: Moderate alcohol consumption is defined as one or two glasses a day, one or two beers, or one shot of distilled spirits. In the previous sentence, I want to emphasize the word *or.* If you substitute the word *and* for the word *or,* you would be drinking heavy alcohol consumption — which increases your risk of heart disease and hypertension as well as the risk of motor vehicle accidents.

Chapter 25

Ten Cardiac Signs and Symptoms: Which Are Worrisome and Which Are Not

*A*lthough medical signs and symptoms can overlap, we can distinguish the two on the basis of who is experiencing it. For example, you might regard a nagging, worrisome cough as a *symptom*. Your doctor, however, may regard that cough as a *sign* of congestion of the lungs. In broad terms, then, *symptoms* are feelings or conditions that a patient experiences and then tries to describe to his or her physician. *Signs* are findings that the physician derives from the physical examination that point toward the proper cardiac diagnosis.

There are a number of symptoms (conditions you experience) that, depending on the circumstances and severity, may represent signs of very serious cardiac disease to your physician or may not be worrisome at all. In this chapter, I look at ten key symptoms and signs.

Chest Pain

Chest pain is probably the most common symptom for which people come to see a cardiologist. Although heart problems are common causes of chest pain, it can also come from a wide variety of structures in the chest, neck, and back that have no relation (other than proximity) to the heart. These include the lungs, skin, muscles, spine, and portions of the gastrointestinal tract, such as the stomach, small bowel, pancreas, and gallbladder. Pain caused by angina or heart attack is usually located beneath the breast bone, but the front of the chest or either arm, neck, cheeks, teeth, or high in the middle of the back are also possible locations. It is also often provoked by exercise, strong emotion, or stress. Very short bouts of pain lasting five to ten seconds are typically not angina or heart-related but are more likely to be musculoskeletal pain. If you have concern about *any* chest discomfort, it is imperative that you go to a medical facility and have it further evaluated. (See Chapters 14 and 15 for more.)

Shortness of Breath

Shortness of breath is a major cardiac symptom. But typically, it's difficult to determine whether or not this symptom comes from problems with the heart, the lungs, or some other organ system. Exertion can cause temporary shortness of breath in otherwise healthy individuals who are working or exercising strenuously or in sedentary individuals who are working even moderately. But an abnormally uncomfortable awareness of breathing or difficulty breathing can be a symptom of a medical problem. Shortness of breath that occurs when you're at rest, for example, is considered a strong cardiac symptom. If shortness of breath lasts longer than five minutes after activity or occurs at rest, have your doctor evaluate it.

Loss of Consciousness

Loss of consciousness usually results from reduced supply of blood to the brain. Perhaps the most common loss of consciousness is what people commonly call a "fainting" episode. This temporary condition may be brought on by being in a warm or constricted environment or in a highly emotional state. Such episodes are often preceded by dizziness and/or a sense of "fading to black." When the heart is the cause, loss of consciousness typically occurs rapidly and does not have preceding events. Cardiac conditions ranging from rhythm disturbance to mechanical problems can potentially cause fainting or a blackout. Because such cardiac problems can be serious, never dismiss loss of consciousness in an otherwise healthy individual as a "faint" until that person has had a complete medical workup.

Cardiovascular Collapse

You can't experience a more dramatic symptom or greater emergency than cardiovascular collapse, also called *sudden cardiac death*. Of course, cardio-vascular collapse results in a sudden loss of consciousness. But the victim typically has no pulse and stops breathing, where the victim of a seizure or fainting spell does have a pulse and continues breathing. Cardiovascular collapse can occur as a complication in an individual who has known heart disease, but sometimes may be the first manifestation of an acute heart attack or rhythm problem. When cardiovascular collapse occurs, resuscitation must occur within a very few minutes or death inevitably follows. This is the greatest reason to learn CPR, or basic cardiac life support. (See also Chapter 19.)

Palpitations

Palpitations, which may be defined as an unpleasant awareness of a rapid or forceful beating of the heart, may indicate anything from serious cardiac rhythm problems to nothing worrisome at all. Typically, an individual who is experiencing palpitations describes a sensation of a "skipped" beat; however, people can also describe a rapid heart beat or a sensation of lightheadedness. Whenever the palpitation is accompanied by lightheadedness or loss of consciousness, it is imperative that a further workup be undertaken to determine whether or not serious, underlying heart rhythm problems are present. Often, the simplest underlying causes of palpitations can be turned around by getting more sleep, drinking less coffee or other caffeinated beverages, decreasing alcohol consumption, or trying to reduce the amount of stress in your life. But take the problem to your doctor for evaluation first.

Edema

Edema is an abnormal accumulation of fluid in the body, a type of swelling, and has many causes. The location and distribution of the swelling is helpful in determining what causes it. If edema occurs in the legs, it is usually characteristic of heart failure or of problems with the veins of the legs. Edema with a cardiac origin typically is symmetric; that is, it involves both legs. If the edema is an abnormal gathering of fluid in the lungs, called *pulmonary edema,* the typical symptom is shortness of breath. This symptom too can be typical in a patient with heart failure. Abnormal gathering of fluid, either in the legs or the lungs, always indicates the need for a complete cardiac workup to determine whether one or both of the main pumping chambers of the heart are not working adequately.

Cyanosis

Cyanosis, the bluish discoloration of the skin resulting from inadequate oxygen in the blood, is both a sign and a symptom. One form of cyanosis occurs when unoxygenated blood that is normally pumped through the right side of the heart somehow passes into the left ventricle and is pumped out to the body. This commonly occurs in congenital abnormalities that create abnormal openings between the right and left side of the heart. The second type of cyanosis is a peripheral form commonly caused by constriction of blood vessels, which may come either from a low output from the heart or from exposure to cold air or water. Whether the cyanosis is central or peripheral in nature guides a physician in the search for which type of underlying condition is causing the cyanosis. Any form of cyanosis is a symptom that should prompt discussion with your physician.

Cough

As anyone who has had a head cold knows, a cough can accompany a viral illness. It can also represent a variety of underlying causes such as cancers, allergies, abnormalities of the lungs, or abnormalities of the breathing tube. The cardiovascular disorders that result in cough are those that cause abnormal accumulations of fluid in the lungs, such as significant heart failure. Take any prolonged or unexplained cough to your doctor. Certainly anytime blood is present in what you've coughed up, you need to have the possible causes checked out. The same goes for any evidence of bacterial infection, typically yellowish, greenish, or blood-tinged sputum.

Hemoptysis

Coughing up blood of any kind — from small streaks in sputum to large quantities — is called *hemoptysis* in medicine. This condition can result from a variety of very serious diseases of the lungs or even some forms of cancer. Whatever the cause, coughing up blood-tinged secretions is never normal and may represent a medical emergency. Should you ever cough up blood in any form — no matter how minor it seems — immediately contact your doctor.

Fatigue

In our busy, hectic lives, fatigue may come from a bewilderingly large number of underlying causes ranging from depression, to side effects of drugs, to physical illnesses including cardiac problems. The ordinary fatigue you feel after working hard is normal, even when you have to crash into bed early. But a significant level of *enduring* fatigue should always prompt a call to your doctor, who may want to do an appropriate medical workup to determine possible underlying causes.

Chapter 26

Ten Secrets of Long-Term Success

In This Chapter

▶ Secrets for winning the race against heart disease

▶ How to use small steps for long-term change

*P*reventing heart disease or effectively treating it requires making a life-long commitment to carry out simple heart-healthy habits and practices from day to day. Affirming the positive habits you already have and making necessary changes to nurture heart health is a race — make that an enjoyable marathon — always won by the tortoise and not the hare. In this chapter, I highlight ten key "secrets" that can make you a world champion tortoise in the marathon battle against heart disease. How can I be so sure? I've seen these strategies work for thousands of patients.

Educate Yourself

Former President John F. Kennedy was fond of saying, "Knowledge is power." This is certainly true when it comes to heart disease. This whole book has been about providing you with both knowledge and, I hope, motivation, to learn about those lifestyle factors and medical therapies that can lower your risk of heart disease or help treat established heart disease. In addition to *The Healthy Heart For Dummies,* there are wonderful books, periodicals, and now the Internet to help you gather the facts that you need to be an effective partner in fighting heart disease. Don't be embarrassed or shy about bringing this information to your physician.

Accumulate, Accumulate

This particular secret applies very specifically to physical activity. Hundreds of scientific studies support the concept that accumulating physical activity in small increments throughout the day is just as effective, in terms of lowering your risk of heart disease, as establishing one period of time each day when you exercise.

But the concept of accumulation applies to other aspects of combating heart disease as well. Each day we make hundreds of small decisions: to eat a piece of fruit or to have a doughnut. To smoke a cigarette or not. To take the elevator two flights or climb the stairs. You get the picture. Such small daily steps add up and can make an enormous difference in long-term success.

Be Prepared

The Boy Scouts had it right when they adopted as their motto, "Be prepared." Most people who have difficulty making changes in their lifestyle falter on simple issues, not profound ones. Most people ignore simple, basic preparation, making it much more difficult to accomplish changes. A good pair of walking shoes or a good all-weather exercise suit, for example, can make the difference between establishing a consistent walking program or faltering. Having the proper ingredients in your pantry makes it more likely that you will choose something low in fat and nutritious rather than a convenience food loaded with salt and fat. Writing down your questions and being prepared to discuss side effects can make the difference between a satisfactory visit to your doctor and a frustrating one. As you see, most preparatory steps are not complex, but neglecting preparation is an invitation to frustration and failure.

Mix and Match

Variety is the spice of life — the spice of making lifestyle changes, too. Boredom sabotages the best intentions. Whether it's keeping lots of fruits and vegetables in the refrigerator to make sure that you get your requisite five a day, mapping out different walking routes, or experimenting with different forms of physical activity, adding variety can prevent things from going stale. The best way to fight boredom is to prevent it in the first place by mixing and matching to add variety to your lifestyle change program.

Be Specific and Prioritize

Remember that most people tend to falter on simple issues, not complex ones, when making positive lifestyle changes. To accomplish any goal, but particularly ones that involve the long-term accumulation of small changes, you must be specific and prioritize. For example, each day, try to have a specific plan for how you are going to get in your physical activity. This may be as simple as establishing a time and place to walk. To stick with eating low-fat food, you can do something as simple as packing your lunch every day or always taking a piece of fruit to make sure that doughnut doesn't tempt you midmorning. It's also important to establish a specific list of priorities. Decide which changes you want make when and take them one by one. Having a vague idea that you'll get "around to it" dooms you to failure.

Include Family and Friends

People are all social beings. There is clear evidence that individuals who are connected to other human beings in positive ways and open up their hearts by sharing and loving others lower their risk of heart disease. Connecting to other people in positive ways is also a wonderful strategy for accomplishing both short- and long-term goals. It is much easier to bring about those changes in your life, whether it be weight management, more physical activity, better nutrition, or even smoking cessation if you share your aspirations with family and friends. These are the people who love you the most and they want to help you. By sharing with them, you stack the deck in your favor when it comes to lifestyle changes.

Be Optimistic

Everyone has heard the definition that an optimist is a person who sees the glass as "half full" while a pessimist sees the glass as "half empty." Over the years, I have become convinced that optimism is one of our great allies in the fight against heart disease. My patients who truly believe that they are going to win the war against heart disease invariably seem to do better. It is one of the reasons why I love to see patients who garden. Gardeners, in my experience, are inevitably optimistic. They plant the seeds and then are filled with hope as they tend them over the course of the growing season, watching the fruits (and vegetables!) of their labors mature to produce food and beauty. Doctors have many wonderful techniques and medicines in modern cardiovascular medicine, but nothing is more powerful than the human spirit in helping to control heart disease. If you have the diagnosis of heart disease, it does not mean the end of anything. It can often be the beginning of taking charge of your life. In this area, attitude is everything. Strive to be an optimist.

Seize the Day

Each day, every one of us faces multiple opportunities to choose between positive and negative lifestyle decisions. If you ask people who are not regular exercisers why they have difficulty establishing this habit, the most common excuse is "I don't have time." In the 1980s, I conducted a survey of physical activity among Fortune 500 CEOs, arguably some of the world's busiest people. Yet the average CEO was three times more likely to exercise on a regular basis than the average American adult. Clearly, these very busy individuals were making time for things that mattered to them. They were truly "seizing the day."

In my opinion, the basis for all stress reduction programs is to "seize the day." By that I mean to live in the present — not to fear the future or regret the past. When it comes to lifestyle changes, people who tend to succeed are those who figure out how to live in the present and make the most of daily opportunities to choose positive heart-healthy lifestyle decisions. They avoid the Alice-in-Wonderland Syndrome — jam yesterday, jam tomorrow but never jam today. And of course, today's all we ever have. So, *carpe diem* — seize the day!

Form Partnerships

As I discuss in Chapter 22, forming a partnership with your physician and other health care workers is one of the best strategies that you can adopt in the war against heart disease. In fact, I am skeptical that anyone can truly succeed who has not formed such a positive partnership. Modern cardiovascular medicine has many wonderful techniques, medicines, and procedures with more being developed regularly, but your cardiologist can not help you get the most out of these unless you work together as active partners. You'll find that such a partnership can also shore you up when you're tempted to backslide while making difficult lifestyle changes.

Reward Yourself

Changing your behavior is tough! When you make changes, therefore, it is important to recognize that you have succeeded; be proud of yourself and reward yourself. When you achieve any of the short-term and long-term goals you set, make a point of celebrating your success. Go out and buy yourself a new CD or treat yourself to a delicious (low-fat!) meal. Find some other way to mark your success. If you are living in a family with a person who is struggling to establish a positive lifestyle, make sure that you participate in celebrating and rewarding every success. Celebrate that lower cholesterol or the first month anniversary of smoking cessation. Make a big fuss over that first ten-pound weight loss, and the next and the next. All these gestures of celebration and reward remind us that small victories lead to large victories and that the largest victory is our victory over the number one killer in our society — heart disease.

Heart-Healthy Cookbook: Great Heart-Healthy Recipes by America's Leading Chefs

• •

Bruschetta

Created by Angela H. Kirkpatrick, RD
Research Dietitian, The Center For Clinical and Lifestyle Research
Shrewsbury, Massachusetts

Preparation Time: *3 hours to marinate the tomato mixture, 15 minutes to prepare*

Yield: *8 servings*

1 medium yellow tomato

3 ripe plum tomatoes, diced finely

1 tablespoon of finely minced garlic

¼ cup coarsely chopped fresh basil

2 ½ tablespoons finely chopped Italian parsley

2 teaspoons lemon juice

Pinch of crushed red pepper flakes

Salt and freshly ground pepper, to taste

8 ¼-inch thick slices of French bread

2 cloves garlic, halved

1 Mix all ingredients except bread and garlic halves in a large bowl. Allow this mixture to "rest" for three hours to intensify and marry the flavors.

2 After the flavors have developed in the tomato mixture, toast the French bread slices in a 300-degree oven until crispy and browned, 12 to 15 minutes.

3 Remove the toasted bread from the oven and rub the surfaces with the halved garlic. (Warming the garlic first will enhance its flavor. You can toss the garlic onto the sheet pan along with the bread while it's toasting.)

4 Top each slice with tomato mixture and enjoy.

(continued)

Nutrition Information Per Serving based on 8 servings

Calories	90	Saturated Fat	0 grams
Protein	3 grams	Cholesterol	0 mg
Carbohydrate	16 grams	Sodium	157 mg
Total Fat	2 grams	Dietary Fiber	1 gram

Chilled Cantaloupe Soup with Honey and Lime

Created by Hans Bergmann
Executive Chef, Cacharel Restaurant
Arlington, Texas

Special Ingredients: Lavender honey (can use orange blossom honey)

Preparation Time: 4 ½ hours (due to 4 hours chilling time)

Yield: 6 servings

3 medium, ripe cantaloupes

3 tablespoons lavender honey

12 mint leaves, julienned

6 mint sprigs for garnish

3 limes, juiced

1 Halve cantaloupes and cut out seeds.

2 Scoop out about 30 melon balls for garnish. Set aside.

3 Cut rind from cantaloupe halves and cut melon into chunks.

4 In a blender, puree the melon chunks until smooth.

5 In a small pan, cook honey until it foams and caramelizes.

6 Reduce heat and add lime juice. Reduce by a third. Allow to cool.

7 Add honey-lime mixture to the melon puree and pass through a sieve.

8 Add mint julienne and stir well.

Lavender honey is honey produced from bees that have fed off of lavender plants. Different flavors of honey come from the perfume of the flower where the nectar has been gathered. Be careful when substituting one honey for another; the flavors of certain honeys (buckwheat, for instance) can be very intense and may not work well in certain dishes. Clover honey is the most commonly available honey in most supermarkets.

9 Refrigerate soup for four hours until the soup is very cold and flavors have blended.

10 To serve, ladle soup into chilled bowls. Float five melon balls in the center of each bowl and garnish with a sprig of mint.

Nutrition Information Per Serving based on 6 servings

Calories	132	Sodium	28 mg
Protein	3 grams	Dietary Fiber	2 grams
Carbohydrate	33 grams	Vitamin A	95% of the Daily Value
Total Fat	1 gram	Vitamin C	201% of the Daily Value
Saturated Fat	0 grams	Folic Acid	27% of the Daily Value
Cholesterol	0 mg		

Chilled Sweet Corn Broth with Crab and Avocado Salad

Created by John Harris
Chef, Gautreau's
New Orleans, Louisiana

This recipe will take very little time to prepare if you make the broth ahead of time. Preparing the salad and assembling the dish will take only minutes, making this a wonderful lunch item even on the busiest day.

Special Ingredients: *White pepper corns*

Preparation Time: *60-75 minutes (due to cooling time for broth)*

Yield: *6 servings*

(continued)

For the broth:

2 tablespoons olive oil

1 cup diced white onion

½ cup diced celery

4 ears fresh corn

4 sprigs fresh thyme

4 ½ cups water

Salt and freshly ground white pepper, to taste

For the crab salad:

Juice of 2 oranges

Juice of 1 lime

Juice of 1 lemon

4 tablespoons extra virgin olive oil (Italian or Californian)

Salt and freshly ground white pepper, to taste

1 pound jumbo lump or lump crab meat (picked)

3 avocados (peeled and roughly diced)

Fresh chives, for garnish

Part I: Prepare the corn broth

1 Shuck the corn and cut off kernels. Set aside.

2 In a medium pan, sauté the onions and celery in olive oil over medium heat for about five minutes.

3 Add corn, thyme, water, and seasonings and bring to a boil.

4 Turn flame down to achieve a simmer for about 15 minutes (until flavors are married and corn is tender). Remove thyme sprigs.

5 Remove from flame, puree in blender while hot (in batches, if necessary). Then push through a fine sieve strainer. Adjust seasonings and chill in the refrigerator.

Chef Harris advises: "Add slightly more salt than you may think is needed — a cold food item always needs more than you think it does when it's hot."

Part II: Prepare the crab salad

1 Prepare the dressing, whisking together the citrus juices and olive oil. Adjust the seasoning with salt and pepper.

2 In a bowl, gently fold together crabmeat, avocados, and the citrus dressing. Adjust seasonings.

Part III: Serve

1 Take six large chilled bowls and lay them out on a table or countertop. Arrange crab salad in a ring mold or just portion out among the six bowls in the center of each bowl.

2 Spoon six ounces (¾ cup) of the corn broth around the salad. Garnish with fresh chives, freshly ground white pepper, and a drizzle of extra virgin olive oil (optional).

Chef Harris recommends serving this dish with a Reisling or Gewurztraminer. Chef Harris writes, "[Both wines] complement the sweetness of the corn and the fruit of the olive oil, and stand up to the fat in the avocado."

Nutrition Information Per Serving based on 6 servings

Calories	429	Sodium	231 mg
Protein	19 grams	Dietary Fiber	7 grams
Carbohydrate	30 grams	Vitamin C	49% of the Daily Value
Total Fat	29 grams	Vitamin E	46% of the Daily Value
Saturated Fat	4 grams	Folic Acid	75% of the Daily Value
Cholesterol	70 mg		

Citrus Quinoa Salad

*Created by Alfonso Constrisciani
Executive Chef-Proprietor, Opus 251 at the Philadelphia Art Alliance and Circa
Philadelphia, Pennsylvania*

Special Ingredients: Quinoa, citrus oil (optional)

Preparation Time: 30 minutes

Yield: 8 servings

(continued)

For salad:

1 ½ cups chicken stock (vegetable stock can be substituted)

¾ cup quinoa, washed and rinsed well

¼ cup red onion, finely diced

¼ cup carrot, finely diced

¼ cup radish, finely diced

3-4 scallions (green onions), washed and diagonally sliced ¼-inch thick

For salad dressing:

Zest of one orange

¼ orange, peeled and minced

Zest of one lemon

¼ lemon, peeled and minced

1 tablespoon fresh lemon juice

1 ½ teaspoon fresh garlic, minced

1 tablespoon citrus oil or canola oil

1 tablespoon olive oil

1 ½ teaspoon rice wine vinegar

1 tablespoon parsley, finely chopped

Salt & freshly ground pepper to taste

1 In a medium sauce pan, bring chicken stock to a boil. Add quinoa until liquid is absorbed and quinoa is tender, about 15 minutes.

2 Prep all salad vegetables while quinoa is cooking.

3 When quinoa is fully cooked, remove from heat, strain and cool quinoa by spreading it out on a sheet tray (cookie sheet) while preparing salad dressing.

4 Zest orange and lemon for dressing by finely grating outer layer of peel. Be sure to wash fruit prior to zesting.

5 Combine all salad dressing ingredients in small bowl and season with salt and pepper.

6 In a large bowl combine all vegetables with cooled quinoa and toss with dressing. Season to taste with salt and pepper.

Quinoa (pronounced KEEN-wah), a grain commonly used in South American cooking, is the most protein-rich grain and contains all essential amino acids. Quinoa is also higher in mono and polyunsaturated fats and lower in carbohydrates than other grains. Quinoa cooks like rice and expands to about twice its original volume (pasta doubles in size and rice triples). Quinoa can be purchased in many health and natural foods stores as well as in some supermarkets.

Nutrition Information Per Serving based on 8 ½-cup servings

Calories	*107*	*Cholesterol*	*0 mg*
Protein	*3 grams*	*Sodium**	*199 mg*
Carbohydrate	*14 grams*	*Dietary Fiber*	*2 grams*
Total Fat	*5 grams*		
Saturated Fat	*0.5 grams*		

* Sodium information based on no added salt.

Creamless Tomato Soup with Chives and Roasted Yellow Tomatoes

Created by Susan Weaver
Executive Chef, Fifty Seven Fifty Seven Restaurant & Bar, Four Seasons Hotel
New York, New York

Preparation Time: *1 hour 15 minutes*

Yield: *6 servings*

3 yellow tomatoes

Dried Italian herbs, such as oregano, basil, and thyme

2 teaspoon olive oil

1 Spanish onion, finely chopped

1 ounce (about 4 tablespoons) shallots, minced

2 cloves fresh garlic, minced

12 Roma tomatoes, destemmed and chopped

8 ounces Pomi Crushed Tomato

8 ounces Pomi Strained Tomato

1 teaspoon tomato paste

5 basil leaves

Salt and freshly ground black pepper

6 chives, cut into 1-inch long "sticks"

1 Cut the yellow tomatoes in half lengthwise and toss with a small amount (½ teaspoon or less) dried Italian herbs (oregano, basil, thyme), freshly ground pepper, and 1 teaspoon olive oil. Lay flesh side down on a roasting rack pan and roast in a 275-degree oven for one hour.

2 Meanwhile, in a large covered saucepan, heat remaining teaspoon of olive oil. When hot, sauté the onions, shallots, garlic, and Roma tomatoes, stirring 3 to 5 minutes over medium high heat.

3 Add the Pomi tomato products and tomato paste and simmer, stirring occasionally, with the fresh basil for approximately 20 minutes.

(continued)

4 Puree the soup in the workbowl of a food processor or blender and adjust consistency by adding additional strained tomato, if necessary.

5 Return blenderized soup to saucepan, adjust seasoning with salt and pepper, and keep warm while tomatoes finish roasting.

6 To serve, place a roasted tomato half in the bottom of each soup bowl. Ladle the soup over the tomato and garnish with chive "sticks."

Nutrition Information Per Serving based on 6 servings

Calories	86	Cholesterol	0 mg
Protein	3 grams	Sodium	331 mg
Carbohydrate	17 grams	Dietary Fiber	3 grams
Total Fat	2 grams	Vitamin A	20% of the Daily Value
Saturated Fat	0 grams	Vitamin C	75% of the Daily Value

Eggplant and Tomato Gratin (Gratin d'aubergines et de Tomates)

Created by Constantin "Chris" Kerageorgiou
Executive Chef, La Provence Restaurant
New Orleans, Louisiana

The preparation and baking time on this dish is two hours, but the gratin will keep for a couple of days in the refrigerator before baking. Prepare the eggplant and tomato sauce ahead of time and then bake the day of serving.

Special Equipment: *Gratin pan, food mill*

Preparation Time: *2 hours*

Yield: *4 servings*

A **food mill** is a counter-top kitchen utensil with a hand-turned paddle that forces food through a strainer. It is often used to remove seeds (for example, from a tomato), skin (for example, from fish), or fiber. Most food mills come with plates with small, medium, or large holes. Food mills can be purchased at kitchen supply stores or from kitchen supply catalog companies, such as Williams Sonoma.

3 pounds (3 large or 5 to 6 medium-size) eggplant

4 teaspoons olive oil

3 large garlic cloves, minced or put through a press

3 pounds (12 medium-size) tomatoes, seeded and quartered

1 to 2 pinches of sugar (nutrition analysis based on using 1 teaspoon of sugar)

½ teaspoon salt

3 tablespoons slivered fresh basil

1 ounce (¼ cup) Parmesan cheese, freshly grated

2 tablespoons fresh or dry, coarse or fine bread crumbs

Freshly ground pepper to taste

1 Preheat the oven to 450° F.

2 Cut the eggplants in half lengthwise, score the flesh on the cut side down the middle, to the skin but not through it, and place cut side down on a large, lightly oiled baking sheet. Bake for 25 to 30 minutes, until thoroughly tender. Remove from the heat and allow to cool. Carefully peel away the skins or scoop the eggplant out from the skins, and cut in ¼-inch-thick lengthwise slices.

3 While the eggplants bake, heat 1 teaspoon of the oil in a large, heavy-bottomed nonstick skillet over medium heat and add the minced garlic. When it begins to color, after about 30 seconds, add the tomatoes, sugar, and salt. Cook, stirring often, for 20 to 25 minutes, until the tomatoes are cooked down and beginning to stick to the pan. Stir in the basil, simmer for a few minutes, and remove from the heat.

4 Put the tomatoes through the medium blade of a food mill. Adjust salt and add pepper.

5 Lightly oil a 3-quart gratin dish. Spoon a small amount of tomato sauce over the bottom and top with one-third of the eggplant. Spoon on a third of the remaining tomato sauce over the eggplant. Make two more layers, sprinkle on the cheese and bread crumbs, season with pepper, and drizzle on the remaining olive oil.

6 Bake for 30 minutes at 425° F, until the top browns and the mixture is sizzling. Remove from the heat and serve hot or warm.

(continued)

Nutrition Information Per Serving based on 4 servings

Calories	228	Sodium	476 mg
Protein	8 grams	Dietary Fiber	10 grams
Carbohydrate	36 grams	Vitamin A	28% of the Daily Value
Total Fat	8 grams	Vitamin C	106% of the Daily Value
Saturated Fat	2 grams	Vitamin E	25% of the Daily Value
Cholesterol	5 mg	Folic Acid	48% of the Daily Value

Fruit and Vegetable Carpaccio with Lemon Dressing

Created by Felicien Cueff
Chef de Cuisine, CITRONELLE
Santa Barbara, California

Special Equipment: *Mandoline or food processor (optional)*

Special Ingredients: *Jicama, chervil leaf*

Preparation Time: *15 minutes*

Yield: *4 servings*

*This recipe calls for uniform thinly cut fruits and vegetables; if you don't feel comfortable hand slicing, feel free to use a **mandoline** or **food processor** to achieve very thin uniform slices.*

½ cup lemon juice	1 firm peach, halved and pitted
⅛ cup olive oil	1 firm tomato with the eye cored
Ground pepper to season (optional)	1 peeled jicama
Pinch of sugar (optional)	½ cucumber
1 firm nectarine, halved and pitted	1 peeled red onion
1 firm plum, halved and pitted	2 tablespoons chopped chervil leaf

Jicama is a Mexican potato that has sweet, nutty flavor. It can be purchased in Mexican markets and most large supermarkets.

Chervil is a member of the parsley family. It has a distinct anise (licorice) flavor. You can find fresh chervil in many supermarkets.

1 Whisk the lemon juice and olive oil together in a bowl. Add pepper and a small amount of sugar if desired; set aside.

2 Slice the nectarine, plum, peach, onion, tomato, and cucumber into very thin slices; set aside.

3 Set the tomatoes first on a clean, cold oval dish. Then set the peaches, then cucumbers, then plums, and then the nectarines. Set a few onion rings over the entire plate. Sprinkle with fresh chervil leaf.

4 Dice the jicama and scatter over fruit. Then drizzle the lemon juice and olive oil mixture over the dish.

Nutrition Information Per Serving based on 4 servings

Calories	196	Cholesterol	0 mg
Protein	3 grams	Sodium	11 mg
Carbohydrate	33 grams	Dietary Fiber	11 grams
Total Fat	7 grams	Vitamin C	103% of the Daily Value
Saturated Fat	1 gram		

Grand Marnier French Toast Stuffed with Banana Cream Cheese

Created by Jeremy Kirkpatrick and Angela H. Kirkpatrick, RD
Research Dietitian, The Center for Clinical and Lifestyle Research
Shrewsbury, Massachusetts

Preparation Time: *15 minutes*

Yield: *4 servings*

2 whole eggs

8 egg whites

¼ cup lowfat (1%) buttermilk

¼ teaspoon Grand Marnier liquor

1 large banana

4 tablespoons low-fat cream cheese

8 slices whole grain bread

2 tablespoons powdered sugar

¼ cup maple syrup

(continued)

1 In a large, shallow bowl, using a fork, beat the eggs and egg whites until lightly frothy.

2 Stir in the buttermilk and the Grand Marnier. Set aside.

3 Peel the bananas, place into a small bowl, and mash with a fork. Mix with cream cheese and spread mixture over four bread slices, leaving a ¼-inch border uncovered on all edges.

4 Top with remaining bread slices and press gently to seal.

5 Place each sandwich in the egg mixture. Turn gently until they evenly soak up the egg mixture.

6 In a large, well-seasoned or nonstick frying pan or griddle over medium heat, cover pan's surface with non-stick spray and fry each sandwich over medium heat until the undersides are golden brown, about 2 minutes.

7 Add more cooking spray to the pan, if needed; then flip the bread with a spatula and fry until the second sides are browned, about 2 minutes longer.

8 Transfer to a warmed platter and keep warm. Repeat with the remaining bread. Use spray as needed.

9 To serve, cut each sandwich in half diagonally and arrange on a dinner plate. Dust with powdered sugar using a small fine mesh sieve. Serve hot, with fresh fruit or a drizzle of maple syrup.

Nutrition Information Per Serving based on 4 servings

Calories	343	Saturated Fat	3 grams
Protein	19 grams	Cholesterol	115 mg
Carbohydrate	51 grams	Sodium	500 mg
Total Fat	7 grams	Dietary Fiber	3 grams

Green Pimento & Mango Salsa

Created by MaryAnn Saporito Boothroyd
Chef/Owner, Saporito's Florence Club Café
Hull, Massachusetts

Chef MaryAnn recommends serving this flavorful, fragrant, and fat-free salsa with grilled chicken or fish or baked tortilla chips. The salsa also makes a wonderful topping for baked potatoes. Don't be confused by the name of this salsa. Pimento is the Spanish term for pepper, hence the name of this salsa that combines three different peppers with fresh herbs and the sweetness of mangoes.

Preparation Time: *25 minutes*

Yield: *8 ⅓-cup servings*

2 green bell peppers

1 ½ cups ripe fresh mango, peeled and diced

½ cup red bell pepper, diced

¼ to ½ cup diced hot pickled cherry peppers (Italian-style in vinegar, not oil)

½ cup pineapple juice

2 tablespoons red wine vinegar

2 tablespoons fresh cilantro, chopped

2 tablespoons fresh basil, chopped

Salt, to taste (analysis based on ¼ teaspoon salt)

Freshly ground black pepper, to taste

1 Roast green peppers by halving and seeding. Arrange the pepper halves on a baking sheet, skin side up and place under broiler for 3 to 4 minutes until skin blisters and blackens; rotate the pan if necessary for even cooking. Place pepper into a bag and close it (or into a bowl and cover tightly with plastic wrap). Set aside for 10 minutes to loosen skins. Peel, discard skins, and dice. Use ½ cup for this recipe.

2 Combine all ingredients in glass bowl and let sit for at least 30 minutes.

Nutrition Information Per Serving based on 8 ⅓-cup servings

Calories	50	Cholesterol	0 mg
Protein	0 grams	Sodium	274 mg
Carbohydrate	12 grams	Dietary Fiber	2 grams
Total Fat	0 grams	Vitamin A	34% of the Daily Value
Saturated Fat	0 grams	Vitamin C	58% of the Daily Value

Grilled Indian Spiced Pork Chop with Sticky Black Rice & Papaya Salsa

Created by Michael Schwartz
Chef/Owner, Nemo Restaurant
Miami Beach, Florida

Chef Schwartz writes: "This dish has long been a favorite at Nemo. The contrasting flavors of the spice-laden pork and the sweet and acidic papaya salsa make a great combination along with the texture of the sticky black rice. If you don't eat pork, try this recipe with a firm fish such as sword, which is equally delicious. I prefer to use the 'strawberry' papayas, which have a pinkish tone to the meat and are much smaller, versus those gigantic ones you sometimes see in the market."

Special Ingredients: *Chinese black rice, coriander, anise, star anise, cardamom, papaya*

Preparation Time: *2 hours to marinate the pork chops, 60 minutes to prepare and cook*

Yield: *6 servings*

For the spice rub (makes enough rub for 36 pork chops):

2 tablespoons ground cumin

½ tablespoon ground coriander

½ tablespoon curry powder

½ teaspoon crushed red pepper

½ teaspoon anise

½ teaspoon ground star anise

½ teaspoon ground cardamom

2 tablespoons canola oil

For the pork chops:

6 5-oz center cut pork chops, trimmed of all visible fat

6 teaspoons spice rub

6 teaspoons honey

For the papaya salsa:

3 ripe papayas, peeled, seeded, and finely diced

1 small red onion, finely diced

1 jalapeno, seeded and minced

1 bunch cilantro, cleaned and chopped

¼ cup fresh squeezed lime juice

¼ cup extra virgin olive oil

6 sprigs cilantro, for garnish

Salt and pepper to taste (optional)

For the sticky black rice:

2 cups Chinese black rice

2 cups water

½ teaspoon salt (optional)

For the carmelized onions:

1 teaspoon canola oil

2 medium red onions, peeled and cut into ½-inch thick wedges

¼ cup honey

Pinch of crushed red pepper

Salt and pepper to taste (optional)

Prepare the spice rub:

Combine all ingredients and store in an airtight container in the refrigerator until ready to use.

Marinade the pork chops:

Rub one teaspoon of spice rub on each pork chop and allow to marinate at least two hours or overnight.

Prepare the papaya salsa:

In a medium-size mixing bowl, combine the papaya, red onion, jalapeno, cilantro, lime juice, and olive oil. Season with salt (optional) and pepper to taste. Allow salsa to sit at room temperature until ready to serve (but for no longer than one hour).

Prepare the sticky black rice:

1 In a small pot combine black rice and water and let sit for 10 minutes. Add salt and bring rice and water to a boil.

2 Turn heat down to a simmer, cover and cook for 30 to 35 minutes or until rice is sticky and tender. Add up to another ¼ cup of water if necessary to continue cooking until tender. Do not stir.

3 Keep covered in a warm place on the stove until ready to serve.

Prepare the carmelized onions:

1 Heat the canola oil in a large skillet over high heat until oil gets wavy and almost smokes.

2 Add onions, reduce the heat, and cook the onions, by stirring constantly, until they brown (about 4 to 5 minutes).

3 Just as the onions begin to get good and brown, add the honey and crushed red pepper. Season with salt (optional) and pepper.

4 Cook for another 1 to 2 minutes. The onions should be dark in color but not burnt. They should still have a bite to them. Remove from heat and let sit at room temperature.

Cook the pork chops:

1 Preheat your gas grill or start your charcoal grill.

2 When your grill is hot, grill pork chops for 5 to 6 minutes per side or until cooked through.

3 When the pork chops are just about done cooking, drizzle about one teaspoon honey on each chop, flip it over, and cook for another minute. Remove from heat and start building the dish.

(continued)

Chinese black rice helps give this dish its unique character. It is available in Asian markets or by mail from Dean & Deluca (1-800-221-7714). You may substitute Himalayan red rice, brown rice, or wild rice, but not white rice, says Chef Schwartz, because white rice would dramatically affect the integrity of the dish.

Assemble the dish:

1 Spoon equal amounts of rice onto the center of six large dinner plates.

2 Make a well in the center of each rice pile and fill it with carmelized onions.

3 Place a pork chop on top of the rice pile.

4 Smother each pork chop with papaya salsa, garnish with cilantro leaves, and serve.

Nutrition Information Per Serving based on 6 servings

Calories	667	Sodium	76 mg
Protein	38 grams	Dietary Fiber	8 grams
Carbohydrate	80 grams	Vitamin A	29% of the Daily Value
Total Fat	22 grams	Vitamin C	193% of the Daily Value
Saturated Fat	5 grams	Vitamin E	23% of the Daily Value
Cholesterol	89 mg	Folic Acid	22% of the Daily Value

Grilled Maine Salmon in Lemongrass Broth

Created by Nora Pouillon
Chef and Owner, Nora — the only certified organic restaurant in the U.S.
Washington, D.C.

Special Ingredients: *Lemongrass, nuoc mam*

Preparation Time: *20 minutes*

Yield: *4 servings*

Lemongrass, with its scallion-like base, adds a sour-lemon flavor, making it a must in Thai cooking. Typically only the tender white part of the stalk is sliced or diced for use in dishes. Use the tougher tops in stock.

Lemongrass is available in Asian markets, specialty stores, and some supermarkets. No worries though if you can't find it in your local market; green onions (scallions) and a touch of lemon juice will do.

Nuoc mam is a fish sauce. When nuoc mam is combined with red chiles, garlic, lime juice, ginger, scallions, and sugar, the popular Vietnamese condiment nuoc cham is created. You can find nuoc mam in Asian markets and specialty markets.

Pad Thai noodles, or rice sticks, is a pasta made from rice flour. Available in Asian markets and many supermarkets.

4 oz Pad Thai noodles or rice sticks

3-inch piece of ginger, peeled and sliced

1 stalk lemongrass, outer leaves removed and thinly sliced

1-2 jalapeno chiles or to taste

6 cups water

2 tablespoons nuoc mam (Thai fish sauce)

2 large carrots, about 6 ounces, peeled and thinly sliced

16 shiitake mushrooms, washed, stemmed, and quartered

4 green onions, trimmed and sliced thinly on the diagonal

4 ounces watercress, stems trimmed

½ cup cilantro leaves, for garnish

4 six-oz salmon fillets, skinned

1 teaspoon canola oil

1 Preheat your grill or broiler.

2 Soak the Pad Thai noodles or rice sticks in hot tap water for about 3 minutes or until softened. Drain and set aside.

3 Put the ginger, lemongrass, and chiles in a small chopper or food processor and process until minced, or mince finely by hand.

4 In a medium saucepan, bring the water to a boil and add the ginger, lemongrass, and chiles. Season to taste with nuoc mam. Add the carrots, shiitake mushrooms, green onions, and the drained noodles. Simmer about one minute.

5 The broth can be made ahead to this point. (If you do make ahead, wait to add the noodles to the broth.) Just before serving, stir in the watercress. This will keep them green and crisp.

6 Brush the salmon with the oil and cook about 3 minutes per side or until the fish turns opaque and medium rare.

(continued)

7 To assemble, ladle the broth into four large soup bowls, dividing the vegetables and noodles evenly. Top with the salmon and garnish with cilantro.

Nutrition Information Per Serving based on 4 servings

Calories	308	Cholesterol	88 mg
Protein	37 grams	Sodium	854 mg
Carbohydrate	23 grams	Dietary Fiber	3 grams
Total Fat	7 grams	Vitamin A	275% of the Daily Value
Saturated Fat	1 gram	Vitamin C	79% of the Daily Value

Grilled Portobello Mushroom with Corn Relish

Created by Nora Pouillon
Chef and Owner, Nora - the only certified organic restaurant in the U.S.
Washington, D.C

Preparation Time: *15 minutes*

Yield: *4 servings*

For the tamari balsamic vinaigrette:

1 tablespoon balsamic vinegar

1 teaspoon tamari

2 cloves garlic, finely minced

¼ teaspoon freshly ground black pepper

2 tablespoons olive oil

For the corn relish:

2 ears corn, silks removed and washed

1 large red pepper, washed, seeded, and diced into ¼-inch pieces

1-2 green onions, washed, trimmed and thinly sliced (about 3 tablespoons)

OR *3 tablespoons minced chives*

2 tablespoons chopped flat leaf parsley

Sea salt and freshly ground black pepper, to taste

1 tablespoon olive oil

For the portobello mushrooms:

4 portobello mushrooms, about ½ pound, stemmed, and wiped clean

Tamari-balsamic vinaigrette marinade (see recipe)

Prepare the tamari balsamic vinaigrette:

1 Combine the vinegar, tamari, garlic, and pepper in a small bowl and whisk with a fork.

2 While whisking, slowly add the olive oil until emulsified.

Prepare the corn relish:

1 Carefully cut the corn kernels off the cobs and place in a medium bowl.

2 Add the red pepper, green onions or chives, and parsley. Stir to combine and season to taste with salt and pepper.

3 Heat the olive oil in a small pan, add the vegetable mixture, and sauté for 1 to 2 minutes or just until the corn loses its raw taste. ***Note:*** If your corn is very fresh, sweet, and tender, this step is not necessary. Just add the olive oil to the raw vegetables and stir to combine.

Prepare the mushrooms:

1 Preheat grill or broiler.

2 Brush the portobellos with the tamari-balsamic vinaigrette marinade.

3 Place the mushrooms on the grill, about 4 inches from the heat source, or on a baking pan about 4 inches from the broiler, and cook for 2 to 3 minutes on each side or until cooked through and softened.

Plate the mushrooms:

1 Place a portobello on each of four large plates.

2 Spoon some corn relish on top.

3 Plating variation: You could top each mushroom with a piece of fresh mozzarella or slice of silken tofu and then top with the corn relish.

Nutrition Information Per Serving based on 4 servings

Calories	162	Cholesterol	0 mg
Protein	4 grams	Sodium	96 mg
Carbohydrate	15 grams	Dietary Fiber	4 grams
Total Fat	10 grams	Vitamin A	55% of the Daily Value
Saturated Fat	1 gram	Vitamin C	150% of the Daily Value

Grilled Vegetable Quesadillas

Created by Bruce Molzan
CEO and Chef, Ruggles Grille 5115
Houston, Texas

Preparation Time: *30 minutes*

Yield: *One entrée serving or three appetizer servings*

½ small zucchini grilled, cut into ¼-inch thick diagonal slices

½ small yellow squash grilled, cut into ¼-inch thick diagonal slices

3 ¼-inch thick slices eggplant, grilled

3 asparagus, bottom stem removed

2 tablespoons red onion, chopped

2 eight-inch flour tortillas

1 tablespoon olive oil

3 tablespoons low-fat mozzarella cheese, grated

½ large steak tomato, cut into ¼-inch thick slices

2 tablespoons chopped cilantro

Salt and pepper to taste

2 tablespoons salsa

1 Arrange rack so that it is 3 to 4 inches from the broiler. Pre heat broiler. Place zucchini, yellow squash, and eggplant on sheet or broiler pan and broil each side for approximately 2 minutes until tender. Remove and set aside.

2 Blanch asparagus in boiling water for one minute, cut in half lengthwise, and cool in ice water. Drain and set aside.

3 In large sauté pan, sauté red onion in 1 teaspoon olive oil over medium heat. Remove from pan and set aside.

4 Brush one teaspoon olive oil on one side of each tortilla, and then place one tortilla — oil side down — in the large sauté pan over medium heat. Sprinkle with half the cheese and arrange the tomatoes on top, followed by the cooked vegtables. Sprinkle on remaining cheese , the cilantro, and season with salt and pepper. Cover with second tortilla, oil side up.

5 When bottom tortilla is crispy, carefully flip quesadilla over and grill second side until crispy.

6 Remove from pan and cut into six wedges.

7 Serve warm with salsa.

Nutrition Information Per Serving based on 1 serving

Calories	456	Cholesterol	13 mg
Protein	14 grams	Sodium	483 mg
Carbohydrate	51 grams	Dietary Fiber	6 grams
Total Fat	23 grams	Vitamin C	37% of the Daily Value
Saturated Fat	5 grams	Folic Acid	46% of the Daily Value

Gulf Fish Court Bouillon

Created by Carl Walker
Executive Chef, Brennan's
Houston, Texas

Special Equipment: *Heavy-duty 18" aluminum foil*

Special Ingredients: *Creole Seafood Seasoning, Louisiana Hot Sauce, Crab Boil Liquid*

Preparation Time: *60 minutes*

Yield: *2 servings*

½ cup roasted red, green, and yellow peppers, julienne cut

¾ cup tomatoes, peeled, seeded, and julienne cut

⅓ cup yellow onions, julienne cut

2 small garlic cloves, shaved thin

⅓ cup celery, cut thin diagonally

½ teaspoon Louisiana Hot Sauce

½ teaspoon Worcestershire sauce

2 tablespoons red wine

Couple of drops Liquid Crab Boil

2-4 bay leaves

¼ teaspoon salt

⅛ teaspoon black pepper (finely ground)

2 lemon wedges

2 five-oz fillets of red snapper (no skin or bones)

6 shrimp 16/20 count (peeled & deveined)

2-3 teaspoons Creole Seafood seasoning

1 Arrange rack so that it sits 3 to 4 inches under the broiler. Preheat broiler. Preheat oven to 350°F.

(continued)

2 Clean, seed, and halve peppers. Place the pepper halves onto a baking sheet or pan, skin side up, and place under broiler for 3 to 5 minutes until skin blisters or blackens; rotate pan if necessary for even cooking. Place the peppers into a bag and close it, or into a bowl and cover tightly with plastic wrap. Set aside for 10 minutes to loosen skins. Peel skins off and julienne flesh.

3 In a glass or stainless bowl, mix tomatoes, onions, peppers, garlic, celery, hot sauce, Worcestershire sauce, red wine, crab boil, bay leaves, salt, pepper, and lemon wedges. Set aside.

4 Take a sheet of heavy-duty 18" aluminum foil and lay out flat on a table. The diameter of the foil should be approximately 18" x 18" for two servings. Season the fish and shrimp with Creole seasoning.

5 Place three shrimp on top of each fish fillet. Spoon a generous amount of the vegetable mixture on top of the fish and shrimp and cover with another sheet of foil. Fold the edges of the foil tightly 2 to 3 times on each side. Then fold each corner of the foil to create a small triangle shape. This helps lock in more heat for the cooking process. *Note:* This dish can be made in a casserole dish with a cover.

6 Place the foil package on a sheet pan and bake for 20 minutes.

7 The foil will puff up when finished cooking. Carefully cut around the edges of the foil and spoon into a bowl or plate. Serve with your favorite starchy side dish.

Nutrition Information Per Serving based on 2 servings

Calories	231	Cholesterol	84 mg
Protein	36 grams	Sodium	493 mg
Carbohydrate	11 grams	Dietary Fiber	3 grams
Total Fat	4 grams	Vitamin A	21% of the Daily Value
Saturated Fat	1 gram	Vitamin C	92% of the Daily Value

Israeli-Inspired Watermelon Salad with Feta, Sage, and Sumac

Created by Danielle Custer
Executive Chef & General Manager
Laurels Restaurant (in the Weston Park Central)
Dallas, Texas

Special Ingredients: Sumac (optional), English cucumber

Preparation Time: 30 minutes

Yield: 4 servings

¼ *of a medium, seedless watermelon*

6 tablespoons feta cheese, diced into small pieces

½ cup English cucumber, diced into small pieces

2 tablespoons red onion, minced

½ bunch Italian parsley, cleaned with stems removed

¾ bunch sage, cleaned with stems removed — ½ bunch set aside for pesto, ¼ cut chiffonade

½ teaspoon fresh garlic, minced

¾ teaspoon shallot, minced

4 tablespoons fresh lemon juice

4 tablespoons olive oil

1 teaspoon extra virgin olive oil

Salt and freshly ground pepper to taste

2 tablespoons ground sumac (optional)

1 Cut the watermelon into quarters. Peel off the flesh from the rind with a sharp knife. Slice into ¼-inch slices and trim to form triangles. Set aside.

2 Combine the cheese, cucumber, and onions in a medium bowl and set aside.

3 To make pesto, place the parsley, whole sage leaves, garlic, shallot, and lemon juice in a blender or small food processor. Pulse to get started. With the motor running, drizzle in the oils and blend until emulsified. Season to taste with salt and freshly ground pepper. Spoon half of the pesto into the bowl of fresh vegetables and toss.

4 Sprinkle the watermelon triangles with a tablespoon of sumac, if using.

5 On four salad plates arrange the watermelon slices (3 or 5 slices depending on the size or shape of the watermelon) on top of each other. Adorn the top of the watermelon with the pesto-vegetable mixture. Spoon the remaining pesto around the edge of the plate. Finally, garnish each plate with the remaining sumac and chiffonade of sage.

(continued)

Sumac is a brick red-colored spice commonly used in Middle Eastern dishes. Sumac bushes, which produce the red berries from which the spice is derived, grow wild throughout the Middle East and in parts of Italy. Sumac is sold in Middle Eastern markets in ground or dried berry form. Sumac can be ordered from Dean & Deluca by calling 1-800-221-7714 or by ordering on line at www.dean-deluca.com.

English cucumbers, also known as hothouse cucumbers, are a seedless variety of cucumbers that can grow up to two feet long. Small cucumbers, whose seeds have not fully developed, or seeded regular cucumbers can be used in place of their more expensive English cousins.

Chiffonade is a French term that literally translated means "made of rags." Chiffonades are usually used for garnishes. Chiffonade herbs by stacking the leaves one on top of another and then cutting into ⅛-inch wide strips. For best results, use a non-serrated knife, such as a French knife.

Nutrition Information Per Serving based on 4 servings

If pesto garnish on the edge of the plate is not eaten, see Nutrition Information in parentheses:

Calories	202	(133 calories)
Protein	3 grams	(3 grams)
Carbohydrate	10 grams	(10 grams)
Total Fat	18 grams	(9 grams)
Saturated Fat	4 grams	(2 grams)
Cholesterol	13 mg	(13 mg)
Sodium*	160 mg	(160 mg)
Vitamin C	50% of the Daily Value	(50% of the Daily Value)

* *Sodium information based on no added salt. Salting to taste will significantly increase the sodium content of this dish.*

Lemon Risotto

Created by Walter Pisano
Executive Chef, Tulio Ristorante
Seattle, Washington

Special Ingredients: *Arborio rice, preserved lemons (optional)*

Preparation Time: *25 minutes*

Yield: *8 servings (½ cup)*

28 ounces chicken stock, warmed (homemade or low sodium canned broth)

1 teaspoon shallot, minced

2 teaspoons unsalted butter

1 bay leaf

10 ounces (1 ¾ cups) Arborio rice, uncooked

½ teaspoon fresh lemon juice

1 teaspoon preserved lemon (optional)

1 teaspoon lemon zest

2 teaspoons fresh Italian parsley, chopped

Salt and freshly ground black pepper, to taste

1 In a small saucepan, warm the chicken stock over low heat until ready to use.

2 In a large sauté pan or medium sauce pan, sauté the minced shallots in butter over medium heat, stirring about 2 minutes or until softened.

Arborio rice is *the* rice to use when making risotto. The kernels have a higher starch content than other types of rice; the starch gives risotto its distinctive creamy texture.

Preserved lemons are lemons that have been preserved in a salt and lemon juice brine, possibly with additional spices such as cinnamon, cloves, or coriander. Preserved lemons have a very distinctive flavor and are commonly used in Moroccan cooking. Preserved lemons may be found in specialty food shops or markets that cater to Moroccan clients.

3 Add the bay leaf and rice and stir until the rice is coated with butter.

4 Slowly add three-fourths of the warmed chicken stock. Stir continuously, and add ½ cup of stock as needed, as the rice absorbs the liquid. Cook for 15 to 18 minutes until the rice is tender and creamy, not soupy.

5 Add remaining ingredients, stir and serve.

Nutrition Information Per Serving based on 8 servings

Calories	161	Sodium*	26 mg
Protein	4 grams	Dietary Fiber	1 gram
Carbohydrate	31 grams		
Total Fat	2 grams		
Saturated Fat	1 gram		
Cholesterol	3 mg		

* Sodium information based on no added salt and use of very low sodium chicken broth. Using regular canned chicken broth or adding salt will significantly increase the sodium content of this dish.

Mark's Low-Fat Oat Bran Muffins with Fresh Peaches

Created by Mark Tarbell
Executive Chef/Owner
Tarbell's and Barmouche
Phoenix, Arizona

Special Ingredients: *Kosher salt (regular table salt can be substituted), 2¾ inch muffin pan*

Preparation Time: *30 minutes*

Yield: *12 muffins*

(continued)

2 cups oat bran

2 teaspoons baking powder

1 teaspoon cinnamon

½ teaspoon kosher salt

1 cup nonfat milk

½ cup maple syrup

2 egg whites

2 tablespoons canola oil

1 cup diced fresh peaches (can substitute strawberries or blueberries)

1 Preheat oven to 425°F.

2 Grease muffin pans with cooking spray.

3 In a large bowl, combine the oat bran, baking powder, cinnamon, and salt and stir to blend.

4 In a separate bowl, whisk together the milk, maple syrup, egg whites, and canola oil. Stir in the peaches.

5 Pour the peach mixture into the dry ingredients and stir very gently, just to combine. It's okay if there are lumps in the batter.

6 Spoon batter into the muffin tins, filling about three-quarters full.

7 Bake 15 minutes or until golden brown on top.

Nutrition Information Per Serving based on 12 servings

Calories	117	Saturated Fat	0 grams
Protein	4 grams	Cholesterol	0 mg
Carbohydrate	24 grams	Sodium	184 mg
Total Fat	3 grams	Dietary Fiber	3 grams

Meringue with Mango Sorbet & Raspberries

Created by Nora Pouillon
Chef and Owner, Nora — the only certified organic restaurant in the U.S.
Washington, D.C.

Special Equipment: Pastry bag fitted with large star tip, ice cream maker

Preparation Time: 4 hours (including baking time)

Yield: 4 servings

Time saver tip: The meringue baskets need to bake for two to three hours. To save time the day of serving, bake the meringue baskets the day before and store in an airtight container.

For the meringue baskets:

A pinch of sea salt (nutrition analysis based on adding ¼ teaspoon salt)

3 egg whites at room temperature

¾ cup superfine sugar

For the mango sorbet:

3 mangoes (2 ½ – 3 ½ pounds)

4 tablespoons sugar

½ cup orange juice

1 teaspoon lime juice

¼ cup rum or tequila

For assembly:

½ pint raspberries

Mint sprigs, for garnish

Prepare the meringue baskets:

1 In a medium mixing bowl, combine eggs whites and a pinch of salt and whip the whites by hand or with a mixer until they hold soft peaks.

2 Add the sugar in a slow, steady stream, continuing to beat the egg whites as they are incorporated.

3 After all the sugar is added, continue beating the egg whites until they become glossy and hold stiff peaks.

4 Preheat the oven to 200°F.

5 Line a 12-x 18-inch baking sheet with aluminum foil, shiny-side-down.

6 Trace four 4-inch circles in the foil. Put the meringue in a pastry bag fitted with a large star tip and pipe out four meringue baskets. Form the baskets by starting at the center of the traced circle and piping around and around to make the base. Pipe another two layers around the edge to make the sides higher than the center. Or shape with a spoon to make a basket.

7 Bake the meringues for about 2 hours or until the meringues are dry but not brown. The meringue baskets should be white. If the meringue baskets begin to color in the oven, lower the oven temperature and continue baking until they are completely dry.

Prepare the mango sorbet:

1 Cut the mangoes in half, cutting around the large pit and removing the flesh from the skin.

2 Combine the mango flesh, sugar, orange juice, lime juice, and rum in a blender. Puree until smooth. Refrigerate to cool.

3 When the sorbet mixture has cooled, freeze in an ice cream freezer according to manufacturer's directions.

(continued)

Assemble the dessert:

1 On four chilled dessert plates, place one meringue basket in the center of each plate.

2 Spoon equal amounts of sorbet into each basket and top with fresh raspberries.

3 Garnish with a mint sprig and serve immediately.

Nutrition Information Per Serving based on 4 servings

Calories	351	Cholesterol	0 mg
Protein	4 grams	Sodium	380 mg
Carbohydrate	82 grams	Dietary Fiber	5 grams
Total Fat	0 grams	Vitamin A	61% the Daily Value
Saturated Fat	0 grams	Vitamin C	111% of the Daily Value

Mizuma Salad with Oranges, Mint & Dried Cranberries

Created by Donna Nordin
Owner/Chef, Café Terra Cotta
Tucson and Scottsdale, Arizona

Special Ingredients: *Mizuma greens*

Preparation Time: *15 minutes*

Yield: *4 servings*

4 cups mizuma greens, washed and patted dry (can substitute mesclun salad green mix)

3 oranges

1 tablespoon fresh mint, julienned

¼ cup sweetened, dried cranberries

Salt and freshly ground black pepper, to taste

1 Fillet two of the oranges. Fillet oranges by peeling away outer rind and inner white skin. Using a sharp paring knife, cut individual sections away from the membranes that encase each section.

2 Juice the third orange. This can be done by hand. Roll the orange on the counter top, gently pressing down, for a few seconds to make it easier to juice. Then cut the orange in half and squeeze each half into a medium mixing bowl until all the juice has been released.

> **Mizuma** is a delicate salad green from Japan that is often included in mesclun salad mixes. Mizuma may be found at farmer's markets or specialty produce markets during the spring and summer.

3 Add julienned mint and cranberries to the orange juice and mix. Season to taste with salt and pepper.

4 Add greens and toss enough to coat leaves. Arrange salad on large platter or four individual serving plates. Top with orange fillets.

Nutrition Information Per Serving based on 8 servings

Calories	*72*	*Dietary Fiber*	*3 grams*
Protein	*1.7 grams*	*Vitamin A*	*24% of the Daily Value*
Carbohydrate	*17 grams*	*Vitamin C*	*88% of the Daily Value*
Total Fat	*0 grams*	*Folic Acid*	*54% of the Daily Value*
Saturated Fat	*0 grams*		
Cholesterol	*0 mg*		
Sodium*	*14 mg*		

* Sodium information based on no added salt. Salting to taste will significantly increase the sodium content of this dish.

Ratatouille (Ratatouia)

Created by Constantin "Chris" Kerageorgiou
Executive Chef, La Provence Restaurant
New Orleans, Louisiana

Special Ingredients: *Coriander seeds*

Preparation Time: *2 hours*

Yield: *4-6 servings*

(continued)

2 pounds (3 to 4 small) eggplant, ends trimmed and cut into cubes

2 tablespoons plus 1 teaspoon olive oil

2 large onions, sliced

6 large garlic cloves, 4 sliced or minced, 2 put through a press or pureed

1 large red bell pepper, cut into slices about 1 inch thick by 2 inches long

1 large green bell pepper, cut into slices about 1 inch thick by 2 inches long

Coarse sea salt to taste

1 ½ pounds (3 medium-size) zucchini, cut in half lengthwise and sliced ½ inch thick

4 large or 6 medium-size tomatoes, peeled, seeded, and coarsely chopped

1 tablespoon tomato paste

1 bay leaf

2 teaspoons fresh thyme leaves or 1 teaspoon crushed dried thyme

2 teaspoons chopped fresh oregano or 1 teaspoon crushed dried oregano

½ teaspoon crushed coriander seeds

1 Heat the olive oil in a large heavy bottom skillet. Add the onions, garlic, and peppers, season with salt, and sauté over medium-high heat for 5 minutes, stirring. Add the zucchini and cook another 2 minutes. Stir in the remaining ingredients and bring to a simmer.

2 Transfer the sautéed vegetables and herb mixture to a large earthenware dish and bake in a 300°F oven for 1½ hours. Check periodically, adding ¼ cup of water here and there to keep ratatouille moist.

Nutrition Information Per Serving based on 6 servings

Calories	171	Dietary Fiber	9 grams
Protein	5 grams	Vitamin A	32% of the Daily Value
Carbohydrate	28 grams	Vitamin C	207% of the Daily Value
Total Fat	6 grams	Folic Acid	24% of the Daily Value
Saturated Fat	1 gram		
Cholesterol	0 mg		
Sodium *	30 mg		

* Sodium nutrition information based on no added salt. If salt is added to taste, sodium content will increase.

Roasted Asparagus Salad with Orange Ginger Dressing

Created by Nora Pouillon
Chef and Owner, Nora — the only certified organic restaurant in the U.S.
Washington, D.C

Preparation Time: *25 minutes*

Yield: *6 servings*

1 pound asparagus, tips cut, ends trimmed, stems peeled if tough, and cut diagonally into ½-inch pieces

Olive oil spray

Herbal seasoning salt to taste

½ cup orange juice

1 tablespoon lime juice

2 tablespoons orange marmalade

½ teaspoon grated ginger root

1-2 tablespoons olive oil

7 cups chopped romaine lettuce

3 tablespoons pine nuts or slivered almonds, toasted

1 Preheat oven to 450 degrees.

2 Spread asparagus on baking sheet in single layer. Mist lightly with olive oil spray.

3 Roast until tender when pierced with a knife, about 10 to 12 minutes.

4 Season with herbal salt and set aside.

5 In a small bowl mix juices, marmalade, ginger, and olive oil and whisk until well blended.

6 Arrange lettuce on dinner plates.

7 Top with roasted asparagus.

8 Whisk dressing again and pour over salad. Garnish with pine nuts.

Nutrition Information Per Serving based on 6 servings

Calories	92	Sodium	13 mg
Protein	3 grams	Dietary Fiber	2 grams
Carbohydrate	11 grams	Vitamin A	41% of the Daily Value
Total Fat*	5 grams	Vitamin C	55% of the Daily Value
Saturated Fat	1 gram	Folic Acid	37% of the Daily Value
Cholesterol	0 mg		* Fat content based on using one tablespoon olive oil.

Roasted Chicken with Caramelized Garlic & Sage

Created by Walter Pisano
Executive Chef, Tulio Ristorante
Seattle, Washington

Shocking! A recipe with chicken skin in a heart health book? Don't despair — although we'd never recommend eating poultry skin, we certainly don't discourage cooking poultry with the skin on to trap in juices. Doing so does not significantly affect the fat content of the meat but does significantly affect the final flavor. This recipe calls for caramelized garlic and sage tucked under the skin while roasting — talk about flavor!

Preparation Time: *45 minutes*

Yield: *8 servings*

4 large whole skin-on chicken breasts (bone-in or boneless), halved

4 cloves garlic (peeled)

¼ cup sugar

2-3 fresh sage leaves, chopped

½ tablespoon unsalted butter

2 tablespoons olive oil

Salt and freshly ground pepper, to taste

1 Preheat oven to 375°F. Peel and slice the garlic paper thin, and then blanch in boiling water for one minute. Heat the sugar in a small heavy saucepan over medium heat until golden brown. Remove from heat and add the blanched garlic, chopped sage, and butter. Mix well and set aside to cool.

2 Prepare each chicken breast by carefully pulling up the skin in one corner, at the thickest point. Slip approximately ½ teaspoon of the caramelized garlic and sage mixture under the skin. Carefully spread it around, keeping the skin attached to the meat as much as possible. You will have extra caramelized garlic and sage, which you can use later or brush on the chicken *after* searing and before baking.

3 Season chicken with salt (optional) and pepper to taste. Heat the olive oil in a large, oven-safe skillet. (If you don't have one, you can transfer the chicken breasts to a baking dish later.) Sear each breast, skin side down, and cook over medium-high heat until skin is browned, about 5 minutes. Turn the breasts over and spread the remaining garlic/sage mixture over the browned tops, if desired.

4 Transfer the breasts in the oven-proof skillet (or in a baking dish) to the oven. Roast for 15 to 20 minutes, or until cooked through. When done, allow chicken to rest 4 to 5 minutes before removing skin, slicing, and serving. Serve over Lemon Risotto, which appears previously in this appendix.

Nutrition Information Per Serving based on 8 servings

Calories	181	Saturated Fat	1 gram
Protein	30 grams	Cholesterol	84 mg
Carbohydrate	2 grams	Sodium	76 mg
Total Fat	5 grams	Dietary Fiber	0 grams

Roasted Pepper and Feta Pizza

Created by Gloria Klein, MS, RD
Senior Research Dietitian, The Center for Clinical and Lifestyle Research
Shrewsbury, Massachusetts

Preparation Time: *1 hour 15 minutes*

Yield: *4 servings*

For the crust:

½ cup milk, warmed

1½ teaspoons yeast

¼ cup water

1 teaspoon sugar

2 tablespoons olive oil

1 teaspoon salt

⅓ cup whole wheat flour

1¼ cup all-purpose flour

¼ cup all-purpose flour, for kneading

For the tomato-pesto sauce:

1 large ripe tomato

¾ cup fresh basil, chopped

1 clove garlic

2 tablespoons fresh Parmesan cheese

2 tablespoons olive oil

2 tablespoons pine nuts

For the toppings:

4 ounces crumbled feta cheese

1 large red pepper

1 large yellow pepper

Freshly ground black pepper

Part 1: Prepare the crust

1 Warm milk on the stove or in the microwave to 110 degrees. (You should be able to comfortably stick your finger in the milk at this temperature.) Pour milk into a large mixing bowl and add yeast. Stir to dissolve yeast and allow to sit for 2 to 3 minutes.

(continued)

2 Add water, sugar, and olive oil to yeast mixture. Whisk together. In a medium bowl, stir together the salt and the whole wheat flour, and then add to the yeast mixture, whisking until well mixed.

3 Add all-purpose flour and stir until a dough ball forms. Sprinkle ¼ cup flour on clean counter and transfer dough to floured surface. Kneed dough for 4 to 5 minutes.

4 Transfer dough to a large oiled bowl. Cover bowl with kitchen towel and place bowl in sink filled with hot water. Allow to rise until doubled in bulk, 45 minutes to an hour.

Part II: Prepare the peppers and pesto

1 Arrange rack so that it sits 3 to 4 inches under the broiler. Preheat broiler.

2 Halve and seed peppers. Cut tomato in half and remove stem. Place peppers and tomato skin-side-up on oven-proof pan and roast under broiler for 3 to 5 minutes until the tomato skins peel back slightly and pepper skins char. The tomato will take less time than the peppers, so watch carefully.

3 Transfer tomato to cutting board when roasted. Transfer peppers to bag and close it, or into a bowl and cover tightly with plastic wrap. Set aside for 10 minutes to allow skins to loosen.

4 Remove skin and seeds from tomato. Transfer tomato flesh to food processor. Add basil, garlic, olive oil, Parmesan cheese, and pinenuts. Puree. Set aside.

5 Remove skins from peppers and cut into long strips. Set aside.

Part III: Assemble the pizza

1 When the dough has doubled in bulk, punch down and transfer to a lightly flour-dusted surface. Stretch dough into a 12-inch circle. To shape, push the dough out from the center, working around the circle to within 1 inch of the edge. Transfer to a lightly oiled pizza pan, baking sheet, or preheated pizza stone. Bake until the crust is lightly browned, about 12 to 15 minutes.

2 Remove crust from oven and cover with tomato-basil pesto. Top with pepper slices and feta cheese. Finish with cracked black pepper.

3 Return the pan to the oven and cook until the crust is golden brown and the cheese is melted, about 10 minutes.

4 Cut into 8 pieces (one serving equals 2 pieces or ¼ of pizza).

Nutrition Information Per Serving based on 4 servings

Calories	469		Dietary Fiber	5 grams
Protein	14 grams		Vitamin A	45% of the Daily Value
Carbohydrate	51 grams		Vitamin C	290% of the Daily Value
Total Fat	24 grams		Vitamin E	44% of the Daily Value
Saturated Fat	7 grams		Folic Acid	53% of the Daily Value
Cholesterol	29 mg		Calcium	32% of the Daily Value
Sodium	991 mg			

Rock Shrimp with Plum Tomato Relish

Created by Mark Tarbell
Executive Chef-Owner
Tarbell's and Barmouche
Phoenix, Arizona

Preparation Time: *25 minutes*

Yield: *4-6 servings*

1¼ pound rock shrimp, cleaned and deveined

3 plum tomatoes, diced

1 small white onion, chopped

¼ bunch cilantro, roughly chopped

1 tablespoon tomato paste

1-2 serrano chili peppers, diced or 2-3 shakes Tabasco sauce

Kosher salt, to taste

Juice of 2 limes

1 Preheat oven to 350°F Place shrimp in a small baking pan. Roast for 10 minutes or until shrimp are pink and firm.

2 In a medium mixing bowl, mix all ingredients together, except the rock shrimp, to make plum tomato relish.

3 Make a ring or mound of the plum tomato relish, and then place the cooked shrimp on top.

4 Serve immediately.

Nutrition Information Per Serving based on 6 servings

Calories	121	Cholesterol	144 mg
Protein	20 grams	Sodium*	148 mg
Carbohydrate	6 grams	Dietary Fiber	1 gram
Total Fat	2 grams	Vitamin C	28% of the Daily Value
Saturated Fat	0 grams		

* Sodium information based on no added salt. Salting to taste will significantly increase sodium content of this dish.

Snapper Escabeche Salad with Olives, Avocados, and Oranges

Created by Norman Van Aken
Chef/Owner, Norman's
Coral Gables, Florida

Chef Van Aken writes: *"There are many kinds of snapper. I like the delicate yellowtail variety, which will have a nice texture with this salad. Note that the yellowtail is a somewhat thin snapper compared to varieties such as the American Red and will cook in a shorter period of time. Above all other considerations, you want to always choose the freshest fish."*

This may surprise many (and disturb some), but the snapper, after being briefly seared, is "cooked" in a marinade. The acid from the fruit juices and the alcohol in the marinade break down the protein fibers in the fish similarly to how heat cooks meat. Is this safe? Yes. Is this easy? Yes!

Special Equipment: *Spice grinder (can use clean coffee grinder)*

Special Ingredients: *Gold tequila, Spanish sherry wine vinegar*

Preparation Time: *1 ½ to 3 ½ hours (due to long marinade time)*

Yield: *6 servings*

Part I: Prepare the Escabeche Spice Rub

This recipe makes enough spice rub to make this dish 15 times, but as Chef Van Aken explains, "The Escabeche Spice Rub is a very versatile spice rub that can be used to flavor chicken or pork dishes for grilling." Be creative and find your own uses for this fragrant rub!

1 cup cumin seeds

1 cup black peppercorns

½ cup sugar

¼ cup salt

1 Put the cumin and peppercorns in a dry skillet and toast over medium heat, shaking the pan frequently until fragrant and slightly smoking, about 30 seconds to one minute.

2 Transfer the toasted spices to a spice grinder and pulverize them until not quite finely ground. Transfer to a bowl and mix in sugar and salt.

3 Store the rub in an airtight container until needed.

Part II: Prepare the Snapper Marinade

3 cloves garlic, peeled and thinly sliced

½ red onion, peeled and thinly sliced

½ bunch cilantro leaves, washed and torn

3 fluid oz (6 tablespoons) gold tequila

¼ cup Spanish sherry wine vinegar

¼ cup fresh lime juice

¼ cup fresh orange juice

¼ cup extra virgin olive oil

1 Mix together all ingredients in a stainless steel, glass, or plastic mixing bowl.

2 Place in refrigerator until ready to use.

Part III: Prepare the Snapper

1 ¼ pounds boneless, skinless snapper, cut into 6 fillets

3 tablespoons Escabeche Spice Rub

1 tablespoon peanut or canola oil

1 Lay the fillets on a plate. Rub the fillets on one side only with the spice rub.

2 Heat a large non-stick skillet to high heat and add oil. When the pan is smoking hot, sear the fish fillets *briefly* on both sides, about 15 seconds per side. Remove to a clean plate and allow them to cool for a few minutes.

3 Transfer the seared yet still raw fish into the marinade and allow to marinate covered in the refrigerator for one to three hours. Check the fish periodically for doneness. The "cooking" time will vary depending on the thickness of the fillets.

Part IV: Prepare the Vinaigrette

½ cup freshly squeezed orange juice

Salt to taste

¼ cup Spanish sherry wine vinegar

¼ cup extra virgin olive oil

2 shallots, peeled and thinly sliced

Freshly cracked black pepper

(continued)

1 In a small sauce pan, bring the orange juice to a boil. Maintain a moderate boil until the orange juice is reduced by half.

2 Put a pinch of salt in a large mixing bowl and add the vinegar and reduced orange juice. Whisk. Add remaining ingredients and whisk again. Adjust seasonings with salt and pepper. Reserve until ready to dress and serve the greens.

Part V: Prepare Salad

6 cups salad greens	*2 Valencia oranges*
1 avocado	*24 olives (choose your favorite)*

1 Fillet oranges by cutting away outer peel and inner skin. Use a sharp knife to cut sections away from inner membrane. Cut over a bowl to reserve the juice and place fillets in bowl. Set aside while prepping avocado.

2 Cut the avocado in half, remove and discard the pit, and scoop out the flesh. Cut into attractive slices. Cover while preparing rest of salad.

3 Remove fish from marinade and slice each fillet into nicely shaped "fingers." Discard excess marinade.

4 Toss the greens and citrus vinaigrette in a large mixing bowl.

5 Mound the greens on six serving plates. Surround the greens with fish, orange fillets, avocado slices and olives.

6 Serve immediately.

Nutrition Information Per Serving based on 6 servings

Calories	*356*	*Sodium*	*561 mg*
Protein	*21 grams*	*Dietary Fiber*	*5 grams*
Carbohydrate	*18 grams*	*Vitamin A*	*29% of the Daily Value*
Total Fat	*21 grams*	*Vitamin C*	*90% of the Daily Value*
Saturated Fat	*3 grams*	*Vitamin E*	*57% of the Daily Value*
Cholesterol	*50 mg*	*Folic Acid*	*71% of the Daily Value*

Spice Rubbed Chicken Breasts

Created by MaryAnn Saporito Boothroyd
Chef/Owner Saporito's Florence Club Café
Hull, Massachusetts

Chef MaryAnn says that this spice rub can be used on chicken, beef, pork, scallops, shrimp, or any firm flesh fish. The meat can be pan-seared, baked, broiled, or grilled after applying the spice rub.

This recipe calls for briefly pan-searing and then baking the chicken to finish the cooking process. If the meat is grilled, no oil is needed, which dramatically reduces the total fat per serving.

Preparation Time: *45 minutes*

Yield: *4 servings*

For the spice rub:

¼ cup ground cumin

2 tablespoons fresh rosemary, finely chopped

¼ teaspoon or less cayenne (red) pepper

Salt, to taste (nutrition analysis based on ⅛ teaspoon salt)

Freshly ground black pepper, to taste

For the chicken:

4 teaspoons olive oil

4 4-5 oz. boneless, skinless fresh chicken breast meat

1 Preheat oven to 400°F. Toast cumin in a small dry sauté pan until it slightly darkens and the aroma heightens. Cool cumin and mix with remaining spice rub ingredients.

2 Coat each chicken breast with spice rub. This can easily be done by placing spice rub and chicken in a plastic bag and shaking vigorously to coat each breast. Discard excess spice rub.

3 In a large skillet, heat olive oil over medium heat. When hot, place the chicken breasts in the pan and evenly brown on both sides, approximately 2 to 3 minutes per side. If your skillet isn't ovenproof, transfer to a baking pan.

4 Finish cooking in the oven until done, about 15 to 20 minutes.

Nutrition Information Per Serving based on 4 servings

Calories	*204*	*Saturated Fat*	*2 grams*
Protein	*26 grams*	*Cholesterol*	*68 mg*
Carbohydrate	*3 grams*	*Sodium*	*146 mg*
Total Fat	*10 grams*	*Dietary Fiber*	*1 gram*

Spicy African Chicken Soup

Created by Garrett Cho
Executive Chef, Palomino Euro Bistro
Minneapolis, Minnesota

Special Ingredients: Bulgar wheat, cinnamon sticks

Preparation Time: 2 hours (mostly simmering time)

Yield: 16 one-cup servings

2 tablespoons olive oil

1 ½ cups diced onion

5 teaspoons minced garlic

8 cups (64 fluid oz) chicken stock

12 ounces chicken breast, cut into strips approximately 1½ inches long and ½ inch thick

3 ½ cups (28 fluid oz) canned tomatoes, diced, with juice

1 cup chopped celery

½ cup + 1 tablespoon minced parsley

½ cinnamon stick

Pinch ground cloves (about ¼ teaspoon)

2 bay leaves

Pinch cayenne pepper (about ¼ teaspoon)

2 cups uncooked bulgar wheat

2 teaspoons salt (omit if using chicken broth with sodium)

1 teaspoon coarsely ground black pepper (use more to add spiciness)

1 In a large saucepan, heat olive oil over low heat. Add onions, celery, and garlic and cook, stirring often, until soft.

2 Add chicken stock, tomatoes, parsley, cinnamon stick, cloves, bay leaves, and cayenne pepper. Increase heat to bring soup to a slow boil.

3 Reduce the heat to low; simmer for 20 minutes, stirring occasionally.

4 Add the bulgar wheat and the chicken and continue to simmer for 15 minutes.

5 Remove cinnamon sticks and bay leaves. Season to taste with salt and pepper.

6 Ladle soup into soup bowls. Top with unsalted, dry roasted peanuts (optional).

7 Extra soup may be frozen for 2 months or kept in the refrigerator 3 to 4 days at most.

Nutrition Information Per Serving based on 16 one-cup servings

Calories	111	Cholesterol	13 mg
Protein	9 grams	Sodium	620 mg
Carbohydrate	12 grams	Dietary Fiber	3 grams
Total Fat	3 grams	Vitamin A	23% of the Daily Value
Saturated Fat	0.7 grams	Vitamin C	21% of the Daily Value

Spinach and Potato Frittata

Created by Amy Myrdal, MS, RD
Senior Research Dietitian, The Center for Clinical and Lifestyle Research
Shrewsbury, Massachusetts

Chef Amy writes, "Frittatas differ from quiches in that they have no pastry crust. This recipe uses potatoes to create a crust. This delicious, nutrient-rich, and easy-to-make brunch dish can be made ahead of time and reheated in a warm oven or microwave. Prepare your frittata in the individual frittata dishes Williams-Sonoma sells and your guests will 'ooh and ahh' over the little darlings."

Special Equipment: *9-inch round quiche/frittata dish*

Preparation Time: *45-60 minutes*

Yield: *6 servings*

3 medium red-skinned potatoes, boiled with skins

⅓ cup chopped onion

½ medium red pepper, chopped

1 garlic clove, finely minced

1 pound spinach, washed, with stems removed and finely chopped

1 tablespoon olive oil

½ cup part-skim Mozzarella cheese

6 large eggs, beaten

1 tablespoon 1% or skim milk

2 tablespoons fresh chives, chopped

¼ cup freshly grated Parmesan or Asiago cheese

½ teaspoon freshly ground black pepper

(continued)

1 Boil potatoes in medium saucepan until tender, about 15 to 20 minutes. Pierce with a paring knife to test doneness — they should be cooked but still firm. Potatoes can be boiled ahead of time to save time on day of serving. Cool potatoes in refrigerator.

2 While potatoes are boiling, prep vegetables. In a medium nonstick skillet, sauté spinach, onion, red pepper, and garlic in olive oil until spinach is wilted. Set aside.

3 Spray and wipe bottom of quiche plate with olive oil.

4 Cut potatoes into ¼-inch thick slices. Line bottom of quiche plate with potatoes.

5 Layer spinach mixture on top of potatoes. Add pepper to taste.

6 Sprinkle mozzarella cheese on top of spinach layer.

7 Whisk together eggs and milk in medium bowl. Pour over spinach mixture.

8 Sprinkle chives and Parmesan cheese over eggs.

9 Bake frittata in a cool 300-degree oven for 35 to 40 minutes, until eggs are set.

10 Cut into six sections. May serve warm or cold.

Nutrition Information Per Serving based on 6 servings

Calories	199	Sodium	188 mg
Protein	11 grams	Dietary Fiber	3.4 grams
Carbohydrate	19 grams	Vitamin A	74% of the Daily Value
Total Fat	9 grams	Vitamin C	72% of the Daily Value
Saturated Fat	3 grams	Vitamin E	25% of the Daily Value
Cholesterol	215 mg	Folic Acid	78% of the Daily Value

Spinach Gnocchi

Created by Alfonso Constrisciani
Executive Chef-Proprietor, Opus 251 at the Philadelphia Art Alliance and Circa
Philadelphia, Pennsylvania

This is a labor-intensive dish, but one definitely worth trying. The lemon zest adds an unexpected zing that will surprise and delight your taste buds. Serve with a mild tomato sauce, one that won't overpower the delicate flavor of the gnocchi (such as Chef Constriciani's Tomato Water, which appears later in this Appendix).

Special Equipment: *Food processor*

Special Ingredients: *Parmigiano-Reggiano*

Preparation Time: *60 minutes*

Yield: *8 servings*

1 pound spinach, de-stemmed, blanched and squeezed dry (can use 1 1/2 cups frozen chopped spinach, thawed and squeezed dry)

2 cups part-skim ricotta cheese

1½ cups grated Parmigiano-Reggiano (or other freshly grated Parmesan cheese)

3 eggs, beaten

¼ teaspoon nutmeg

4 tablespoons fresh parsley, minced

Zest of one lemon, minced

3½-4 cups all-purpose flour

½ teaspoon salt

Freshly ground black pepper, to taste

1 In a food processor, puree spinach. Add ricotta, Parmesan, eggs, nutmeg, parsley, and lemon zest. Pulse in 3 cups of the flour until dough forms a ball.

2 Turn out onto a clean counter and use remaining flour as necessary to knead dough to correct consistency — it should be smooth and not sticky. Quickly knead just until tender and smooth.

3 Cut dough into quarters and roll each quarter into a long log, about ½ inch in diameter. Cut into ½-inch slices and roll each piece into a ball using the palms of your hands. Use thumb to slightly flatten each gnocchi ball. Place formed gnocchi on a floured baking sheet. When all gnocchi are formed, cook in small batches in salted (optional) boiling water for 2 to 3 minutes. The gnocchi will float when they are fully cooked. Strain gnocchi and serve immediately with Tomato Water or other light tomato sauce.

Nutrition Information Per Serving based on 8 servings

Calories	437	Vitamin A	58% of the Daily Value
Protein	25 grams	Vitamin C	23% of the Daily Value
Carbohydrate	53 grams	Calcium	61% of the Daily Value
Total Fat	13 grams	Folic Acid	65% of the Daily Value
Saturated Fat	7 grams		
Cholesterol	113 mg		
Sodium*	631 mg		
Dietary Fiber	3 grams		

* Sodium information based on not adding salt to the water. The salt in the dough plus the cheeses contribute a lot of sodium, so adding salt to the water is probably not necessary.

Tomato Salad with Grilled Wild Leeks

Created by Mark Tarbell
Executive Chef-Owner
Tarbell's and Barmouche
Phoenix, Arizona

Special Equipment: *Grill (stovetop grill, grill pan, or outdoor grill)*

Special Ingredients: *Balsamic vinegar*

Preparation Time: *30 minutes*

Yield: *4 servings*

3 medium yellow tomatoes, washed, with stem base removed

4 scallions (green onions) or small wild leeks, well cleaned

1 red onion, finely diced

3 thin (young) carrots

¼ bunch pea shoots or alfalfa sprouts

¼ cup extra virgin olive oil

Juice of 1 lemon

Salt, to taste (optional)

1 tablespoon balsamic vinegar

1 Slice tomatoes into ¼-inch thick rounds and lay flat on individual salad plates to make a base.

2 Place the green onions or leeks over a clean, hot grill for about 2 to 3 minutes, turning frequently. Thinly slice, and then transfer to a bowl of cold water for 5 minutes; remove from water and drain. Place in a medium bowl.

3 Toss the carrots in 1 tablespoon of olive oil and sprinkle with salt (optional). Roast in a 350°F. oven until slightly tender, about 15 to 20 minutes. Let cool and cut into 1-inch pieces. Add the carrots, red onion and pea shoots (or sprouts) to the bowl with the green onions.

4 Make a dressing combining the remaining 3 tablespoons olive oil, and lemon juice, and season to taste with salt (optional). Pour the dressing over the vegetables and toss to coat evenly.

5 Place on tomato base and drizzle balsamic vinegar around the outside of the plate.

Leeks look like giant scallions (green onions) and are related to both the garlic and onion families. Compared to garlic and onions, leeks have a milder, sweeter, subtler flavor. Leeks are available year-round in most supermarkets. Choose leeks that have firm green leaves and unblemished white bulbs.

Pea shoots are the delicate, crisp tendrils and tender uppermost leaves of pea plants. Pea shoots are used in Chinese cooking and have a flavor akin to peas and spinach. Chinese markets carry pea shoots (also known as *dau miu*, the Cantonese word for pea shoots) in the spring.

Nutrition Information Per Serving based on 4 servings

Calories	184	Cholesterol	0 mg
Protein	2 grams	Sodium	29 mg
Carbohydrate	15 grams	Dietary Fiber	4 grams
Total Fat	14 grams	Vitamin A	135% of the Daily Value
Saturated Fat	2 grams	Vitamin C	57% of the Daily Value

Tomato Vinaigrette

Created by MaryAnn Saporito Boothroyd
Chef/Owner Saporito's Florence Club Café
Hull, Massachusetts

Use this zesty vinaigrette on tossed salads, as a simple dipping sauce for baguette bread, or on a pasta and vegetable salad.

Preparation Time: *10 minutes*

Servings: *15 servings, 2 tablespoons per serving*

1 cup canned plum tomatoes and juice

½ cup roasted red peppers, canned in water, not oil

¼ cup or less balsamic vinegar

1 teaspoon fresh garlic, chopped

2 tablespoons olive oil

Salt to taste (nutrition analysis based on ⅛ teaspoon salt)

Freshly ground black pepper, to taste

1 Place the tomatoes and roasted red peppers in the workbowl of a food processor and puree until smooth.

2 Add the balsamic vinegar and garlic, and pulse to combine. With the motor running, drizzle the olive oil through the feed tube, blending until well emulsified.

3 Season with salt and pepper.

4 Use within 3 to 4 days.

(continued)

Nutrition Information Per Serving based on 15 servings

Calories	21	Saturated Fat	0 grams
Protein	0 grams	Cholesterol	0 mg
Carbohydrate	1 gram	Sodium	43 mg
Total Fat	2 grams	Dietary Fiber	0 grams

Tomato Water

Created by Alfonso Constrisciani
Executive Chef-Proprietor, Opus 251 at the Philadelphia Art Alliance and Circa
Philadelphia, Pennsylvania

Special Equipment: *Juicer (optional, can use blender)*

Preparation Time: *15 minutes*

Yield: *6 servings*

2 cups fresh tomato juice (this will take about 4-6 tomatoes depending on their size)

2 tablespoons olive oil

1 tablespoon shallot, peeled and minced

¼ cup Chardonnay wine

¾ cup vegetable stock (canned or homemade)

1 tablespoon fresh basil leaf, finely julienned

Salt and freshly ground black pepper, to taste

1 Juice tomatoes. If using a blender, blanche the tomatoes in boiling water for 2 to 3 minutes to loosen skins. Transfer them to a bowl filled with ice water to stop cooking process. Peel the skins from the tomatoes. Cut them in half and squeeze out seeds. Transfer to a blender and puree until smooth. Set aside.

2 Heat medium sauce pan over medium-high heat. When warm, add olive oil and shallots. Cook shallots for 2 to 3 minutes, stirring, until they soften.

3 Add Chardonnay and simmer for 2 minutes over medium heat.

4 Add tomato juice and simmer lightly for 2 minutes.

5 Add vegetable stock and simmer for another 2 minutes. Stir in the basil and season with the salt (optional), and freshly ground black pepper.

Nutrition Information Per Serving based on 6 ½-cup servings

Calories	73	Cholesterol	1 mg
Protein	1 gram	Sodium	201 mg
Carbohydrate	5 grams	Dietary Fiber	1 gram
Total Fat	5 grams	Vitamin C	26% of the Daily Value
Saturated Fat	1 gram		

Watermelon Gazpacho with Lime & Mint Dressing

Created by Nora Pouillon
Chef and Owner, Nora — the only certified organic restaurant in the U.S.
Washington, D.C

Preparation Time: *25 minutes*

Yield: *4 servings*

1 medium watermelon
(approximately 5-6 pounds)

2 tablespoons lime juice

2 tablespoons lemon juice

1 whole red chili pepper

½ cup sliced red onion

2 garlic cloves, minced

⅓ cup minced fresh mint leaves

1 zucchini, seeded and diced

1 green pepper, seeded and diced

Sea salt and freshly ground black pepper

Mint sprigs, for garnish

1 Cut the watermelon into wedges, peel the fruit from the rind, and remove the seeds.

2 In batches, put the watermelon in a blender and puree until smooth.

3 Pass the puree through a colander or sieve to remove any remaining seeds.

4 Set aside one-half of the puree in a large bowl and pour the other half back into the blender.

5 Add the lime and lemon juice, chili, onion, and garlic and puree until smooth.

6 Pour this seasoned puree into a large bowl with the reserved puree and stir in the mint, zucchini, and pepper.

(continued)

7 Season to taste with salt and pepper.

8 Refrigerate until ready to serve.

9 To assemble, divide the soup among four bowls. Garnish with mint. Serve chilled.

Nutrition Information Per Serving based on 4 servings

Calories	148	Cholesterol	0 mg
Protein	4 grams	Sodium	20 mg
Carbohydrate	33 grams	Dietary Fiber	4 grams
Total Fat	2 grams	Vitamin A	53% the Daily Value
Saturated Fat	0 grams	Vitamin C	248% of the Daily Value

Whole Wheat Pappardelle with Shrimp and Chickpeas

Created by Mario Nocera
Executive Chef, Terramia Ristorante
Boston, Massachusetts

The whole wheat flour in the pasta gives this dish a nutty, hearty taste. Whole wheat flour has a higher fat content than all-purpose flour and should be stored in the refrigerator in an airtight container to keep it from turning rancid. The majority of fat in whole wheat flour is unsaturated and is found in the nutrient-dense germ section of the wheat kernel. The germ of a wheat kernel can be compared to the yolk of an egg; it's where the nutrients for growth are stored. Regardless of whether you're a wheat stalk or a human, the fat-soluble vitamins and minerals contained within the germ are very beneficial!

Preparation Time: 90-120 minutes

Yield: 8 servings

1½ cups whole wheat flour

1½ cups all-purpose flour

2 large eggs, lightly beaten

⅓ to ½ cup of water, as needed

2 tablespoons extra virgin olive oil

5 cloves garlic, minced

2 cups cooked dried chickpeas (may substitute canned, rinsed chickpeas)

2 pounds large shrimp, shelled and deveined

1 teaspoon fresh parsley, chopped

Salt and freshly ground black pepper, to taste

Sprigs of fresh parsley for garnish

1 Stir the flours together in a large bowl, and then pour onto a work surface. Make a well in the center and place the eggs and ⅓ cup of water in the well. Use a fork to slowly work the flour into the liquid. Knead for 2 to 3 minutes, adding more water if necessary, to make a smooth, stiff dough. Compact the dough to a disk, wrap in plastic and refrigerate for at least 20 minutes.

2 While dough is resting, fill a 10-quart put three-quarters full of water. Bring water to a rolling boil.

3 Divide the dough in half and place it on a floured surface. Press one of the dough halves down to flatten it into a rectangular shape of even thickness. Using a rolling pin, start to flatten and spread out the dough, maintaining the rectangular shape and dusting with the flour as needed to prevent sticking. Roll until the dough is a large paper-thin rectangle. (If the dough starts to rip or tear, it is too thin. Gently push dough together to cover the tear and roll the spot again.) Repeat with the second half of the dough. (If you have a pasta machine, it's easier to cut the dough into quarters and work each quarter through the machine until you have a long sheet at the narrowest setting, about 4 times. After you make the long sheet, use a pizza cutter to cut the pasta into one-inch ribbons.)

4 Cut the rectangle of dough into one-inch wide by six-inch long strips. Sprinkle with all-purpose flour and let rest on counter top.

5 Sauté garlic in olive oil in a large sauté pan over low heat until garlic has lightly browned, 2 to 3 minutes. Increase the heat to medium and add chickpeas and shrimp, and cool until shrimp turns pink, about 2 to 3 minutes.

6 While shrimp is cooking, add pasta to boiling water and cook for 1 to 2 minutes or until tender but firm. Drain the pasta and add it to the sauté pan. Add parsley, freshly ground black pepper, and salt (optional) to taste. Cook, gently tossing, over low heat for 2 minutes.

7 Serve immediatcly. Garnish plates with fresh parsley sprigs.

Nutrition Information Per Serving based on 8 servings

Calories	*335*	*Sodium**	*143 mg*
Protein	*22 grams*	*Dietary Fiber*	*7 grams*
Carbohydrate	*46 grams*	*Folic Acid*	*24% of the Daily Value*
Total Fat	*7 grams*		
Saturated Fat	*1 gram*		
Cholesterol	*160 mg*		

* Sodium information based on no added salt. Salting the pasta water and salting to taste will significantly increase sodium content.

Index

angina. *See also* unstable
  angina
  angioplasty, 181–182, 193
  as CAD symptom, 187
  causes, 19, 189
  defined, 187
  described, 17, 188
  diagnosis, 189–190
  ECG for, 173
  emergency chest pain, 191
  heart damage and, 189
  other causes of chest
    pain, 191
  physical activity programs
    and, 77
  plaque and, 131
  risk factor reduction, 192
  treating, 192–193
  types, 190
  warning signs during
    exercise, 94
angiography
  after heart attacks, 207
  for angina, 190
  for heart failure, 241
  overview, 177–178
angioplasty
  after heart attacks, 207
  for angina, 193
  overview, 181–182
  for peripheral vascular
    disease, 250
  for unstable angina, 198
angiotensin converting
    enzyme (ACE) inhibitors.
    See ACE inhibitors
anti-arrhythmic drugs, 233
anticoagulants
  after heart attacks, 206
  for stroke, 248
antidepressant
    medications, 105
antioxidants
  cholesterol and, 277
  in fruits and vegetables, 46
  low levels as risk factor, 35
anti-platelet agents
  after heart attacks, 206
  for stroke, 248
anxiety
  caused by heart
    problems, 104
  medications for, 105
  states mimicking heart
    disease, 105
aorta, diseases of, 252–254
aortic dissection, 253

aortic valve, 18
apple-shaped people, 158
arborio rice, 333
arm discomfort during
  exercise, 94
arrhythmias
  after heart attacks, 205, 208
  arising in atria, 229–230
  arising in the ventricles, 231
  conduction problems, 232
  described, 20
  diagnosis, 228–229
  electrical system of the
    heart and, 224–227
  heart attacks and, 200
  insignificant, 224
  life-threatening, 224
  people at risk, 103
  psychological-physiological
    link, 102–103
  rehabilitative exercise
    training for, 218
  statistics, 224
  stress and, 99
  symptoms, 227
  treatment, 232–234
  ventricular fibrillation, 103
  ventricular tacchycardia, 103
arterial catheterization, 184
arteries, anatomy of, 21–22
arteriovenous malformation,
  248
ASD (atrial septal defect), 257
asparagus salad, roasted,
  with orange ginger
  dressing, 339
aspirin
  after heart attacks, 205, 206
  for angina, 193
  as preventative therapy,
    277–278
  for unstable angina, 197
atherectomy, 182
atherosclerosis. *See*
  coronary artery disease
  (CAD); coronary heart
  disease (CHD)
athletes, nutrition for, 53
atria
  defined, 17
  rhythm problems arising in,
    229–230
atrial fibrillation, 180, 230
atrial flutter, 230
atrial septal defect (ASD), 257
atrial tacchycardia, 180,
  229–230

atrioventricular node,
  224–225
attention, getting your
  physician's, 288
auscultation, 171–172
automated external
  defibrillators (AEDs), 179
AV (atrioventricular) node,
  224–225
avocados
  salad, crab and, with
    chilled sweet corn broth,
    311–313
  snapper escabeche salad
    with olives, oranges and,
    344–346

• *B* •

B vitamins, 299
balloon angioplasty. *See*
  angioplasty
balloon valvuloplasty, 252
balsamic vinegar, 62
banana cream cheese, Grand
  Marnier French toast
  stuffed with, 319–320
basic cardiac life support
  (BCLS), 178–179
Batista procedure, 243
BCLS (basic cardiac life
  support), 178–179
Bergmann, Hans, 310
beta blockers
  after heart attacks, 205, 207
  for angina, 193
  exercise and, 78
  for heart failure, 243
  for high blood pressure, 123
  for unstable angina, 197
bile acid sequestrants, for
  elevated cholesterol,
  137–138
black rice
  about, 324
  sticky, with grilled Indian
    spiced pork chop and
    papaya salsa, 322–324
bleeding after heart
  attacks, 209
blood, coughing up, 304
blood clots, cerebral
  embolism and, 246
blood clotting, abnormal, 35

• F •

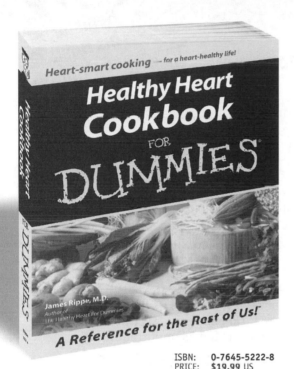

IDG BOOKS WORLDWIDE BOOK REGISTRATION

Register This Book and Win!

We want to hear from you!

Visit **http://my2cents.dummies.com** to register this book and tell us how you liked it!

✔ Get entered in our monthly prize giveaway.

✔ Give us feedback about this book — tell us what you like best, what you like least, or maybe what you'd like to ask the author and us to change!

✔ Let us know any other *...For Dummies*® topics that interest you.

Your feedback helps us determine what books to publish, tells us what coverage to add as we revise our books, and lets us know whether we're meeting your needs as a *...For Dummies* reader. You're our most valuable resource, and what you have to say is important to us!

Not on the Web yet? It's easy to get started with *Dummies 101*®: *The Internet For Windows*® *98* or *The Internet For Dummies*®, 6th Edition, at local retailers everywhere.

Or let us know what you think by sending us a letter at the following address:

...For Dummies Book Registration
Dummies Press
7260 Shadeland Station, Suite 100
Indianapolis, IN 46256-3917
Fax 317-596-5498

BESTSELLING BOOK SERIES